Super Nezh
Chess Assassin

by

Alex Pishkin
ICCF-IM

Thinkers' Press, Inc.
Davenport, Iowa 52802

Super Nezh, Chess Assassin
September 2000

ISBN: 0-938650-91-2 (f)
ISBN: 0-938650-94-7 (h)

THINKERS' PRESS

Bob Long, Editor-in-Chief
Thinkers' Press, Inc.
P.O. Box 8
Davenport, IA 52805-0008 USA
office phone: 319-323-1226
e-mail: tpi@chessco.com

Contents

Explanation of Symbols

x	=	captures
†	=	check
+—	=	White has a winning advantage
—+	=	Black has a winning advantage
±	=	White has a definite advantage
∓	=	Black has a definite advantage
⩲	=	White has the better game
⩱	=	Black has the better game
∞	=	Unclear
N/f3	=	Knight on f3 (for example)

A triptych by Galin Satonin of the clash between Polugaevsky (left panel) and Nezhmetdinov (right panel) which was heard round the world. As Polugaevsky said on page 36:

> **"Sunk in thought for a long time, I understood that I was to say good-bye to all hope and that I was losing a game that would be spread all over the world."**

Preface

The world of chess is multifaceted. Yet, of all its sides, three are considered the most important: sport, science, and art. It is impossible to achieve complete success by developing your mastery in only one of these areas. Any outstanding master combines in himself these three sides to this or that extent. Happy are those in whom they have been harmoniously developed: Fischer, Spassky, and Kasparov.

Lasker and Petrosian were outstanding sportsmen, and from the present—Karpov. Steinitz, Euwe, and Botvinnik were distinguished by their scientific approach.

Alekhine and Tal can be called brilliant high priests of chess art.

It goes without saying that these champions were blessed by additional chess qualities as well, otherwise the list of champions would be different.

There are masters in whom certain chess qualities are developed to such a phenomenal extent that few of the recognised geniuses of chess can challenge them.

Are there many among the greatest who can compete in the theory of the endgame with Yuri Averbakh, Nikolai Grigoriev or André Cherón? Perhaps, only Smyslov and Rubinstein.

Are there many among the greatest who might surpass in the field of analysis Isaac Boleslavsky, Igor Zaitsev or Mark Dvoretsky?

But chess theory and analysis are still the applied side of chess. They are certainly necessary for a chessplayer, no less than the mastery of versification is necessary for a poet, and solfeggio, for a musician. What we value most of all in the poet and musician is the gift of creativity, that intangible, ephemeral thing which is called "a God's spark."

Among those who were endowed with "the God spark," and created many unforgettable masterpieces (though they never became world champions) were: Chigorin, Réti, Bronstein, Larsen, Ljubojevich ... To this list we should undoubtedly add Spielmann, Simagin, Tolush, Kupreichik and especially Nezhmetdinov.

The name of Rashid Gibyatovich Nezhmetdinov is not as well known to the western lover of chess. Indeed he is not included among "the greatest" of the chess world. He wasn't a grandmaster, though in the former Soviet Union one can count about two hundred owners of this title.

He wasn't famous in the international arena, simply because he had few chances to play outside of his own country.

Still, if you ask any chess master, no not even that, if you ask any man who likes art in chess and has become acquainted with the creative heritage of the chess masters of the past, he will surely say, "Ah, he is that master who regularly defeated Tal and who attacked so beautifully!"

And that is true.

Despite his lack of the grandmaster title, Rashid Nezhmetdinov was a unique personality in the chess world.

• In the USSR and, quite possibly, in the whole world, he was the only "master squared," that is, he was a chess master and a checkers master at the same time. Once Mikhail Tal jokingly called chess "algebra" and checkers "arithmetic." He hinted at a certain second-rate quality of a checkers game in comparision with a chess game, a game which many consider the "royal game." After Nezhmetdinov had finally given up checkers, he noted one time that all checkers contests can be reduced to Rook endgames. On the other hand, checkers players have often commented on the depth of calculations of variations in their favorite game, and especially its oriental varieties, like the Japanese "Go," as surpassing chess. We won't argue about this; these arguments increase the significance of Nezhmetdinov's double mastery of both games.

• His talent fully blossomed and revealed itself when he was no longer young. He was 37 when he received the title of chess master. At that age, and even at a younger age, many famous chess masters disappeared from the scene (remember Fischer, Morphy, Pillsbury, Mecking… ?).

Nezhmetdinov gained his best results after 40. He made his debut in the USSR chess championship at 41, and the last time he became the Russian champion was at the age of 45. The last time he played in the finals of the all-Union championship was when he was almost 55!

In chess history you will seldom find similar cases of a chess player going on the "big stage" at such an "elderly" age. Some might remember Georg Salwe, the Russian champion of 1905, who also became a master after the age of 40.

Contemporary chess practice shows that chess champions "are younger and younger," and that a chess player reaches his peak by the age of 25-30, and after 35, his sporting form slowly decreases. At that age, the ability to accurately calculate variations lessens. The ability to endure many hours of intensive mental exercise also declines, something which a chess master seriously needs. If this is true, and we cannot doubt the truthfulness of the conclusions of specialists, then how can we account for the phenomenal chess of Nezhmetdinov? This is even more remarkable if we take into consideration that his style of playing chess was primarily based on the increase of tension on the chessboard and the extremely intensive calculation of variations.

It is impossible to explain this, just as it is impossible to answer the question "How can one become a genius?"

• Rashid Nezhmetdinov holds an unequaled record: he was chess champion of Russia five times. All in all, he played in the finals of the Russian championships 16 times.

Besides those five first places, another five times he was among the prize-winners. Here also should be added a silver medal in one, the checkers championship. His closest rival among Russian chess champions is the great Chigorin, who won three championships at the beginning of the century.

• His chess talent was unique. Lev Polugaevsky called him "the greatest master of the initiative."

M. Tal says: "His games reveal the beauty of chess and make you love in chess not so much the points and high placings, but the wonderful harmony and elegance of this particular world." Tal was a good friend and admirer of Nezhmetdinov's creative activity. In the preface to Nezhmetdinov's book *Selected Games* he wrote: "In Nezhmetdinov, more than in anybody else, you can see the difference between his creative and sporting achievements."

When a game was dry and there was much maneuvering, he got bored and sometimes played negligently. As a result, he lost more often than was expected. There were tournaments in which he never experienced a feeling of inspiration and creative enthusiasm. He didn't win laurels in those events.

On the other hand, when he managed to achieve a position that aroused the desire to create, when he succeeded in luring his opponent onto the slippery ice of combinational complications, when he obtained the initiative, then he was fearsome and irrepressible. It didn't matter then who was facing him across the board.

Rashid Nezhmetdinov's talent resembles a tree that, by some miracle, has grown on a bare cliff. He had a difficult childhood and was a youth of hunger. During his best years for chess he was in the army, and then came the war. He gained access to serious chess competitions only when he was 35. It was much later when young talents in the Soviet Union could achieve wonderful conditions for growth and blossoming. They had experienced teachers in the Pioneer palaces, regular training meetings during school vacations, *Chess Informants*, and computers.

Rashid had no dreams of anything like that. Practically speaking, he alone created the brilliant chess master Nezhmetdinov. This might explain why Nezhmetdinov was not only a master, but also a brilliant coach who trained many masters and gave many young people their access to chess.

I hope this book will broaden the circle of admirers for the creative abilities of this wonderful chess player and perhaps arouse in some ambitious young man an aspiration to achieve something in the cruel and beautiful world of chess. Perhaps, another Super Nezh.

Personal Thoughts for the Westerner

I have never been Rashid Nezhmetdinov's pupil or friend. I met him only twice at team championships, but not at the chessboard.

In the 50s when I was making my first steps in chess, Nezhmetdinov's games appeared quite often on the pages of chess magazines. It so happened that it was through his creative play that I began to comprehend the beauty and depth of chess. Since that time I have always remained an unfailing admirer of his wonderful talent.

Unlike many other great Soviet masters, Nezhmetdinov enjoyed the respect of his contemporaries, and many of his games have become known to thousands of chess lovers; some very famous grandmasters cannot boast that. During his lifetime he had a book published about his life in chess (Kazan, 1960). The book was published by the provincial publishing house and the circulation was small. Unfortunately, not all of his best games were included. As for the second edition of that book, which was considerably expanded, Nezhmetdinov never saw it for he had passed away. It was republished in 1978, and this printing was larger, 50,000 copies.

Later J. Damsky authored an excellent book in 1987 to commemorate Nezhmetdinov's 75th birthday. *Rashid Nezhmetdinov* was published in an edition of 100,000 copies where Nezh is presented not only as a bright chess master, but also as a self-made man who devoted his life to chess, enduring many difficulties along the way.

Before I decided to write one more book about Rashid Nezhmetdinov, I studied thoroughly all that had been published, and primarily his games and commentaries on them. Nezhmetdinov's own notes are characterized by a laconic, terse style, and concrete analysis. My task was to remove some analytical inaccuracies and some very rare mistakes, as well as to refresh his opening theories.

Damsky's commentaries on some games are also good, especially if he himself witnessed those games or saw them demonstrated by Rashid. Unfortunately, Damsky's commentaries on some games are too curt and fail to fully reveal the depth of their contents. There are some analytical mistakes as well in Damsky's book. Some of Nezhmetdinov's brilliant games didn't get into Damsky's book or were only given as fragments.

In the end I came to the conclusion that it would be necessary to reselect the games and to comment on them all over again.

I tried to use Nezhmetdinov's original analyses on those parts of the games that required detailed analysis. I also used his brilliant evaluations of positions which disclosed the real situation with utmost clarity and in few words. In these cases Nezhmetdinov's notes were quoted.

The selection of games has been changed according to their composition, as well as order of their arrangement. I have rejected the common method of chronological order in arranging the games. This approach to chess art is a good one for those great men of the chess world whose creative work is many-sided, and whose mastery is universal. The average level of games of those type of masters is high. Thus, even at the peak of their creative work, their very best games do not offer a sharp contrast to the other games in their game collections.

Nezhmetdinov was a player of inspiration. Such masters cannot have, and don't have, an even graph of first-rate games. A chronological graph of Nezh's games looks rather like a mountain range in which alongside with the highest peaks of his creative achievements—his eight thousand meter high mountains—there are quite a lot of modest hillocks and separate rocks. Therefore, I divided select samples of Nezhmetdinov's creative work into several approximately equal sized groups.

In the first group I included genuine masterpieces. I am not afraid to call them masterpieces, as any of the chess greats might envy these games.

In the second group I put games which are saturated with big fights. They are distinguished by the high quality of play from both combatants, though not devoid of mistakes.

The remaining games and fragments are divided among: attack, defense and counterattack, strategy, the opening, the endgame, and "small raisins."

Alex Pishkin
Syktyvkar, 1999

Editor's Note: It must be noted with sorrow that Alex Pishkin died June 7, 1999 and that it was necessary for Mr. Chuchin (his translator), Don Aldrich and myself to finish up the polishing of Alex's prose, suggestions and changes. In some cases (near the back of the book), I began to make editorial decisions to clarify questions he had left unanswered. May Alex rest in peace. He is survived by his wife Zina. She referred to this work as Alex's "third child."

An Appreciation

by IM Rashid Ziyatdinov

"Nobody sees combinations like Rashid Nezhmetdinov."

—*Mikhail Botvinnik*

Rashid Gibyatovich Nezhmetdinov was famous among professional players for his way of creating warfare on the chessboard. Masters understand that combinations will only appear after preparation. His style of fight was so specific that many world class players had unexpected and very beautiful losses to him.

Maybe he never thought or talked about the following; but for me it is clear. Let's introduce a European chronicle about some of Rashid Gibyatovich's ancestors.

First of all Nezhmetdinov was a Tartar. Tartar is a collective name applied to the peoples of Turkic origin who invaded parts of Asia and Europe under Mongol leadership in the 13th century. Also known as Tartars, the original Tartars probably came from east-central Asia or central Siberia, and, unlike the Mongols, spoke a language belonging to the Turkic branch of the Altaic languages family. In conjunction with the encyclopedia *Encarta*, I would like to introduce two stories. One is very interesting to me. It is the game *Flohr—Nezhmetdinov USSR ch. 21, Kiev, 1954* (by the way, to qualify for a USSR championship you had to win at least 3 tournaments against strong Russian masters).

Flohr was in his prime and preparing to play a match with Alekhine. Alekhine was from a group of chess gods or at least their messenger.

The second story is a historic chronicling and we will try to make a parallel.

Poland still celebrates April 9 *[Ed. Note: Brittanica.com gives April 15 as the Battle of Liegnitz.]* as the day they repulsed an Asiatic invasion of Europe in 1241. Their Tartar enemies saw things differently—at Liegnitz, they won their third victory in a row over a European army, all with only a diversionary force of 20,000 warriors.

On April 9, 1241, Duke Henry II of Silesia, marched out of his city of Liegnitz to meet the dreaded Tartars. The invaders from the East had already attacked Lublin and sacked Sandomir. Henry had known of that weeks earlier. His army was about 30,000. Opposing him was a host of about 20,000 Tartars, commanded by Kaidu, a great-grandson of Genghis Khan. The real mastermind of the expedition, however, was Subotai, longtime lieutenant of Genghis Khan.

A Tartar commander might be anywhere in his formation, directing his troops as he saw fit.

Salo Flohr—Rashid Nezhmetdinov
E 60
21st USSR Championship
Kiev 1954

1. Nf3 Nf6 2. c4 d6 3. d4 g6 4. b3 Bg7 5. Bb2 0-0 6. g3 Bf5 7. Bg2 Qc8.

To contrast, the leader of the European army often fought alongside his men in the thick of battle where he was easily identified, in danger, and unable to respond to developments in the fight. Such leadership by example made a certain amount of sense where battles were seen as opportunities for the display of personal bravery, and the object of the contest was honor as well as victory.

But to the Tartars, victory was all that mattered. Consequently, their approach was to kill or defeat the enemy as efficiently as possible—that is, with the least cost to themselves.

8. 0-0 Bh3 9. Nbd2 a5 10. a3 Qg4 11. e3 Qh5 12. Nh4 Bg4 13. f3 Bc8 14. f4 Qxd1 15. Raxd1.

Tartar tactics resembled those of the hunter, who uses speed, finesse and deception to herd his prey where he will, and then kill it with as little risk to himself as possible. In the case of their confrontation with Duke Henry's army, Kaidu decided to try a common steppe tactic—attack, false flight and ambush. When the engagement began, the Europeans were disconcerted because the enemy moved without battle cries or trumpets; all signals were transmitted visually.

15... Ng4 16. Rfe1 c6 17. Nhf3 Nd7 18. Ba1 Rb8 19. e4 b5 20. h3 Ngf6 21. e5 Nh5 22. Kh2 Nb6 23. exd6 exd6 24. c5 Nd5 25. Ne4 Bf5 26. Nxd6 Bc2 27. Rc1 Bxb3 28. Nd2 Bc4 29. N2xc4 bxc4 30. Rxc4 Nhf6 31. Ra4.

The overall Tartar discipline was greater than that of the knights, their formations were looser in appearance, making it difficult to accurately count their numbers. The first of Duke Henry's divisions charged into the Tartar ranks to begin hand-to-hand combat, but the more lightly armed Tartars on their agile ponies easily surrounded them and showered them with arrows. A second charge by the second and third divisions was mounted under Sulislav and Meshko of Opole. Unlike the first, this assault seemed successful—the Tartars broke into what appeared to be a disorderly retreat. Encouraged, the knights pressed on with their attack, eager to meet the Tartars with lance and broadsword. Their adversaries continued to flee before them, evidently unable to face the charge of the heavy horsemen. Then, an odd thing happened. A single rider from the Tartar lines rushed about the Polish lines shouting "Byegaycze! Byegaycze!" or "Run! Run!" in Polish. The Polish chronicler is uncertain whether the man was a Tartar or one of the conquered Russians pressed into their service.

31... h5 32. Rxa5 h4 33. g4 Nxf4 34. Bxc6.

Meshko did not take the outburst for a trick and began to retire from the battlefield with his knights. Seeing Meshko's retreat, Henry led his fourth battle group into the Tartar lines and once again engaged in close combat. After a fierce fight, the Tartars again began to flee. Their standard was seen to pull back—its bearer had joined the retreat, and the Polish knights pressed ahead.

34... Rb3 35. Bg2 Nxg2 36. Kxg2 Nd5 37. Re4.

Things were not as they seemed. The European knights had fallen victim to one of the oldest tricks in the Tartars' book—the feigned retreat. The riders of the steppes, unlike the knights, had been taught to retreat as a tactical move, and in so doing, they drew the knights away from their infantry. Once that was accomplished, the Tartars swept to either side of the knights, who had strung out and lost their own measure of order, and showered them with arrows. Other Tartars had lain in ambush, prepared to meet the knights as they fell into the trap.

37... f5 38. gxf5 gxf5 39. Rxh4 f4 40. Rb5 Rxa3 41. Rb1 f3† 42. Kf1.

The dismounted knights were then easy prey for the Tartar heavy cavalrymen, who ran them down with lance or saber with little danger to themselves. The Tartars employed one further trick—smoke drifted across the battlefield between the infantry and the knights who had charged ahead, so the foot soldiers and horsemen could not see each other as the Tartars fell upon the knights and virtually annihilated them.

42... f2 43. Nc4 Ra4 44. Rh5 Nf6 45. Rf5 Rxc4 46. Rxf2.

Duke Henry tried to gallop off the field, but he was run down by Tartars who killed him, cut off his head and paraded about Liegnitz with it on top of a spear as a trophy. With the aid of catapults, the Tartars occupied the only bridge over the Sajó. On April 10, however, the Hungarians charged the bridge, and the lightly armored Tartars, having little room to maneuver, took a beating. Again improvising a fortified camp on the west side of the river by lashing wagons together, Béla pushed on and established a strong bridgehead on the east side as well. Even while the Tartars were being driven from the bridge, however, Subotai had found a fording point to the south.

46... Kh7 47. Kg2 Rg8 48. Kh2 Nd5 49. Rb7.

Just before dawn on April 11, he led 30,000 of his horsemen across. Batu then swept to the left flank of the Hungarians, causing them to turn, while Subotai's men hurried northward to strike at the Hungarian rear. By 7 a.m., the Europeans, completely outmaneuvered, were falling back and took refuge in their camp.

49... Kh6 50. Rd7 Nf6 51. Re7.

For the next several hours, the Tartars assailed Béla's camp once more with catapults, throwing stones, burning tar, naphtha and even Chinese firecrackers.

51... Nh5 52. Bb2 Bf6 53. Re6 Rg6 54. d5 Bh4 55. Rxg6† Kxg6 56. Rd2 Bg5 57. Rg2 Nf4 58. Rd2 Nh5 59. Rg2.

Then another strange thing occurred. The Hungarians discovered that the Tartar army that now surrounded the camp had left a conspicuous gap to the west. Cautiously, a few of the Hungarians tried to escape through the gap and passed through without difficulty. Others followed and soon the flight became uncontrollable.

59... Kf5 60. Be5 Rxc5 61. Bb8 Rxd5 62. Re2 Rb5 63. Bc7 Rb7 64. Bd6 Rb3 65. Re5† Kg6 66. Re6† Kf7 67. Re2 Be3 68. Bc7 Kg6 69. Ra2 Nf6 70. Kg2 Nd5 71. Bd6 Kf5 72. Ra3 Rb6 73. Bg3 Ke4 74. Ra4† Kd3 75. Ra5 Nc3 76. Kf3 Rf6† 77. Kg4 Rf8 78. Bd6 Rf7 79. Ra3 Bc1 80. Ra1 Bd2 81. Ra8 Ne4 82. Bh2 Nf2† 83. Kh5 Rf6 84. Rh8 Ke4 85. Bc7 Kf5 86. Bd8.

As the Hungarians retreated they became strung out—at which point the Tartars reappeared in force, riding along their flanks and showering them with arrows. The Hungarian retreat degenerated into a panicky, disorderly rout—just as Subotai had calculated it would when he deliberately left them that tantalizing but deceptive escape route.

86... Ne4 87. Bc7 Bg5 88. Rh7.

Now, moving in for the kill, the Tartars rode the Hungarians down and killed them with lance and saber.

88... Rf8 0-1.

Depending on the source, anywhere from 40,000 to 65,000 Hungarians and other European men-at-arms were killed. Almost as astonishing as the Tartars' invasion of Europe was their sudden disappearance. After their victory at Liegnitz, the northern army left Poland and never returned. The truth was that Kaidu and Baidar had no intention of venturing deeper into Europe—that had never been their objective. They had, in fact, carried out their assigned task brilliantly.

Source Used With Permission: *Warriors of the Steppe, A Military History of Central Asia, 500 B.C. to 1700 A.D.* by Erik Hildinger, Sarpedon Publishers (Aug. 1997), 272 pgs. ISBN: 1-885119-43-7.

Two of the Spartak Team.
Tigran Petrosian and
Rashid Nezhmetdinov

7th Russian ch. / Yaroslavl 1947

	Players	1	2	3	4	5	6	7	8	9	10	11	12	13	14	Points	Place
1	Novotyelnov	•	■	■	■	▒	■	■	▒	■	▒	■	■	■	■	11.5	1
2	Ivashin		•	■	▒	■	■	■	▒	▒	▒	▒	■	■	■	9.5	2-3
3	Nezhmetdinov			•	▒	■	▒	■	■	▒	■	■	■	■	■	9.5	2-3
4	Ilivitsky		▒	▒	•	▒		■		■	■	■	▒	■	■	8	4
5	Aronin	▒			▒	•		▒	■	▒	▒	■	■	■	■	7.5	5
6	Dubinin			▒	■	■	•		▒	■		▒	▒	■	■	7	6-8
7	Sedov					▒	■	•	■	■	▒		■	■	■	7	6-8
8	Suetin	▒	▒		■		▒		•		■	■	■	▒	■	7	6-8
9	Aratovsky		▒	▒		▒			■	•		■	■	■	■	6.5	9
10	Isakov	▒	▒			▒	■	▒		■	•			▒	■	5.5	10-11
11	Liskov		▒				▒	■			■	•	▒	■	■	5.5	10-11
12	Nogovitsin				▒		▒				■	▒	•	■	■	4.5	12
13	Iasvoin								▒		▒			•	■	2	13
14	Petrov														•	0	14
		1	2	3	4	5	6	7	8	9	10	11	12	13	14		

Candidate to Master / Yaroslavl 1947

	Players	1	2	3	4	5	6	7	8	9	10	11	12	13	14	15	Points	Place
1	Holmov	•		▒	■		▒	■	■	■	■	■	▒	■	■	■	10.5	1
2	Nezhmetdinov	■	•	▒			■	■		■	■	■	▒	■		▒	8.5	2-4
3	Tarasov	▒	▒	•		■	▒		■	▒	■	■	■	▒	■		8.5	2-4
4	Zefirov		■	■	•		▒	■	■	▒		▒	■	■	▒	▒	8.5	2-4
5	Borisenko	■	■		■	•		▒	■		■	▒	■	▒	▒		8	5
6	Sopkov	▒		▒	▒	■	•	▒	■	■		▒		▒	▒	■	7.5	6
7	Nogovitsin			■		▒	▒	•	▒		■	▒		■	■	■	7	7
8	Bastrikov		■					▒	•		■	▒	■	■	■	▒	6.5	8-12
9	Ivashin			▒	▒	■		■	■	•				▒	■	■	6.5	8-12
10	Estrin				■		■			■	•	▒	■	▒	▒	■	6.5	8-12
11	Magergrut				▒	▒	▒	▒	▒	■	▒	•	▒	▒	▒	■	6.5	8-12
12	Gorenstein	▒	▒				■	■		■		▒	•	▒	▒	■	6.5	8-12
13	Zherlev			▒		▒	▒			▒	▒	▒	▒	•	■	■	5.5	13
14	Bogdanov		■		▒	▒	▒				▒	▒	▒		•	■	5	14
15	Lapin		▒	■	▒	■			▒							•	3.5	15
		1	2	3	4	5	6	7	8	9	10	11	12	13	14	15		

Board 8 Team ch. / 1948

	Players	1	2	3	4	5	6	7	Points	Place
1	Nezhmetdinov	•	■	■	■		▒	■	4.5	1
2	Kogan		•	■	▒	■	▒	■	4	2
3	Klaman	[1]		•	▒	■[1]	■[2]	■	3.5	3
4	Kan	[3]	▒	▒	•	▒	▒[3]	■	3	4
5	Gongadze	■[4]			▒	•	■[4]		2.5	5-6
6	Perevoznikov	▒	▒		▒		•	■	2.5	5-6
7	Farber					■[5]	[5]	•	1	7
		1	2	3	4	5	6	7		

[1] Played Shamaev.
[2] Played Chekhover.
[3] Played Konstantinopolsky.
[4] Played Buslaev.
[5] Played Tinovskis.

Publisher's Foreword

We've published nearly 100 books on chess since 1973. In none of them do I recall writing a foreword, but there is always that first time.

I don't exactly recall how Pishkin and I got hooked up, but it began with his huge history of chess championships in Russia and the former Soviet Union. This book, when we finally publish it, will have about 400 games, photos, and lots of commentary about the championships, the games, the players, and the history of chess behind the scenes—it will be called *100 Years of Gladiatorial Chess.*

Because that work took awhile to translate accurately from Alex's Russian into American English by Alex Cherniak, and because it was so big, I wanted to see if I could get another project to press before that one.

So was born *Super Nezh.*

For a number of years I wanted to start an auxiliary publishing firm called Ninja Press, and its works would be devoted to true chess assassins such as Nezhmetdinov, Kurt Richter, and Leonid Stein. These artistic geniuses would just as soon pound you into chessic ground beef as to look at you. And, they did it with originality, flair, eagerness, and repeatedly.

It helped that Alex knew Nezhmetdinov and his games. It helped that he also had the requisite enthusiasm for the project. And, it helped that he could unearth games not found in the regular chess databases.

I have worked on some wonderful projects in my life as a chess editor, but I haven't had as much fun and horror as this one.

Retranslating the "translation" was taxing, but it made me learn so much more, and appreciate more—Nezh, the games, and the job Pishkin did.

Nezhmetdinov was a creator, of that there is no doubt—look at the games. The man was also a shark, a killer, and a magician. He can terrify you—will *right now* be the time when the "bomb" is dropped?

Even when the bomb was dropped the repercussions weren't always immediately felt. Sometimes he would be two pawns down in a late middlegame, or early endgame, and tell himself, "I am going to win this, it is all calculated." And sure enough, the opponent's advantage would drift away like smoke. His rival would become desperate and fight back with incredible energy, but generally to no avail.

His input on the Poisoned Pawn Variation preceded Fischer's by years. In fact, his imprimatur was established in a seminal game way back in 1954! His other ideas in the openings also inspired a new generation of players in the Soviet Union.

But most of all, I picked this guy because he was just your average-looking giant killer! When the conditions were right he was afraid of no one.

The list of bigshots he defeated, a number of them repeatedly, is like a *Who's Who of Important Chess Fatalities*:

Bagirov
Boleslavsky
Bronstein
Estrin
Flohr
Geller
Gurgenidze
Holmov
Krogius
Lein
Lutikov
Mikenas (many times)
Polugaevsky
Savon
Shamkovich (many times)
Spassky (twice)
Suetin
Tal (three times)
Vasiukov
Yudovich

Yet, this talented chess assassin never received the title of grandmaster! Many of his opponents were, or became, grandmasters and world champions. And there are many I have not listed (check the disk, available from Thinkers' Press). As Purdy would've said, "There must be something wrong with chess."

Only Furman, Korchnoi, and Taimanov seemed to know how to handle him. He played some well known opponents many times while some others most of us never knew.

Playing through his games is exhilarating. The opening ideas and the proof that many games aren't over until they are over— is proven time and time again—the fat lady was always warming up for Super Nezh's opponents!

Even the endgames fascinated me. I wish I could play like Nezh [I borrowed the name from the game playing systems, SUPER NES®, because this guy is action personified].

While proofing the games in the *Masterpieces* section I was awestruck not only by their complexity, but by the idea that some were conceived so far in advance that even chess analysis programs couldn't find some of his diabolical winning moves, even if they were left running all day!

Pishkin emphasizes Nezh's unrestrained imagination. While Nezh had his losses, he must have scared most of his opponents witless! Even if you might "see" his coming hammerblow, the complications seemed to be something he relished. He would think, and think, and think—then, it would be over.

He had perseverance in spades, and an indomitable will for self discipline even when losing. It didn't matter who you were—he sat down at that table with one idea: To Beat You.

Bob Long
Davenport, 2000

Information about the disk of 450+ games is on the Colophon page.

1

Biography

The fate of the chess world would be shaped by chance and not immediately. Until age 11 Rashid Gibyatovich Nezhmetdinov had never played chess; more than that, he hadn't even had a chance to see what it was or know anything about it.

He was born on December 15, 1912 of a poor Tartar family, of a farm-hand in Aktubinsk, an out-of-the-way steppe town. He remembered little of his parents; they died while he was young. His elder brother Kavi took the orphaned children (there were four of them) to his father's native land, to a small village in the Nizhegorodskaia province where his father's brother lived, his uncle Gumer.

It was a time of horror and famine: 1919, the Civil War, and devastation. Little Rashid had remembered an unpretentious fish soup on the bank of a lake as a big deal.

Some months later his brother Kavi took Rashid to an orphanage in Kazan, the ancient Tartar capital on the Volga. He always recalled that home with warm feelings since it was there that he was saved from starvation during the 1921 famine in the Volga area. He was taught to read and write in the native Tartar language, as well as Russian. He made friends and received an education.

Rashid lived in the orphanage for three years, then his brother brought him to his own family.

Kavi was much older than Rashid and was like a father to him. All his life Kavi helped him, fostering in him a love for literature and music. Rashid had much to learn from his brother, who later became the famous Tartar writer, Kavi Nadzhmi (1901- 1957). He wrote a number of novels and stories about the years of the revolution and the Civil War on the Volga and was even awarded the Stalin prize for them.

Rashid got acquainted with chess quite by accident. Once, while running on the staircase during hide-and-seek, he noticed a sheet of paper lying on a stair, with some signs and drawings. Rashid mechanically put the paper in his pocket and forgot about it. In the evening he remembered the mysterious signs, but he was having trouble understanding what was written—he still could read Russian, though he couldn't read it well. It turned out that the sheet of paper was torn out of the magazine "Smena" and contained the rules of chess.

Some days passed. Having come to a pioneer meeting at the "Communist Club" before the appointed time, Rashid entered the reading hall and there saw people sitting at small tables. On the tables there were nearly the same "thingummies," as he said, that he had seen on the scrap of paper.

Rashid came closer to them and began to watch with interest the movements of the people sitting around the tables. In a couple of minutes he guessed that they were moving the pieces exactly as was explained on that scrap of paper.

From then on Rashid, as if magnetized, was drawn to the chess tables. He would stand by for hours, silently watching them play. Finally, he dared, in a tremulous voice, to ask permission to play a game when one of the adult players stood up from the table.

Unexpectedly, for himself and for all those present, he won! The game was played on the condition that the loser leaves, so another player sat dawn at the boy's table. Again a victory! It goes without saying, the chess level of those amateurs was not high, but all of them were shocked that they were defeated by a youngster who could barely be seen over the table.

A chessplayer by the name Samsonov, well-known in the city, came up to see what all the noise was about. Having realized what was going on, he immediately wrote a note for Rashid, addressing it to the city chess club. The note went: "I ask you to accept him. He is very promising."

Overwhelmed with delight, Rashid went home and the next day he hurried back to the chess club. However, he was disappointed as he lost one game after another.

Later Nezh recalled: "Everybody beat me until 1927." Could anything different be expected from him? At that time he didn't have any idea of chess theory and was fascinated with blitz. Beaten and discouraged, he stopped playing for a year.

At the end of 1927 Rashid took part in his first tournament. It was a city championship of Pioneers. Nobody expected him to be a success. Rashid himself couldn't even imagine that he would win all his games—15 victories out of 15! For this result, Nezhmetdinov immediately became a third category player, even though before the tournament he wasn't even a fourth category player.

After this success his chess career stopped without actually getting started. Checkers was to blame. He began playing checkers at the beginning of 1928, and for some time his passion for checkers caused him to turn away from chess. In addition, his success in checkers came to Nezhmetdinov at once, literally at the first tournament.

Within a month, after he had played checkers for the first time, Rashid won the semi-finals of the city championship, and after that he was second in the city finalé.

He had further successes such as in the RARO championship held in Kazan (RARO—the area of autonomous republics and regions). There was at that time on the Volga such a territorial structure, with an unclear name, that united seven republics and regions.

Even the famous V. Medkov, who was at that time checkers champion of the USSR, came to take part in that championship.

All of Rashid's 14 rivals were much more experienced than he.

As it was to be expected, the country's champion won the tournament, but Nezh took second place and the title of the RARO champion. Maestro Medkov gave high praise to the young checkers player and even published his games.

For several months Rashid was invited to the Russian checkers championship in Moscow. The newcomer did not disgrace himself—he tied for sixth place and became a first category checkers player.

Checkers was not enough for Nezh. Chess attracted him no less than checkers. In his heart these two passions were fighting, and sometimes checkers got the upper hand, but most often chess won out.

In the spring of 1929 Rashid, encouraged by his victories at checkers, turned to chess again and began to get successes there as well. To begin, he won the small championship of Kazan, and a year later he scored a victory in the "big" championship of the city, and with it he became a first category player.

Still, checkers once again took the lead. In his memoirs Nezh remarked: "In checkers my improvement came quicker, and by 1931 I was close to mastership in skill." By this time the 18-year old Rashid had finished school, and the time came for him to look for his own place in life. He could no longer stay with his brother's family—he had to make his own way.

And so he went south, to Odessa. First he worked there as a stoker and spent every evening until the late hours at the chess club. At last, luck favored him and he got a modest job at the club. Rashid became a "professional," so to speak, chess and checkers player at the same time.

And then began a merry-go-round of continuous contests. Nezhmetdinov's unique, sparkling style of playing gradually began to take shape. Pretty soon all the leading players of Odessa felt Rashid's heavy hand. In 1933 Rashid became the double champion of Odessa which had a glorious tradition of checkers and chess.

Odessa's tough opponents helped Rashid when he returned to Kazan. According to him, he learned to defeat first category players regularly, and in the outlying districts of the country where there weren't any masters, that meant a lot. Checkers continued to occupy first place in Nezhmetdinov's activities. In 1934 he managed to get into the final tournament of the Russia championship where he took fourth place. It's interesting that newspapers didn't praise his results much. They wrote: "The former infant prodigy Nezhmetdinov took only the fourth place playing, in our opinion, beneath his potential..."

At the beginning of 1936 Rashid again won the city championships in chess and checkers. He began to feel that, for him, it was such a familiar situation that it was time to take a more aggressive approach in more than just checkers.

The first category chess tournament in Rostov-on-Don at the end of 1936 became a touchstone. Despite the modest qualification level for the tournament, in reality it wasn't a modest affair since in a few years many of its participants became famous masters who participated in the USSR championships.

Nezh started well, scoring three victories. Then the more experienced contestants sized him up and the sweet life was over. As a result, he didn't even get into the group of the top ten players, having lost the majority of his games. The tournament threw light on the flaws of his game: poor knowledge of opening theory, the lack of solidity, and self-control. Going back home he sat down to study theory and spend sleepless nights over analyses. It was at that time that Rashid managed to develop a taste for tedious analysis and constant theoretical research. At a mature age, these qualities compensated, to some extent, for the classical heritage of the chess culture he didn't receive in his youth.

Rashid keenly became aware of his lack of general education: it was required for his job since he worked at a standards' bureau; it was also required during his contact with students of the local university since he ran a chess circle there. He entered the department of physics and mathematics of a teaching institute. That workload at two places, and studying too, would have been more than enough for any ordinary man. Rashid's impetuous nature wasn't like that. In addition, he took part in all the tournaments that he could.

In 1937, the Kazan team won the chess tournament for the Volga region, and it's leader, Nezhmetdinov, became a winner on a personal basis. Next year Rashid was allowed to take part in the All-Union tournament for first category players. In the 30s such annual tournaments were a good school for chess mastery for the many chess players who later became famous. In the 1938 tournament, held in Gorki, the 16-year old Smyslov (he became a master the following year), Ufimtsev (the author of the Pirc/Ufimtsev Defense), Stohlberg (a very talented chess player who was killed in the war), and many others played.

Nezhmetdinov didn't succeed in getting into the winners circle. Summing up his results, P. Romanovsky, twice a USSR champion, wrote a couple of lines about Rashid: "Nezhmetdinov's playing in Kazan was very interesting. Far-sighted calculation, resourcefulness, and a fiery imagination have made him very dangerous for every player. Unfortunately, a rather poor knowledge and understanding of opening problems turned out to be a serious stumbling block for him."

Yet, in the next tournament of this kind, held in the summer of 1939, Nezh was beyond compare: he scored 9 points out of 10. For this success he got the ranking of candidate-master, a title which had only been recently introduced. Many will read that and smile, since now there are thousands of candidate-masters and even in very small towns there are plenty of first-category players. However, a smile is inappropriate here, since a present day candidate-master cannot be compared with his counterpart of 1939, just as a present day ruble can not be compared with a ruble of that era. Suffice it to say, that almost all participants of that pre-war tournament period became masters, and again, masters of the coinage of the 40s, not of the present-day.

Again, history repeated itself as in the first category tournament of 1936. The All-Union candidate-master tournament of 1940 was equally unsuccessful for Rashid. He took a place in the bottom part of the tournament crosstable. He again lacked theoretical knowledge and a well-prepared opening repertoire. Who would have believed that Nezhmetdinov would become *the Nezhmetdinov*, the one who would inflict defeat on even the greatest players of the day if he had not become so battle hardened?

Failures only shook Rashid up. He developed a habit in which he analyzed his defeats thoroughly. After the 1940 tournament he decided not to try to do everything at once and for awhile he gave up checkers.

That year he graduated from the teaching institute and was immediately called up for military service. He was to serve in the army in the faraway Baikal region. In the first months of his service Rashid managed to play chess, and he won the championship of the Baikal military district. It was his last tournament for many years to come, June 1941 came, and with it, the war.

The war was favorable for Nezh. He served on the Amur banks, far away from the battlefields. It goes without saying though that it was no picnic there, since on the other bank of the river, in China, was the mighty Kwang-tung army of Imperial Japan. A small number of garrisons posted along the river were required to be ready for action on a moment's notice. In general, chess would be put off until a better time.

He spent nearly five years of his military life on the border of China. In the summer of 1945, Lieutenant Nezhmetdinov got a new appointment—he was sent to do Soviet military administration in Berlin. In a year he returned to the world of chess. The first tournament in which he took part was a championship for military administrators in Germany.

Quite surprisingly the tournament composition turned out to be rather a good one, because many fine chessplayers had not yet taken off their military uniform. Hungry for chess, Nezh attacked his opponents and won all his games but two which ended in draws. Only Isaac Lipnitsky, who in a couple of years became one of the best masters in the USSR and a notable theoretician, could compete with him.

At last, in the fall of 1946, Rashid was demobilized and returned to Kazan to resume a peaceful life. He was already 34, and a half a lifetime was behind him. It was necessary to reflect on what he had been through and to choose what he wanted to do. He had not yet achieved much success in chess. Besides, to a great extent, he had lost the experience and knowledge he had gained before the war.

Unfortunately, many records of games that Nezhmetdinov had played before the war were lost. Only a few were published, and his personal archives had not been preserved during the war.

Essentially, Rashid was to start his chess career over again. His name was not on the list of highly qualified chess players who might count on support from the state. On the other hand, could Nezhmetdinov make another career... in chess? Like in the humble position of a school teacher? It goes without saying his indomitable nature, that of a fighter and a sportsman to the core, couldn't be satisfied with such a future. Thus, Rashid had made his choice long before, in the years of his youth, and it was his choice for all his life. He was sorry for the lost years, but nothing could be done about that.

Nezhmetdinov set a benchmark in which it was necessary to begin playing chess so seriously as to achieve his long cherished goals, to become a Master of Sport first in chess, and then in checkers. He understood how difficult this task was after his first tournament during peacetime.

In the Kazan championship he managed to take only third place out of the six participants. However, this result can hardly be considered a failure. Among the contestants was S. Furman, who later became a famous grandmaster and a coach for the world champion Karpov. Master V. Saigin also took part in the tournament, and in a few years it would be no other but Saigin who would pave the way to the highest chess mountain for Mikhail Tal when Saigin lost a master qualification match to Riga's young chessplayer. Later, and for many years, a creative friendship connected Nezhmetdinov and Saigin; they often analyzed games together and prepared for tournaments.

A signal success came to Rashid in 1947 when he won the zonal tournament for the Volga area in Gorki and got into the championship of the Russian Federation. In the finals tournament held in Kuibyshev, Nezh startled all with his start: 7 points out of 7. His finish was much less spectacular, and master N. Novotyelnov won the champion's title. Even sharing the second place was evidence of success for the debutante of the championship. However, the title of master was still far away. The reason was that... only three masters took part in the championship for the whole of all Russia. It's not that they didn't want to play in the championship of the republic, but the fact was that in the post-war years there were few masters still continuing to play.

The second place in the championship of Russia didn't bring Nezh the title of master. Nevertheless, it gave him a chance to be in the almost inaccessible circle of the bearers of the cherished title: he was given a right to play a qualification match with a master.

Requirements for the challenger for the title were extremely severe. They were the same Carl Schlechter was to meet in his famous match with Lasker for the world championship: he was not just to win the match, but to achieve a victory by two points. *[Ed.: This is still being debated, but at this time it appears that this two point advantage was a myth.]*

The Chess Federation appointed Georgy Lisitsin to examine Nezhmetdinov. It was difficult to select a more dangerous rival. Even before the war Lisitsin successfully played in the USSR championships and the tournaments of masters. He possessed a wonderful feeling for positions and was brilliant in his play and understanding of the endgame. He later wrote a basic manual, *Finishing Part of a Chess Game.* In the artistic aspects, Lisitsin was Nezhmetdinov's exact opposite; he preferred, and brilliantly oriented himself in, those positions which Rashid had never liked and in which he wasn't very strong. However, Nezh wasn't distressed when he learned the name of his rival. He even joked that he would play with the champion of... China, Li-Si-Tsin.

Rashid thoroughly prepared for this match. For three months he had been studying the games of the Leningrad master, especially the endgame. His fate, in the guise of chess bureaucrats, presented him with a surprise a couple of days before the beginning of the match: a telegram came from Moscow stating that the international master V. Mikenas would come instead of Lisitsin.

As the old saying goes, it's not worth choosing between two evils. The Lithu-

For the ultimate leadership... Championship of ZabVO. At the chess board is Nezhmetdinov (left) and V. Baturinsky.

anian master had gotten a high international reputation as far back as the 30s. At that time, for many years running, he had been a leader for the Lithuanian team at chess competitions and even defeated the great Alekhine at the prestigious tournament in Kemeri. Rashid had no time to study his new rival, he was to play on sight. The only help he had was Mikenas's article on Alekhine's Defense, published in the magazine *Chess in the USSR* shortly before the match.

The study of the article brought Nezhmetdinov success in the first game of the match (February, 1948), and it was a great success. The experienced master was defeated in his favorite Alekhine's Defense in 17 moves. The unexpected result encouraged both rivals: it made Nezhmetdinov more confident, and the examiner more angry. And, it deprived Mikenas of an easy assurance of his superiority. In the next game Mikenas took his revenge on Nezh. Later the match went on with variable success in a sharp and lively struggle.

The result was an honorable draw: +4, –4, =6, which to some extent satisfied both sides. The venerable master retained his reputation, and though the ambitious competition didn't succeed in getting Nezh the title of master, still he understood that he had reached the level of master play and a formal presentation of the title was just a question of time.

Yet, two years passed before Nezhmetdinov acquired the master's norms. During those two years he played a lot in tournaments (for that time). He took part in two Russian championships and in the semifinals for the 17th championship of the USSR. He didn't score big successes there. The reasons were his charged emotions and the unsettled state of his life.

It was necessary to make a new dash—now or never—Rashid was almost 38. Success came to him and came to him where nobody, including himself, expected him to become a success—in checkers. For 15 years (!) Nezh hadn't taken part in any checkers tournament, and was not going to take part in any more. Then fate offered him an opportunity.

In the fall of 1949 in Kazan, there was held a semifinal for the USSR championship in checkers. One of the masters couldn't come to the tournament and Nezhmetdinov was offered to take the vacancy. None of the favorites of the tournament objected to including him into the competition, a notorious outsider who hadn't played checkers in a long time.

It's quite possible that what happened at that tournament will never be repeated, though there are precedents of a participant who is included into the tournament at the last moment being a success. Nezh didn't have any sports goal in his mind and he played quite freely, following his intuition. He defeated one favorite after another. The result was absolutely spectacular: he didn't have a single defeat and he took first place, leaving his competitors far behind. He reached the master's norm scoring many more points than were necessary.

In the spring of 1950 a collision appeared in his world of chess and checkers. Almost simultaneously there was to be held a final for the USSR checkers championship and a final tournament for the Russian chess championship. This collision touched only one man; once again Rashid was to choose between chess and checkers. In similar situations he always chose chess. The same thing happened that time, and there was a chance to become unique—to become a double master. So Nezhmetdinov went to the chess championship in Gorki.

The tournament composition was notable. There was one of the world's most famous grandmasters at that time, Boleslavsky; also international masters Kan, Aronin, Dubinin, Novotyelnov, the experienced Ilivitsky and many others. This didn't discourage Rashid. In the first half of the tournament he had already broken away from the contestants and he gained the master's norm long before the finish. Playing with enthusiasm to the very end, Nezh took first place.

Nezhmetdinov, 1950
(from *Chess in the USSR)*

It came true—he was a master and champion of the Russian Chess Federation. With a rush he tried to duplicate the title of champion in the finals of the Russian checkers championship of 1950. Nezh led all the way through, but at the end he caved in and finished second, although a draw in the last game could have made him champion.

The people of Kazan, and all the people of Tartaria who were fond of both chess and checkers, rejoiced. Many Tartar admirers of ancient games, and not only Tartar fans but Moslem fans as well, now had their own hero. A hero? Isn't it an overly impressive phrase about a chessplayer who had not smelled powder at international tournaments, or who had not yet played in the USSR championships, and only recently became a master?

Of course, for a present day chess fan who is spoiled by a continuous sequence of great tournaments, who hears the names of scores and hundreds of grandmasters, it would be funny to hear such an epithet describing just a master. Stalin's stern era is almost as far away from us as the era of Peter the Great and Catherine the Great. It may so happen that even the pre-revolutionary years of the beginning of the century are perceived as something closer than the phantasmagoric period of the decline of the Stalin regime.

In those days "an iron curtain" was raised, but only in one direction—to let an elite group, hardly including more than a dozen of the best chessplayers, go to foreign tournaments. Even the world champion, and best known Soviet claimants of that title, couldn't go abroad every year. In the period between 1948 and 1956 no international tournaments were held inside the country.

The intramural calendar of competitions was very limited even for the leading masters. There were the championships of Moscow, Leningrad and the Union Republics. Then there were the individual victory and team championships, but the latter weren't held every year. There were championships of sport societies, but only some of them could boast of being composed of masters. There were also quarter-finals, semifinals, and finals for the USSR championship and some rare masters' tournaments. That was about it. An active master could hardly play in more than 2 or 3 tournaments a year.

It must be clear now why even an ordinary master's tournament became an event, especially if it was held not in Moscow or Leningrad, but in some provincial city. If grandmasters took part in such a tournament, it was regarded as the descent of gods to the earth. A halo of grandeur, of something unattainable by ordinary mortals accompanied leading masters too. It is possible to understand the delight of Kazan fans when Nezhmetdinov was ordained into the dignifed group of "immortals."

This delight increased even more after Rashid's victory in the next Russian championship (Yaroslavl, 1951). He didn't start the tournament in the best possible way, but he made a dash toward the finish line and left behind his main rival, N. Krogius.

It was time to get into the main tournament of the country, the USSR championship. He didn't make this leap though it was certainly quite possible for him to do so. He didn't manage to get into either the 19th or 20th championships of 1951 and 1952. As Nezh himself acknowledged, "some underestimation of opponents who made poor showings at the tournaments" had let him down.

There was another reason which, in our country, was diffidently called a "violation of tournament regimen." How many chess players can go about from one tournament to another, and from one hotel to another, and say that they never have spent all night playing cards and have never drank a glass of alcohol?

Can we reproach this man who became used to the unsettled life of a bachelor, for whom a nomadic way of life in hotels and dormitories was quite normal? It was this bachelor's nomadic life which trained him to endure Spartan-like conditions in his life. He took his teapot from one hotel to another and learned to make wonderful tea. Nezhmetdinov's tea was famous among chessplayers.

When he was approaching 40, his life radically changed—Nezh married. Now he had to put an end to the bachelor parties and all-nighters. In addition, Rashid had gotten tired of the nomadic tournament life. At that same time he had gotten a forced break in competitions, such as during the semifinals of the USSR championship, when he, together with masters Tarasov and Holmov, ventured into "weakenings of their character." This became known to those chess functionaries who were "observers" of communist ethics. As a result Tarasov, who had especially "distinguished himself" (he was a brilliant chessplayer, a participant in a number of USSR championships and a winner of one of Russian championships) was deprived of the title of master, and in those years it wasn't, of course, the worst punishment one could get. Nezhmetdinov and Holmov were forbidden to play in tournaments for a year. When the period of their disqualification had expired, and the selection of participants for the USSR championship semifinals into groups was being made, they were dispersed to different cities as a precaution.

Rashid decided not to lose any time

and began writing his first book. It was a chess manual in the Tartar language, the first serious book on chess for his nation. It was hard work because some terms didn't exist in the Tartar language. At the same time work on this book enriched Nezhmetdinov's storehouse of chess knowledge; he was very much preoccupied with the analyses of games and real opening ideas.

The year passed and at the beginning of 1953 Rashid returned to the chess world. He started off by playing successfully in the championship for the sports' team "Spartak," where he took second place after Holmov, ahead of a large group of masters. Then he took part in the Russian championship which was held in April in Saratov. In the first half of the tournament there shone the 18-year old Lev Polugaevsky. After 9 rounds Rashid lagged behind him by 1.5 points. Nezh won the remaining six games and once again, for the third time, he became champion of Russia, thus equalling the legendary Chigorin in number of titles.

Finally the last divide was conquered: in the semi-finals of the 21st USSR championship, Rashid managed to get a placing which gave him the right to play in the finals.

Thus, at 41 he was making his debut in the USSR championship.

Could he hope to succeed? It goes without saying Nezh understood it was nearly impossible. It was inconceivable to expect to get a grandmaster's title, as one had to become the champion for that. Even second place would get one a medal (!). Those were the classification strata in those times. He was going to fight even if it was just for the sake of his own self-esteem. And he fought. He defeated Geller (Game No. 54), Flohr (Game No. 82), and Lilienthal (game No. 55), scoring 4.5 points out of 7 in the games against grandmasters. Only Taimanov's extraordinary perseverance allowed him to draw.

He was less successful with the (international) masters, although Nezh didn't spare either himself or his opponents. For instance, playing against Bannik he made 144 moves, finishing the time controls repeatedly and spending sleepless nights in adjournment analysis. He derived no benefit from that undertaking. Sometimes he didn't have the strength to play other games. In the course of the tournament Rashid had successes as well as failures, but in general, the result was not bad—he got into the group of the top ten best players. Some other masters also performed well, among them Korchnoy, Furman, Holmov, and Suetin.

Then something totally unexpected happened: for the first time in many years the decision had been made to send a contingent of completely unknown masters abroad to the prestigious international tournament in Bucharest. Undoubtedly, changes in the political climate had played a certain role in that decision. The icy atmosphere of the Stalin era was substituted by Khrushchev's wish, although still a very weak wish, for a thaw. Nezhmetdinov was among the lucky ones.

Before going to Bucharest, the participants in the coming tournament among who, besides Nezh, were Korchnoy, Furman, and Holmov, were invited to Moscow for preparation under the guidance of D. Bronstein and I. Boleslavsky. There was such emphasis attached to the performances of Soviet chessplayers at that time that no money, and no time or strength, even from the elite grandmasters, was spared in their preparation. Only a small group of Soviet chess-players, including the world champion M. Botvinnik, members of the Soviet Olympic team, and a number of older grandmasters, enjoyed renown in the West.

This time the Soviet functionaries decided to demonstrate to the world that the Soviet chess elite had powerful reserves. The "novices" didn't do too badly. Viktor Korchnoy most assuredly was the winner of the tournament, and Nezh came immediately behind him, considerably overfulfilling the norm for an international master. Indeed, all four Soviet participants fulfilled that norm.

In Bucharest Rashid played with enthusiasm and many wonderful games resulted. His wife Tamara's telegram saying that a son had been born to him, which he received at the beginning of the tournament, was also an excellent encouragement.

1954 was a lucky year for Nezh. He became the hero of another tournament. It was a USSR team tournament held in Riga. The team "Spartak," for which Rashid played, won. Those who play very well in team tournaments are especially respected by chessplayers at any level. Nezh was a real team player. His playing on a team made him more strict and responsible. He didn't spare himself, not only in the analysis of his own adjourned games, but as a rule, he would become the team analyst. It was so in that championship as well. Rashid not only won playing on his board, but also brought his team points in the games with the higher placed boards, which was especially valuable.

The years from 1950 to 1954 were another peak in Nezh's career. It was unlikely that he would achieve anything more at his age with regards to sporting titles, but there are no age barriers for creative activity, and Rashid Gibyatovitch would demonstrate that for many years to come. Although with the passage of time, his creative successes considerably outshone his sporting

Sochi, Chigorin Memorial. Marina Bronnikova, Anatoly Lein, Tamara Ivanovna (wife), Iskander (son), Rashid, and arbiter Karen Ogadzhsanian.

achievements.

Nezh didn't manage to win the 1954 and 1956 Russian championships. He took second place and tied for second place, respectively. In both cases it was felt that he lacked the strength to even go the distance. Then he had success in the semi-finals of the 24th USSR championship where he divided first place honors with Boleslavsky and his friend Tarasov.

The finals tournament which was held in Moscow at the beginning of 1957 went down in the annals of Soviet chess history as one of the most important and interesting among the Soviet Union championships. Its significance lay in the fact that it became a springboard for the swift upward flight of Mikhail Tal. The 20-year old master, for the first time, became champion of the country, leaving the grandmaster elite behind. Nezhmetdinov didn't win laurels in that championship, placing in the lower half of the tournament table, but he did manage to create a stir by defeating the freshly baked champion Tal and his rival, Boris Spassky. Spassky was the same age as Tal and, at that time, was the youngest grandmaster in the world as well as world junior champion.

Throughout the whole of Soviet history, the country's leaders, whoever they might be, Stalin, Khrushchev, or Brezhnev, had always treated the leading sportsmen very favorably, and from time to time showed them many kindnesses, awarding them prizes and medals. In 1957 Rashid Nezhmetdinov got his turn on the list. It is true, he was not awarded the highest of orders, he was honored only with a medal. However, for a Soviet man, it was not the rank of the award that was important, but the very fact it was being awarded. An award raised the social status of the citizen, and Rashid was very proud of his medal.

Who knows whether the govermental award inspired his further chess success, but the years of 1957 and 1958 became, again, another peak in his career. Nezhmetdinov won, twice in a row, the championship of Russia and became a 5-time champion. The magazine *Chess in the USSR* wrote about him: "One can become a competition winner if he plays especially attentively and energetically, and in an interesting way."

With the same creative enthusiasm he was now known for, Nezhmetdinov played in the semi-finals of the 26th USSR championship and tied with Spassky for first place. In the same fighting mood Rashid went to the finals of the championship which was held in Tbilisi in 1959. At the opening ceremony he learned with regret that he was the oldest participant. Of course, that couldn't encourage him. The composition of the tournament was remarkable and it was easy to be lost among its participants where any one could better than any other. Still nobody expected that Nezh would come to such a disaster—last place but one. In the majority of cases the game would follow this scenario: a well played opening, a promising middlegame, and then near the end there would be mistakes and time trouble.

One had to note that Nezh reached that point when, as one master who was his age put it, "When I am at the chessboard, I see everything, I understand everything, but... " Success left him even in the Russian championships, his favorite tournament. In 1959 he could only split fifth place, and it was even worse in 1960 when he tied for ninth.

Yet, there was a third peak of success, the year 1961. Seven years after his first international tournament, Rashid played in his second international competition. It was the Chigorin Memorial in Rostov-on-Don. Foreigners who were not used to his impetuousness were defeated, one after another. He was also successful when he played against his compatriots as well. As a result, he took second place after Taimanov. Just like Bucharest 1954, he made spectacular attacks and sacrifices. With this same enthusiasm Nezh played at the next Russian championship in Omsk. The tournament was also a semi-final for the 29th USSR championship. He didn't become a champion for a sixth time, but with a powerful finish he managed to take second place even though it was divided among four other contestants. These five were to play for two "tickets" to a Union championship in another competition. The veteran Nezhmetdinov turned out to have the best tie-breaks.

Nezh didn't have any ambitious plans in the country's championship where he again was the oldest. But he was always eager to fight; he used to say: "Our day will come." He defined his tournament fate exactly: his result was very modest, but still he had his successful moments! When Rashid Gibyatovich was playing his famous game with Mikhail Tal (Game No. 10), the commentators nicknamed him "Evergreen Rashid."

Some years later Tal, who by that time was an ex-world champion and who had experienced to the fullest all sorts of troubles under the sun, was asked when was the happiest day of his life. Usually one would expect an answer like: "When I became the world champion."

Nothing of the kind. Tal replied: "When I lost to Nezhmetdinov(!!)."

That was Tal all over—the objective knight of chess beauty. At the same time it was the highest praise for Nezh who also belonged to that limited circle of Caissa's priests. Before the 1960 World championship match between Tal and Botvinnik, Tal could have chosen any of the leading grandmasters as his assistant in preparing for the big match. He invited Nezhmetdinov, whom he began to greatly respect after their memorable game in the 24th USSR championship, and he considered it a wise decision. He recalled: "Nezhmetdinov hasn't been a theorist in the usual sense—he hasn't got card indexes or overly thick notebooks, but his ideas are remembered. They attract attention because they are out of the ordinary; they have not always withstood the test of time, but at the beginning they have always been very dangerous for the opponent."

In the last ten years of his life he was rarely a success at tournaments. The logical train of struggle in his games was more and more often distorted by mistakes and time trouble. Even though the sporting results of his performances were modest, at any tournament, as a rule, he was one of the first to get a prize for the best game.

Grandmaster V. Simagin, who was one of the admirers of Nezh's play and who himself was a bright, creative chessplayer, wrote: "A youthful freshness is characteristic of play by the chess veteran Nezhmetdinov. His talent doesn't lose its luster with the years. For many years running I have been observing Nezh's creative activity and I have come to the conclusion that in the sphere of sharp combinational play he doesn't finish second to the best grandmasters in the world."

Some scattered tournament successes continued to come to Rashid Gibyatovich: he was third in the Baku international tournament in 1964; he won in the championship of the sports league "Spartak" in the same year; he took part in the 35th USSR championship in 1967. Nevertheless, the successes of his pupils and his team, the combined team of the Tartar Republic, were gradually becoming more and more important to him.

In the 60s some young chess players from Kazan (Damsky, Voloshin and Smirnov) became masters. Each of them was schooled by Rashid Gibyatovich. He trained them in chess, not only sharing with them his knowledge and experience, but influencing them with his personal example. In those years the Tartar team was young. The chess veteran played only on Board One. If we look at the games of the team players, we can see that it was Nezhmetdinov who demonstrated the most energetic and crucial play. One cannot measure his contribution to the team's success only by looking at the points he brought to the team's scorebox. The team's general attitude, created by the victories of their leader and the example of his desire to struggle to the end without sparing himself, was even more important. The other participants of the team just could not slacken or avoid the struggle. If they did, they would forever lose the respect of their coach and idol. Though the Tartar team of the 60s were considered underdogs to other teams in terms of qualification and sports titles, quite often those same teams finished lower in the tournament tables than the Tartars.

Rashid Gibyatovich was 60 when he took part in his last tournament. It was an open championship in Latvia in 1972. He divided third and fourth places. He didn't finish his last game.

Super Nezh

Shortly before he died he started a game with the readers of the newspaper *Socialistic Tatarstan*. Nezhmetdinov never refused to meet with amateur chessplayers and fans. He never played carelessly in those games, such as by using only half of his strength, either in the performance of a simultaneous exhibition or with a group of amateurs. He never showed them any difference in his level of mastery. In the very same way, he played that last game in earnest. Making moves, he even commented on them, thus turning a game into an original chess lesson for thousands of inexperienced readers of the newspaper. Even when bedridden in the hospital, he didn't stop playing the game.

In June of 1974 the readers didn't see the next move of the Master; instead, in the place of a blackened chess diagram there was an obituary. The game was still played to the end—his pupils finished it.

The author of this book has often thought: what if Rashid had been born 50 years later? Would he have been the same Nezhmetdinov? Could he have been able to create masterpieces at the chess board of the same high standard?

Had he been born in the 60s, he might have gone to Botvinnik's school, from which came Kasparov. He might have received immeasurably better conditions for developing his talent: better coaches, a great number of chess books and magazines, a lot of competitions and constant contacts with leading figures...

There is no doubt he would have become a grandmaster, which he never achieved during his lifetime. He might have even become a great and prominent grandmaster. Could he have become *the* Nezhmetdinov? It's seems hardly possible; the multifaceted person seldom creates masterpieces.

At present, chess is, in essence, different from chess in the times of Rashid Gibyatovich. At present, results (sporting rationalism) reigns supreme, and creative improvisation is contraindicative. At present, ratings and prizes are foremost in the minds of almost every master, and everything else is secondary. Tournament organizers prefer to invite mediocre players who have a high rating, but not those romantics who do not. It is a pity, but chess Don Quixotes, like Nezhmetdinov, Tolush, Simagin, and later Kupreichik, could not survive in the present chess climate.

I would like to conclude this short biographical excursion with some of Nezhmetdinov's statements:

"With every game a door to a mysterious world of fantasy, adventure, enigma and exact mathematical calculations is opened for me."

"For me chess is an eternal enigma and a miracle. Space flight doesn't impress us today. It has become ordinary. It's nearly impossible to predict a move in a chess game. Even chess pieces are capable of behaving in the most incomprehensible way for us chessplayers, as well as for outside spectators."

"For playing well, I need inspiration. Like a capricious woman, it either visits me or it stands me up. Without inspiration there is no playing well. I am not rational enough; therefore games where one should play positionally and capture necessary squares, and hold back the opponent, most often end unhappily for me."

"I think, many of my chess colleagues have experienced the following feeling: you think you are close to success; all you need is to extend a hand and a firebird will be caught. All of a sudden, everything falls to the ground. Your hand is empty, and the firebird of luck has flown to another."

In commentaries to his game with Tal, Nezh devoted the following curious eulogy to a chess knight which was one of the main heroes of that remarkable chess performance:

"There is nothing more enigmatic than a knight. Its possibilities in a definite situation surpass any imagination. A knight is presented sometimes as a dragon, as a force that cannot be either held back or tamed."

Isn't it true to write that it is not enough to be a chessplayer, one should also be a real artist?

2

Masterpieces

The largest collection of Nezhmetdinov's pearls of creative activity have been gathered into this chapter. There aren't many, but each one will suit the varied tastes of the lovers of art in chess.

Even in this array of brilliant works Game No. 1 stands apart—it's distinguished as Rashid Gibyatovich's calling card.

1.

L. Polugaevsky—Super Nezh

A 53

18th Russian ch.

Sochi 1958

1. d4 Nf6 2. c4 d6 3. Nc3 e5.

This is one of the ways of avoiding Sämisch's system. Black should be ready for an early exchange of Queens. Usually Nezh regarded this prospect without enthusiasm, but he still chose this variation quite often.

4. e4

Nezh preferred 4. Nf3.

4. ... exd4
5. Qxd4 Nc6
6. Qd2 g6
7. b3 Bg7
8. Bb2 0-0
9. Bd3 Ng4
10. Nge2

In the game *Alatortsev—Boleslavsky, 18th USSR Ch., 1950,* there was: 10. Nf3 Nge5! 11. Be2 Nxf3† 12. Bxf3 Nd4 13. Bd1 f5, and Black captured the initiative.

10. ... Qh4!

That is just so! Despite the usual conceptions of opening strategy, proceeding from the concrete peculiarities of the position, Black makes an early move with the Queen without completing the development of his pieces, thus making White determine the position immediately. Now the game enters a period of violent tactical complications.

R. N.

It can be added here that after 10... Nge5 White would simply retreat to 11. Bc2, retaining the possibility of driving the Knight away by f2-f4.

11. Ng3 Nge5

Nezh rejected the more active 11... Nce5 because of 12. Bc2 Bh6 13. f4! for fear that after White castles long he might lose the initiative. The fact is, on 13... Nxh2 there was 14. Nce2 and 14... Nhf3† 15. gxf3 Qxh1† 16. Nxh1 Nxf3† 17. Kd1 Nxd2 18. Kxd2 was not dangerous. After the move in the game, castling is not yet possible because of Bh6.

However, 11... Bd4!? should be taken into consideration. After 12. Nd1 Bxb2 13. Qxb2 [if 13. Nxb2, then 13... Nxh2 14. Be2 Be6 and White will not be able to castle long] Nce5 14. Bc2 Nxh2 15. Ne3 then Black had the nice 15... Qf6 with the threat of ...Nd3†.

12. 0-0

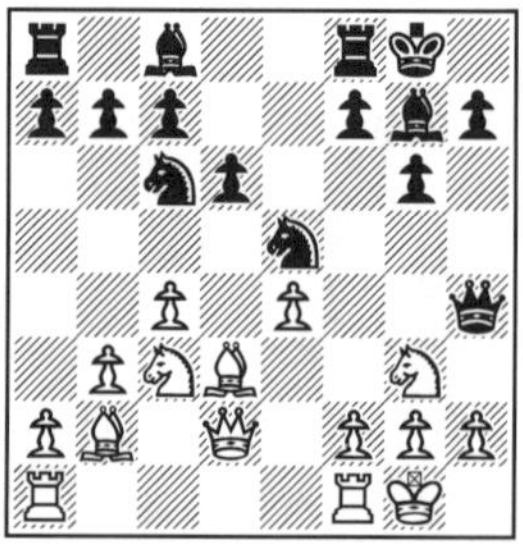

It was necessary to castle as there was no time to make moves like 12. Bc2 because of 12... Nd4!, or 12. Be2 Bh6 13. Qd1 f5.

12. ... f5!

In this position few would refuse the "easily winning" move 12... Ng4. It appears that after 13. h3 Nxf2 Black might win a pawn in the unceasing attack [14. Kxf2 Bd4† 15. Kf3 Ne5†, or 14.

Rxf2 Qxg3, or at last, 14. Qxf2 Bd4]. If you consider the position more deeply, you can understand that all this is not as simple as it appears to be at first sight. After 12... Ng4 13. h3 Nxf2 14. Qxf2 Bd4 White may suddenly sacrifice the Queen for two minor pieces: 15. Qxd4!! Nxd4 16. Nd5!. Here the usual material considerations recede into the background and the concrete peculiarities of the position come to the foreground. Despite Black's solid material advantage, White's position is in no way worse than that of Black, and psychologically a sudden turn of events is only in White's favor.

R. N.

It was a pity, but the sacrifice of the Queen, suggested by Nezh, was fantasy of the first order. After 16... c5! 17. Ne2 Nxe2† 18. Bxe2 f5 19. Rf4 Qd8 20. exf5 Bxf5 21. g4 Qg5, and 22... Rae8, White has no compensation for the Queen. That's why 12... Ng4 was good, and may well be the best move. After 13. h3 Nxf2 14. Rxf2 Qxg3 15. Ne2 Qh4 16. Bxg7 Kxg7 17. Raf1. Sure, Black can't attack, but as compensation he had a healthy extra pawn.

13. f3

White had to defend, but the move played was not best. Now Black gets the initiative for a long time. There was a way to equalize: 13. exf5 Nxd3 14. Qxd3 Bxf5 15. Nxf5 Rxf5 16. Rae1.

13. ... Bh6!

No doubt Black can win the pawn with 13... Nxd3 14. Qxd3 Bd4† 15. Kh1 Be5 16. Qd5† Rf7 17. f4 Bxf4. Yet, after 18. Nce2 Bxg3 19. Nxg3 White would create some serious counterplay.

14. Qd1 f4

It was worth paying attention to 14... Be3† 15. Kh1 and only now 15... f4 16. Nge2 Nxd3 17. Qxd3 Nb4.

15. Nge2 g5
16. Nd5 g4
17. g3!

White's crafty defense certainly increased the worth of the game and presented serious problems to Rashid because if Black's pieces were driven away from the attacking position, White's counterattack wouldn't take long to begin.

Of course White couldn't play 17. Nxc7? because of 17... g3. Then 18. h3 Bxh3! with a decisive attack.

17. ... fxg3
18. hxg3 Qh3
19. f4 Be6!

The stereotypical continuation of 19... Nf3† can be ruinous for Black because of the attack 20. Kf2 Qh2† 21. Ke3. Instead of that, Black found a witty resource allowing him to keep the Knight at the most important e5-square.

20. Bc2?

20. fxe5 was forbidden because of 20... Bxd5 threatening 21... Be3.

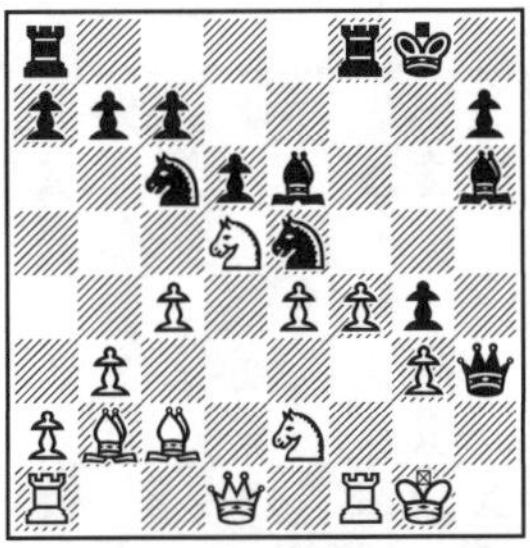

As the game went on to show, this retreat was unsuccessful. It would be difficult for White to defend, mainly because of the different ways of attacking the f4-square. So, in the event of 20. Bc1, then 20... Bxd5 21. cxd5 Nd4!. The fork wouldn't work either: 20. Nxc7? Rxf4! 21. Rxf4 Bxf4 22. Nxf4 Qxg3† 23. Ng2 Rf8, and Black's threats were irrefutable.

20. Bxe5 wasn't any better because of 20... Nxe5! And again, 21. Nxc7 wouldn't work because of 21... Rxf4!.

The position in this diagram has been analyzed by many. Another retreat was offered by 20. Bb1!? It was clear that the white Bishop must be moved because of 20... Bxf4. After 20... Bxd5 21. Qxd5† Rf7 22. Kf2 Bg7 23. Bc3 Nf3 24. Bxg7 Kxg7. Black's attack was dangerous, but White can still defend himself.

20. ... Rf7

Black takes a time out to make a defensive move. Now there won't be a check on d5.

21. Kf2 Qh2†
22. Ke3 Bxd5
23. cxd5

In case of 23. Qxd5 [23. exd5? Re8] there is 23... Nb4 24. Qd2 Rxf4! 25. gxf4 Bxf4 26. Nxf4 Nxc2†, and it would be over. That would be the result of the mistake on move 20.

23. ... Nb4
24. Rh1

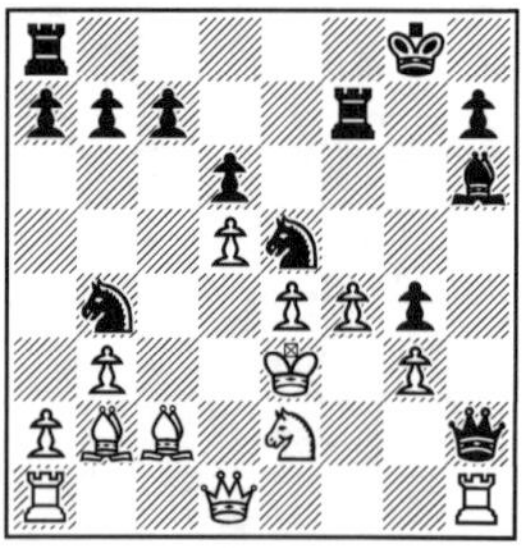

24. ... Rxf4!!

Sunk in thought for a long time, I understood that I was to say good-bye to all hope and that I was losing a game that would be spread all over the world.

L. Polugaevsky

25. Rxh2

All this time the helpless position of the Bishop on c2 had been telling upon White's position: 25. Nxf4 Nxc2†; 25. gxf4 Bxf4† 26. Nxf4 [26. Kd4 Qf2† 27. Kc3 Qc5#] Nxc2†.

25. ... Rf3†
26. Kd4 Bg7!!

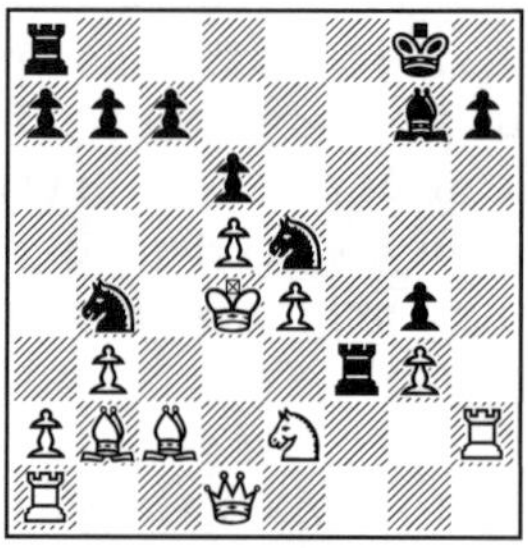

Black has few men for his Queen, and still... he makes a quiet move! A threat had been prepared: 27... c5† 28. dxc6. If 28... bxc6, then 29. Bd3 would stop the immediate mate, but not the loss of the game. On 28... b5, then 29... Nexc6#.

27. a4

Alas, this would have warded off only the second threat, not the first. Let's put ourselves in Polugaevsky's place. It's our move, we have an extra Queen. How can White be finished off? Let's try something:

• 27. Ng1 Ned3† [certainly it was possible to include 27... Rxg3 28. Ne2 Rf3 29. Ng1 c5† 30. dxc6 Ned3†−+] 28. Kc4 Nxb2† 29. Kxb4 Bc3† 30. Ka3 b5! 31. Qd4 Bxd4 32. Nxf3 Bc3! 33. b4 Nc4†

34. Kb3 Bxa1 35. Ng5 Be5!, and Black would be winning.

• Or 27. Nf4 b5 28. Qxf3 Nxf3† 29. Ke3 Bxb2–+.

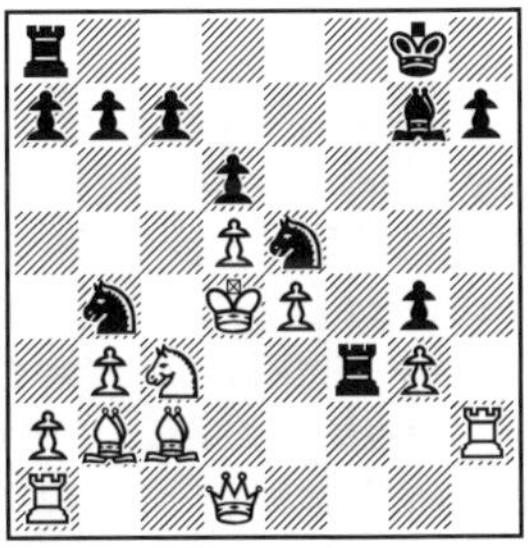

After 27. Nc3!? (analysis below)

• Or lastly 27. Nc3!? Rxg3 [threatening 28… a6!!, followed by 29… Nec6† 30. Kc4 Rxc3†! 31. Bxc3 b5#!] 28. Rh5 Nbd3!, or 28. Nb5 a6!, or 28. Ne2 Rf3 with a transposition after 29. Ng1 to the first variation already considered.

The variations are fantastically complicated. Certainly, in the interests of the chess truth they ought to be studied to the end. Is it in our power to do this? Let's give this opportunity to the meticulous reader. We shall confine ourselves to Nezhmetdinov's quote:

> **It goes without saying it was impossible to consider at the chessboard (!) all probable continuations. The combination was intuitive, therefore it was because of this that it was hard to decide upon it.**
>
> ***—R. N.***

27. ...	**c5†**
28. dxc6	**bxc6**
29. Bd3	**Nexd3**
30. Kc4	**d5†!**
31. exd5	**cxd5†**
32. Kb5	**Rb8†**
33. Ka5	**Nc6†.**

White resigned **(0-1).**

> **I think this is the most beautiful game of all I have played.**
>
> ***—R. N.***

As for most us, we think that he is too modest in the evaluation of the game. Let everybody who considers himself a more powerful chess player than Rashid Gibyatovich ask himself: "Can I ever create anything like it?".

However, a chess game is a canvas made by two artists, and to create such a masterpiece the opponent's composure and persistence are necessary as well. So Polugaevsky should certainly be considered the co-author.

2.

Super Nezh—A. Suetin

B 62

7th Russian ch.

Kuibyshev 1947

1. e4 c5 2. Nf3 Nc6 3. d4 cxd4 4. Nxd4 Nf6 5. Nc3 d6 6. Bg5 e6 7. Bc4.

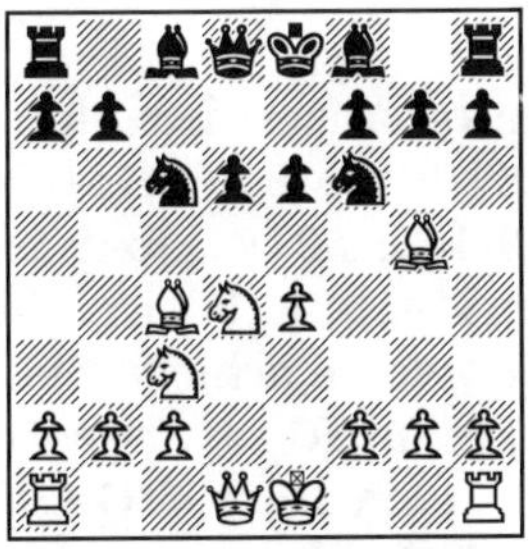

This move is justly condemned by theory. Black can get a comfortable position by a natural and logical way: to castle soon and then Nf6xe4 and d6-

d5 with a release of the tension. Nezh himself recommended this particular plan. Another promising idea was demonstrated by *Larsen* in one of his games at the *Olympiad* in *Siegen, 1970:* 7... Qb6 8. Bxf6 gxf6 9. Ndb5?! [9. Nb3 was better though it's high time for White to struggle for equality] Ne5 10. Bb3 Rg8, and White had gotten into difficulties.

Nezh's choice of his seventh move could very likely be explained by his desire to entice his young rival, who later became a prominent opening theorist, to still unknown paths.

7. ... a6?!

White's intention was justified: Black lost time in vain.

8. Nxc6 bxc6
9. e5 Qa5

Nezh considered this move best, but the course of the game didn't confirm this viewpoint. If 9... dxe5 he proposed the following:

10. Qf3 Bd7 11. 0-0-0 Be7 12. Bxf6! Bxf6 13. Rd3 Qc7 14. Rhd1 Rd8 15. Ne4 Be7 16. Nd6† Bxd6 17. Rxd6 Ke7 18. Qg3, and White restores the material equilibrium in a considerably better position.

Damsky proposed reinforcement: 10... Be7! 11. Bxf6 [or 11. Qxc6† Bd7 12. Qf3 0-0 13. 0-0 Qc7] Bxf6 12. Qxc6† Bd7 13. Qf3 0-0 14. Rd1 Qc7 15. Bd3 Rab8, and Black would achieve good play.

10. Bxf6 gxf6
11. exd6 Qe5†
12. Kf1!

Playing without prejudices. After 12. Qe2 Bxd6 13. 0-0-0 Rb8, White would castle but lose the initiative.

12. ... Qxd6?

A new loss of tempo which placed Black into a difficult situation. Though 12... Bxd6 13. Qf3 would give White an opportunity to develop an attack in the center, it would still allow Black to defend.

13. Qf3 f5
14. Rd1 Qc7
15. g4!

For the sake of opening lines, White was ready to weaken the cover of his own King. There was no fear of a counterattack on Black's part because of Black's lack of development.

15. ... fxg4
16. Qxg4 Bb7?

A critical moment in the game. Black has serious defensive problems which are difficult to solve by simple means. Black's passive move can only be explained so: Suetin saw White's opportunity to begin a direct attack with the Bishop sacrifice on e6. However, he also saw that the attack was not necessarily deadly, and knowing Nezh's passion for swift attacks, he played Bb7 provoking the sacrifice.

If we reject psychological speculation, we see that Black's move is not good. He should have looked at 16. ... Rb8, and if 17. Ne4 then 17. ... Qe5 with Be7 to follow. White retains the initiative, but Black retains defensive opportunities.

Now comes a combination calculated far ahead, which befittingly crowns the game. After 16... Bd7 17. Ne4 Be7 18. Qg7 Black probably wouldn't escape either, but would have retained practical chances for defense. Transferring the Bishop away from defending the e6-square, Black certainly saw the subsequent outcome but hoped to refute it ...

17. Bxe6?!

The tempting bishop sacrifice leads to the win, but should have lost the advantage. 17. Qh5! is a clever maneuver which makes it difficult to defend against the threatened Bxe6. Perhaps 17. ... Bc8 must be played, when Black must regret his provocation, and now after 18. Rg1 or 18. Ne4 White has a siginificant advantage.

17. ... fxe6
18. Qxe6† Be7

For 18... Qe7 Nezh had prepared 19. Qf5! Bc8 20. Qf3! [But not 20. Qh5† Qf7 21. Rd8† Ke7 22. Qg5† Qf6 23. Re8† Kf7 24. Qh5† Qg6 and Black is winning, or 21. Qe5† Qe7 22. Qxh8? Bh3†.] with the following effective variant: 20... Qc7 [Ed.: The defensive move 20... Ra7 poses some real problems for White as there is no obvious killer reply such as in Nezh's response to 20... Qc7.] 21. Re1† Be7 22. Rg1 Rf8 23. Qh5† Kd8 24. Rg7 Re8 25. Nd5! Qa5 26. Qxe8!!.

19. Ne4 Bc8
20. Nf6† Kf8
21. Rd7!

Now there would be nothing to defend the white squares.

21. ... Bxd7
22. Nxd7† Ke8
23. Nf6† Kd8

After 23... Kf8 White would have won immediately with 24. Rg1.

24. Ke2!

Starting the sacrifice at move 17, White had to have foreseen this "royal" move after which Black would have had to part with his Queen.

24. ... Qd6
25. Rd1 Qxd1†
26. Kxd1 Bxf6
27. Qxf6† Kc7
28. Qe7† Kb6
29. c4

After several more moves Black surrendered. **(1-0).**

The game was awarded a prize for "its beauty."

3.

Super Nezh—M. Kamyshov
B 10
10th Russian ch.
Gorki 1950

1. e4 c6 2. Nf3 d5 3. Nc3 Nf6.

Just like 3... d4, this continuation was not the best one. The line with a safe reputation is 3... Bg4 4. h3 Bxf3 5. Qxf3 e6, a position which is solid and for which there are no problems. If 3... d4, White gets the advantage by playing 4. Ne2 c5 5. Ng3 Nc6 6. Bc4 e5 7. d3 Be7 8. 0-0.

4. e5 Ne4
5. Ne2!

This idea, which is now universally acknowledged, belongs to master L. Savitsky. This talented chessplayer only lived 24 years yet managed to play in two USSR championships in the 30s. On 5... Bg4, Savitsky answered 6. Nfg1(!!) and Black was obliged to retreat, though the black Knight's path of retreat was awkward: 6... Bd7 7. f3 Nc5 8. d4 Nca6 9. c3. The Knight's wandering led Black to be restrained in his play, *Savitsky—Veresov, 9th USSR Ch., 1934.*

5. ... Qb6

Nezh considered this move to be weak, but here it looks as if the question isn't about one isolated move. After 5... e6 [or 5... g6] 6. d3 Nc5 7. d4 White would get an advantage in the center, since on 7... Ne4 we would get the already familiar 8. Nfg1!.

6. d4 c5

7. dxc5 Qxc5

Boleslavsky considered 7... Nxc5 as preferable, but still not sufficient for equalization: 8. Nf4 e6 9. Be2 Be7 10. 0-0 0-0 11. c4 dxc4 12. Bxc4 Nc6 13. Qe2 Na5 14. Nh5! with White having the initiative.

8. Ned4 Nc6

9. Bb5!

It was possible to play more quietly: 9. Be2, as in the game *Sokolsky—Holmov, 17th USSR Ch., 1949.* Nezh didn't like the unclear complications which could come from 9... g5!?.

9. ... Bd7

If 9... a6, then 10. Bxc6† bxc6 11. 0-0 Bg4 12. Be3 Qc4 13. c3 e6 14. b3! Qxc3 15. Rc1 Qb2 16. Rc2 Qa3 17. Nxc6 with the threat Bc1.

R. N.

10. 0-0

Here there was no going back: it was necessary to sacrifice a pawn, as 10. Bxc6, can not be seriously regarded.

10. ... Nxe5!?

Of course, this is risky, and Nezh put a question mark to this move. What he recommended, namely 10... e6, is even worse: after 11. Be3 Nxd4 [11... Qb4 12. c4 dxc4 13. Qc2] 12. Bxd7† Kxd7 13. Nxd4 the position of the black King in the center is fraught with danger.

11. Nxe5 Bxb5

12. Nxb5 Qxb5

13. Re1! Nf6?!

13... e6 looked better, but ... it would have lost immediately because of 14. c4! Qa5 [or 14... Qb6] 15. Rxe4! and not 15... dxe4, due to 16. Qd7#!. The only chance to resist [and to resist with persistence] was 13... Rd8!. Damsky points out the following: 14. Nxf7 Kxf7 15. Rxe4 dxe4 16. Qxd8 g6 17. Qd4 Bg7 18. Qxe4 Rd8 19. Qf3† Kg8 20. c3 a5, and White should make a great effort to use the extra pawn. After 13... Rd8!, White shouldn't have sped up the play. 14. Qf3 was worth considering, and if 14... Nf6, then there was 15. g4 h6 16. h4, and on 14... Nd6—15. a4 Qa5 16. c3 White would have strong pressure for the pawn.

14. Bg5 e6

15. c4!

A calculated blow in the center was the beginning of the final assault. Black shouldn't take that pawn: 15... dxc4 16. Bxf6 gxf6 17. a4! Qd5 18. Qxd5 exd5 19. Ng6†.

15. ... Qa5

16. Bxf6 gxf6

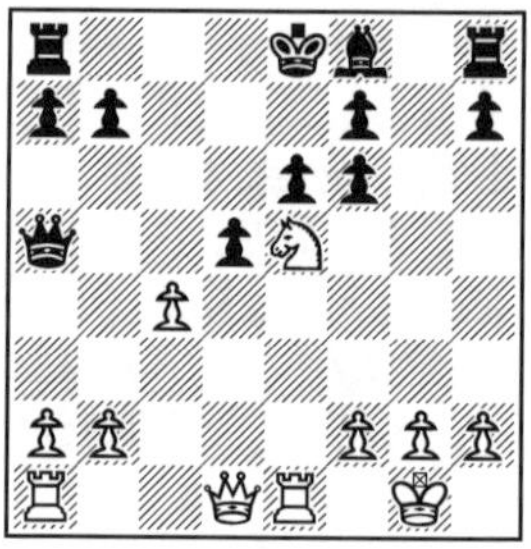

17. Nxf7!!

With the King stuck in the center of the board, this sacrifice was as logical and natural as it was spectacular.

17. ... Kxf7

18. Qh5† Ke7

18... Kg8 would have been followed

by 19. Qg4† Bg7 20. Qxe6† Kf8 21. Qd6† Kg8 22. Re7 and, it would have been all over.

19. cxd5 e5
20. f4 Qxd5

[Ed.: If 20… Qb6†, then 21. Kh1 Bg7 draws. We do not know why Black didn't play it except he probably thought that 20… Qxd5 wins because of his extra Rook.]

21. fxe5 f5
22. e6 Kf6
23. h4!

Using very limited forces, White attacked successfully, and now came the final touch.

23. ... Bc5†
24. Kh1 Qxe6
25. Qh6†

Black surrendered **(1-0).**

4.
A. Lilienthal—Super Nezh
A 54
Semi-finals 19th USSR ch.
Baku 1951

1. d4 Nf6 2. c4 d6 3. Nc3 e5 4. Nf3 Nbd7 5. g3 exd4?!.

This was, by no means, a forced surrender of the center. The usual continuation is 5… c6 6. Bg2 e4 and 7… d5.

6. Nxd4

Taking into account that the Knight could no longer attack the Queen, it was worth looking at 6. Qxd4.

6. ... g6
7. Bg2 Bg7
8. 0-0 0-0
9. b3

After 9. e4, White could have moved into the usual positions of the King's Indian Defense.

9. ... Nc5
10. b4

Sharp play with the intention to attack on the Queen's wing. As Black had no weaknesses, such a move could allow counterplay as well.

10. ... Ne6
11. Nb3 Nd7
12. Bb2 Ne5
13. Na5 Nd4

This is an attempt to maneuver the Knight to c6.

But of course Black has at his disposal the "normal" 13... Rb8 14. Rc1 f5 with approximately equal chances.

14. Na4

The flanking attack of a Knight's detached force on the queenside looks rather suspicious when opposed to the centralization of the black Knight on d4. Nevertheless, it is not a bad idea as Black must defend against the pressure along the h1-a8 diagonal. Perhaps 14. Nb5?! Nxb5 15. cxb5 Rb8 16. Bd4! is more energetic, and Black has some difficulty defending his queenside. If the game were to follow this line, Black would probably regret his Knight's raid in the center [13… Nd4]. In this position, Nimzovich's well known aphorism 'A threat is stronger than its execution' finds real confirmation. The fact is that the immediate exchange on b7, i.e., 14. Nxb7 [14. Bxb7 Bxb7 15. Nxb7 Qb8 16. Nd5 Qxb7 17. Bxd4 c6 18. Ne3 Qxb4 is equal] Bxb7 15. Bxb7 Rb8 16. Nd5 Ne6 17. f4 Rxb7 18. fxe5 c6 gives White nothing.

14. ... c5?!

Nezh excitedly pours oil on the flame of the battle. Objectively, 14… Ndc6 15. Nxc6 Nxc6 16. Bxg7 Kxg7 is stronger. Though Black's position remains solid, it loses active play, something Nezh would never consent to voluntarily.

15. a3

Solid, but 15. Nxb7! is more energetic—now this exchange is convincing: 15... Bxb7 16. Bxb7 Rb8 17. bxc5! dxc5 18. Bd5 and White has an extra pawn and a nice position.

15. ... Bg4!

Black again tempts his rival with the b7-pawn. From a chess expediency point of view it would be 'better' to continue 15... Qe7 16. Bxd4 cxd4 17. Rc1 leaving White with a pawn advantage on the queenside, but material equality. As a matter of fact, psychology begins to play the leading role. It reminds one of poker, where each of the players, acting with an assurance of success, raise the bet higher than their cards warrant, and finally an opponent folds, taking his word for it.

16. Bxd4 cxd4

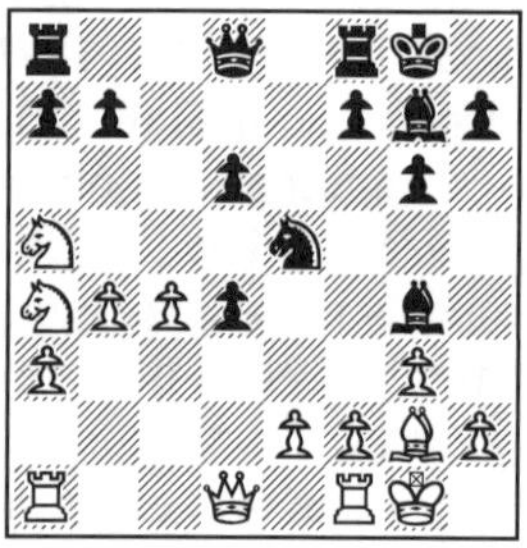

17. h3

After a long think, Lilienthal believed his opponent and refused to take the b7 pawn. It's a critical point in the game. Let's examine what this decision means—was it a fatal hesitation or prudence? Observe:

A. 17. Bxb7 Re8! [Nezh gives the following variation in his analysis: 17... h5 but this is hardly correct: 18. Bxa8 Qxa8 19. f3 Bh3 20. Rf2 d3 21. e4 Nxf3† 22. Qxf3 Bxa1 23. Nb3 Be5 24. Qxd3. The attack wasn't a success; the move 17... h5 derives no benefit for Black] 18. Bxa8 [18. f3 doesn't strengthen the position: 18... Bh3 19. Bxa8 Qxa8! 20. Rf2 d3 21. Ra2 Bh6! 22. f4 Ng4 23. exd3 Nxf2 24. Rxf2 Bg7 25. Nb3 Re3! with the most dangerous threat of Qe8.] Qxa8 19. f3 Bh6!. And now:

a) 20. Qxd4 Nxf3† 21. exf3 Be3† 22. Qxe3 Rxe3 23. fxg4 Re2 24. Rf2 Qe8 25. Nb2 [Bad are 25. b5 Re1† or 25. Nc3 Re1†.] Qe3, and Black's chances are better;

b) 20. Kh1 d3! 21. e4 Bxf3† 22. Rxf3 Qxe4 23. Kg2 d2 with a dangerous attack, e.g., 24. Nc3 Qxf3† 15. Qxf3 Nxf3 26. Nd1 Nd4;

c) 20. Kg2 d3 21. e4 Nxf3 22. Qxd3 Rxe4! and here White's position is in trouble.

B. 17. Nxb7 Qd7 18. Na5 d3 19. Nc3 dxe2 20. Nxe2 Nf3† 21. Bxf3 Bxf3 22. Ra2 Rfe8 23. Qd3. This position is preferable for White, but instead of 19... dxe2 Black can play 19... Rac8 20. Rc1 Rfe8 with compensation for his pawn.

So, we can conclude that Lilienthal made the wrong decision by not taking on b7. It would have been better to play 17. Nxb7 with equal chances. Now, the initiative is in Black's hands.

17. ... Be6

18. c5

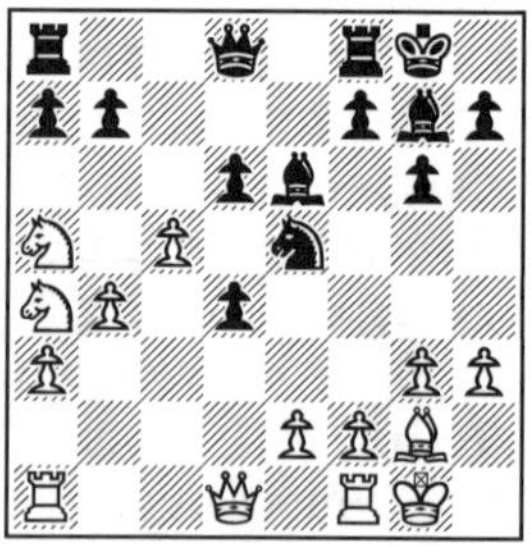

18. ... b5!

The decisive blow. Now White was

forced to take material and leave his King without a defender.

19. cxb6?

Taking on a8 in such a position is no doubt unacceptable. White should have stepped back: 19. Nb2 dxc5 20. Nb7 Qc8 21. Nxc5 Bxh3 and Black has the advantage but after the move in the game White's position quickly worsens.

19. ... axb6

20. Bxa8

At last White takes the exchange offered by Black. However, it is practically forced. There is nothing good for White after 20. Nc6 Nxc6 21. Bxc6 Rc8 22. Rc1 [22. Bg2 d3] Bxh3.

20. ... Qxa8

21. Nxb6 Qa6

22. Na4 Bxh3

23. Rc1

On 23. Re1 there would have followed the same blow [23... d3] as in the game.

23. ... d3!

24. exd3

On 24. e3, Nezh had prepared 24... d2!!, putting a stop to any remaining resistance.

24. ... Qa8

25. f3 Ng4!

By energetic strokes Rashid Gibyatovich finished the canvas with a powerful attack. White was helpless.

26. Nc4

A beautiful variation finished the game after 26. Rf2 Bd4 27. Rcc2 Re8 28. Nc4 Qxf3!! with an inevitable mate.

26. ... Bd4†

27. Kh1 Qd5

28. Rc2 Bxf1

White resigned **(0-1)**.

5.

Super Nezh—Lusikal

D 85

Simultaneous Exhibition

Kazan 1951

1. d4 Nf6 2. c4 g6 3. Nc3 d5 4. cxd5 Nxd5 5. e4 Nxc3 6. bxc3 c5 7. Bb5†.

It's interesting to note that this very continuation is now at the center of attention of both practical players and theorists.

7. ... Nc6

Nowadays 7... Bd7 is usually played.

8. d5 Qa5

9. Qa4 Qxc3†

10. Ke2 Bd7

Black can't take the Rook: 10... Qxa1 11. dxc6 Kd8 12. Nf3 Qf6 13. Rd1† Kc7 14. Bf4† Qxf4 15. cxb7 Bxb7 16. Qa5† Kb8 17. Qd8† with a quick mate. A better continuation was found not long ago. The game S. *Kiselev—Dvoirys, Russian ch., Elista, 1994* continued: 10... Bg7!? 11. dxc6 0-0 12. cxb7 Bxb7 13. Rb1 c4! 14. Bxc4 Rac8 15. Bb5 a6 16. Bd2 axb5 17. Qxb5 Qc2 18. Qxb7 Rfd8 19. Nf3 Qd3† 20. Kd1? [20. Ke1!=] and now 20... Rc2 and White surrendered.

11. dxc6 bxc6

12. Bxc6 Rd8!

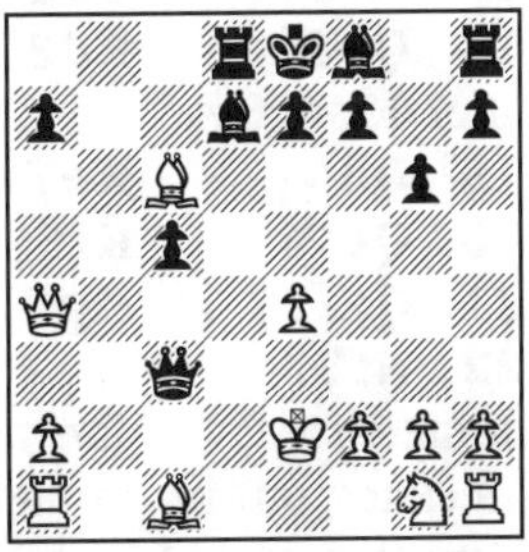

Here *ECO* stops its analysis, taking a stand in favor of Black. True, on the expected 13. Rb1, Black prepared 13...

Qd3†!! 14. Kxd3 Bxc6† and 15... Bxa4, getting an endgame with an extra pawn.

It cannot but arouse admiration how Nezh, in an offhand manner during the simul (!!), found the correct solution of a position which was beyond such venerable theoreticians as A. Karpov, an author of the corresponding section in *ECO*, and Boleslavsky, who had written a monograph on Grünfeld's Defense (Berlin, 1976) and who recommended 13. Bxd7† Rxd7 14. Nf3 Qd3† with a perpetual check.

13. Qb3!! Qxa1

After 13... Qxb3 14. Bxd7† Black would have remained down a piece.

14. Bb2 Qb1

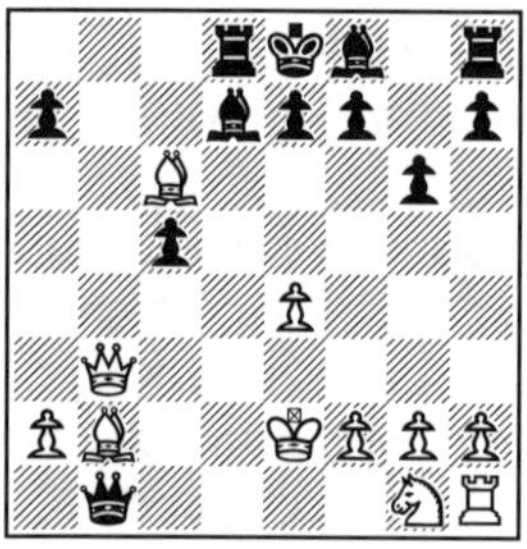

15. Nf3!!

Brilliant! The romantic games of the 19th century immediately come to mind.

15. ... Qxh1
16. Ne5 e6
17. Bxd7† Rxd7
18. Qb8† Rd8

18... Ke7 19. Nc6#.

19. Qb5† Ke7
20. Qb7† Kf6
21. Qxf7† Kg5
22. Nf3†

The game *Yusupov—Morenz, Graz, 1981* is an exact, but incomplete copy of Nezh's masterpiece. It's incomplete because Black offered no resistance and resigned here. Well, there are reasons to study the old masters! Yusupov did not make one of his own moves, and he received a prize for 'Beauty.'

22. ... Kh5
23. g4†! Kxg4
24. Qxe6† Kf4

In *Klarenbeek—Van Gaalen, Ghent, 1992,* Black played 24... Kh5 and was mated.

25. Be5† Kxe4
26. Ng5#!

(1-0). Anderssen would have envied such a game.

6.

Super Nezh—E. Paoli

B 95

Bucharest 1954

1. e4 c5 2. Nf3 d6 3. d4 cxd4 4. Nxd4 Nf6 5. Nc3 a6 6. Bg5 e6 7. Qf3.

The continuation 7. f4, later recognised as the main one, was just paving its way at that time. It was Nezh who, together with Tolush, first discovered this new idea, which later became very popular.

7. ... Be7
8. 0-0-0 Qc7

It was very risky to leave the Queen in the line of fire from the white Rook: 8... Nbd7 [It was no good to play 8... Bd7 9. e5! dxe5 10. Nxe6! fxe6 11. Qxb7 Nc6 12. Bxf6 Bxf6 13. Rxd7!, and White would quickly win, *Khavin—Borisenko, Riga 1954.]* 9. Rg1 Qc7 10. g4 b5 11. a3 Bb7 12. Bxf6 Nxf6 13. g5 Nd7 14. Qh3, with an obvious advantage in White's favor, *Rossetto—Letelier, Mar del Plata 1955.*

9. Rg1

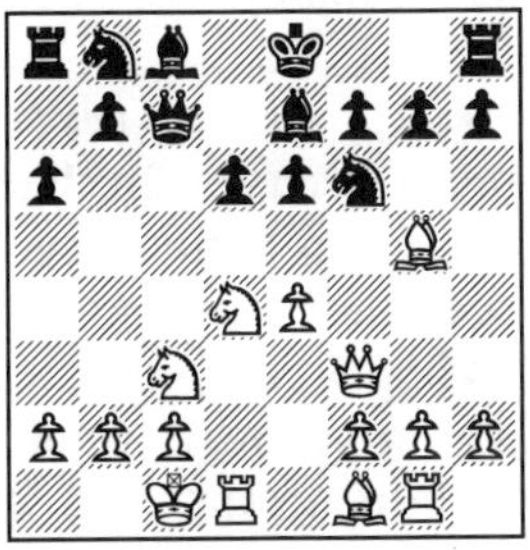

9. ... Bd7?

This was a passive and senseless move. It might have been better if Black, instead, simply missed a move. In such dynamic systems only purposeful, brisk play has a right to live. In reply to White's attack on the kingside it was necessary to prepare a counterattack in the center: 9... 0-0 10. g4 b5 11. a3 Bb7 12. h4 with sufficient counterplay for Black.

10. g4 Nc6
11. Be3 h6
12. h4 Rc8?

It was suicide for Black to castle short. His last move doomed his King to a difficult trial in the center. In essence, it was the losing move. Meanwhile, Black still had a choice of acceptable continuations: 12... Ne5 13. Qe2 [after 13. Qh3 there was no threat of g4-g5 because of the simple answer hxg5] 13... 0-0-0 and White would have a spatial superiority, but not a decisive advantage; 12... h5 13. gxh5 Nxh5 14. Bg5 Nf6 with definite counterplay in *Roizman—Polugaevsky, Leningrad 1953.*

13. g5 hxg5
14. hxg5 Ne5
15. Qg2

15. Qe2 is a little better because after 15... Nfg4 16. g6! [Nothing comes of 16. Rxg4 Nxg4 17. Qxg4 e5 18. Nf5 g6.] Nxe3 17. gxf7† Nxf7 18. Qxe3 Bf6 White will gain a considerable advantage.

15. ... Ng8?

Black should have tried the lunge 15... Nfg4!. After 16. Bf4 Qc5 17. Be2 Ng6! 18. Qxg4 Rh4 19. Bxd6 Bxd6 20. Qf3 Bf4† 21. Kb1 Bxg5 Black should be okay.

16. f4 Nc4
17. Bxc4 Qxc4
18. f5

Not bad, but not the only path of attack. It would have been acceptable to play 18. g6 f6 19. f5, or 18. Rh1 Rxh1 19. Rxh1 Bf8 20. Rh8 Ne7, and White would have the h-file.

18. ... b5
19. Kb1

Nezh's biographer, Master J. Damsky, who was always rapturously commenting on Nezh's creative ability, put two exclamation marks to this move asserting that Rashid had by this time calculated all the moves remaining to mate!

Of course, I too am delighted by the brilliant attacks played in this game, but I don't think that it was possible to make this King move only by having calculated the whole attack to the very end.

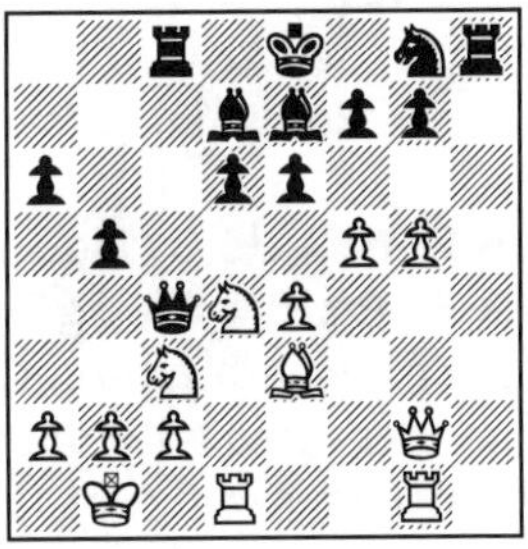

19. ... b4
20. g6!

The beginning of the final assault. Why hadn't Nezh made this move earlier? As we shall soon see, 19. Kb1 took away Black's hopes for counterplay.

20. ... e5
21. b3!

This move deprived the f7-square of the Queen's protection. There was another move, though less spectacular: 21. Nd5 f6 22. b3.

21. ... Qxc3
22. gxf7† Kd8
23. Qxg7 exd4

When the white King was on c1 it might have been possible to play 23... Qxe3† 24. Kb1 Qh3, dragging out the resistance.

24. Bxd4!

The shortest way to victory as the King could not run away through the c7-square.

24. ... Qxc2†
25. Ka1 Rh2
26. Bb6† Rc7
27. Qxg8†

Black resigned **(1-0).**

This game was awarded the first prize for beauty. Nezhmetdinov's son was born the day before, and the happy father dedicated this victory to him.

7.

Super Nezh—G. Kasparyan

B 11

Riga 1955

1. e4 c6 2. Nf3 d5 3. Nc3 Bg4 4. h3 Bxf3 5. Qxf3 e6 6. g3 g6.

This is Kasparyan's patent, which nowadays is covered with dust on the shelf. In the *return-match of 1958, Botvinnik* successfully used it against *Smyslov.* Smyslov developed his Bishop with less success on e2.

7. Bg2 Bg7
8. 0-0 Nd7
9. Qe2

Black had been ready to take the initiative, for example: 9. Rd1? Ne5 10. Qe2 d4 11. Nb1 d3!.

9. ... d4?!

This move deserved no cheers. The Knight goes into temporary retreat, but on the other hand, nothing will prevent White from initiating an attack on the kingside. He should have shown more restraint with, say 9... Ne7.

10. Nb1 e5
11. d3 Ne7
12. f4 Qc7
13. a4 0-0?!

A debatable decision. It was on this very wing where White had the advantage. It would have been safer to play 13... 0-0-0.

14. f5 f6
15. Nd2

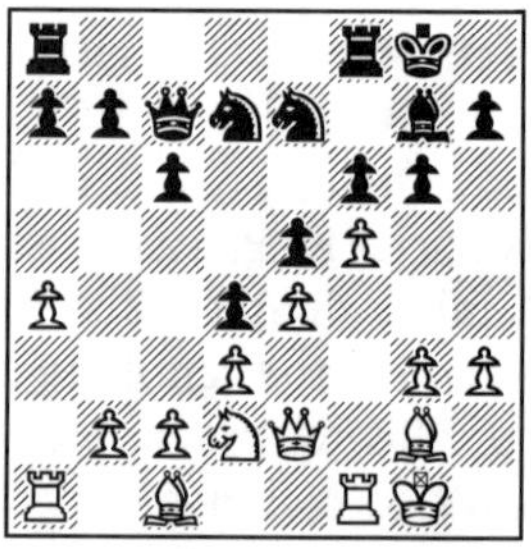

15. ... Bh6!

To exchange black-squared Bishops was a strategically correct decision, as the c1-Bishop might be more dangerous than its opponent.

16. Kh2 Kh8?!

After an impressive move he made a dull, unconvincing one. It might have been better to play 16... Kg7, so that if 17. fxg6 hxg6, it was possible to have the h-file for counterplay.

17. fxg6 hxg6
18. Nf3 Bxc1
19. Raxc1 Nc5?!

Black wanted to make the Knight

more active yet it had nothing to do but allow his opponent to have the initiative. It was worthwhile to think about 19... c5, preparing a pawn storm on the queenside, or 19... Kg7, correcting the inaccuracy which was made at move 16.

20. c3! Nb3

Accepting the sacrifice of a white pawn would have been a very weak-minded idea: 20... dxc3 21. bxc3 Nxa4 22. d4, as Black will have to continue yielding even more: 22... exd4 23. cxd4. With a powerful mobile center White had all the chances for a successful attack.

21. Rcd1 Rad8
22. Nh4 Qc8

It was necessary to switch over to defense as it would have been dangerous to let the white Queen get to g4.

23. Bf3 Qe6
24. Bg4 Qf7?

This was an inaccuracy which resulted in the loss of a tempo. It would have been better to play 24... Qg8 immediately.

25. Nf3 Qg8
26. h4 Kg7
27. Rf2 Rd6?!

Black has no counterplay and can make no headway, still, 27... c5 might have been better.

28. Rdf1 Rdd8
29. Qc2 b6
30. h5 c5

Strategically this was a hopeless attempt to close off play. Upon 30... g5, White, with the help of a very simple regrouping, might move his Knight to g4 and onto f6 where Black would have awaited a catastrophe.

31. hxg6 dxc3
32. bxc3 c4!

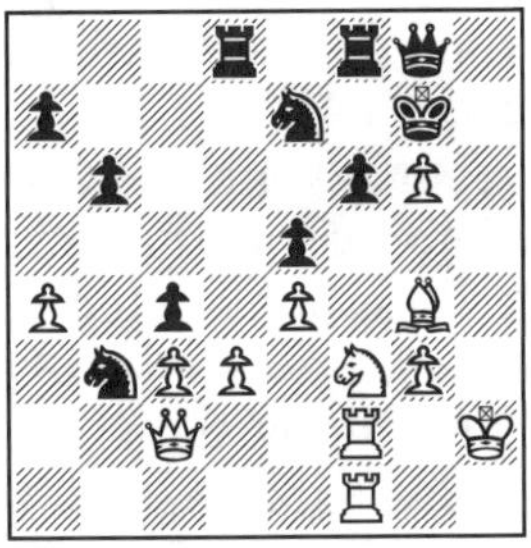

After incomprehensible play, Black finally realized that he was on the verge of defeat and his only chance was in some sort of counterplay. The tension grew.

After a prolonged reflection I managed to realize a multifaceted combination.

R. N.

33. d4! exd4
34. cxd4 Nxd4
35. Nxd4 Rxd4
36. e5 f5
37. Bxf5 Qd5!

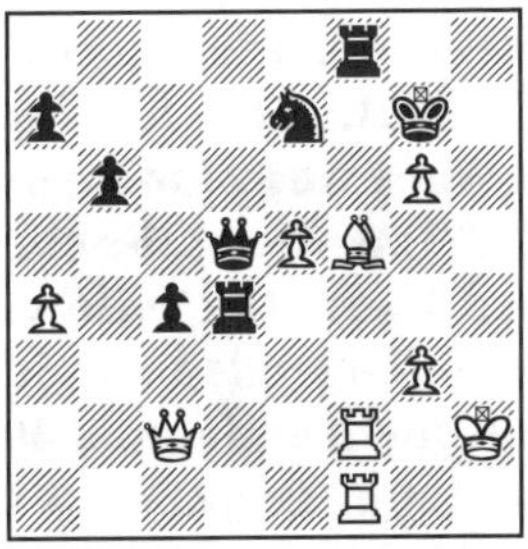

This is a strong move which had to be seen in all its detail before starting the combination.

R. N.

And really, the impression was that White "had gone too far:" the e5 pawn was hanging, and counterthreats could have sprung up along the h-file.

38. Be6!!

The resource which Nezh had earlier taken into account. This move proved the correctness of his attack.

38. ... Rh8†

The following wouldn't be of any use here: 38... Rxf2† 39. Qxf2 Qxe6 40. Qf8†, or 39... Rd2 40. Bxd5 Rxf2† 41. Rxf2 Nxd5 with an easy victory for White in the endgame.

39. Bh3

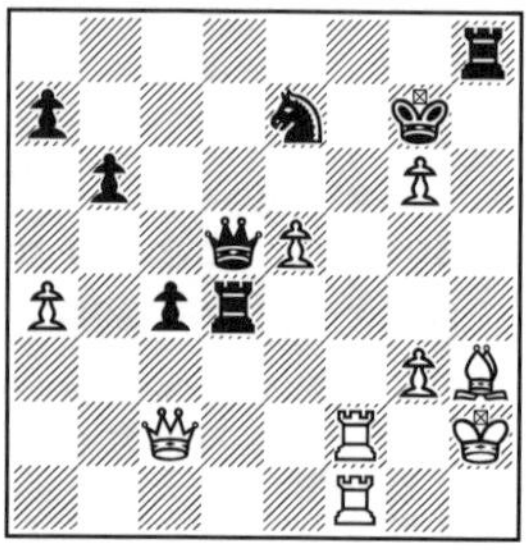

39. ... Nxg6

This lead to the end at once.

The most complicated lines of the combination start with 39... Rd3!. First I thought that White was winning after 40. Rf7†. While at the chessboard I saw the following line which leads to a victorious pawn endgame: 40... Kg8 41. Qg2 Qxg2† 42. Kxg2 Rd2† 43. R1f2 Rxf2† 44. Kxf2! Nxg6 [44... Rxh3 45. Rxe7 with a winning Rook endgame] 45. Be6 Rh7 [I will add such a feature: 45... c3 46. Ke3 c2 47. Kd2 Rh2? 48. Rf2†!—A. P.] **46. Rxa7† Kh8 47. Rxh7† Kxh7 48. Bf5 Kh6 49. Bxg6 Kxg6 50. g4! and White is winning. But when I was mentally checking the position once again and calculating this line again, I suddenly found out that instead of 41... Qxg2†? Black might play even more powerfully: 41... Rd2 42. R1f2 Rxf2! 43. Rxf2 [On 43. Qxf2 Nxg6, Black has the advantage.] and then after 43... Qxg2† 44. Kxg2 Nxg6, White hasn't got anything, as after 45. e6 there is simply 45... Ne7 46. Rc2 [46. Rf7 Rh7] Nd5! 47. Rd2 Rh5.**

Only after checking and rechecking did I find the following line: 40. Qe2 Nxg6 [a thematic mate is discovered in the line 40... Rh6 41. Rf7† Kh8 42. g7† Kh7 (42... Kg8 43. Rxe7†) 43. Qg4 Ng8—or 43... Rd2† 44. Kg1 Qc5† 45. R1f2 Ng8, which leads to the same result—44. Qf5† Rg6 45. Qh5† Rh6 46. Bf5#.] 41. Rf7† Qxf7 [Damsky amended Nezhmetdinov's extensive analysis: 41... Kg8 42. Qg4 Rd2† 43. Kg1 Qd4† 44. Qxd4 Rxd4 45. Be6, or 41... Kh6 42. R1f5 with mate coming.] **42. Rxf7† Kxf7 43. Qg4.**

This position is favorable for White. Only after having checked all the variations did I decide to continue 33. d4!.

This is the longest combination in my practice.

R. N.

The game ended so:

40. Rf7† Kh6

41. Qxg6†!!

Black surrendered **(1-0)**, because there was a mate in six moves: 41... Kxg6 42. R1f6† Kg5 43. Rf5† Kg6 44. R7f6† Kh7 45. Rh5† Kg7 46. Rg5† Kh7 47. Bf5#.

8.

Super Nezh—Y. Kotkov

C 67

17th Russian ch.

Krasnodar 1957

1. e4 e5 2. Nf3 Nc6 3. Bb5 Nf6.

It was a "Berlin Defense," rare nowadays, also sometimes called the "Rio de Janeiro System." It was used as far back as *1886* by *Zukertort* in a *match* with *Steinitz* at the world championship. Nearly one hundred years later the Berlin Defense again appeared at the highest level—in the second game of the match of *Karpov* against *Korchnoy, Merano 1981.*

4. 0-0 Nxe4

5. Re1

Karpov preferred 5. d4 Be7 6. Qe2 Nd6 7. Bxc6 bxc6 8. dxe5 Nb7 9. Nc3 0-0, achieving little advantage.

5. ... Nd6

6. Nxe5 Be7

7. Bd3

More "natural" continuations 7. Bf1 Nxe5 8. Rxe5 0-0 9. d4 Bf6 doesn't give White any advantage. *ECO* gives 7. Nc3 Nxb5! 8. Nd5 0-0 9. Nxc6 dxc6 10. Nxe7† Kh8, but this is erroneous as after 8... Nbd4! Black keeps the extra piece.

7. ... 0-0

8. Nc3 Nxe5

From the point of view of theory this was an inaccuracy. Preferable was either the age old 8... Ne8 9. Nd5 Bf6 10. Ng4 d6 with equal chances, *Janowsky—Lasker, Nuremberg 1896*, or 8... Bf6 9. Ng4 Bd4 10. Ne2 Bb6 11. Nf4 Ne8 12. Nd5 d6, also with equality, *Stein—Smyslov, 1961.*

All the same, one cannot say that the continuation chosen by Black is hardly worse than those recommended by theorists.

9. Rxe5 Bf6

10. Re3 g6

11. Qf3 Bg7?!

Steinitz long ago recommended the preliminary attack on the Rook—11... Bd4!, making it leave the active position on the third rank where it is ready to support the attack on the King.

12. b3 Ne8?!

Even though losing a tempo it would have been better to play 12... Bd4 to prevent the white pieces from gaining active posts.

13. Ba3 d6

14. Rae1

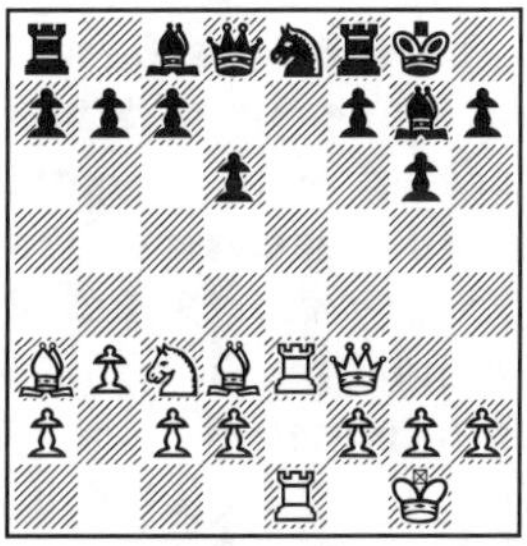

A picturesque parade of white pieces on the third rank is unusual to the eye of a present-day chess-player! Such notions as "the pawn center" and "pawn structure" don't mean anything here. White has an overwhelming advantage in development, and it was very difficult for his opponent to defend.

14. ... Nf6

15. h3

Maybe it is emphasized too much,

and deliberately basic, but the Bishop on c8 hasn't had a chance to move because it would lose the b7-pawn. It was possible to skip over to the main plan of the attack: 15. Bc4 Rb8 16. Nd5.

15. ... Nd7
16. Nd5 f5?

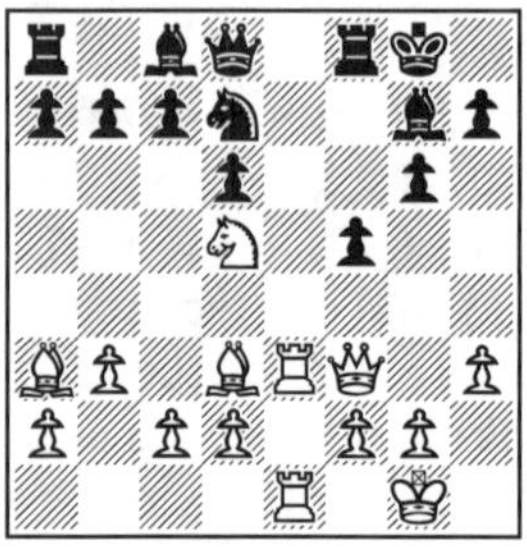

This was a mistake which can be fully explained by the extreme defensive difficulties. It allows White to go over to a combinational attack.

After 16... Ne5 there might have followed 17. Rxe5! Bxe5 [17... dxe5 18. Be7 Qd7 19. Nf6† Bxf6 20. Qxf6, which might have given White a chance to win at least a pawn in a better position.] 18. Rxe5! dxe5 19. Be7 Bg4 20. hxg4 Qb8 [Ed.: 21. Nf6† leads to mate! 21... Kg7 22. Nh5†! gxh5 23. Qf6† Kg8 24. Qg5† Kh8 25. Bf6#.]**... One should remember to try and develop the queenside by 16... Rb8 and then b6.**

R. N.

17. Nxc7!! Qxc7
18. Qd5† Kh8
19. Re8!

Of course not 19. Bxd6? because of 19... Nb6! 20. Qc5 Qxc5 21. Bxc5 Rg8 22. Re8 Bd7.

19. ... Nf6
20. Rxf8† Bxf8
21. Bb2!

The pinning of the Knight turned out to be fatal, though it looked as if Black had a way to defend.

21. ... Bg7

21... Kg7 was rejected because of 22. Bc4, and the Queen breaks through to g8.

A win, on 21... Qg7, is achieved in a very interesting way. White prepared the following forced variation: 22. Qd4! Ne4 [22... Be7 23. Qe3 Bf8 (or 23... Bd8 24. Qe8† Qg8 25. Bc4!) 24. Qg5 Be7 25. Rxe7] 23. f3 d5 24. fxe4 fxe4 [if 24... dxe4, then 25. Qd8!] 25. Bxe4! [Ed.: Nezh misses 25. Qf2!!] **dxe4 26. Qd8! and so on.**

R. N.

Nezh's analysis is convincing, but nevertheless, instead of 23... d5, the following line is even stronger: 23... Qxd4† 24. Bxd4† Bg7 25. Bxg7† Kxg7 26. fxe4 and 26... Kf6 avoids the mating net and keeping unpretentious hopes for saving the game in the ending.

22. Qd4, which was suggested by Nezhmetdinov, was good. A. Magergut's recommendation of 22. Bxf6 Qxf6 23. Bc4 Kg7 [23... Qg7 24. Re8 with a threat 25. Qxd6.] 24. Qg8† Kh6 25. Re8 Bg7 26. Rxc8 Rxc8 27. Qxc8 Qa1† 28. Bf1 Qxa2 29. Qd8!, and 29... Be5 was bad because of 30. d4!.

22. Bc4! Bd7
23. Bxf6

White might carry out the beautiful blow 23. Qf7 Rf8

24. Re8!!. but he didn't want to prolong Black's resistance by playing 24... Bxe8 25. Qxc7, and besides, the end of the game is no less interesting.

R. N.

23. ... Bxf6
24. Qf7

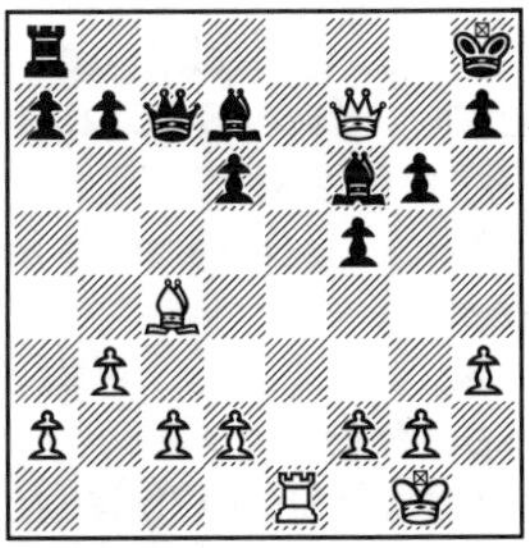

24. ... Qd8

Black didn't have a wide choice; the more persistent 24... Bg5, still required checking, and Nezh gave the following line: 25. g3! [The exclamation mark is mine.] Rc8 26. h4 Bc6 27. Re8†! Rxe8 28. Qxc7 Re1† 29. Bf1 Bxd2 30. Qxd6 Bh6 31. Qd4† Bg7 32. Qd2 Re7 33. Bg2 followed by the win. I can add that after 25... Qd8 [instead of 25... Rc8] 26. h4 Bc6 [26... Bh6 27. Re7!] 27. hxg5 and 27... Qxg5 is bad because of 28. Re7. After 27... Qf8 28. Re7 Qxf7 29. Bxf7 and White's advantage should be sufficient for the win.

25. Re8†!!

An unusually effective blow: any taking of the Rook leads to mate.

Black surrendered **(1-0).**

Nezh liked this game and often showed it at meetings of his fans.

9.

L. Belov—Super Nezh
C 59
21st Russian ch.
Omsk 1961

1. e4 e5 2. Nf3 Nc6 3. Bc4 Nf6 4. Ng5 d5 5. exd5 Na5 6. Bb5† c6 7. dxc6 bxc6 8. Be2 h6 9. Nf3.

Over a hundred years ago there was a major discussion about this variation between Steinitz and Chigorin. The then champion Steinitz persistently defended the position of White after 9. Nh3?!, but in games with the Russian champion he made no headway. In spite of the unfavorable conclusions of theory and practice on the effectiveness of Steinitz' move, *Fischer* tried to bring it back to life. In his game with *Bisguier, New York 1963*, after 9... Bc5 10. 0-0 [Later Fischer preferred 10. d3.] 0-0 11. d3 Bxh3 12. gxh3 Qd7 13. Bf3 Qxh3 14. Nd2 Rad8 15. Be2 Qf5 16. Qe1, he got the better chances, but then he was Fischer!

9. ... e4
10. Ne5 Bd6
11. d4 exd3
12. Nxd3 Qc7

In different published versions of this game there are differences in move order, therefore, I prefer to stick to the sequence of moves which was given by Nezh himself, though there certainly isn't any difference in principle compared to the version 10... Qc7 11. d4 exd3 12. Nxd3 Bd6.

After a hundred-year old research of this variation, the verdict of the theorists was as follows: Black's initiative is sufficient to compensate for the missing pawn, but no more.

Certainly, this evaluation, however

fair it may be, was not indisputable for Nezhmetdinov—he always placed possession of the initiative as superior to material losses; and, it must be confessed, sometimes he went too far.

13. Nd2

This was an obvious move, but not the best. The best move is considered to be 13. b3, for example: 13… 0-0 14. Bb2 Nd5 15. h3 Bf5 16. 0-0 Rad8 17. Nc3, and the prospects are approximately the same, *Honfi—Ciocaltea, Wijk aan Zee 1969*.

13. ... Ba6

In the well-known game *Ragozin—Botvinnik, 14th USSR ch., 1945*, Black played 13… 0-0. The move made by Nezhmetdinov was not appreciated by theorists: it is not mentioned in the Yugoslavian *ECO*. The aim of the move was to be able to play Nc4 in case of the push b2-b4.

14. Nf3 0-0
15. 0-0 Rad8
16. b3 Rfe8
17. Re1?

White doesn't take into account that the f2-square is now weakened, and Black would have made immediate use of that. Certainly, 17. Bb2 was correct, finishing development without any complications as yet. Damsky recommended 17. Be3?, asserting that Nezh would have answered that with 17… Ne4. Hardly so. Nezh would certainly have played 17… Ng4, which makes the recommendation senseless.

17. ... Ng4
18. h3

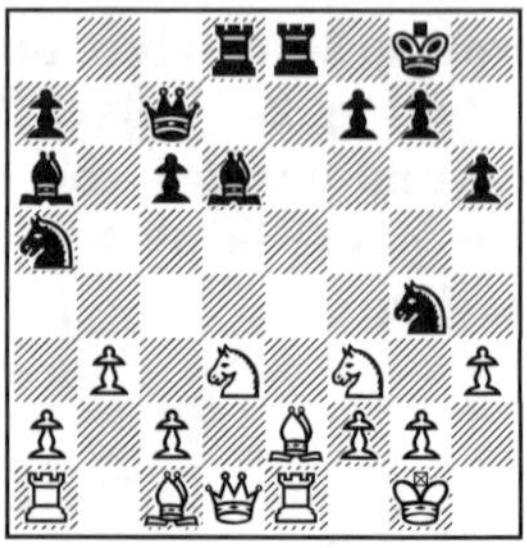

Another attempt at defense, 18. g3, would have lost quickly and simply: 18… Bc5 19. Rf1 Qb6 20. Qe1 [or 20. Kg2 Nxf2 21. Qd2 Rxe2! 22. Qxe2 Nxd3 23. cxd3 Bxd3 24. Qe1 Bxf1†] Rxd3! 21. cxd3 Bxd3.

18. ... Nxf2!
19. Kxf2

After 19. Nxf2 Bh2† White would lose his Queen without any compensation.

19. ... Qb6†
20. Kf1 Bg3
21. Qd2

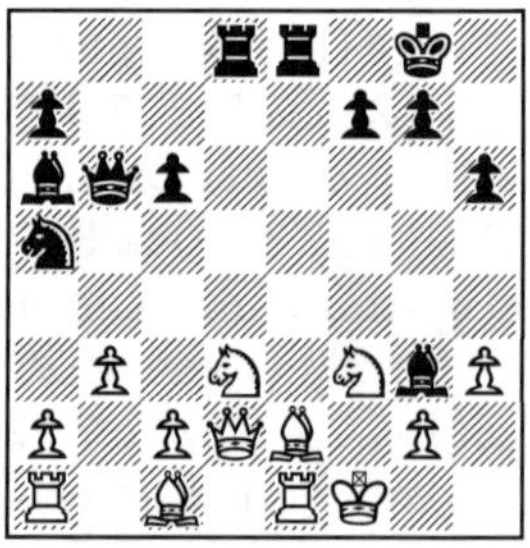

White had escaped the mate [21… Bxd3 22. Bxd3, and the f2-square was defended.], but,

The idea of the combination is quite different, the attack won't go along "weak" black squares, but along the "strong" white squares!

R. N.

21. ... c5!!

It's a surprise, but a very important resource in the attack: there is the threat of 22… c4 23. bxc4 Nxc4 with a quick and complete defeat.

22. c4

An attempt to blockade the pawns doesn't ease the position. There is another, more stubborn defense: 22. Bb2! c4 23. Qc3 f6 24. Nd4 cxd3 25. Bxd3 Rxe1† 26. Rxe1 Bxe1 but little by little, Black still would have had winning chances.

22. … Bxe1
23. Kxe1

It was worth noting that [23. Nfxe1] would be terrible because of 23… Qf6† and 24… Qxa1.

23. … Nxc4!

Black literally rammed the defensive fortifications of his opponent.

24. bxc4 Bxc4
25. Kf2

If 25. Kf1, one more sacrifice would have been required from Black: 25… Rxe2 26. Kxe2 Rxd3 27. Qxd3 Bxd3† 28. Kxd3 and, 28… Qf6! wins a whole Rook.

25. … Bxd3
26. Bxd3 c4†
27. Kg3 Rxd3
28. Qb2

White was in a deplorable state from other threats as well: 28. Qf2 Qf6 29. Bb2 [29. Rb1 Qg6 30. Kh2 Rxf3 and 31… Qxb1] Qd6† 30. Be5 Qxe5†.

28. … Qg6†
29. Kf2

Or 29. Kh2 Qd6† 30. Kg1 [30. Kh1 Rd1† 31. Ng1 Ree1] Rxf3 31. gxf3 Qg3† and then 32… Re1#.

29. … Qe4
30. Bd2 Rxf3†!
31. gxf3 Qh4†

White surrendered **(0-1)**.

Nezh received a prize for the most beautiful game in this championship.

10.
Super Nezh—M. Tal
B 84
29th USSR ch.
Baku 1961

1. e4 c5 2. Nf3 d6 3. d4 cxd4 4. Nxd4 Nf6 5. Nc3 e6 6. Be2 Nbd7.

Nezh preferred 6… Nc6 with the exchange on d4 and the transference of the Bishop through d7 to c6. A similar plan: [6… Nc6] 7. 0-0 Be7 8. Be3 0-0 9. f4 Qc7 10. Kh1 Bd7 11. Qe1 Nxd4 12. Bxd4 Bc6 is considered one of the best even today.

7. 0-0 a6
8. f4 Qc7
9. g4

A more reserved setup is usually preferred, connected with 9. Bf3, then Kh1, Qe1 and Be3. The move g2-g4 was one of Nezhmetdinov's favorite methods against the Sicilian.

9. … b5
10. a3

The "active" 10. g5? b4 11. gxf6 bxc3 would be to Black's profit.

R. N.

10. … Bb7
11. Bf3 Nc5

Later, opening theorists recommended 11… e5 12. Nf5 g6 13. Ne3 exf4 14. Ned5 Bxd5 15. Nxd5 Nxd5 16. Qxd5 Rc8 with equal chances. In response to 11… e5 Nezh recommended 12. Nde2 Nc5 13. Ng3 exf4 14. Bxf4 Nfd7 15. Nf5 Ne5 16. Ne3!, considering that in the struggle for the center, White has the better prospects. Damsky had suggested an intermediate leaping away of the Knight, that is, 14… Ne6! 15. Be3, and now White couldn't transfer the Knight on g3 for a hold on the d5-square via g3-f5-e3.

12. Qe2 e5

This was very courageous, but risky. Spassky's recommendation 12... Nfd7, preventing the advance e4-e5, is more reliable.

13. Nf5 g6

Later Spassky suggested the more solid 13... exf4 14. Bxf4 Nfd7.

14. fxe5 dxe5

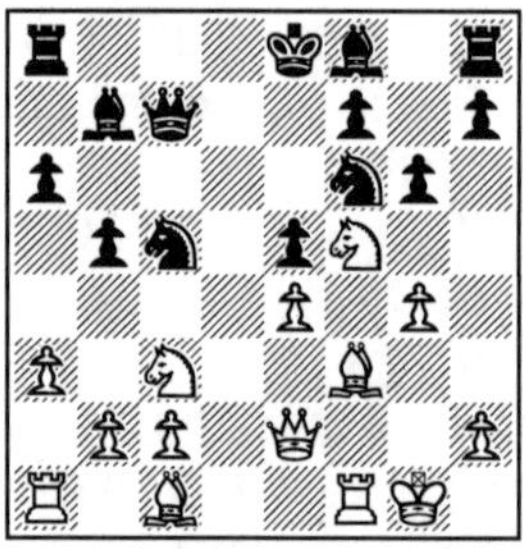

15. Nh6!?

Tal confessed that he hadn't envisaged this jump of the Knight onto the edge of the chessboard. Meanwhile, the Knight stands quite well there, and more than that, it was a dangerous attacking piece. Rashid Gibyatovich was good at finding similar exceptions to generally accepted rules of strategy.

Nevertheless, it should be admitted that in this position the line 15. Bg5 Nfd7 16. Ne3 Ne6 17. Ned5 is considered to be the more usual continuation with approximately equal play.

15. ... Ne6

16. Bg2 Bg7

The attempt to close the f-file doesn't work out: 16... Nf4 17. Bxf4 exf4 18. e5! with a powerful attack. For example, 18... Bxh6 19. exf6† Kf8 20. Qe7†! with the win of a piece, or 18... Nd7 19. e6 Bxh6 20. exd7† Kf8 21. Bxb7 Qxb7 22. Qe5 with irresistible threats.

17. Rxf6!

This non-evident sacrifice for equality was the introduction to a powerful attack on the black King stuck in the center.

One must notice that after the extravagant jump 15. Nh6 the logic of the struggle demands White continue in the same way. The fact is that an ordinary continuation gives White nothing: 17. Qf2 Bxh6 18. Qxf6 Bg7 19. Qf2 0-0; or 17. g5 Bxh6 18. gxf6 Nf4 and both players feel fine.

17. ... Bxf6

18. Nd5 Qd8

It is one of the most important moments in the game. Tal didn't take either Knight, and it was to no avail. After 18... Bxd5 19. exd5 Black chooses between 19... Nd4 and 19... Qc5†:

A. 19... Nd4 20. Qf2 Qd6 [20... Qa7 21. Be3 is worse for Black. 21... Bg7 (Ed. Note: 21... Bh4 is mind-boggling, but if Black plays like a genius, he can probably draw.) 22. Re1 0-0-0 23. c3 and Black is the loser.] 21. g5 Be7 22. Nxf7 0-0! 23. Nxd6 Rxf2 24. Kxf2 Rf8† 25. Kg3 Nxc2 26. Rb1 Bxd6 27. Be4 and the ending is equal.

B. 19... Qc5†! [In order to deprive White of the opportunity d5-d6] 20. Kh1 [After 20. Be3 Nf4 21. Qf2 Qd6 White has no compensation for the exchange.] Nd8 21. Bg5! Qd6 22. Bxf6 Qxf6 23. Rf1 Qd6 24. g5 Ra7 25. Rf6, or 24... f5 25. gxf6 Rf8 26. Ng4. In this variation (B) White would have to prove his initiative was worth more than the lost material.

19. Qf2 Nf4

Quite possible was 19... Bxd5 20. exd5 Nf4 21. Bxf4 exf4 22. Qxf4 [Nezh analyzed 22... Qb6† 23. Kh1 0-0-0 24. c3! Rhe8 25. g5 Be7 26. Nxf7 as giving White a strong advantage.] Ra7! 23. Rf1! [23. Re1† Re7 24. Rxe7† Qxe7 doesn't go anywhere.] Bg7 [23... Bxb2 is dangerous for Black because of 24. Nxf7 Qb6† 25. Kh1 Rg8 26. Nd6† Kd8 27. Qg5†.] 24. Qf2! Qd7 25. Re1† Kd8 26. d6 Qxd6 27. Qxa7 Bd4† 28. Kh1 Bxa7 29. Nxf7† Kc7 30. Nxd6 Kxd6 and White doesn't have much for his extra pawn. Perhaps more flexible piece play through 27. Nxf7† [instead of 27. Qxa7] Rxf7 28. Qxf7 Bxb2 is worth considering.

20. Bxf4 exf4

Even here it would have been possible to take on d5.

21. e5! Bxe5?

Tal could no longer stand the psychological stress and made an error. White's threats are dangerous. For instance, bad is 21... Bxd5 22. exf6 f3 [22... Bxg2? 23. Re1†] 23. Bxf3 and 23... Bxf3 or 23... Qxf6 both fail to 24. Re1†. However, the cool headed thrust 21... Bh4! gives Black defensive chances. In my analysis, I cannot find any decisive continuations: 22. Qd4 Rf8 23. Rd1 Rc8! [23... Bxd5? 24. Bxd5 Rc8 25. Nxf7! Rxf7 26. Bxf7† Kf8 27. Bb3, and White has nice chances to win; or 23... Bg5? 24. Qf2! Bxd5 25. Bxd5 Qd7 (25... Qc8 26. Qb6!) 26. Bf3 Qc7 27. Bxa8 Bxh6 28. Rd6 and Black is unprotected.] 24. Qa7 Bxd5 25. Rxd5 [25. Bxd5 Qc7 26. Qxa6 Ke7! and Black has successfully defended.] Qc7 26. Qxa6 Rb8 27. Rxb5 Bg5 28. Rxb8† Qxb8 29. Qc6† Kd8 30. Qd5† Ke8, and White has nothing but a draw, as the Knight is in a precarious place.

22. Re1 f6
23. Nxf6† Qxf6
24. Qd4!

It goes without saying, such play is art.

24. ... Kf8
25. Rxe5 Qd8

After 25... Rd8, the end would be like this: 26. Re8†! Kg7 27. Re7†.

26. Rf5† gxf5
27. Qxh8† Ke7
28. Qg7† Ke6
29. gxf5†

Black surrendered **(1-0)**.

It was clear why this game was awarded a prize as the best in the championship.

11.

D. Ciric—Super Nezh
C 72
Chigorin Memorial
Rostov-on-Don 1961

1. e4 e5 2. Nf3 Nc6 3. Bb5 a6 4. Ba4 d6 5. 0-0 Bg4 6. h3 Bh5.

Many lances had been broken around the 6... h5 gambit until it was finally rejected. What is interesting is that Nezh, who was an aggressive, attacking chessplayer, didn't accept nor use this gambit.

7. c3 Nf6
8. Qe2

This is a rare continuation. Usually

8. Re1 or 8. d4 are played at once.

8. ... g5?!

A dubious experiment whose only aim was to thrust onto his opponent a non-standard move. A good solid continuation is 8... Be7.

9. g4 b5
10. Bb3 Bg6
11. d4 h5!?

In essence, Black should continue in the same aggressive style; if 11... h6 12. dxe5 dxe5 and the Bishop on g6 is turned into a big pawn.

12. Bg5?!

After 12. Nxg5 hxg4 13. hxg4 exd4 14. Rd1 dxc3 15. Nxc3 Ne5 16. f3 Be7 Nezh's risky experiment with 8. ... g5 proves to be correct as the play would be equal. [Ed. Note: While the B/g6 appears to be incarcerated it's also true that White's piece play is somewhat limited. White might consider 16. f4!?.]

12. ... hxg4
13. Nh4

The tempting thrust 13. Bd5 is nicely refuted by 13... Nxd5! 14. Bxd8 Nf4 15. Qe3 Nxh3† 16. Kh1 Bxe4! 17. Bf6 Rh6 18. Nbd2 Bxf3† 19. Nxf3 gxf3 20. Kh2 Nf4† 21. Kg3 Rxf6 and Black, with sufficient material compensation for the Queen, has brilliant attacking prospects.

Ciric's move is hardly good. 13. hxg4! is more convincing. With that move White could achieve some advantages: 13... Be7 14. Bxf6 Bxf6 15. dxe5 dxe5 16. Rd1 Qc8 17. Nh2 and Black has no compensation for the pawn; or, 13... Na5 14. Bd5! c6 [Here the Queen sacrifice 14... Nxd5 15. Bxd8 isn't enough: 15... Nf4 16. Qe1 Rxd8 17. dxe5 Nh3† 18. Kg2 Nf4† 19. Kg3 and Black has no attack.] 15. dxe5 Qc8! 16. e6! [16. Nh2 is worse: 16... Nh7 17. Bf6 Nxf6 18. exf6 cxd5 19. exd5† Kd8, and Black has the advantage.] Nh7 17. exf7† Bxf7 18. Bxf7† Kxf7 19. Bf4 Qxg4† 20. Bg3 Nf6 21. Re1 and Black is down a pawn with no compensation. At least 13... Qd7 or 13... Qc8 are completely unsuccessful only because of the surprising 14. Nxe5! dxe5 15. Bxf6.

13. ... Bh5
14. Bd5

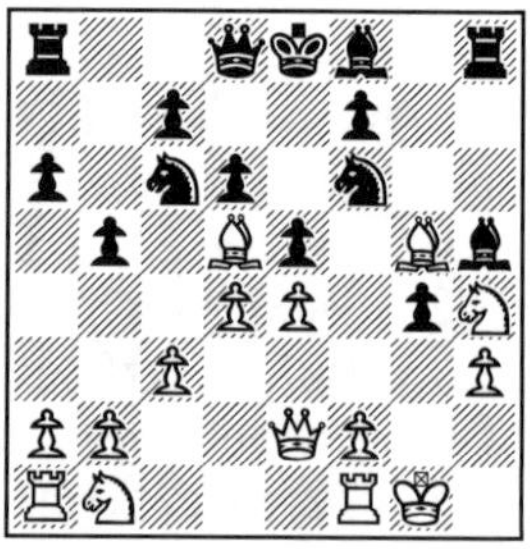

14. ... Nxd5!!?

By playing 12. Bg5, White certainly had no inkling of this Queen sacrifice, carried out in the best traditions of the great romanticists of the previous century.

We can't say the Queen sacrificed was forced. Black could play 14... Kd7, and after 15. a4! Rg8! 16. Bxc6† [16. Bxf6? gxh3† and 17... Bxe2] Kxc6 17. axb5† Kd7 [17... axb5 loses to 18. d5† Kb6 19. Rxa8 Qxa8 20. Qe3† Kb7 21. Bxf6] 18. Qe3 gxh3 he can calculate to an advantage. Of course, Nezh didn't calculate and simply was not able to realize all the after effects of his decision. Had he seen the main point of this sacrifice, that it abruptly changes the nature of play, gives the probability of obtaining future compensation, and places him on the attack with a psychological advantage, he would have believed in his opportunities.

15. Bxd8 Nf4
16. Qe3 Nxh3†
17. Kg2

Upon 17. Qxh3 gxh3 18. Bxc7 Rg8† 19. Kh1 Rg4, all the chances were with Black.

17. ... Nf4†

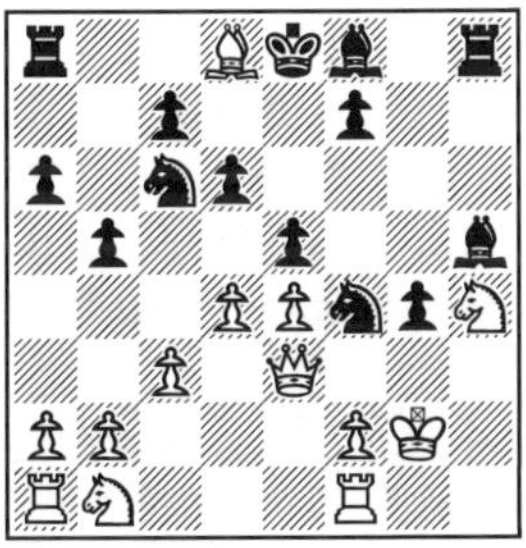

18. Qxf4?

Shocked by the recklessness and fantasy of his rival, Ciric prefers to stay down a pawn. It was possible to display composure and try to cast doubt on the sacrifice of the Queen. For this, it was necessary to choose correctly between 18. Kg3 and 18. Kg1.

The continuation 18. Kg1?! was unanimously rejected by all the commentators because of 18… Bh6. However, after 19. Bf6!, nothing results from the attack. 19… Nh3† 20. Qxh3 and after 21. Bxh8 Black is done for. If 19… Rh7 White might simply play 20. Kh1! as the Knight on h4 is defended by the Bishop and dams the h-file. Black must choose between 18… Rxd8 and 18… Nh3†.

A. 18… Rxd8 19. Nf5 Bg6 20. Rd1 Bxf5 21. exf5 Nh3† [21… Rh3 22. Qe1 g3 23. fxg3 Rxg3† 24. Kf2 (The straightforward 24. Qxg3 gives nothing: 24… Ne2† 25. Kf2 Nxg3 26. Kxg3 exd4 and the ending is not bad for Black.) Rg2† 25.Kf3 Re2 26.Qh1 Rxb2 27. Rd2 and White has the better position.] 22. Kf1 Nf4 and after 23. Kg1 it's a draw.

B. 18... Nh3†! 19. Kh1 Rxd8 20. a4 Nf4 21. Kg1 [21. axb5 Bg6 22. Kg1 Rxh4 23. bxc6 Nh3† draws] Bh6 [21... Nh3† 22. Kh2 Bh6 23. Qe1 Nf4 24. Rh1 and White has beaten off the attack and has the advantage.] 22. Qe1 g3! 23. f3 g2! 24. Nxg2 Rg8 25. Rf2 Bxf3! 26. Rxf3 Nxg2 27. Qf2 Be3! and Black has an even better position. In this beautiful variation, Black's attacking potential is completely realized. So, after 18. Kg1?! Black does not lose.

18. Kg3! is stronger: 18… Rxd8 19. Rh1! [19. Nf5? Bg6 20. Kxg4 (20. Qd2 Rh3† 21. Kxg4 Bh5† 22. Kg5 Ne6† 23. Kf6 Rf3! and 24... Be7 is mate.) Rg8! and there are no satisfactory defenses from threats of 21… Bh5† 22. Kh4 Rg4# or 21… Bf5† (after 21. Kg5) 22. Kxf5 Ne7† 23. Kf6 Rg6#. 19. Nd2 looks better than 19. Rh1!, but it is difficult to correctly evaluate the complex lines: 19. Nd2 Bh6 20. Nf5 Bg5 21. Rh1 Nh3 22. Qe2 Kd7!. Tal, who analyzed this position with interest, remarked, "I'd rather play the Black pieces here!" However, 19. Rh1! is stronger, and this is difference between 18. Kg3 and Kg1—the Rook can take part in the defense.] Bh6 20. Nf5 Bg5 21. a4. Black's attack has gotten him nothing, and White's material advantage must give him a win. So, Nezh's courageous project was not irreproachable, but it is difficult to find a refutation even in post mortem analysis. Thus, the risk over the board was minimal.

18. ... exf4
19. Bg5

A pawn would not have been gained back by 19. Bxc7, because of 19… Kd7 20. Bb6 Rb8.

19.	**...**	**Be7**
20.	**Bxe7**	**Nxe7**
21.	**Nd2**	**Kd7**
22.	**Rh1**	**f6**
23.	**b3**	**Bf7**
24.	**d5**	**Rh6**

25. Rh2 Rah8
26. Rah1 Nxd5!
27. exd5 Bxd5†
28. f3 g3

White surrendered **(0-1)**.

12.

Super Nezh—O. Chernikov
B 35
Russian Team ch.
Rostov-on-Don 1962

1. e4 c5 2. Nf3 Nc6 3. d4 cxd4 4. Nxd4 g6 5. Nc3 Bg7 6. Be3 Nf6 7. Bc4 0-0 8. Bb3 Ng4.

Now 8... a5 is preferable, and on 9. f3 a blow would have been dealt in the center: 9... d5.

9. Qxg4 Nxd4
10. Qh4

Then, more than thirty years ago, as well as today, 10. Qd1 was considered to be the strongest move, after which it is difficult for Black to equalize.

10. ... Qa5

Nezh recommended 10... Nxb3.

11. 0-0 Bf6

Long ago this position was known to be drawn because White could choose between 12. Qh6 Bg7 13. Qh4 Bf6 with a repetition of moves, or 13. Qg5 Qxg5 14. Bxg5 Nxb3 15. axb3 Bxc3 with a drawn endgame. If 12. Qg3 or 12. Qf4, Black would reply 12... Qxc3!.

Chernikov was sure that his opponent wanted to rest that day. Therefore he quietly strolled about in the tournament hall. Meanwhile time went on and Nezh continued to think. Everyone was puzzled "what was Rashid Gibyatovich thinking about," there was no avoiding a draw... At last a boy, out of breath, ran up to Chernikov and said: "Dyadya, a Queen was sacrificed to you!"

12. Qxf6!

White only has two pieces for the Queen, but he hoped to attack the weakened black squares near the enemy King.

12. ... Ne2†!

An obligatory check which makes White expend an unnecessary tempo. If 12... Nxb3, White might win without any difficulty: 13. axb3! Qxa1 14. Qxe7 Qa5 15. Bh6 Qd8 16. Nd5!.

13. Nxe2 exf6
14. Nc3 Re8

Immediately after the game, and later, this position underwent numerous analyses, and Nezhmetdinov's idea was given practical study. The main conclusion drawn on the basis of these analyses was that 14... d5! was stronger. After 14... d5 15. Nxd5 Rd8 16. Bd4 Rxd5 17. exd5 Kg7 18. Rae1 Bf5, the chances of both sides turned out to be approximately equal in *Chervinsky—Grabczewski, Poland ch. 1963*. Or 15... Be6 16. Nxf6† Kg7 17. Bd4 Kh6, *Petzh—Medler, DDR ch. 1963*. After 18. Be3† Black will probably have to agree on 18... Kg7 19. Bd4 with a repetition of moves.

Thus, Nezhmetdinov didn't succeed in overturning the conclusions of theory. Does that belittle the depth of his plan? Does that make the flight of his fantasy more prosaic?

Rashid Gibyatovich was ready to play this line again. He thought that even after 14… d5 there might appear positions in which it is more difficult for Black to play than for White.

15. Nd5 Re6
16. Bd4 Kg7
17. Rad1 d6

17... b5! was the most efficient continuation. Now 18. Bc3 Qd8 19. Nxf6? doesn't work because of the intermediate stroke 19... b4! and 20. Nh5† doesn't work: 20… Kh6 21. Bxe6 bxc3 22. Bd5 Ba6 and Black must win. In the echo variation 20. Ne8† Kf8 21. Bxe6 bxc3 22. Bd5 Ba6 Black is on top.

Instead of 19. Nxf6?, 19. Nb4! is better. However, after 19… a5! 20. Bxe6 fxe6 21. Nd3 b4 22. Bd4 e5 23. Be3 d6 Black must realize his advantage. After the text move, Black's position begins to deteriorate.

18. Rd3 Bd7
19. Rf3 Bb5
20. Bc3 Qd8
21. Nxf6! Be2?

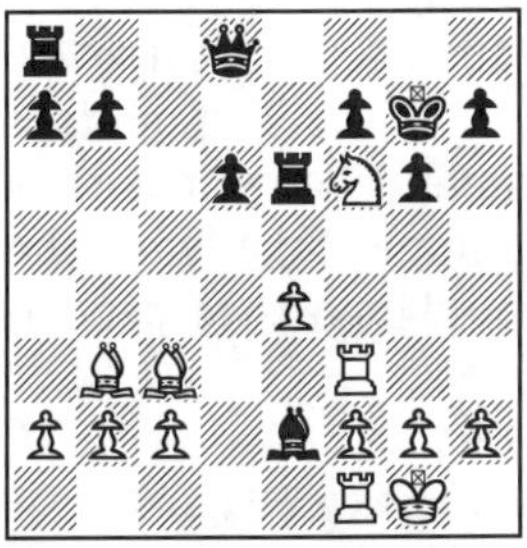

White's advantage cannot be repulsed in such a way. It would better to use the alternative: 21... Rc8! [Bad is 21... Bxf1 22. Ng4† Kf8 23. Bxe6.] 22. Bxe6 Rxc3! 23. bxc3 Bxf1 24. Nh5† Kh6! 25. Rxf7 Qg5 and Black's position, at a minimum, isn't worse.

22. Nxh7†! Kg8

Before taking the pawn, Nezh thought over the following: 22… Kxh7 23. Rxf7† Kh6 24. Bd2† g5 25. Bxe6 Bxf1 26. Bf5 Qh8 [26… Qg8 27. Rf6† Kh5 28. g4 and 29. Rh6#] 27. h4! Be2 28. Bxg5† Kh5 29. f3 Bxf3 30. gxf3, and the King was in a mating net.

23. Rh3 Re5

23... Bxf1 didn't suit Black in view of 24. Ng5 Re5 25. Nxf7, a complete defeat. In the very same way 23... Bh5 wasn't good either because of 24. Bxe6 fxe6 25. Nf6† and then 26. g4!

R. N.

24. f4! Bxf1
25. Kxf1

25. Ng5! is stronger and with dangerous threats.

25. ... Rc8
26. Bd4!

Certainly, the Bishop was more valuable than any of the Rooks. However, for a victory the prosaic 26. fxe5 dxe5 27. Rd3 Qh4 28. Bxe5 Qxh7 29. Rh3 is certainly sufficient.

26. ... b5
27. Ng5 Rc7

An attempt to close the diagonals with the Rooks would not have been successful: 27… Rc4 28. Bxc4 bxc4 29. Bxe5 dxe5 30. Rh8†!.

27... Qf6 wouldn't save either because it would be followed by 28. Bxf7† Kg7 29. Rh7† Kf8 30. Ne6† Ke7 31. Bxg6†! Kxe6 32. f5, and Black loses the Queen and the Rook.

R. N.

28. Bxf7†! Rxf7
29. Rh8†! Kxh8
30. Nxf7† Kh7

31. Nxd8 Rxe4
32. Nc6 Rxf4†
33. Ke2

Black surrendered **(1-0).**

The game produced such an impression on the many participants of the championship team that none of them presented their games to the judges for the beauty prize—it was guaranteed in advance to Nezh.

13.
B. Kalinkin—Super Nezh
C 76
Vologda 1962

1. e4 e5 2. Nf3 Nc6 3. Bb5 a6 4. Ba4 d6 5. c3 Bd7 6. d4 g6 7. 0-0 Bg7 8. Be3 Nf6 9. Nbd2 0-0 10. Re1.

In Game No. 65 (Boleslavsky—Nezhmetdinov) White played 10. dxe5. Rejection of this pawn exchange would have been favorable for Black as it facilitated creation of counterplay on the kingside.

10. ... Nh5
11. Nf1 b5
12. Bc2 exd4!

However White might have taken on d4, Black would have gotten some advantage: when taken by a pawn, the activity of the Bishop on g7 increases, and if taken as in the game, Black gets the strong point e5. Black wouldn't have gotten all of this if White had exchanged in a timely manner on e5.

13. Nxd4 Ne5
14. Nf5!

White was struggling desperately to keep his initiative from slipping.

14. ... Bf6
15. Bh6 Re8
16. N1e3 Bg5!

White threatened to drive the Knight back by f2-f4 giving him the advantage. Black's task is to prevent this.

17. Nd5 c6!

17... Bxf5 doesn't look bad, but after 18. Bxg5 Qxg5 19. exf5 Nf4 20. Nxf4 Qxf4 21. Re4! White has achieved a stable advantage in a calm position, as 21... Qxf5? is bad because the Knight is lost after 22. f4.

18. Nc7

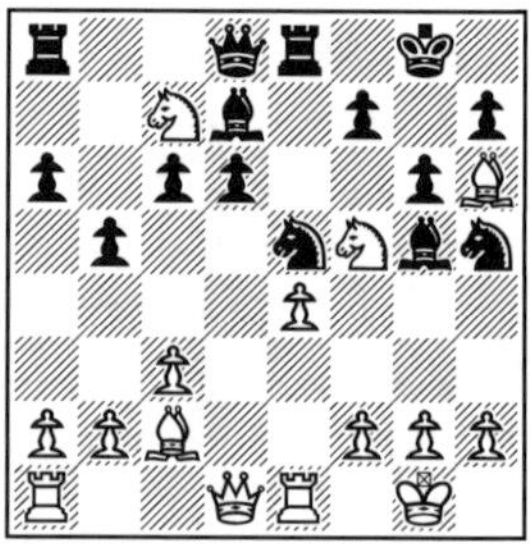

The most important point in the game. With great excitement and optimism, Nezh is risking complications in preferring not to be led by his opponent. In case of 18... Qxc7 19. Bxg5 Bxf5 20. exf5 Ng7 21. fxg6 fxg6 White would have a better position due to the advantage of the two Bishops, and Black would have to forget about winning.

18. ... Nf4!
19. Bxg5?!

Yes, Nezh evidently excelled over his young rival in strength of character. The only way to call Black's bold plan into question is by 19. Nxe8! Bxe8 [19... gxf5 20. Qxd6 is weak, as mate is now threatened on f8.] 20. Re3! [20. h4 doesn't work: 20... Bxh6 21. Nxh6† Kg7 22. Ng4 Qxh4 23. Qxd6 Qxg4 24. Qxe5† f6 25.Qe7† Bf7 26. g3 Nh3† 27.Kh2 (27. Kg2 Nf4†) Nxf2] Bxh6 [Finally, 20... gxf5 doesn't work because of 21. Bxg5 Qxg5 22. Rg3 Ng4 23. exf5 h5 24. h3] 21. Nxh6† Kg7

22. Ng4 Qg5 23. Rg3 Nh5 24. Nxe5 Nxg3 25. Nf3 and Black's position is a disaster.

19.	**...**	**Qxg5**
20.	**Ng3**	**h5**
21.	**Nxa8**	**Rxa8**
22.	**Qxd6**	**h4**
23.	**a4**	

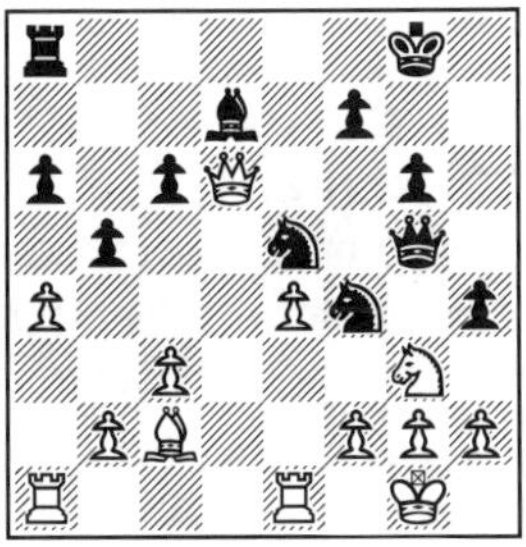

23.	**...**	**h3!!**

This was startling! Black doesn't need the Knight at all, just the g2-square. It has become clear that it was the main weak square in the vicinity of the King. Even looking at the diagram it is difficult to find such a shot, but Nezh had found it as far back as the 18th move! If White had foreseen the opponent's idea, he would have probably played 23. Re3, trying with all his strength to defend the f3 square.

24.	**axb5**	**cxb5**
25.	**Rxa6**	**Rxa6**
26.	**Qxa6**	**hxg2**
27.	**Bd1**	

There was another way to defend h3: 27. Re3 but Black has 27... Bg4 and there is no satisfactory defense from the terrible check on f3.

27.	**...**	**Bg4**
28.	**Qa1**	**Bf3**
29.	**Qa8†**	**Kh7**
30.	**Qc8**	**Bxd1**

White surrendered **(0-1).**

14.
V. Timofeev—Super Nezh
E 67

Leningrad 1969

1. d4 Nf6 2. Nf3 d6 3. c4 Nbd7 4. g3 g6 5. Bg2 Bg7 6. Nc3 0-0 7. 0-0 e5 8. Qc2 c6 9. Rd1 Re8 10. h3?!.

After this passive move White had virtually lost the advantage of the first move. Universally acknowledged continuations today are 10. e4 or 10. d5.

10.	**...**	**e4**
11.	**Nh2**	**d5**
12.	**cxd5**	**cxd5**
13.	**Bf4**	**a6**
14.	**Ng4?!**	

The active position of the Bishop on f4 made the plan of preparing for an invasion on the c7-square promising. For this to succeed it was first necessary to secure the stability of the Bishop on the h2-b8 diagonal, and so White had to play 14. g4. But instead, White had something else on his mind: he saw a temping tactical idea...

14.	**...**	**Nxg4**
15.	**Nxd5**	**Ndf6!**
16.	**Nc7**	

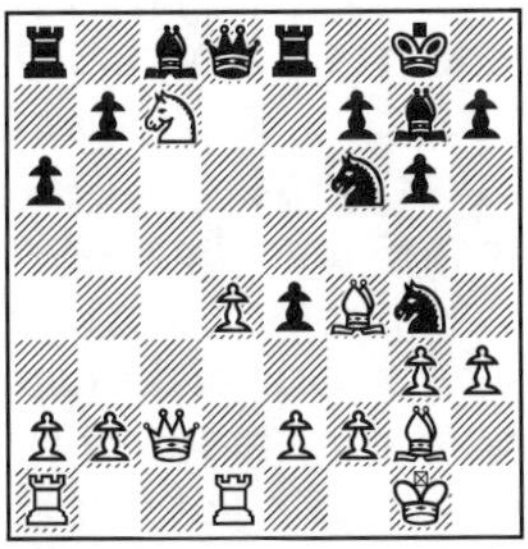

16.	**...**	**e3!!**

White had sown the wind and reaped the whirlwind! Nezh was not only ready to accept the combinational challenge of his opponent, but having calculated the variations, he found some shots which had not been taken into account by White.

17. hxg4 exf2†
18. Kf1 Nxg4
19. Nxe8!

White was right to reject 19. Nxa8. Now on 19… Bxd4 20. Bf3 Ne3†! 21. Bxe3 Bh3† 22. Kxf2 [22. Bg2 Qd5!!] Bxe3† 23. Ke1 Qg5 24. Qc7 Bf2† 25. Kxf2 Qe3† 26. Ke1 Qxf3 and Black is winning. White might have tried: 20. e3, but then 20… Bd7! [Better than 20… Bxe3 which meets with 21. Rxd8! Nh2† 22. Ke2 Bg4† 23. Kd3 Bf5† 24. Be4!.] 21. Rxd4 [21. Bxb7 Nxe3† 22. Bxe3 Bh3† wins.] Bb5† 22. Rc4 Rxe3 23. b3 g5 wins.

Black had a wonderful resource [after 19. Nxa8] in 19… g5!!. Suddenly it becomes clear that after this non-obvious move, White's affairs at once go bad. For example, 20. Qc7 [20. Bf3 gxf4 21. Bxg4 Bxg4, or 20. Bc1 Qf6 with the threat of 21… Nh2# and sending the black Queen on the route f6-h6-h2.] gxf4 21. Qxd8 Rxd8! [Damsky's suggestion was also good: 21… Ne3† 22. Kxf2 Nxd1† 23. Rxd1 Rxd8 24. gxf4 Bxd4† 25. Kf1 Bf6, and because of the bad Knight, White would have lost a pawn at the very minimum.] 22. gxf4 Bxd4 with a strong attack even without the Queens.

19. … Qxe8
20. Qb3?!

How many games have been spoiled by excessive optimism! First of all, White should have thought of the danger concealed in the combination around the f2-pawn and the Knight. The e3-square was defended only by the Bishop. Therefore, it was worthwhile to pay attention to 20. Qe4 or even 20. e4.

20. … h6
21. Bxb7

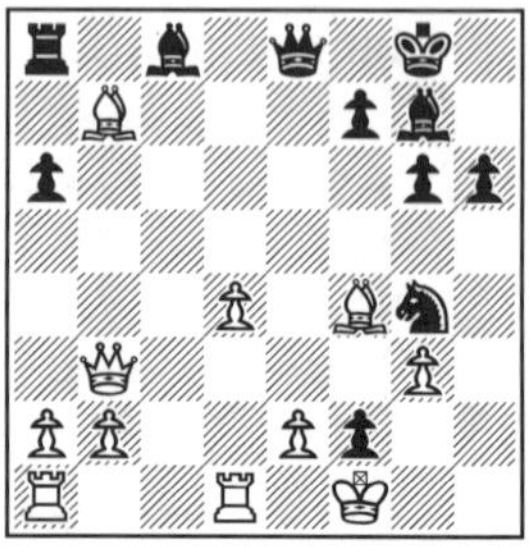

21. … g5!!
22. Bxa8

There was nothing better than this. On 22. Bd6 or Bc7 there might have followed 22… Qe3!. For example: 23. Bxa8 Nh2† 24. Kg2 Qxe2 25. Rf1 Nxf1 26. Rxf1 Bh3† 27. Kxh3 Qxf1† 28. Kg4 [28. Bg2 g4†] h5†! 29. Kxg5 Qc1† 30. Bf4 Qb1! with a quick victory.

On 22. Bc1 there was the simple 22… Rb8 23. Bc6 Qxc6!, with the threat of mate on h1.

22. … gxf4
23. gxf4 Be6!
24. Qb7

Neither 24. d5 Qxa8, and after 25. dxe6 [Ed.: On 25. e4, after 25… Bd7 Black has White tied down.] there was a mate on h1, nor 24. Bd5 Bxd5 25. Qxd5 Ne3† work.

24. … Bc4
25. Qe4 Qd8
26. Kg2 f5!
27. Qc6 Kh7!
28. Kf3 f1=Q†!!

White had struggled honorably and had repulsed nearly all the brilliant blows of his 57-year old rival, but he was in no condition to withstand Nezh's unrestrained imagination.

29. Rxf1 Qh4

In view of the inevitable mate, White surrendered **(0-1)**.

The Fight

The games collected in this chapter are not as brilliant as the first 14. Neither combatant played beyond reproach, thus, fine play wasn't always constant; but these games are interesting for their drama, and the battle between two characters and personalities. Here we can find fighting spirit, risk, will to win, and resolve. Qualities like these attract our attention during contests between worthy rivals.

15.
V. Mikenas—Super Nezh
E 91
Match, 14th game
Kazan 1948

1.	**d4**	**Nf6**
2.	**c4**	**d6**
3.	**Nf3**	**g6**
4.	**Nc3**	**Bg7**
5.	**e4**	**0-0**
6.	**Be2**	**c6**

This was the last game of the match. The score was 6-1/2–6-1/2 and even a victory wouldn't bring Nezhmetdinov master status, since the exceptionally rough norms of those times required a win by a margin of two points. Nevertheless, a victory over such a favored rival was very important.

That fact can explain Black's refusal to play the theoretically preferable 6… e5. That same fact also explains Black's extravagant play at various points in the game.

7.	**h3**	**Nbd7**
8.	**Be3**	**e5**
9.	**d5**	

Of course, even Mikenas, an experienced player, didn't think about the draw, which could have been foreseen if 9. dxe5.

9.	**...**	**cxd5**
10.	**cxd5**	**Nc5**
11.	**Nd2**	**a5?!**

An unnecessary weakening and loss of time. Better would have been 11… Ne8 at once.

12. a3

White still wanted to drive the Knight from c5, and this vindicates the preceding mistake by Black. More logical was 12. 0-0, and on 12… Ne8, 13. Nc4, organizing an attack on the queenside.

12.	**...**	**Ne8**
13.	**b4**	**axb4**
14.	**axb4**	**Rxa1**
15.	**Qxa1**	

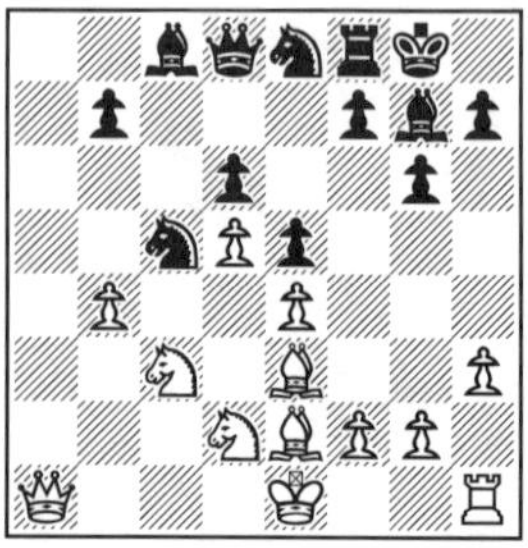

15. ... Nxe4?!

The play follows the principle "all or nothing." Ten or fifteen years later, Tal surprised everybody with the same unexpected approach. It was quite plausible to play the very good move 15… Nd7, but that evening Nezh wouldn't play cautiously.

16.	**Ndxe4**	**f5**
17.	**Nd2**	

Boleslavsky advised 17. 0-0! fxe4 18. Nxe4, and White's position would be better due to the firm grip on e4. This was nice advice, but it's always easier to give away someone else's pieces.

17.	**...**	**e4**
18.	**Nb3!**	

White must be precise in his defense. 18. 0-0 f4 19. Ba7 f3! was unsuitable, as the piece must retreat [20. gxf3 Qg5† and 21… Qxd2]. 18. g3 Qf6 19. Ndb1 g5 can't be recommended either, as over the long haul White's position will become difficult.

18.	**...**	**f4**
19.	**Bd4**	**f3**
20.	**gxf3**	**exf3**
21.	**Bd3**	**Qg5!**

As the game moves on, Black's initiative increases. It was clear the white King will be in trouble. The threat was 22… Bxd4 23. Nxd4 Qe5†.

22. Be3 Qh4
23. Kd2 Qxb4
24. Rb1 Qh4
25. Qa7 Be5
26. Nd4 Bf4!

A strong move, which gives new momentum to Black's attack in connection with the threat ...Qxf2.

27. Kc2

27. Rf1 Bxh3 or 27. Nd1 Bxe3† 28. fxe3 f2 wouldn't have helped.

27. ... Bxe3
28. fxe3 Qf2†
29. Kb3 Qxe3

Chasing the King, Black won two pawns which equalized material and preserved the attack. It can be assumed that Black's position was now won.

30. Bf1 f2
31. Ndb5 Qg3
32. Qa2 Rf3?!

A *zeitnot* [time pressure] move. Black continues to attack, though the light pieces don't take part. After 32... Bxh3, the victory would have been achieved without considerable difficulty.

33. Qa8 Bd7
34. Ka2 Qe5?

This was from the same series of misadventures because of the hanging flag. The Knight should have been protected by the Rook, 34... Re3; then ...Bxh3 would have been possible.

35. Rb4 Re3
36. Qxb7 Bf5?

The pawn could have been taken on h3: 36... Bxh3 37. Bxh3 Rxh3 38. Re4? f1=Q. 36... Bxb5 was very good also.

37. Ra4 Re1?

The question mark was put here for the same reason. After 37... Rxc3 38. Nxc3 Qxc3 39. Ra7 Qd2† there was a perpetual check.

38. Ra7

Here Black saw with horror the threatened mate, and during the next few seconds wasn't able to find the maneuver 38... Qg7 39. Qb8 Qh6.

38. ... Bb1†?

As revealed during the postmortem, this led to the defeat. In time trouble, Nezh didn't realize that it was high time to pull his legs in, and head for the ending. 38... Qg7 was obligatory. Then 39. Qxg7† Nxg7 40. Bc4 [40. Nxd6 Rxf1 41. Ra8† Ne8 42. Rxe8† Kg7 43. Re7† Kh6 44. Nxf5† gxf5 45. Re3 Ra1† 46. Kxa1 f1=Q†] Ne8 41. h4 Bh3 42. Kb3 f1=Q 43. Bxf1 Bxf1. Black's chances were better.

39. Nxb1 Re2†!

At the last moment Nezh takes himself in hand and decided to take the draw, though it was too late.

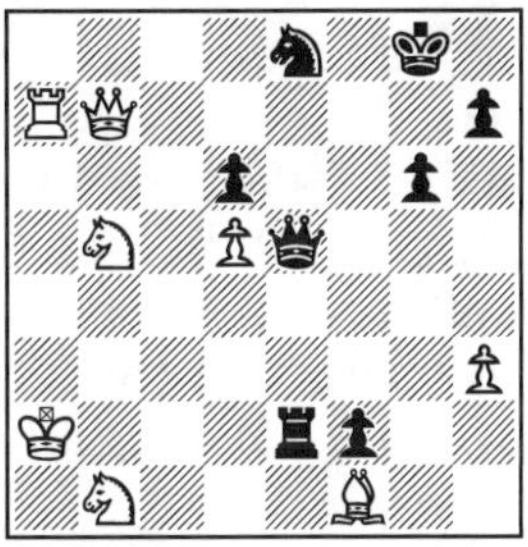

40. Bxe2!

Mikenas felt the danger just in time: 40. Kb3 [40. Ka3 Qa1†] Qb2† 41. Ka4 [41. Kc4 Re4† 42. Kd3 Qxb1†] Qa2† 42. N1a3 Re4† 43. Ka5 Qd2† 44. Ka6! [If 44. Kb6, then 44... Qe3† forces 45. Ka5 as 45. Kc6 [45. Ka6 Ra4#.] Qc5† 46. Kd7 Nf6† leads to mate.] Ra4† 45. Kb6 Qe3† 46. Kc6 Qc1†! 47. Kd7 Rxa7 and 48... Qxf1.

R.N.

Alas, Nezh's analysis was inexact. 40. Kb3 won. 40... Qb2† 41. Ka4 Qa1† 42. N5a3 Re4† 43. Kb3 Re3† 44. Kc4 Re4† 45. Kd3! Qd4† 46. Kc2, and the checks would have been over.

40. ... Qxe2†
41. Ka1?

Time pressure had eased, but this didn't stop White from losing the opportunity to win [nobody mentioned this opportunity].

Now we get a draw, the goal of both players, and deserved by both. But for the sake of chess truth, I'll point out that 41. Kb3! could have brought home the victory: 41... Qf3†! [41... Qe3† loses simply because of 42. N5c3!, and Black would be obliged to play 42... Qxa7† 43. Qxa7 f1=Q 44. Qe3, which would end Black's chances.] 42. N5c3! Qf6 43. Qxh7† Kf8 44. Qh6† Kg8 45. Nd2, and Black wouldn't get an extra Queen.

41. ... Qe5†

Here a draw was agreed **(1/2-1/2).** The Queen now controls the h8-square; that's why there was no mate, and White has to give perpetual check: 42. Ka2 f1=Q 43. Qxh7† Kf8 44. Qh6† Kg8 45. Qh7†.

16.
I. Boleslavsky—Super Nezh
A 77
10th Russian ch.
Gorki 1950

1. d4 Nf6
2. c4 e6
3. Nc3 c5
4. d5 exd5
5. cxd5 d6
6. e4 g6
7. Be2

The "Modern Benoni" system was used for the first time by F. Marshall in the 1927 New York tournament, but didn't gain popularity and would seldom be encountered until the 1950s. The revival of this system is usually connected with the names Tal, Fischer, Boleslavsky, Gligorich, and other GMs. The merits of other masters, whose rank is lower, shouldn't be underestimated—namely, their important contributions to the creation of the system [and, more specifically, the rebirth of interest in it] as played in this game.

7. ... Bg7
8. Nf3 0-0
9. 0-0 Re8
10. Nd2 b6

In his famous 1984 monograph, *Indian Defences*, A. Kapengut said this position was "a seldom occurring and comparatively passive continuation." This conclusion, based on many years of intensive research and practice, is probably indisputable. "But," says A. Suetin, "it shouldn't be forgotten that this game was the very first one." Nowadays, we more often see the plan wherein the Knight moves Nb8-a6-c7, and b7-b5 is prepared; this helps preserve defensive positions in the center and on the kingside.

11. a4 Ba6

Black's exchange of white-squared Bishops is not approved of theoretically, because the current pawn structure makes Black's white-squared Bishop "better" than White's. Preferable was 11... a6, intending to transfer the b8-Knight to e5 and the a8-Rook to e7.

12. Bb5!

The same idea can be seen in the French Defense: White shows his willingness to exchange Bishops and creates pressure on Black's flank at the same time.

12. ... Bxb5

More precision would be shown with 12... Re7 13. Re1 Bb7! 14. Bf1 Nbd7 15. Nc4 Ne5 and some advantage to White, *Bobotsov—Bilek, Moscow 1967.*

13. axb5 Nbd7
14. Qc2 Ne5
15. f4 Ned7

Black instigated White's 15. f4 to weaken the g1-d4 diagonal and create counterplay by an eventual ...Ng4. White could have deprived his rival of these opportunities by the simple 16. h3 and would have gotten a stable advantage.

16. Nf3?! c4!

A typical pawn move, which White should have prevented as soon as possible. Black made the c5-square available for his Knight.

17. Re1

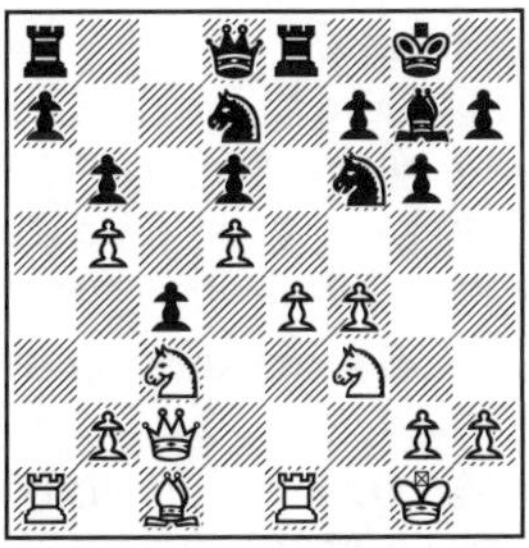

17. ... Qc7

A move characteristic of Nezhmetdinov's playing style. He wrote in his commentaries: "It is possible that I missed a chance to win here." This move illustrates not only optimism, which is characteristic of chess players who prefer an attacking style, but also Nezh's confidence in both his power and the rectitude of his assessment of the position. This was a type of confidence without which no creative risk or courage in carrying out one's intentions is possible.

Still—was Nezh right, did the Black position give him a chance to win? Instead of the game move he offered 17... Nc5!, and in case of 18. Nd4, 18... Nfxe4! 19. Nc6 Qh4 20. Rf1 with one extra pawn and an active position for Black.

Instead of 18. Nd4, better would have been 18. Bd2 Qd7 19. Re2, and it would be too early to talk about the possibilities of a Black win.

Unfortunately, the possibility of overestimating his chances never bothered Rashid Gibyatovich. He dealt with his 17... Nc5 18. Nd4 annotation inaccuracy by failing to mention the reply 18... Nfxe4!.

18. Ra4 a6!
19. Rxa6!

Boleslavsky found the right way to stop Black's initiative. 19. bxa6 was a false lead: ...b5! 20. Nxb5 Qc5† 21. Nbd4 Nb6 22. Ra3 Nfxd5! and Black stands better. An example could have been: 23. Qd1 Nf6! 24. Be3 Ng4 25. Qd2 Rxe4.

19. ... Rxa6
20. bxa6 b5
21. Nxb5!

In spite of the apparent danger, this was the only way White can preserve the balance.

21. ... Qc5†
22. Nbd4 Nxd5
23. exd5 Rxe1†
24. Nxe1 Bxd4†
25. Kf1 Qb5

An attempt to get the advantage by 25... Qxd5 26. Qa4 Nf6 [26... Nb6 27. Qe8† Kg7 28. a7 Qa8 29. Qb8!] 27. a7 Qa8 28. Qxc4 was not successful.

26. Qe2 Qxa6
27. Nc2 Bf6
28. Na3

Now the position was equal.

28. ... Nb6

29.	**Qe8†**	**Kg7**
30.	**Qb5**	**Qxb5**
31.	**Nxb5**	**Be7**
32.	**Na3**	**Bf6**
33.	**Nb5**	**Be7**

(1/2-1/2).

17.
L. Polugaevsky—Super Nezh
E 68
13th Russian ch.
Saratov 1953

1.	**d4**	**Nf6**
2.	**c4**	**d6**
3.	**Nf3**	**Nbd7**
4.	**g3**	**g6**
5.	**Bg2**	**Bg7**
6.	**0-0**	**0-0**
7.	**Nc3**	**e5**
8.	**Qc2**	**Re8**
9.	**Rd1**	**c6**
10.	**e4**	**Qe7**
11.	**b3**	**a5**

For more than 40 years, the Qc2 variant didn't undergo any serious change. Today, this position is considered one of the main lines.

12.	**Bb2**	**exd4**
13.	**Nxd4**	**Nc5**
14.	**Re1**	

Inconsistent, but Polugaevsky was afraid of the flank attack h7-h5-h4 after 14. f3.

14.	**...**	**Qc7**
15.	**Rad1**	**Qb6!**

A good repositioning of the Queen, providing Black with active play on the Queen's flank.

16. Nde2

White's reply is aimed at the backward d6-pawn.

16.	**...**	**a4**
17.	**Nc1**	**axb3**
18.	**axb3**	**Rd8**
19.	**h3**	**Be6**

More energetic was 19... h5.

20.	**Kh2**	**h5**
21.	**N3a2**	

Black played a good opening and seized the initiative; that's why it was difficult for White to find the right way. So, the response for the pseudoenergetic 21. f4 was the unpleasant move 21... h4! The same move could have followed on 21. Rd2: 21... h4! 22. Red1 Nh5! 23. N3e2 Bxb2 24. Qxb2 Nxe4! 25. Bxe4 Qxf2† 26. Kh1 Bxh3 with a strong attack [mentioned by Polugaevsky].

21. ... d5

Black decides to open the center, but it was a pivotal decision for both players. 21... h4 would have been good here, and White could have responded with 22. Bd4.

22.	**cxd5**	**cxd5**
23.	**exd5**	

23. Bd4 wouldn't work: 23... Nfxe4! 24. Rxe4 dxe4 25. Bxc5 Qc7 26. Rxd8† Rxd8 27. Bxe4 Rc8.

23. ... Bf5

23... Nxd5 was bad because of 24. Bxg7 Kxg7 25. Re5.

24.	**Qc4**	**Nxb3**
25.	**Nxb3**	**Rxa2**
26.	**Bd4**	**Qd6**
27.	**Bc5**	**Qb8!**

Worse was 27... Qd7 28. Re7 Qc8 29. d6 Be6 30. Qd3 with the advantage to White.

28. Na1!?

Black had a good choice of active replies: ...b5, ...Bc2, ...Rc2. If 28. Rd2, then 28... b5 29. Qb4 Ra4. If 28. Nd4, then 28... Rxf2! 29. Ne2 Rxg2†! 30. Kxg2 Be4†. Instead 28. Na1!? is an extraordinary move by White to repel direct threats.

28. ... Qa8

29. d6 Be6

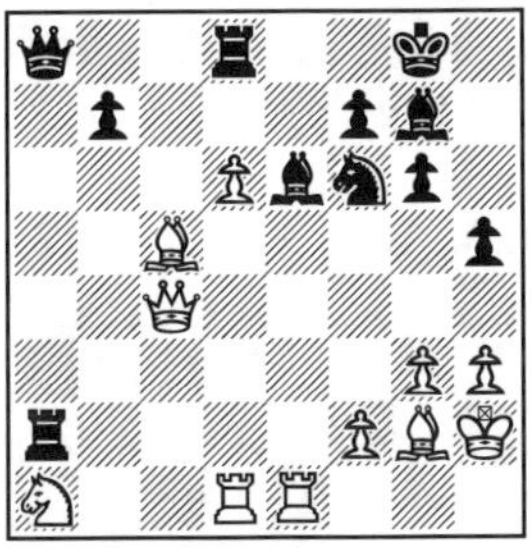

30. Rxe6!

The eighteen-year-old Polugaevsky was very resourceful in defending. It wasn't easy to find a good retreat for the Queen: 30. Qb5 Rb2!, 30. Qf4 Ra4.

30. ... fxe6
31. Qxe6† Kh7
32. Bd4 Re8
33. Qb3?!

A prolonged struggle brings both rivals to *zeitnot*. Best is 33. Qf7 Rf8 34. Qe7! [worse was 34. Qxb7 Qxb7 35. Bxb7 Nd7! and White was in a difficult position] with adequate chances.

33. ... Qa4?

This returned the favor. A resolute 33... Ree2! gives Black the advantage, for example, 34. Qxb7 Qxb7 35. Bxb7 Nd7 followed by ...Red2.

34. Qxa4 Rxa4
35. Nb3 Rb4
36. Nc5 Ng4†

An instinctive tendency in time pressure *[zeitnot]* to simplify the position. Black had already lost his chance to win anyway.

37. hxg4 Rxd4
38. Rxd4 Bxd4
39. Nxb7 Bb6
40. gxh5 gxh5

Zeitnot had passed, and so has the smoke from the battle. White's endgame was better, but he couldn't have won.

41. d7 Rf8
42. Kh3 Kg6
43. f4 Kf5
44. Kh4 Bd8†
45. Nxd8 Rxd8
46. Bc6 Rh8
47. Bf3 Kf6
48. Be4

On 48. Bxh5, 48... Kf5! and White would be in *zugzwang*.

48. ... Rd8
49. Bc6 Kf5
50. Ba4 Rh8
51. Bd1 Kf6
52. Bc2 Rd8
(1/2-1/2).

18.
Super Nezh—L. Shamkovich

C 84

16th Russian ch.
Kislovodsk 1956

1. e4 e5
2. Nf3 Nc6
3. Bb5 a6
4. Ba4 Nf6
5. 0-0 Be7
6. d4 b5
7. Bb3 d6

The text of this game, as well as Game No. 9 [Belov—N.], involves some confusion as to move order. Nezh maintained that the game line was 5... b5 6. Bb3 Be7 7. d4 d6, but his biographer, Damsky, witnessed that Rashid Gibyatovich never recorded his games—he just remembered them. In this case we should rely on Damsky, since he compared the text of the game with the tournament form.

8. c3 Bg4
9. h3

This was a pawn sacrifice, but no

other way to fight for the advantage in this frequently occurring position has been found.

9. ... Bxf3

It's interesting to compare different commentaries on this exchange. *Nezh* believed that this is exactly where Black's troubles began, and recommended 9... Bh5 10. d5 [He considered 10. Re1 stronger here, however] Na5 11. Bc2 c6 12. dxc6 Qc7 with equal chances, as in his game with *Zhilin, semi-finals 26th USSR ch., Rostov 1958.*

Matanovich, the author of this section in *ECO*, prefers the game move, and offers 9... Bh5 [by the way, seen for the first time in *Geller—Keres, 1947]* as preferable for White because of the weakness of the d5-square.

10. Qxf3 exd4

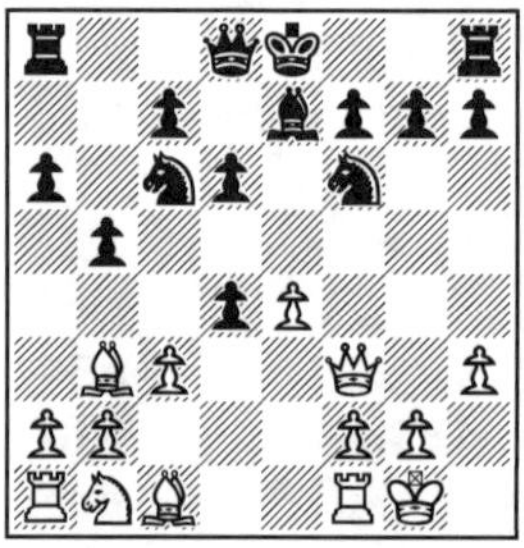

11. Qg3!

Nezhmetdinov's idea, which was accepted at once by many chess players.

11. ... 0-0

Other possibilities are not so good: 11... g6 12. Bd5! Qd7 13. Bh6 Rb8 14. f4 with the initiative to White, *Tal—Teschner, European ch., Vienna 1957;* 11... Qd7 12. Qxg7! 0-0-0 13. Qxf7 Kb7 14. Be6, and Black had no compensation for the pawn, *Pietzsch, W—Spassky, Havana 1962.*

12. Bh6 Ne8

Worse would have been 12... Nh5 13. Qg4 dxc3 14. Nxc3 Nd4 15. Qxh5 gxh6 16. f4, when White preserves the advantage and Black has no compensation for the damaged pawn structure.

13. Bd5 Qd7

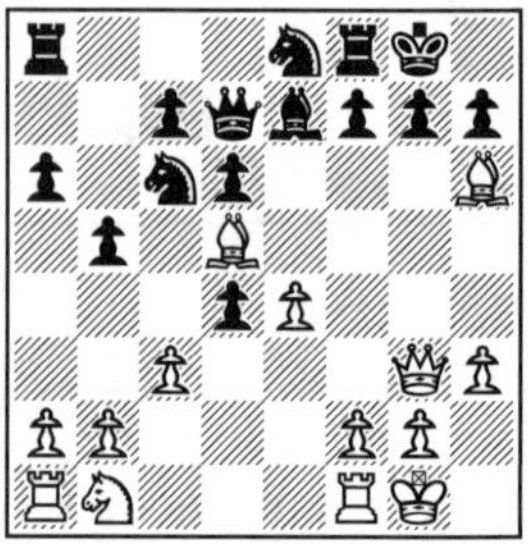

14. Qg4!

A typical Nezhmetdinov tactic: the abrupt offer of a Queen exchange at a moment most inconvenient for his rival. It looks like a wrestler's chop—the opponent loses the initiative at once. The same thing can be seen in Games 80 [N.—Krogius, 25th move] and 67 [Shishov—N., 18th move].

14. ... Qxg4
15. hxg4 gxh6
16. Bxc6 dxc3!

Forced; otherwise White just wins back the pawn, preserving all positive aspects of the position.

17. Nxc3 Rb8
18. Nd5 Bd8

Here Black's material advantage means nothing; White had a considerable positional and spatial advantage. The only imperative here was accurate play.

19. f4?

Being in a joyful mood he makes a mistake.

R.N.

The right method was demonstrated

by *Nezh* in the game with *G. Zhuravlev, Cheboksary 1959:* 19. f3 Kg7 20. b4!, strengthening the advantage that White had lost.

19. ... Nf6
20. Ne3 Nxe4!
21. Nf5!

Not 21. Bxe4, because of 21... Re8.

21. ... Nc5
22. Nxh6† Kh8
23. b4 Ne6

Dangerous was 23... Nd3 24. Rab1 and the Knight would be out of moves.

24. Rad1 Bf6
25. Bd5 Rbe8
26. Bc6 Rd8
27. g3 Nd4
28. Bd5 Rd7

Black missed his chance to simplify: 28... Ne2† 29. Kf2 Nc3 30. Nxf7† Rxf7 31. Bxf7 Nxd1† 32. Rxd1 c5, retaining adequate chances.

29. g5 Bg7
30. Rfe1 c6
31. Bg2 c5?

A mistake caused by an incorrect evaluation of the situation. Now the d5-square would be in White's hands. With 31... d5!, Black could have limited the activity of the white Bishop and had good chances.

32. Ng4 f6?

As the proverb says, "When it rains, it pours." For the second time in the game, the advantage was White's. Black himself destroys the main drawing factor: opposite-colored Bishops.

32... a5! would be good, as recommended by Nezhmetdinov, and if 33. bxa5, then 33... Ra7 with equal chances for Black.

33. gxf6 Bxf6
34. Nxf6 Rxf6
35. Re8† Kg7
36. Bd5 Rf8
37. Re4 Kf6?

Again Black doesn't grasp the essence of the position—he shouldn't allow g4.

38. g4 h6
39. Kg2 Rc8

To prevent the loss of the pawn; White intends 40. Rc1, and 40... Rc8 was no good because of 41. Rxd4.

40. Rh1 Kg7
41. f5 Rf8
42. Rc1 Rfd8
43. Kg3 Kf6

The attempt to undermine with 43... h5 might have deplorable results: 44. Rf1 Rf8 45. Rxd4! cxd4 46. g5, and White would get a pair of dangerous passed pawns.

44. Kf4 Kg7
45. Rc3 Kf6
46. Rh3 Kg7

47. g5!

A change in piece activity which was so great that it gave White an opportunity to attack the King.

47. ... hxg5†
48. Kxg5 Rf8
49. f6! Rxf6
50. Rh7†! Kxh7
51. Kxf6

The attack had reached its goal—the Knight must be sacrificed to escape mate.

51. ... Nf3
52. Rf4 Rg7

53. **Rxf3** **Rg6†**
54. **Kf7** **Rg7†**
55. **Kf8** **Rg4**
56. **Rf6** **cxb4**
57. **Be6** **Rh4**
58. **Kf7**

Black resigned **(1-0)**, as his King was trapped in a mating net.

19.

Super Nezh—L. Shamkovich

B 63

17th Russian ch.

Krasnodar 1957

1. **e4** **c5**
2. **Nf3** **Nc6**
3. **d4** **cxd4**
4. **Nxd4** **Nf6**
5. **Nc3** **d6**
6. **Bg5** **e6**
7. **Qd2** **Qb6?!**

A Shamkovich experiment, now largely forgotten; it's not mentioned in modern opening reference books. At that time, Black experienced some definite difficulties in traditional lines of Rauzer's system: 6. Bg5 e6 7. Qd2 Be7 or 7... a6. That's probably why Shamkovich, who always worked extensively on opening problems, decided to test a new idea. Its lifetime was short, and the reason was this game.

8. **Nb3**

White gets nothing after 8. 0-0-0 Nxd4 9. Qxd4 Qxd4 10. Rxd4 a6. It's early for 8. Ndb5 a6 9. Be3 [but not 9. Nxd6†? Bxd6 10. Qxd6 Qxb2] Qd8 10. Nd4 Ng4, and Black gets an excellent position. Besides the game continuation, Nezh considered 8. Bxf6 gxf6 9. Nb3 as worthy of attention.

8. **...** **a6**

Necessary to stop 9. Bxf6 gxf6 10. Nb5 from winning the d6-pawn.

9. **Be2** **Bd7**
10. **0-0** **Be7**
11. **Kh1!**

A move both useful and expected: White let his opponent decide where to put his King—a difficult problem. If 11... 0-0-0 12. Be3 Qc7 13. Na4! Nxe4 14. Qd3 Nc5 15. Naxc5 dxc5 16. Nxc5 Bxc5 17. Bxc5, White would get a big advantage.

11. **...** **h6**

Black decided to leave his King in the center, where its position [as will be shown] was not sufficiently secure. In spite of the apparent danger, it was easier to provide protection for the King after castling short: 11... 0-0!? 12. Bxf6 gxf6 13. f4 Kh8 14. Bh5 Be8. Then Black could transfer the Rook to g7 and successfully defend, due to the "hedgehog" pawn structure. Also important was the absence of White's black-squared Bishop.

12. **Bxf6** **gxf6**
13. **Bh5!**

This was the best place for the Bishop. Nowadays, this maneuver has become standard in similar positions.

13. **...** **Ne5**
14. **f4** **Nc4**
15. **Qe2** **Rc8**

It would be dangerous to take on b2 [15... Nxb2] because of 16. f5!

16. **f5?!**

16. Rae1! first, would be stronger, discouraging ...Qe3. Perhaps Nezh was afraid of an invasion of the white Queen to e6.

16. **...** **Qe3!**

And here 16... Nxb2 wouldn't work: 17. fxe6 Bxe6 18. Nd5 Bxd5 [18... Qd8 19. Nd4 Bxd5 20. exd5 Kf8 21. Bxf7!; 18... Qb5 19. c4! Nxc4 20. Nd4 Qd7 21. Nxe6 Qxe6 22. Bg4] 19. exd5 Kd8 20.

Rab1, and Nezh gives the following fine continuation: 20... Na4 21. Nc5! Qxc5 22. Rxb7 Rc7 23. Rb8† Rc8 24. Re1! Qc7 25. Rxc8† Kxc8 26. Qxa6†.

17. Qg4 Kf8

18. Rae1

An inaccuracy taken advantage of very resourcefully by Black. Better was 18. Rf3, for after 18... Rg8, 19. Qh3.

18. ... Rg8!

Based on the fact that if 19. Rxe3 Rxg4 20. Re2 Rg5, then 21... Nxb2 would make it unprofitable for White.

19. Qh4 Qg5

20. Qh3 Nd2?

Black tenaciously strove for a defendable position. 20... Nxb2! would have offered equal chances after 21. Re3 Qg7. The game move was a serious tactical mistake, and it led to defeat.

21. Nxd2 Qxd2

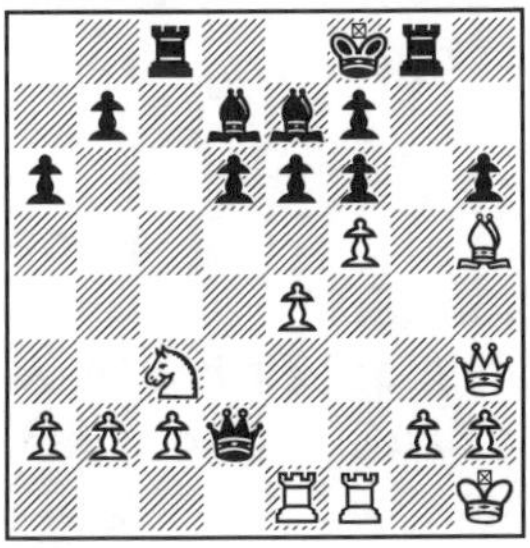

22. e5!!

A terrific shot, blowing up Black's entire defense.

22. ... Bc6

Sadly, it was not a good idea to take on e5: 22... fxe5 23. Re2 and 24. fxe6, and after 22... dxe5 23. Rd1 the Bishop would be lost.

23. Re2 Qg5

24. fxe6 fxe6

25. exf6 Bxf6

26. Ne4

Easier was 26. Bf3!, stifling Black's counterplay.

26. ... Bxe4

27. Rxe4 Rxc2

28. Rxe6 Rf2?

A *Zeitnot* cheapo which sped his defeat. More chances were offered by 28... Kg7.

29. Re8† Kg7

30. Rxg8† Kxg8

31. Qc8† Kg7

32. Rxf2 Qxh5

33. Qxb7† Kg6

34. Qf3 Qxf3

35. gxf3 1-0.

20.

G. Borisenko—Super Nezh

A 42

17th Russian ch.

Krasnodar 1957

1. d4 g6

On 1. d4 Nezh usually chose the King's Indian Defense. This time, he played a different way...

The choice of this order of moves is explained by sporting and tactical reasons. G. Borisenko ... was my main rival ... that's why I was obliged to play only for victory.

G. Borisenko is an outstanding theorist who knows well how to play the opening stage of a game... He seldom loses when playing White. Having studied his games, I came to the conclusion that Borisenko is very uncertain when playing the games with unfamiliar schemes and a com-

plicated tactical beginning. That's why I made up my mind to choose a new order of moves.

R.N.

2. c4	**Bg7**
3. Nc3	**c5**
4. d5	**d6**
5. g3	**Nd7**
6. Bg2	**Bxc3†!?**

And here, an unfamiliar situation for Borisenko emerged from the position. It resembled a Nimzo-Indian Defense, but with an unpromising placement of the Bishop at g2.

R.N.

Nezh certainly managed to move the famous theorist away from his studied and well-known ways. Still, his decision to part with the "Indian" Bishop was risky from a strategical point of view—White's black-squared Bishop possesses the c1-h6 diagonal, where it can act unopposed.

7. bxc3	**Qa5**
8. Qb3	**Ngf6**
9. Nf3	**Nb6**
10. 0-0	**Bg4**
11. Re1	

11. Bh6!? was worth thinking about.

11. ... h5!?

12. e4?!

Done without considering the plans of his rival, who was eager to open the h-file. It would have been better to protect the Knight from a Bishop exchange: 12. Nd2! h4 13. h3 Bd7 14. g4, and if 14... Ba4, then 15. Qa3 with better chances for White since he would be avoiding opening the h-file and could create a pawn-roller in the center after f4 and e4.

12. ... Nfd7?!

Based on the previously mentioned points, 12... Bxf3 and 13... h4 would be stronger.

13. Be3

Again, 13. Nd2 was preferable; Nezh offered 13... Ne5 14. f4 Nd3 15. Re3 Nxc1 16. Rxc1 Bd7 17. e5 "with equally sharp positions." We can hardly agree with this estimation. The strong center gives White better chances.

By the way, Nezh himself recommended 13. h3 Bxf3 14. Bxf3 0-0-0 with equal chances.

13. ... h4!

14. Nxh4

With 14. gxh4 Bxf3! 15. Bxf3 Ne5 16. Be2 Rxh4 17. f4 Ng4 Black has a big initiative. Safer would be 14. Nd2 hxg3 15. hxg3 0-0-0 with mutual chances.

R.N.

14. ... Ne5

15. Qb5†

An obligatory exchange. After 15. Bf1, 15... Rxh4! and 16... Nf3†.

15. ... Qxb5

16. cxb5

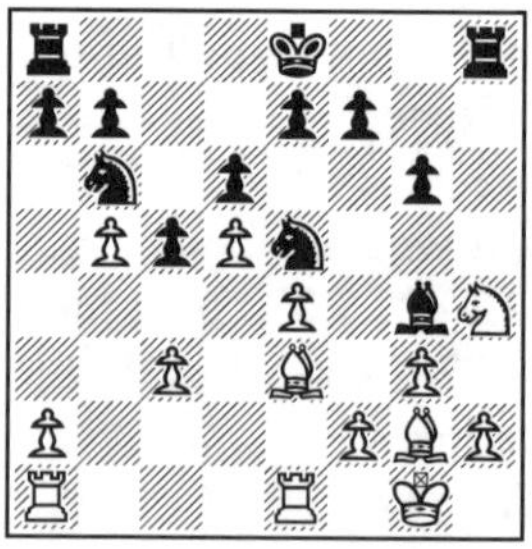

Black preceded this position with the sacrifice of a pawn.

The endgame is convenient for him because of White's numerous weaknesses on the queenside.

R.N.

16. ... Na4
17. Rec1

Looking toward the endgame, Nezh often examined long, concrete continuations: 17. f4 Nd3 18. Reb1 Nxc3 19. Rb3 Ne2† 20. Kf1 c4 21. Ra3 Nexf4 22. gxf4 Rxh4 with difficult play for White.

17. ... Nc4
18. Bf1?

Being in an unfamiliar situation, White was in time trouble by this time and he committed an error. He should have chosen 18. Bf4 Rg8 19. Nf3 Bxf3 20. Bxf3 or 18. Nf3 Nxe3 19. fxe3 Nb6.

Black had excellent compensation for the pawn, but nothing more.

18. ... Nxe3
19. fxe3 g5!
20. Ng2

Not good would have been 20. Nf5, since after 20… Kd7 the Knight would be in danger by ...e6.

20. ... Bf3
21. Ne1 Bxe4
22. Bg2 Bxg2
23. Kxg2

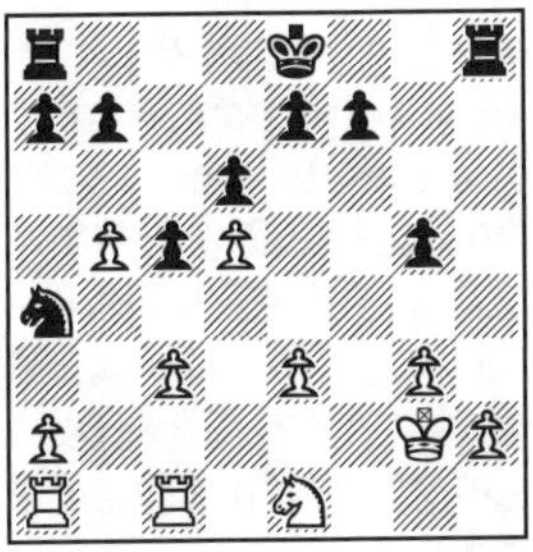

23. ... c4!

An important move, which fixes the weak position in White's camp.

R.N.

24. Rab1

Nezh offered a more definite plan of defense: 24. Nf3 g4 25. Nd2 Nb6 26. e4 Rc8 27. a4 Nd7 28. a5 Ne5 29. Ra4, but even here Black preserved opportunities to reinforce his position.

24. ... Nb6
25. Rd1 g4
26. Rd4 f5
27. Nc2 Rh5
28. a4 Nxa4
29. Rxc4 Nb6
30. Rd4

On 30. Rc7, there was the simple 30… Rb8 followed by ...Kd8.

30. ... Rc8!

The a-Rook must be forced to take a passive position at b3.

R.N.

31. Rb3 Kd7
32. e4 Rch8
33. h4 gxh3†
34. Kh2 fxe4
35. Ne3 Rf8
36. Rb2 Rf3
37. Re2 Rg5
38. c4 Rgxg3
39. Rxe4 Rg5
40. Ng4 Rg7
41. Ra2

Here the game was adjourned; upon resuming the game, Nezh demonstrated the most efficient way to win.

41. ... Kc7!
42. Rxa7 Rc3
43. Ne3 Nd7
44. Ra2 Nf6
45. Nf5 Ng4†

White resigned **(0-1).**

21.
Super Nezh—M. Tal
B 48
Spartakiade USSR
Moscow 1959

1. e4 c5
2. Nf3 Nc6
3. d4 cxd4
4. Nxd4 Qc7
5. Nc3 e6
6. Be3 Nf6
7. Bd3 a6
8. 0-0 Ne5
9. h3 b5
10. f4 Nc4
11. Bxc4 Qxc4
12. Qd3

It was determined in the 1960s that 12. e5 Nd5 13. Nxd5 Qxd5 14. Qe2 Bb7 15. Nb3 was better with a small advantage for White, *Vasiukov—Suetin, USSR ch., 1965.*

12. ... d5
13. exd5

Another approximately equal reply was used by *Fischer* against *Petrosian, Santa Monica 1966:* 13. e5 Nd7 14. Qxc4 dxc4 15. f5 Nxe5 16. fxe6 Bxe6 17. Rae1 with compensation for the lost pawn.

13. ... Qxd3
14. cxd3 b4!
15. Ne4 Nxd5
16. Bd2

White didn't manage to gain the advantage, and, because this was a team tournament, Nezh [as a team leader for Russia] offered a draw. Tal, the leader of the Latvian team [and also twice-champion of the USSR by that time], also defending his team's interests, decided to continue the game. It's interesting to note that, having misunderstood that Tal refused the draw, Nezh started analyzing and began to move pieces—but the game was to be continued.

16. ... a5?!

Not the best move. Nezh recommended 16... f5! 17. Ng5 Bc5 18. Ngf3 with approximate equality and disruption of the attacking ideas involving f4-f5.

17. Rac1 Ba6
18. Rfe1! g6

Black didn't have the stomach for 18... Bxd3 because of White's possible 19. f5 with a dangerous initiative. The move played can't stop this pawn's push. Therefore it was worth thinking about 18... Be7, and if 19. f5, then 19... 0-0 20. fxe6 Bxd3, though it looked dangerous.

19. f5?!

This was a typical Nezh pawn sacrifice in order to create a sharp position. Subsequent play showed that White had no advantage. The balanced player would have preferred 19. Nc5 Bxc5 20. Rxc5 0-0 21. Nc6 Bxd3 22. Ne5 Ba6, and now after 23. Rxa5 or 23. Nc6, it would probably be drawn.

19. ... Bg7

If 19... gxf5, then 20. Nxf5!, and if 20... exf5?, then 21. Nf6† and mate in one.

20. f6

The alternative pawn sacrifice [he had to give up a pawn] doesn't give White chances to get an advantage either: 20. Nc6 gxf5 21. Nd6† Kf8 22. d4 Rg8 23. Ne5 Bxe5 24. dxe5 Ke7.

20. ... Nxf6

Not 20... Bxf6? 21. Nxf6† Nxf6 22. Nxe6! fxe6 23. Rxe6† Kf7 24. Rcc6.

21. Nd6†

Here, the similar combination 21. Nxf6† Bxf6 22. Nxe6? fxe6 23. Rxe6† Kf7 24. Rcc6 Bxd4† was flawed because of the check.

21. ... Ke7

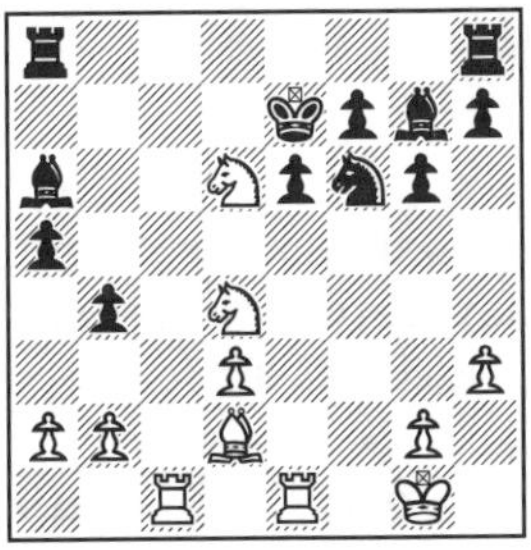

22. Nxf7?!

White decided on a questionable sacrifice of the Knight having found nothing good in 22. Rc7† Nd7 [22... Kxd6 23. Bf4† Kd5 24. Nb3 with an irresistible White attack] 23. N6b5 Bxb5 24. Bg5† Bf6 25. Bxf6† Kxf6 26. Nxb5 Rhd8, and Black would keep the extra pawn.

22. ... Kxf7
23. Rc7† Kg8
24. Nxe6 Ne8
25. Rd7 Bf6?

A mistake which would lead to defeat. Meanwhile, after 25... Bb5 26. Rd5 Bc6 27. Rc5 Bd7 and then 28. Nxg7 Nxg7 29. Re7 Be8 30. Bh6 Bf7 [30... Nf5? 31. Rxf5 gxf5 32. Rg7† Kf8 33. Ra7†+−] 31. Rcc7 Nf5 32. Rxf7 Nxh6 33. Rfd7. The activity of the white Rooks are at a maximum here, but it's not clear if that's enough to balance the position on the board.

26. Rf1!

Black didn't take into account the threat 27. Rxf6 Nxf6 28. Rg7#, and even 26... Bb5 doesn't help because of 27. Rxf6 Bxd7 28. Rf8#.

26. ... Ng7
27. Rxf6 Nxe6
28. Rxe6 Bb5
29. Rc7 h5
30. Rxg6†

After some meaningless moves **(30... Kf8 31. Bh6† Ke8 32. Re6† Kd8 33. Rc5 Kd7 34. Rb6 Bxd3 35. Bf4 Rhf8 36. Rd6† Ke7 37. Rc7† Ke8 38. Bg5 Rf1† 39. Kh2 Bb1 40. Rh6)**, Black resigned **(1-0)**.

22.

Super Nezh—I. Boleslavsky

B 62

USSR Team ch.

1960

1. e4 c5
2. Nf3 Nc6
3. Nc3 d6
4. d4 cxd4
5. Nxd4 Nf6
6. Bg5 e6
7. g3 Be7

In Game 30 [N.—Zilber], Black played the weaker 7... Qa5?

8. Bg2 0-0
9. 0-0 Bd7

After 9... Nxd4 10. Qxd4 h6, Black achieved equality without problems in *Bronstein—Geller, 1954.*

10. Nb3 Qb8

More exacting was 10... Qc7, and Boleslavsky corrects himself with the next move, unafraid of losing a tempo.

11. f4 Qc7
12. Qe2 a5
13. a4 Nb4

In spite of the loss of tempo, it should be assumed that Black had solved his opening problems and achieved good play.

14. Rf2!?

An unusual move which solves two problems: it closed the g1-a7 diagonal [usually, the players put the King in the corner] and protected the c2-pawn.

14. ... Rac8

15. Rd1 Rfd8
16. Nd4 Qb6

More accurate would be 16... h6.

17. e5!

It should be noted that for quite some time both sides couldn't begin active play because they were busy with the improvement of their pieces' positions. The right of the first move makes White obliged to attack first.

17. ... dxe5
18. fxe5 Nfd5
19. Ne4! Bxg5
20. Nxg5

It was now evident that Boleslavsky didn't play ...h6 in time, giving his opponent a chance to organize a strike.

20. ... Be8
21. c3 Nc6
22. Qe4 g6
23. Rdf1

There was a threat to the black King. In addition to the pressure on f7, there was the threat of Ndxe6 unless ...

23. ... Nxd4!

The timely exchange of an active Knight.

24. cxd4 Ne7!

This calmly defended. If 25. Nxf7, 25... Bxf7 26. Rxf7 Nf5 and 27... Qxd4†.

25. Qh4 h5
26. Nxf7!

And still the pressure was on.

26. ... Nf5

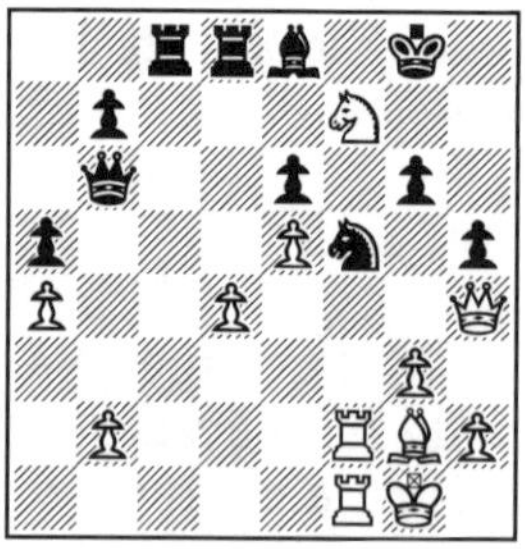

27. Nh6†!

A resource previously considered by Nezh. After 27. Rxf5 exf5 28. Nxd8 Rxd8 29. Rd1 Bxa4; and after 28. Nd6 Rxd6 29. exd6 Qxd6 Black's chances were preferable.

27. ... Kh7

The Knight can't be taken because of the mate threat 27... Nxh6 28. Rf8† Kh7 29. Qe7† Nf7 30. R1xf7† Bxf7 31. Rxf7†, etc.

28. Nxf5 exf5
29. d5

Here was the difference in comparison with 27. Rxf5: the d-pawn was not pinned and can move in tandem with its neighbor.

29. ... Rc2

The Black position hung by the thread called "pinning the Rook." Now everything depended upon the strength of the thread.

30. Qe7† Kh6
31. d6 Bxa4!

Black had no time for 31... Rxb2 because of 32. Bf3 Bxa4 33. Kg2 and White would be free from the pin. Now after 31... Bxa4! there was the threat 32... Bb5; White should have done something until the pair of pawns in the center could advance.

32. Qxb7 Qc5
33. Qd5 Qb6
34. Qf3 Bb5
35. Kh1

Black wouldn't equalize with 35... Bxf1 because of 36. Rxc2.

35. ... Rdc8!

The activity of the black pieces is offset by the potential of the pair of white pawns. If 36. Rxc2 Rxc2, the threat was Rxg2! and Bc6.

36. Qf4† g5!

A decisive response, after which White had nothing better but to try to draw.

37. Qxf5 Rxf2

38. Rxf2

If 38. Qe6†, then on 38… Kg7 39. Qe7† Kh8! it would have taken a lot of precise checks by Black to force the win.

38. … Rc1†
39. Bf1 Rxf1†
40. Rxf1 Bc6†!

The last detail. In case of 40…Bxf1? 41. Qxf1 Qc6† 42. Kg1 Qc5† 43. Qf2 Qxe5 44. Qd2 Black couldn't have saved the Queen and pawn endgame.

41. Rf3 g4

(1/2-1/2), as White had only the perpetual check.

This excellent game did credit to both players. Still, neither considered it important enough to include in their collection of selected games. It was worth mentioning that, even for the top masters, the result was more important than the dynamics of any one game.

23.
Super Nezh—N. Padevsky
B 76
Sofia 1961

1. e4 c5
2. Nf3 Nc6
3. d4 cxd4
4. Nxd4 g6
5. Nc3 Bg7
6. Be3 Nf6
7. Bc4 0-0
8. Bb3 d6
9. f3 Na5
10. Qd2 Nd7
11. Bh6 Nb6
12. Bxg7 Kxg7
13. h4

A dangerous move. White didn't want to lose a tempo by castling, but did let his opponent make his move.

13. … Nbc4
14. Qe2 Nxb2
15. Rb1?!

The Knight got stuck in White's camp, and Nezh hoped to punish it. As will be clear later, it wasn't worth the loss of time. Preferable at once was 15. h5.

15. … Qc7

In his commentaries of this game, Damsky rejected 15… Qb6 as a losing move after 16. Qd2 Nbc4 17. Bxc4 Nxc4 18. Rxb6 Nxd2 19. Rb4 a5 20. Ra4 Bd7 21. Ndb5 and the black Knight would be lost. In reality it was not so: 21. Kxd2! and both sides would have had chances.

16. Ndb5 Qc5
17. Rxb2 a6
18. h5!

The expedition for the stray Knight was not successful, and White, though late, got back on the right path of the King hunt.

18. … axb5
19. Qd2 gxh5!

A cool-headed defense. 19… Rh8 wouldn't work because of 20. hxg6 hxg6 21. Rxh8 Kxh8 22. Qh6† Kg8 23. Qxg6†.

20. Nd5 Kh8
21. Kf1!

Freeing the Rook from its watch over g1.

21. … Nc4
22. Qh6! Rg8
23. Rxh5 Rg7

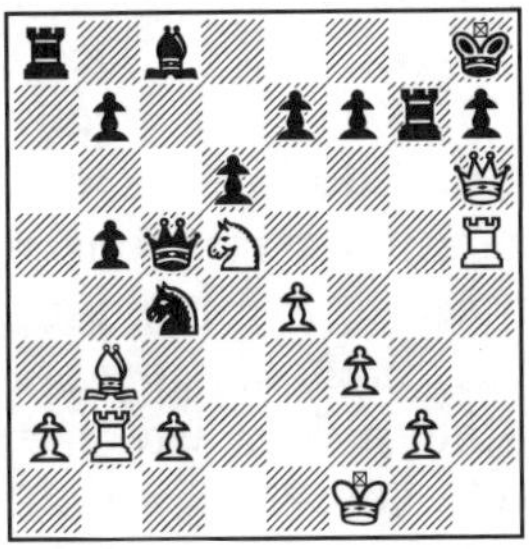

24. Rg5!

As Nezh confessed later, he was about to fall into the devil's trap here. In planning 24. Nf6 he worked out 24… Ne3† 25. Ke2 Rxg2† 26. Kd3 with a win. But at the last moment he saw the poisonous 24… Bf5!!, after which White would be left with nothing: 25. Rxf5 Ne3†; 25. exf5 exf6.

24. … Ne3†?!

Here Black could think of victory. He had to play 24… Rxg5 25. Qxg5 Be6 [but not 25… Nxb2? 26. Qxe7 Be6 27. Qf6† Kg8 28. Ne7† Kf8 29. Bxe6], and if 26. Qxe7, then 26… Bxd5 and White's attack would be busted.

25. Ke2 Rxg5
26. Qxg5 Nxd5
27. Bxd5 Be6
28. Qxe7 Qc3!

Full equality can be achieved after 28… Bxd5 29. Qf6† Kg8 30. Qg5† Kf8 31. Qxd5.

29. Bxe6!

Nezh saw the dangers and realizes that he must play for a draw, so he sacrificed.

29. … fxe6

On 29… Qxb2 there follows 30. Bb3, and all the black pawns were weak, though it is unclear as to whether White could win.

30. Rb3 Qxc2†
31. Ke3 Qc5†
32. Kd3 Qc4†
33. Ke3 Qc1†
34. Kd3 Qc4†
35. Ke3 Qc5†
36. Kd3 Qe5

Having entered into time pressure, Padevsky decides to continue the battle, but Nezh assured his opponent, very quickly, that a draw was certain.

37. Qxb7! Rxa2
38. Qxb5 Qxb5†
39. Rxb5 Rxg2
40. Rb6 Kg7
41. Rxd6 Kf6
42. f4 Rg3†
(1/2-1/2).

On the whole, a well played and eventful game.

24.
B. Shipov—Super Nezh
E 83
22nd Russian ch.
Cheliabinsk 1963

1. d4 Nf6
2. c4 g6
3. Nc3 Bg7
4. e4 d6
5. f3 0-0
6. Be3 Nc6
7. Qd2 a6
8. 0-0-0 Re8

A prophylactic move to prevent the black-squared Bishop from being exchanged. Usual is 8… Rb8 followed by ...b5.

9. g4 e5
10. Nge2 Na5?!

Not a successful novelty. Nezh had made up his mind to provoke Ng3 by attacking the pawn, exchanging on d4, and, after the Bishop took the pawn, move the Knight back to c6 to push away the Bishop. Afterwards, the long diagonal would be in Black's hands. All this took a lot of time, which White used for offense on the kingside. Standard play was needed with the idea of 10… b5!, striving to open the lines.

11. Ng3 exd4
12. Bxd4 Nc6
13. Be3 b5

Being behind for three moves, Black gets back to the standard plan.

14. g5 Nd7

15. f4 Na5
16. h4! Bb7

After 16... Nxc4 17. Bxc4 bxc4 18. h5 White "takes the bull by the horns" without any obstacles.

17. h5

The situation had sharpened considerably. White's chances were looking better as he managed to bring his pawns into the fray.

17. ... b4!
18. Nd5! c6
19. hxg6!

Nezh's young rival was not shy and was not going to give in.

19. ... hxg6

After 19... cxd5 20. gxf7† Kxf7 21. Rxh7 the black King finds himself in a desperate position.

20. Bd4!

A good continuation of the attack. A mistake would have been 20. Nxb4 c5 21. Nd5 Bxd5!, and after any capture Black would seize the initiative with 22... Rb8.

20. ... cxd5
21. Qh2

White also had another line of attack: 21. Bxg7 Kxg7 22. Qd4† but, 22... f6! would have created a deadlock. Now an attack on the h-file fails because Black can always play Re8-h8.

21. ... Ne5?!

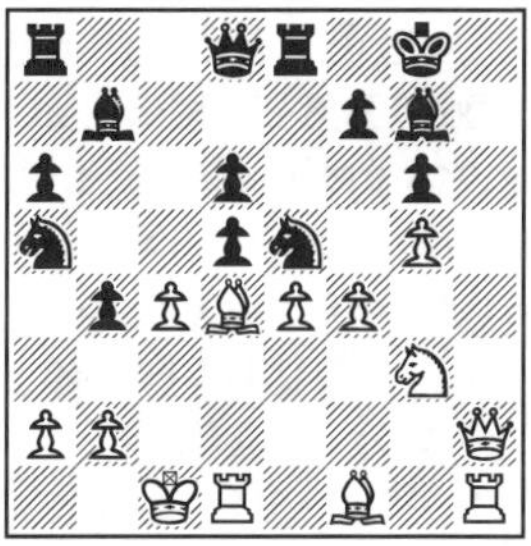

There was the threat of 22. Qh8† and mate to follow, but Black shouldn't be in a hurry to return his extra piece. 21... f6!? was worthy of a serious examination. 22. Qh7† Kf7 23. f5 Rg8 24. Qxg6† Kf8 25. Nh5 Qe8 [Weaker was 25... Bh8 26. Qh6† Ke8 27. gxf6 Ne5 28. Qh7 Rf8 29. Ng7† Bxg7 30. fxg7, or 28... Kf8 29. Nf4! Bc8 30. Qxh8!. Black would lose with either variation.] 26. gxf6. Now Black had two opportunities.

A. 26... Qxg6 27. fxg7† Qxg7 28. Nxg7 Rxg7 29. Bxg7† Kxg7 30. cxd5.

B. 26... Nxf6 27. Nxf6 Qxg6 28. fxg6 Bxf6 29. Bxf6 Rxg6 30. e5!.

In both variations there appeared positions in which White's chances were better, but Black kept certain resources for his defense.

22. exd5?!

Here we can see various possibilities to capture something, but the move chosen by Shipov was unsuccessful and he lost the chance to win. After the correct 22. fxe5! it would have been doubtful if

Black could have avoided defeat:

A. 22... Qxg5† 23. Kb1 Nc6 [23... Rxe5 24. cxd5 Rc8 25. Bh3 and White's position was preferable] 24. Nf5! gxf5 25. Rg1 Qg6 26. Rxg6 fxg6 27. exf5 Nxd4 28. f6! with a decisive attack.

B. 22... b3 23. Qh7† Kf8 24. e6! [not so clear was 24. Qxg7†Kxg7 25. e6† f6 26. Bxf6† Qxf6 27. gxf6† Kxf6 28. exd5 bxa2 29. Kc2 because of 29... Rac8] Qxg5† 25. Kb1 f6 26. exd5 bxa2† 27. Kxa2 Qxg3 28. Rh3! Qg5 29. Be3. White's threats were numerous and dangerous.

22. ... b3

After the strongest 22... Rc8! Black was to be preferred: 23. Qh7† Kf8 24. Kb1 or 24. b3 Bxd5. Not a trace of White's attack remains.

23. Kb1?

All of a sudden there was a changing of the board situation, causing White to weaken his confidence in himself. He stumbled on an even playing field.

Meanwhile, after 23. fxe5 bxa2 [worse was 23... Qxg5† 24. Kb1 Kf8 25. e6 Bxd4 26. Rxd4 fxe6 27. dxe6! with a strong attack, or 24... Rxe5 25. Bd3] 24. Qh7† Kf8 25. Qxg7† Kxg7 26. e6 f6 27. gxf6† Qxf6 28. Bxf6† Kxf6 29. Kc2 Rac8 there appeared the position which was examined in the notes to the 22nd move, part (B), the parenthetical move 29... Rac8. At least this was not worse for White.

However, there was another interesting opportunity: 25. Kc2 [instead of 25. Qxg7†] Rxe5 26. Ne4 Qc7 27. Bxe5 Bxe5 28. Nf6! Nxc4 29. Qg8† Ke7 30. Qxf7†! Kxf7 31. Rh7† Kf8 32. Rh8†!, and a perpetual check. In any event, after 23. fxe5 White was safe from losing. After the timid retreat of the white King, Nezh the Assassin did not miss his chance.

23. ... bxa2†
24. Kxa2 Qd7
25. Bd3

Other attempts wouldn't help either: 25. b3 Nxb3! 26. Kxb3 Rab8 and the King would be threatened everywhere; 25. Qc2 Qg4!

25. ... Naxc4
26. fxe5 Bxd5!
27. Kb1

27. Qh7† Kf8 28. Qxg7 Kxg7 29. e6† was not dangerous because of 29... Ne5†.

27. ... Na3†!
28. bxa3 Rab8†
29. Kc1 Qa4
30. Bb2 Rec8†

White surrendered **(0-1).**

25.
Super Nezh—V. Zagorovsky
C 90
Russian Spartakiade
Gorki 1963

1. e4 e5
2. Nf3 Nc6
3. Bb5 a6
4. Ba4 Nf6
5. 0-0 Be7
6. Re1 b5
7. Bb3 0-0
8. d3

When playing White, Nezh usually preferred the classical Chigorin setup resulting from 8. c3. The choice of a more restrained continuation was probably due to psychological considerations.

8. ... d6
9. c3 Na5
10. Bc2 c5
11. Nbd2 Re8
12. Nf1 h6
13. a4 b4

Yielding the c4-square; 13... Rb8 was preferable.

14. cxb4 cxb4
15. Ne3 Bf8

16. d4 Qb6
17. b3 exd4

Another positional concession. Instead of building the center, Black was eager to create pressure on the e4-pawn. As a rule, strategic advantages outweigh tactical ones. Worthwhile attention could have been given to fianchettoing the black-squared Bishop to put pressure on the e4-pawn.

18. Nxd4 Bb7
19. Bb2!

White was not interested in protecting the e4-pawn, but in developing the initiative.

19. ... Nxe4
20. Ndf5 d5
21. Ng4!

The serious threat 22. Nfxh6† gxh6 23. Bxe4 and 24. Nf6† was created by two Knight moves.

21. ... h5?!

Energetic, but a very risky defense. Now the game enters a period of tactical complications which are advantageous for White. There were some other possibilities which could have been used to stop White's attacking impulses: 21... Re6, protecting the important points, or 21... Rad8.

22. Bxe4 Rxe4
23. Rxe4 dxe4

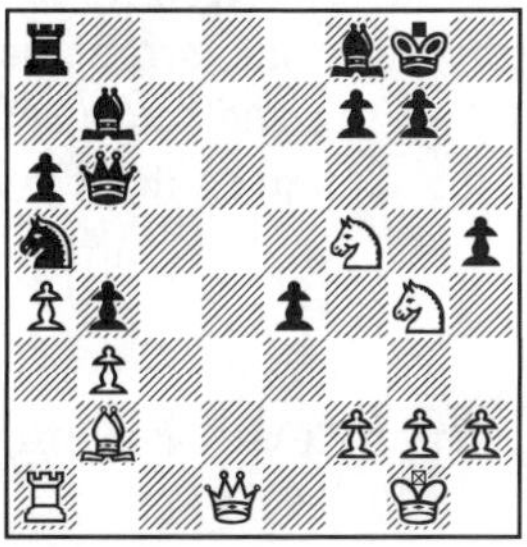

24. Nf6†!?

White began a direct onslaught on the King's position. In fact, he had no choice: a Knight retreat would have added the loss of initiative to the absence of the pawn. However, he had a draw up his sleeve.

24. ... gxf6
25. Qxh5 Rd8?

This was a fatal piece of carelessness. Perhaps Black supposed that White had to give a perpetual. White's win was forced, and he missed it! White's threats were extremely dangerous but Black did have the opportunity for a defense, it was just that a better move was difficult to find in the time remaining. He could have tried 25... e3!.

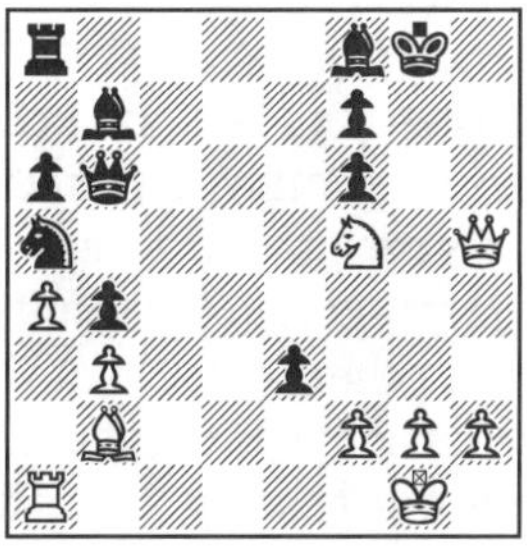

(Analysis after 25... e3)

After the forcing sequence, 26. Qg4† Kh8 27. Qh4† Kg8 28. Bxf6 exf2† 29. Kh1 Bg7 there were two continuations:

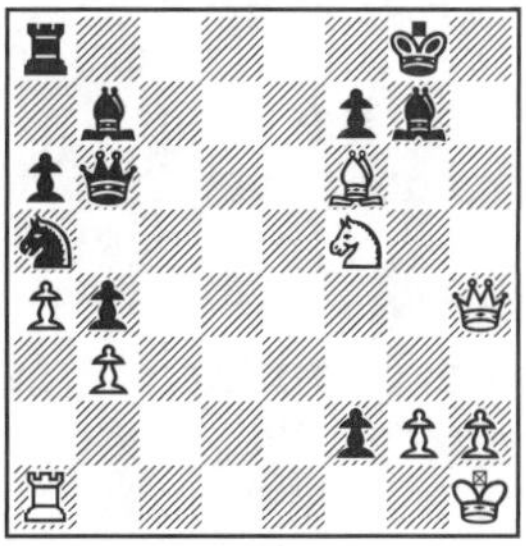

(Analysis after 29... Bg7)

A. 30. Bxg7 Bxg2† 31. Kxg2 Qg6† 32. Kf1 [32. Kh1? Qc6† and mate next move] Qg1† 33. Ke2 Re8† 34. Ne7† Rxe7 [34...

Kxg7?! 35. Qd4† Kf8 36. Rxg1 fxg1=Q 37. Qxg1 Rxe7† 38. Kf3 Nc6 (38... Nxb3? 39. Qd1 Nc5 40. Qd4+–) 39. Qc5 Ne5† 40. Kg3+–] 35. Qxe7 Kxg7 36. Qe5† Kg8 37. Qg3† Qxg3 38. hxg3 Nxb3 39. Rb1 f1=Q† 40. Rxf1 Nc5. In spite of White's material advantage he could hardly win since the position should be Rook and g-pawn against Knight and f-pawn. Instead of 37. Qg3†, stronger would be 37. Rf1. Then 37... Nxb3 38. Qe3 Qg4† 39. Kxf2 Qf5† 40. Kg2 Qg6† 41. Qg3 Qxg3† 42. Kxg3 Nc5. The ending was also Rook versus Knight, but this time it is the h-pawn against the f-pawn. Possibly this could have been in White's favor.

B. 30. Nxg7 Qc6 31. Qg5 Kh7 32. Rf1 Nxb3 33. Qh4† Kg8 34. Qxf2 Rc8 35. Be5 Qc4! This not only defended, but it planned the exchange of Queens. 36. Ne8 Qxf1† 37. Qxf1 Rc1. In the resulting ending there are chances for both sides, but the presence of opposite-colored Bishops made a draw possible too. This long analysis shows that the move 25... e3 was necessary to clear the h1-a8 diagonal, and to obtain counterplay against the white King by any means.

26. Re1?!

Such carelessness was not typical of Nezh's play when he was attacking. However, the win wasn't gone. 26. Qg4† Kh7 27. Qh4† Kg8 [27... Kg6 28. g4! with mate ahead] 28. Bxf6!

26. ... Rd2

27. Qg4†

This was better than 27. Re3 Qxe3! [weaker is 27... Rd3 28. Qg4† Kh7 29. Qh4† Kg8 30. Rg3† Rxg3 31. Qxg3† Kh7 32. Qh4† Kg8 33. Bxf6] 28. Nxe3 Rxb2 29. Qxa5 Rb1† 30. Nf1 Rxb3 31. Qb6 Bc8 32. Qxf6 Rc3 33. Qg5† Bg7 34. Ng3 e3! 35. h4! White should win, though there could be difficulties.

27. ... Kh7

28. Qh4† Kg6

28... Kg8 offered more opportunities to oppose White. 29. Bxf6 Qxf2† 30. Qxf2 Rxf2 31. Kxf2 Nxb3 32. Rb1 Nc5 33. a5 Kh7 34. Be7. White's chances in the ending were better.

29. Bd4!

A tactical nuance, which ensured the way to a win. Its essence was that 29... Rxd4 would lose to 30. g4 and mate would come. With the threat of mate, the sacrifice of the Queen was inevitable in this disadvantageous situation.

29. ... Qxd4?
30. Qg4† Kh7
31. Nxd4 Rxd4
32. Qf5†

The Knight was lost and there was no compensation for the Queen.

32. ... Kg8
33. Qxa5 Rd3
34. Qb6 Bc8
35. Qxf6 Be6
36. Qg5† Bg7
37. h3 Rxb3
38. Rxe4 Rb1†
39. Kh2 b3
40. Qd8† Bf8
41. Re5 b2
42. Rg5† Kh7
43. Qxf8

Black surrendered **(1-0).**

One would say, "Nezhmetdinov won by chance!" Luck likes strong people: he fought up to the end and used all his chances, and Caissa smiled upon him.

26.
Super Nezh—A. Lein
C 14
Chigorin Memorial
Sochi 1965

1. e4 e6

2. d4 d5
3. Nc3 Nf6
4. Bg5 Be7
5. e5 Nfd7
6. Bxe7 Qxe7
7. f4 0-0
8. Nf3 c5
9. dxc5

White wanted to follow Nimzovich's way: relinquishing the pawn center to gain a piece blockade or pressure on the squares d4 and e5. More often we see 9. Bd3 or 9. Qd2, aiming to preserve the pawn center and prepare, under its cover, piece pressure on the central squares.

9. ... f6

White had now lost his grip on the pawn center.

10. exf6 Qxf6
11. g3 Nc6
12. Qd2!?

Nezh chose the sharpest plan with opposite-side castling. After 12. Bd3, a transposition of moves yielded the position from *Keres—Lilienthal, 17th USSR ch., 1949:* 12... Nxc5 13. 0-0 Bd7 14. Qd2 Be8 15. Rae1 Rd8 16. Ne5 with a small but firm advantage for White based on control of the d4- and e5-squares.

12. ... Nxc5
13. 0-0-0 Rd8
14. Qe1!

This not only parried the threat 14... Ne4, but, more importantly, contributed to the gradual success of the plan to control the center.

14. ... Bd7?

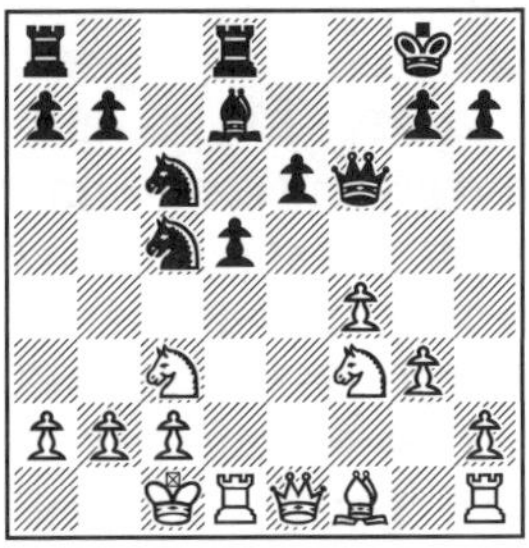

Wrong in principle, as it eliminated a piece which was important for the control of d4 and e5. White managed to control these squares. It was necessary to play 14... a6.

15. Bb5! Rac8
16. Bxc6 Bxc6
17. Nd4

17. Qe3 was not better because of 17... d4! 18. Qe2 dxc3.

17. ... b5!

Having lost the battle for the center, Black tried to find counterplay on the flank. It was no use taking the pawn: 18. Ncxb5 Bxb5 19. Nxb5 Rb8 20. Nd4 Ne4, and Black would stop White's initiative.

18. Qe5!

Nimzovich would have been glad to see this systematic move which goes hand in hand with White's fight for the center.

18. ... b4

Black still hopes to create counterplay. However, when White predominates in the center, it's impossible. That's why now, and during the usual moves, a defensive Queen exchange deserves attention, after which the white e5-pawn could become a weakness.

19. Nce2 Be8
20. g4 a5
21. Qxf6

White considered the consequences of a subsequent ...e5 in refusing to blockade the center.

21. ... gxf6
22. Ng3 e5?

In this case the counterattack was wrong since it just lost a pawn. Black probably missed something. The more tranquil 22... Bf7 could sufficiently preserve the position.

23. fxe5 fxe5
24. Ndf5

The threats Rxd5 and Ne7† put both central pawns in danger.

24. ... Rc7
25. Rhe1 Bb5!

On the verge of defeat, Black remained elusive and so complicated the fight.

26. Kb1

It was early for 26. Rxe5? because of 26... Nd3†.

26. ... d4
27. Rxe5 d3!

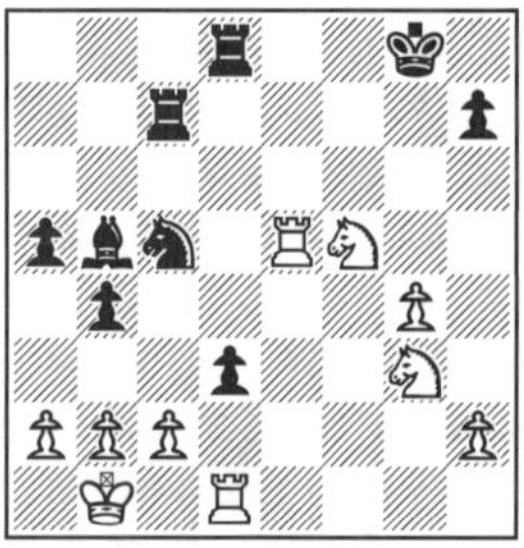

A witty counterattack which made White more cautious.

28. Ka1 Rdc8

On 28... a4 Nezh planned 29. Ne3 b3 30. cxd3 Bxd3 31. Nd5!

29. cxd3 Nb3†

In reply to this attempt to force the draw, White found the best way out. Better was 29... Nxd3; Nezh considered that after 30. Ne7† Kh8 31. Nxc8 Nxe5 32. Nd6 Rd7 33. b3 White's chances were better [33... Nxg4? 34. Rd4 and 35. Nxb5], but stronger was 32... Bd3! and it was hard for White to do anything with his extra pawn.

30. axb3 Rc1†
31. Rxc1 Rxc1†
32. Ka2 Bxd3

Black's goal was in sight: perpetual check. White was to move, and he brings his threats home in time to escape the draw. It was interesting that Black was hindered by his own h-pawn: if it hadn't been there, White wouldn't have managed to attack, and Black would have been able to draw.

33. Re8† Kf7
34. Nd6† Kg6

If 34... Kg7 there was a forced win: 35. Nh5† Kh6 [35... Kg6 36. Rg8† and 37. Nf7#] 36. Nf7† Kg6 37. Ne5† Kh6 38. Nxd3.

35. Re6† Kg5
36. Nf7†! Kf4

36... Kxg4 37. Ne5†; 36... Kh4 37. Rh6† Kxg4 38. Ne5† Kg5 39. Rh5† and 40. Nxd3.

37. Ne2† Bxe2
38. Rxe2

It was time to surrender, but the game continued:

38. ... Kxg4
39. Ne5† Kh3
40. Nxd3 Rc7
41. Nf4† Kg4
42. Nd5 Rf7
43. Re3 Rf2
44. Rg3† Kh4
45. Ne3 Rxh2
46. Rg7

Black surrendered **(1-0).**

27.
Super Nezh—L. Shamkovich
B 13
Moscow 1970

1. e4 c6

2. d4 d5
3. exd5 cxd5
4. Bd3 Nc6
5. c3 Nf6
6. Bf4 Bg4
7. Qb3 Qc8
8. Nd2 e6
9. Ngf3 Be7
10. Ne5 Nxe5

An alternative was an idea offered by Larsen, 10… Bh5 and ...Bg6.

11. Bxe5 0-0
12. Qc2 Bf5!

Weaker was 12… h6 or 12… g6, which would have created opportunities for White to open the g- or h-file after the march of pawns on the kingside. The continuation 12… Kh8 13. h3 Bh5 14. Bxf6 Bxf6 15. Bxh7 g6 16. g4 wouldn't work in this case because White is probably winning after 16… Bxd4 [16… Kxh7 transposes] 17. gxh5 Kxh7 18. Rg1!.

13. Bxf5 exf5
14. Qb3

White can't achieve an advantage this way, but after 14. 0-0 g6 15. Rfe1 Qc6 16. Re2 Ne4 Black would have gotten good chances.

14. ... Qc6

Possibly more precise would have been 14… Re8; after 15. 0-0 Qc6 16. f3 Nh5 17. c4 Rad8 18. cxd5 Qxd5 19. Qxd5 Rxd5, as in *Baier—Kramer, 1974*, Black might have had the better endgame chances.

15. 0-0

15. a4 was worthwhile to prevent ...b5.

15. ... b5
16. a4 a6
17. Rfe1 Ne4
18. Nf1 Bg5

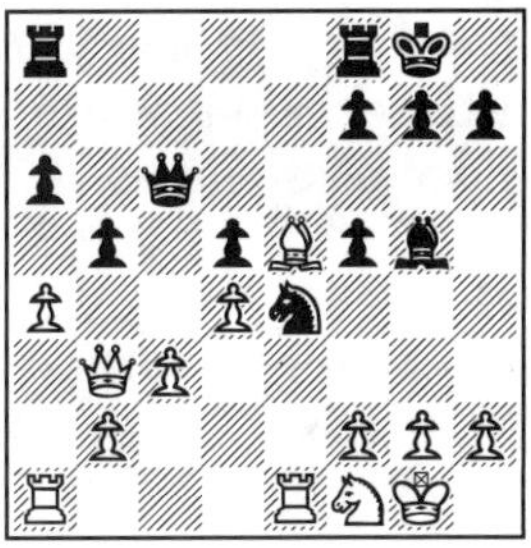

To counter the threat 19. Ne3, yet it allowed White to sharpen the play.

19. f4!?

White decides to make a calculated push, cutting off the retreat squares for his own Bishop because he saw no other prospective opportunities. On 19. axb5 axb5 [weaker was 19… Qxb5 20. Qxb5 axb5 21. f3 Nd2 22. f4 Nxf1 23. Kxf1 Bh6 and White would have a small advantage] 20. f3 Nd2 21. Qc2 Nxf1 22. Kxf1 f6 23. Bg3 f4 24. Bf2 g6 and the play would be about equal; and there was no advantage from 19. f3 Nd2 20. Nxd2 Bxd2 21. Re2 Bh6.

19. ... f6

Black missed an opportunity with 19… Bh4!. Then 20. g3 [20. axb5 Bf2†! 21. Kh1 axb5 22. Rec1 Rxa1 23. Rxa1 f6 24. Bc7 Qxc7 25. Qxd5† Kh8 and White wouldn't have had enough compensation for the lost piece.] bxa4! 21. Rxa4 [21. Qxa4 Qxa4 22. Rxa4 and after 22… Bd8 the Bishop on d5 would be lost: 23. Ne3 f6 24. Nxd5 fxe5 25. fxe5 Rf7! and Black would have chances for victory.] Bd8 [If Black played the straightforward 21… f6, then 22. Bc7! Qxc7 23. Qxd5† and 24. Qxf5! would be in White's favor because the Bishop on h4 would have nowhere to go.] 22. Ne3 Nd2! 23. Qd1 f6 [Black should not try to win with 23… Nf3†? because 24. Qxf3 Qxa4 25. Qxd5 would give White a strong attack.] 24. Bd6! Re8 25. Rb4

Ne4. It should be noted that these moves were not obligatory but have been shown to demonstrate the potential of Black's double-edged possibilities.

20. fxg5 fxe5
21. Ne3 exd4
22. Nxd5 Kh8
23. cxd4 Rad8
24. Nf4

The game was equal. White might hope for a minimal advantage after 24. Nb4 Qd6 25. Nc2 Rb8 26. axb5 Rxb5 27. Qa3 Qxa3 28. bxa3 Nxg5 because of a little better ending.

24. ... Rxd4
25. axb5 axb5
26. Qe3!

The attractive 26. Ne6? would bring difficulties to White because of 26... Rd2 27. Qe3 [27. Nxf8? Rxg2† 28. Kxg2 Nd2†] Rc8! and the initiative would soon pass to Black..

26. ... Rfd8
27. h4 Qd6

Perhaps 27... Rd2 would be more energetic, but after 28. Re2 Rd1† 29. Re1 Rxe1† 30. Rxe1 Rd2 31. g4! White would have equalized.

28. Ra7 Qc5

Owing to active play, Black prepared to seize the initiative.

29. Ne6!

Wrong would have been 29. Rxg7? because of the winning 29... Rd1!.

29. ... Qxa7
30. Nxd8 Qd7?

Both sides were fighting very resourcefully, and after 30... Rd7 the natural outcome of the Queen exchange would have been a draw. Black's game move, however, allows his rival to launch a dangerous attack.

31. Nf7†! Kg8
32. Ne5 Qd6!

Shamkovich cooly defends. "A more reliable" 32... Qd5 would actually be beaten at once because of the knockout punch 33. Nc6!

33. Qb3† Qd5
34. Ra1! g6!

Again, the only way to defend. All other lines would have lost: 34... h5 35. Ra8† Kh7 36. g6† Kh6 and 37. Rh8#; 34... Kf8 35. Ra8† Ke7 36. Qa3† with the decisive invasion of the Queen, as 36... Qc5 37. Qxc5† followed by 38. Nc6† would be the end.

35. Ra8† Kg7
36. Ra7† Kg8
37. Qxd5† Rxd5
38. Nf7! Rd1†

38... Rd2 would have been better.

39. Kh2 Rf1
40. Nh6† Kf8
41. Rxh7 f4

The only hope would be to create counterthreats to the white King. It seems the draw was easy to achieve after 41... Rf4. For example: 42. Kh3 [42. g3 Rf2† 43. Kh3 Rxb2 44. Rf7† Ke8 45. Rg7 Nf2† 46. Kg2 Ng4† 47. Kf1 Ne5] Rf1 43. g4 f4 44. Kg2 Rf2† 45. Kh3 Rf1.

There was more subtle play after 41... Rf4: 42. Rf7†! Ke8 43. Rg7 Rxh4† 44. Kg1 Rh5 [44... Nxg5 45. Rxg6 followed by 46. Nxf5] 45. Rxg6 Nxg5 46. Nxf5 Nf3† 47. gxf3 Rxf5 48. Kf2 Rc5 49. Rg2! and it would have been difficult for Black to achieve the draw.

42. b4 Ke8?!
43. Ng4

Now the game was quickly becoming drawn. However, on 43. Rg7! Black had serious, perhaps unsolvable problems. For example, 43... Ng3 44. Kh3 Ne4 45. Kg4 Nf2† 46. Kxf4 Nd3† 47. Ke4 Nf4 48. g3 and then 49. Rxg6.

Only not 43. Kh3?? Nf2† 44. Kh2 Rh1#.

43. ... Ng3
44. Nf6† Kf8
45. Kh3 Nf5
46. Rd7

It was still possible to lose: 46. Nd5? Ne3!.

46. ... Ne3
47. Kh2 Rf2
48. Nh7†

and White declared **perpetual check.**

A game wherein both rivals showed themselves at their best.

9th Russian ch. / Yaroslavl 1949

	Players	1	2	3	4	5	6	7	8	9	10	11	12	13	14	15	16	Points	Place
1	Dubinin	•	▒	▒	▒	▒		■	▒	■	▒	▒	■	▒	■	▒	■	9.5	1-2
2	Ilivitsky	▒	•		▒	▒	■		■	▒	▒	▒	▒	■	■	■	■	9.5	1-2
3	Aratovsky	▒	■	•	■		■	▒			▒	▒		■	■	■	▒	8.5	3-4
4	Konstantinov	▒	▒		•	▒	▒		■	■	▒	▒		■	▒	■	■	8.5	3-4
5	Aronin	▒	▒	■	▒	•		■	▒		▒		■	■	▒	▒	▒	8	5-8
6	Grechkin	■			▒	■	•			▒		▒	■	■	■	■	▒	8	5-8
7	Kamyshov		■	▒	■		■	•		▒		■	■	▒	■		▒	8	5-8
8	Sopkov	▒		■		▒	■	■	•		▒	▒	▒	▒	▒	▒	■	8	5-8
9	Knishenko		▒	■		■	▒	▒	■	•	■	▒	▒			▒	▒	7.5	9-10
10	Krogius	▒	▒	▒	▒	▒	■	■	▒		•	▒		■	▒		▒	7.5	9-10
11	Nezhmetdinov	▒	▒	▒	▒	■	▒		▒	▒	▒	•	▒	■			▒	7	11-12
12	Novotyelnov		▒	■	■				▒	▒	■	▒	•			■	■	7	11-12
13	Bastrikov	▒						▒	▒	■			■	•	■	■	■	6.5	13
14	Zagorovsky				▒	▒			▒	■	▒	■	■		•	■		6	14
15	Ivashin	▒				▒		■	▒	▒	■	■				•	▒	5.5	15
16	Lyublinsky			▒		▒	▒	▒		▒	▒	▒			■	▒	•	5	16
		1	2	3	4	5	6	7	8	9	10	11	12	13	14	15	16		

Semi-finals,17th USSR ch. / Tbilisi 1949

	Players	1	2	3	4	5	6	7	8	9	10	11	12	13	14	15	16	17	Points	Place
1	Geller	•	▒	▒		▒	▒	■	■	▒	▒	■	■	■	■	▒	■	■	11.5	1
2	Petrosyan	▒	•	▒	■		▒	▒	▒	▒	▒	■	■	■	■	▒	■	■	11	2
3	Holmov	▒	▒	•	▒	■	■	▒		■	■	▒	▒	■	▒		■	▒	10	3
4	Novotyelnov	■		▒	•			■	■	▒	▒	▒		■	■	▒	■	▒	9	4-5
5	Chistyakov	▒	■		■	•	■		■	▒			■	▒	▒	■	▒	▒	9	4-5
6	Grechkin	▒	▒		■		•	▒	▒	▒	▒		■	▒		■	■	■	8.5	6-9
7	Ilivitsky		▒	▒		■	▒	•	■	▒	▒	▒	▒	■	▒	▒	▒	▒	8.5	6-9
8	Makagonov		▒	■			▒		•	▒	▒	▒	■	▒	▒	■	■	■	8.5	6-9
9	Ebralidze	▒	▒		▒	▒	▒	▒	▒	•	■	■	▒		■	▒	▒	▒	8.5	6-9
10	Vasiliev	▒	▒		▒	■	▒	▒	▒		•	■		▒	▒	■	▒	▒	8	10
11	Klaman			▒	▒	■	■	▒	▒			•	▒	■		■		■	7.5	11
12	Nezhmetdinov			▒	■			▒		▒	■	▒	•		■	■		■	7	12
13	Kasparyan					▒	▒		▒	■	▒		■	•	■		▒	■	6.5	13
14	Lubensky			▒		▒	■	▒	▒		▒	■			•	▒	▒	▒	6	14-15
15	Solmanis	▒	▒	■	▒			▒		▒				■	▒	•	■		6	14-15
16	Pogrebiddky					▒		▒		▒	▒	■	■	▒	▒		•	▒	5.5	16
17	Aramanovich			▒	▒	▒		▒		▒	▒				▒	■	▒	•	5	17
18	Pirtshalava	■	▒	▒	—	▒		—	—	—	—	—	—		—		—	▒	withdrew	
		1	2	3	4	5	6	7	8	9	10	11	12	13	14	15	16	17		

4

Attack

"Attack!"
This was Nezh's motto in hundreds of games. That's why this chapter is the longest.

28.

Super Nezh—N. Novotyelnov
B 83
Semi-finals 17th USSR ch.
Tbilisi 1949

1. e4 c5 2. Nf3 Nc6 3. d4 cxd4 4. Nxd4 Nf6 5. Nc3 d6 6. Be2 e6 7. 0-0 Be7 8. Be3 a6 9. f4 Qc7.

Nowadays the Scheveningen line is played with an attempt not to lose a tempo on a7-a6. For example: 8… 0-0 9. f4 Qc7 10. Ndb5 Qb8 11. a4 Rd8 12. Bf3 Bd7 13. Qd2 Be8, with approximately equal chances, *Larsen—Korchnoy, Lone Pine 1981.*

10. Qe1 0-0
11. Qg3

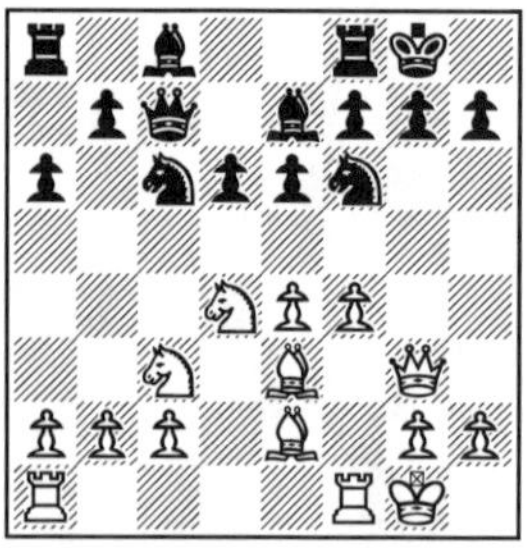

11. … Kh8?

A trite, non-concrete preventive move. It's bad to play this way in the dynamic Sicilian Defense. A good plan is 11… Bd7 with the aim 12… Nxd4 and 13… Bc6.

12. Rad1 Bd7
13. Kh1 Rac8

Also playable was 13… Nxd4 14. Bxd4 Bc6.

14. Nf3 b5
15. e5!

Just in time. Now White would have excellent prospects for attacking the King.

15. … Ne8
16. Ne4 f5?

"Fear has big eyes." This weakening wasn't necessary yet. The most passive black piece was the Bishop on d7. That was why it was worth paying attention to 16… Nb4 17. c3 Nd5 to vacate the c6-square for the Bishop.

17. Neg5 dxe5
18. fxe5 Nb4
19. c3 Nd5

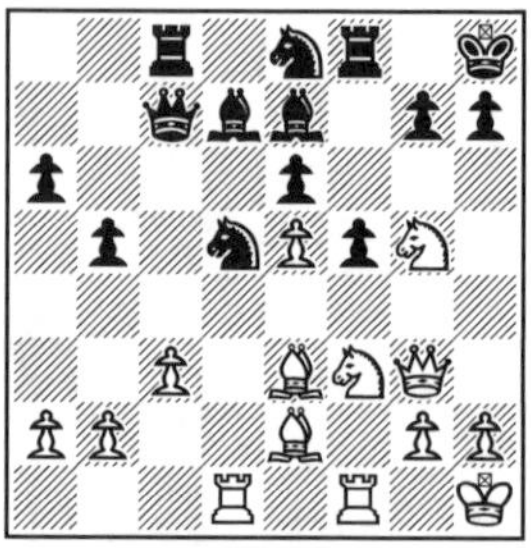

20. Rxd5!

The sacrifice of material was correct owing to the weakening of the e6-square. An energetic attack begins.

20. … exd5
21. Qh3 h6
22. e6! Bxg5
23. Nxg5 Bc6
24. Bh5 Qe7
25. Nf7† Kg8
26. Qxf5

The position was hopeless for Black: 26… Nd6 27. Qg6 Nxf7 28. exf7† Kh8 29. Bd4; 26… Qf6 27. e7 Qxe7 [27… Rxf7 28. Bxf7† Kh8 (28… Kxf7 29. Qh5† and 30. Rf6†)] 28. Qxc8; 26… Rc7 27. Qg6 Nf6 28. Nxh6† Kh8 29. Nf7† Kg8 30. Bd4.

26. … Nf6
27. Nxh6†! gxh6
28. Bf7† Rxf7
29. exf7† Kxf7
30. Qxc8 d4
31. Bxd4 Bxg2†
32. Kxg2 Qe4†
33. Rf3 Qg6†
34. Kh1 Qb1†
35. Bg1

Black resigned **(1-0).**

29.

Super Nezh—L. Shamkovich
B 94
14th Russian ch.
Rostov-on-Don 1954

1. e4 c5 2. Nf3 d6 3. d4 cxd4 4. Nxd4 Nf6 5. Nc3 a6 6. Bg5 Nbd7 7. Bc4.

By 1954 this system was very topical and its theory was making its first steps. Nezh actively participated in the process. He wrote that he had studied it since 1950 and had prepared some interesting ideas in the line: 7... e6 8. 0-0 b5 9. Bxe6!. This sacrifice is so effective, that 7... e6 vanished from tournament practice.

7. ... h6

Today even this move has lost its reputation, and in the majority of cases you'll see 7... Qa5 8. Qd2 e6 9. 0-0-0.

8. Bh4

Literally each move in this game's opening needs comment, because in the last 40 years its theory has advanced considerably. Now it's admitted that 8. Bxf6 Nxf6 9. Qd2 or 9. Qd3 is stronger.

8. ... e6
9. 0-0 Nc5

The "natural" 9... Be7 almost leads to catastrophe: 10. Bxe6! fxe6 11. Nxe6 Qa5 12. Nxg7† Kf7 13. Nf5, with three pawns and the initiative for the piece. The same sacrifice of the Bishop was possible after 9... b5, namely 10. Bxe6.

10. Re1 g5?

Being afraid of 10... Be7, 11. b4 Ncd7 12. Bxe6, Black wants to fully get rid of the sacrificial threat on e6 by means of weakening his flank. This could hardly be a good idea. Also dangerous was 10... b5 because of 11. Bd5! exd5 12. exd5† Kd7 13. Nc6 Qb6 14. Qf3! with a strong attack.

11. Bg3 e5
12. Nf5

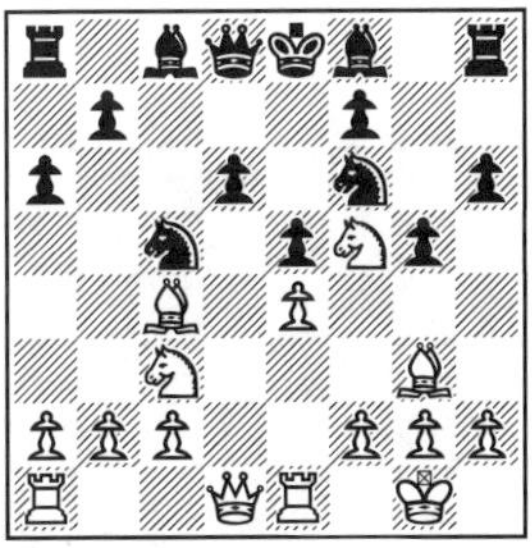

12. ... Be6

Bad was 12... Ncxe4 13. Nxe4 Nxe4 because of 14. Qd5.

13. Bd5!

The main advantage in White's position was his possession of the d5 and f5 squares.

13. ... Bxf5

Black's troubles were illustrated by 13... Bxd5 14. Nxd5. After 14... Nxd5 15. Qxd5 his position was strategically hopeless, and if 14... Nfxe4 15. b4! Nxg3 16. bxc5 Nxf5 17. Qg4! he threatened not only to take the Knight, but also to give a lethal check at a4. On 14... Ncxe4 possible was 15. Qf3 Nxd5 16. Qxe4 Nf6 17. Qxb7 Rb8 18. Qxa6 with 18... Rxb2 being no good because of 19. Bxe5!.

In the spirit of playing the best line, Nezh recommended 13... Nxd5 14. Nxd5 Bxf5 [14... Nxe4 15. Rxe4 Bxf5 16. Rxe5†! dxe5 17. Bxe5 with the strongest attack.] 15. exf5 Nd7, and considered this position as plausible for defense. This was a rare case of mistaken advice in his analysis. After 16. f6! Black was close to surrender, as 16... Nxf6 17. Bxe5! dxe5 18. Rxe5† wouldn't have given him any chance.

All these variations led to the conclusion that Black's position was hopeless, and the decisive mistake was probably 10... g5. Instead, 10... Bd7 could have been recommended, preparing b7-b5 and then ...Be7.

14. exf5

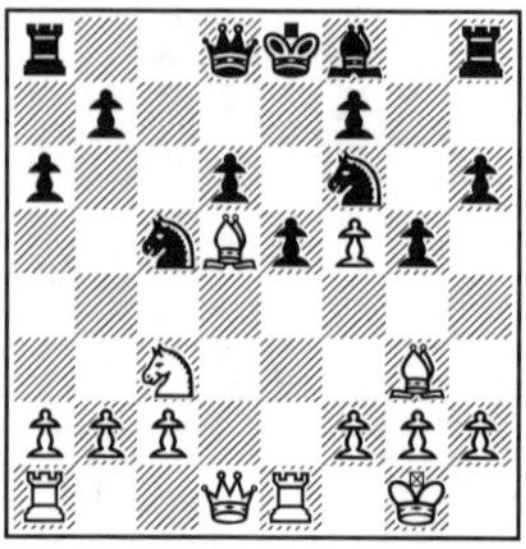

14. ... Qc8

By protecting the b7-pawn, Black made it easier for his opponent to begin an attack. A lesser evil would have been 14... Be7 15. b4 Ncd7 16. Bxb7 Rb8 17. Bxa6 Rxb4.

15. Bxe5! dxe5
16. Rxe5† Be7
17. Qe2 Qc7
18. Re1 Nce4

Worse was 18... Ng8, because of 19. f6.

19. Rxe4

19. Bxe4 is also very good for White.

19. ... Nxe4
20. Qxe4 Kf8
21. Bxf7!

This not only provided the continuation for the attack, but enough material advantage to win.

21. ... Bf6

If 21... Kxf7, good was 22. Nd5 and 23. Qxe7†.

22. Bg6 Qe7
23. Qxe7† Bxe7
24. Nd5 Bd8
25. Re6 Kg7
26. Rd6

Even after the Queen exchange, White's attack wouldn't weaken.

26. ... h5
27. Rd7† Kh6
28. g4!

Not being satisfied with the extra material, White prepared mating threats.

28. ... h4
29. Bh5 Rc8
30. Rd6† Kg7
31. f6† Kh6
32. Ne7! Rb8

Other lines: 32... Rxc2 33. Nf5† etc.; 32... Rc7 33. f7† Kg7 34. Nf5† and it would be mate in one.

33. Nf5† Kh7
34. f7

Black surrendered **(1-0)**.

30.

Super Nezh—I. Zilber
B 62
USSR Team ch.
Voroshilovgrad 1955

1. e4 c5 2. Nf3 d6 3. d4 cxd4 4. Nxd4 Nf6 5. Nc3 Nc6 6. Bg5 e6 7. g3.

Like any other self-respecting researcher, Nezh was very jealous about the correct attribution of authorship for opening ideas, of which he had plenty. In this line he declared:

> **White repeats a peculiar line by fianchettoing his white-squared Bishop, which I used against G. Ilivitsky in 1947. This variant was worked out by me, but since my game with Ilivitsky was not well-known, some theorists announced in 1954 that it was founded by D. Bronstein.**

R.N.

Of course, the practical value of this variant was low, as Black could have easily equalized, but it was the principal that mattered, and of course, Nezh was right. The reason for this claim was Koblents' book *Sicilian Defense*, published in 1955. In it the origin of 7. g3 was said to be the game between *Bronstein* and *Geller* from the *1953 Candidates' Tournament*. There is no reason to look for hidden meanings. In those times there were no computers and *Informants*, the majority of a master's games weren't found anywhere, and many opening discoveries were "found" again by others.

Speaking about the authorship of the 7. g3 variant, I should add that having looked through the *Encyclopedia of Chess Openings*, I saw that only one line [without noticing any names] was devoted to this move.

"Everything has gone before..."

7. ... Qa5?

Having come across this surprise, [Koblents' book was issued a bit later, and the famous book by Bronstein about the Candidates' Tournament appeared only the next year.] Zilber reacted unsuccessfully. In the mentioned game *Nezhmetdinov—Ilivitsky*, Black played better: 7... Be7 8. Bg2 0-0 9. 0-0 Nxd4, and Black got the better game.

8. Bxf6 gxf6
9. Nb3 Qc7

On a recommendation by A. Koblents after the game, that 9... Qg5 would be better, 10. f4 Qg7 11. Nb5 prevents Black from castling.

R.N.

10. Qh5! a6
11. Be2!

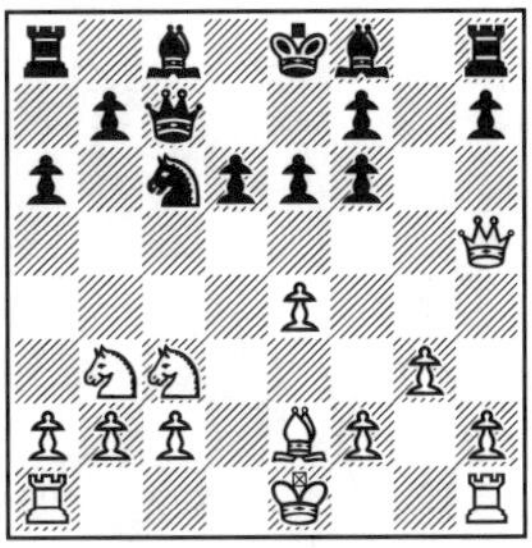

White reacted strongly to Black's inaccuracy. In similar pawn structures with the isolated h-pawn, the h5-square can often be a good place for the Queen, and the Bishop located on the diagonal f1-a6 would be more active. The move g2-g3 doesn't necessarily imply that a fianchetto of the Bishop was obligatory.

11. ... Be7?!

If Black was planning to castle short, castling long is more difficult here, it would have been better for him to move the Bishop to g7.

12. f4 Bd7
13. f5 0-0
14. Rf1 Ne5
15. Rf4 Kg7

Black finds the only move which allowed him to escape immediate destruction.

16. Rh4 Rh8
17. Qh6† Kg8

Paying for the inaccuracy at move 11, and walling in the Rook.

18. 0-0-0 Qd8
19. Nd4 Bf8
20. Qh5 Qe7
21. Nf3 Bg7
22. Nxe5 dxe5
23. Bc4

Here we clearly see Nezh's prudence. He chose exactly, in the opening, the correct diagonal for the Bishop.

23. ... b5

24. fxe6

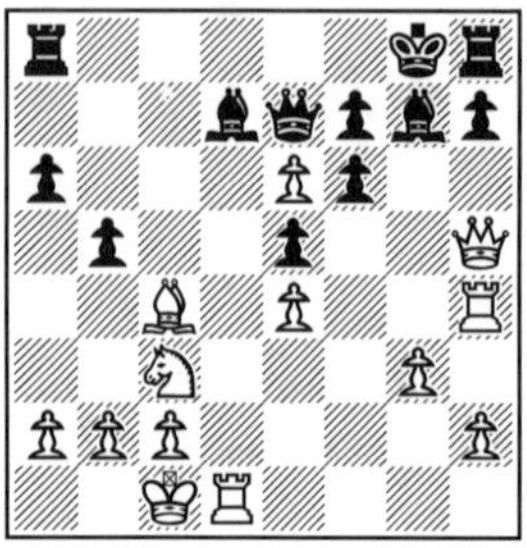

24. ... fxe6

After 24... Bxe6, the d5-square would have been in White's possession for free.

25. Nd5!

A splendid combinational shot, given exactly in the most painful spot. The Knight couldn't be taken, but to not take it would also be bad.

25. ... Qf7
26. Nc7! Qxh5
27. Rxh5 Be8
28. Bxe6† Kf8
29. Nxa8 Bxh5
30. Rd7

The invasion of the Rook decided the outcome, but some accuracy in the realization of the advantage was needed.

30. ... Bh6†
31. Kb1 Be3
32. Nc7 Be8

White was obliged to agree upon the appearance of opposite-colored Bishops. However, the difference in the power of the Rooks was so obvious, that this "opposite-color" couldn't have saved Black.

33. Nxe8 Kxe8
34. Rb7 Kf8
35. c3 h5
36. Bd5

Here it was also possible to make a calm exchange of Rooks. This possibility was given by Damsky: 36. Rb8† Kg7 37. Rxh8 Kxh8 38. Bf7 Bg1 39. h3 Bf2 40. Bxh5. Then, after 40... Bxg3, White would play b2-b4 and Bh5-g4-c8, picking the pawns off the queenside.

36. ... Rh6
37. Kc2 h4
38. Kd3 Bg1
39. gxh4 Rxh4
40. Rf7† Ke8
41. Rxf6 Rxh2
42. b4 Rh3†
43. Kc2 Rh2†
44. Kb3 Be3
45. Rxa6 Bc1
46. Bc6†

Black surrendered **(1-0)**.

31.

Super Nezh—M. Vasiliev
B 47
16th Russian ch.
Kislovodsk 1956

1. e4 c5 2. Nf3 a6 3. Nc3 e6 4. d4 cxd4 5. Nxd4 Qc7 6. Be2 Nf6 7. 0-0 b5?.

> **Premature. He should have played either 7... Nc6, or 7... Bb4.**
>
> *R.N.*

8. Bf3 Bb7
9. e5!

White was ready to begin active play.

9. ... Ng8
10. Bxb7 Qxb7
11. Re1 Ne7
12. a4!

One more result of an early pawn move on the flank—Black was obliged to make a further weakening of his pawn structure.

12. ... b4
13. Ne4 Ng6
14. Qf3

Nezh considered this as provocative, but not the best way of developing the initiative, so he recommended 14. Nf3! Nc6 15. Nd6† Bxd6 16. Qxd6, capturing important squares. The move in the game was not bad.

14. ... Nc6

Another idea was 14 ...Qd5. For this Nezh gave: 15. Nf5! Nxe5 16. Ned6†! Bxd6 17. Qxd5 exd5 18. Nxd6† Ke7 19. Nxf7! Kxf7 20. Rxe5 Re8 21. Rxe8 Kxe8 22. Be3 Nc6 23. Rd1, winning the pawn. Easier was 15. Nd6† Bxd6 16. Qxd5 exd5 17. exd6† with an overwhelming White advantage.

15. Ng5 Nd8
16. Qg3 Qd5
17. c3 Nc6
18. Nxc6 dxc6
19. h4 h6

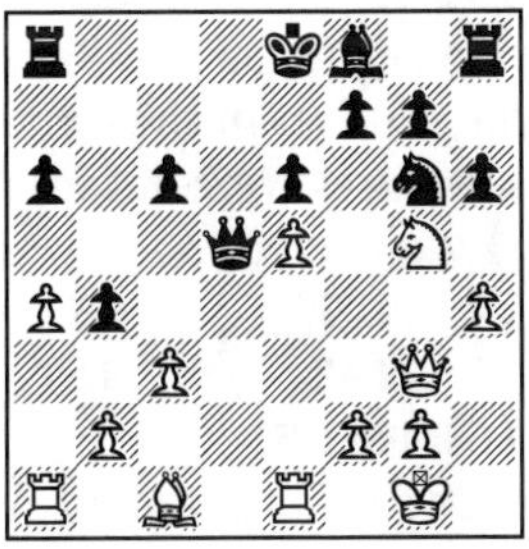

20. c4!

A driving away sacrifice, done for the transference of the Knight to a powerful position in the center.

R.N.

20. ... Qxc4
21. Ne4 Qd5
22. h5!

The sacrifice of one more pawn was needed to add to the attack of the undeveloped pieces.

22. ... Nxe5
23. Bf4 Nd3

All the white pieces were at last joined in the attack. Now, in the middle of the board, they have a decisive effect. This was proven in Nezhmetdinov's analysis of other retreats by the Knight.

For example, 23... Nc4 24. b3! Nb6 25. Bc7 Nc8 26. Rad1 Qxh5 27. Rd8† Ke7 28. Red1. If 23... Nd7, then 24. Rad1 Qxh5 25. Qd3!, and in spite of the three extra pawns, Black's position is hopeless: 25... Qd5 26. Qc2; 25... Rd8 26. Bc7; 25... Nb6 26. Nd6† Ke7 [26... Bxd6 27. Qxd6 Rc8 28. Rxe6† fxe6 29. Qxe6† Kf8 30. Bd6#] 27. Nf5† Ke8 28. Qc2 Rc8 29. a5 Nd5 30. Rxd5!, and White wins.

R.N.

24. Rad1 Nxe1

After 24... 0-0-0 25. Re3 Nxf4 26. Rxd5 Nxd5 27. Rd3 f5, resistance would have been more persistent.

25. Rxd5 cxd5
26. Nd6† Bxd6
27. Bxd6 Nc2
28. Bc5!

A note, explaining this position: 29. Qd6 was threatened, and the Knight had no way to escape.

28. ... Rd8
29. Qc7 Rd7
30. Qc8† Rd8
31. Qc6† Rd7
32. Bb6 Ke7
33. Qxc2 d4
34. Qc5† Kf6
35. Qxb4 d3

36. Qf4†	**Ke7**
37. Bc5†	**Ke8**
38. Bb4	**Rg8**
39. Qb8†	**Rd8**
40. Qb7	**Rd7**

The time control move was made and Black, having no wish to adjourn a hopeless game, surrendered **(1-0)**.

32.

Super Nezh—V. Zhilin
B 43
18th Russian ch.
Sochi 1958

1. e4 c5 2. Nf3 e6 3. d4 cxd4 4. Nxd4 a6 5. Nc3 Qc7 6. a3.

The history of this move in Paulsen's system has seen peaks and valleys. It was first seen in the game *Aronin—Konstantinopolsky, 20th USSR ch., Moscow 1952.* The new move went unnoticed until it was given a second life by Nezh in this game. Then the move gained some definite popularity, and it continued for a short period of time. In the 70s it again disappeared from tournament practice, and not only from there. It wasn't even mentioned in the second edition of *ECO*, so today we can consider the move 6. a3 as a forgotten one. The reason for that, the threat of the pinning 6… Bb4, was of no danger for White, so it was not necessary to lose a tempo to avoid it.

Nezh analyzed a lot and used this system with White. 6. Bd3, 6. Be2 and 6. g3 also were played in his practice.

6. ... Nf6

Preferable was 6… b5 7. g3 Bb7.

7. Be2

In the game *Olafsson—Bilek, Stockholm 1962*, White played more aggressively: 7. f4!? d6 8. g4 h6 9. Bg2 Nc6 10. h3 Bd7, but he didn't get any advantage.

7. ...	**d6**
8. 0-0	**Nbd7**

This opened things up a little bit. Black's inventiveness did not include castling short, though 8… Be7 9. f4 0-0 was, of course, possible.

9. f4	**b5**
10. Bf3	**Bb7**
11. g4	**h6**
12. Re1	**Nb6**
13. Qe2	

13. ... e5?!

In search of counterplay Black weakened some squares in the center. Such serious measures were not needed yet. 13… Nc4 was better.

14. Nf5	**g6**
15. Ne3	**Be7**
16. Ned5!	

White began active play first. After the forced Knight exchange, Black will be obliged to castle long to escape problems on the e-file, and then White will make a solid plan to open up play on the queenside. It should be clear that White had won the opening battle.

16. ...	**Nfxd5**
17. exd5	**0-0-0**
18. a4!	**b4**
19. a5	**Nd7**

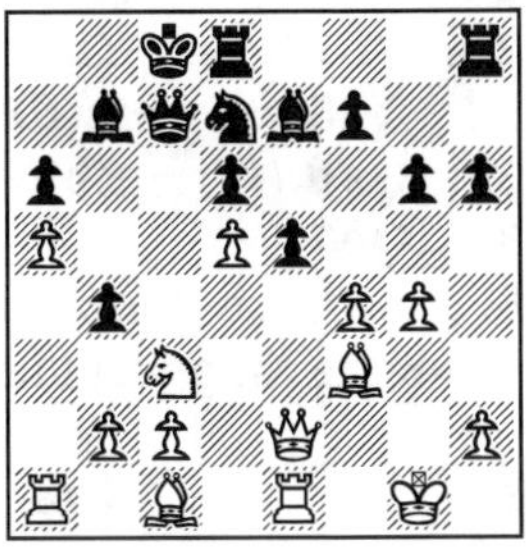

20. Na2!

A sudden retreat. White, without worrying about the loss of a pawn, was eager to get in c2-c3, important for the attack and an advanced outpost for the Knight on b4.

20. ... Bh4
21. Rf1 exf4
22. Bxf4 Bg5

It was important for Black to exchange the black-squared Bishop, as it could have been dangerous in an attack.

23. Bg2 Qxa5?

Absolutely unexplainable and even suicidally greedy. White hadn't yet broken open a single file on the queenside and Black did it for him! It was worth noting that 23... Kb8 24. Qd2 Qc5† 25. Kh1 Ne5 presented opportunities for a persistent defense. After the move played in the game White used the open file energetically.

24. Kh1! Qc5
25. c3 b3
26. Nb4 Rhe8
27. Qd3 Bxf4
28. Nxa6!

Necessary, otherwise Black would have gotten to play ...Ne5.

28. ... Qb6
29. Rxf4 Nc5
30. Nxc5 dxc5
31. Rxf7

The work was done: the Rooks had taken their ideal positions, the only thing left was to remove the black Bishop.

31. ... Re5
32. d6!

32. Rxb7 and then 33. d6 led towards victory, but the text move chosen by White was easier.

32. ... Bxg2†
33. Kxg2 Qc6†
34. Kg1 Rd5
35. Ra8†!

Black surrendered because of an inescapable mate in 3 **(1-0)**.

33.

Super Nezh—V. Sergievsky

B 47

Russian Spartakiade
Joshkar-Ola 1963

1. e4 c5 2. Nf3 e6 3. d4 cxd4 4. Nxd4 a6 5. Nc3 Qc7 6. Be2 Nc6 7. Be3 Bb4 8. Nxc6 dxc6?!.

Better was 8... Bxc3† 9. bxc3, and only then 9... dxc6.

9. Qd4 Bf8

Inexact. This gave White a complimentary tempo for development.

10. 0-0 e5
11. Qd2 Nf6
12. f4! Be7
13. Qe1 exf4

Black decided against castling because he was afraid of an attack. Still, he should have castled.

14. Bxf4 Qb6†
15. Kh1 Be6
16. a4!

It turned out that on 16... 0-0-0 he faced the very unpleasant 17. a5 and 18. Na4.

16. ... a5
17. e5 Ng4
18. Bxg4 Bxg4

19. Ne4! Be6
20. Nd6† Bxd6
21. exd6 Qc5?

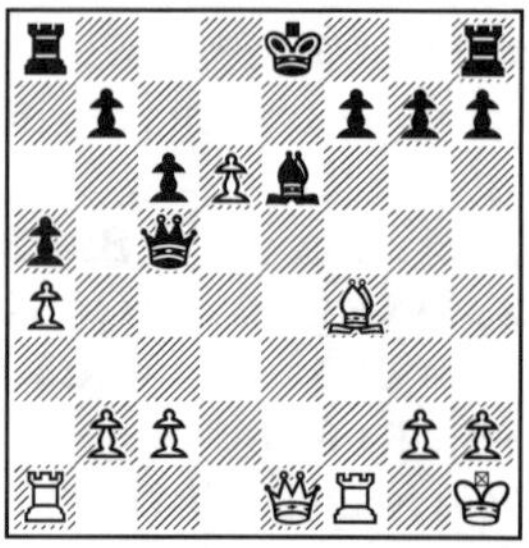

Black had a final chance to castle. After 21... 0-0 22. Be5 Black would have been in trouble, but he would have been able to offer resistance.

22. d7†!

Now the black King had problems.

22. ... Kxd7
23. Rd1† Kc8

After 23... Ke8, then 24. Bd6 and the weakness of the black squares would have quickly decided the matter.

24. Qg3 b6

Black was trying to get the King to a7, but now he created a new weak square at b6. It was instructive to see how Nezh, like a tick, clung to this weakness.

25. Be3 Qb4
26. Rf4!

Forcing the capture at b2 and opening up one more file for the White attack.

26. ... Qxb2
27. Rff1!

In a few moves Black's position looked like a ruins. Nezh achieved this by sacrificing only two pawns. The concluding stage began: the breakthrough of pieces into the camp of the opponent and smashing the King.

27. ... Ra6

Very awkward, but 27... Rb8 was no better.

28. Qd6 Kb7
29. Qe7† Ka8
30. Rd8† Rxd8
31. Qxd8† Kb7
32. Qe7†

32. Bf4 at once was too soon, as after 32... Ra8 the King would hide on a6.

32. ... Ka8
33. Qd8†

By checking White saved time in *zeitnot*, while 33. Rd1 was easier.

33. ... Kb7
34. Qe7† Ka8
35. Rd1 Bd5
36. Qd8† Kb7
37. Qd7†

Accurate to the end: not 37. Bf4?, because of 37... Ra8.

37. ... Ka8
38. Bf4

Black surrendered **(1-0).**

34.

Super Nezh—A. Nikitin

B 53

Kaluga 1970

1. e4 c5 2. Nf3 d6 3. d4 cxd4 4. Qxd4.

In this game with a famous candidate master, Nezh preferred to abandon traditional systems and wanted to test the inexperienced opponent in his play, where all book lines would be set aside.

4. ... Nc6
5. Bb5 Bd7
6. Bxc6 Bxc6
7. c4 Nf6
8. Nc3 g6
9. 0-0 Bg7
10. Re1

The game has come to regular systems, which have appeared in Maroczy's [Bind] system or could turn into the English Opening. White's last move was not necessary. The scheme, recommended by theorists, provided for a retreat of the Queen to d3, then Nd4, b3, and lastly, Bb2.

The resulting position was a very firm yet flexible setup. It was hard for Black to find an effective plan of counterplay. In the main, Nezh provided the same plan, but it has some bias.

10. ... 0-0

11. Qd2

So that's why 10. Re1 was played, to protect the e4-pawn and to make it possible for the Queen to retreat to a more prospective square.

11. ... Rc8

12. h3

The almost closed position made it unnecessary to hurry. Moreover, Black couldn't find other active opportunities.

12. ... b6?!

A passive move. Black was preparing the retreat of the Bishop in case of Nf3-d4, but even in a closed position tempi should be taken into account. 12... Nd7 or 12... a6 would have been more active.

13. Nd4 Ba8

14. b3 Qd7

Even here 14... Nd7 would have been more expedient, though White's advantage was solid.

15. Bb2 Rfd8

16. Nd5

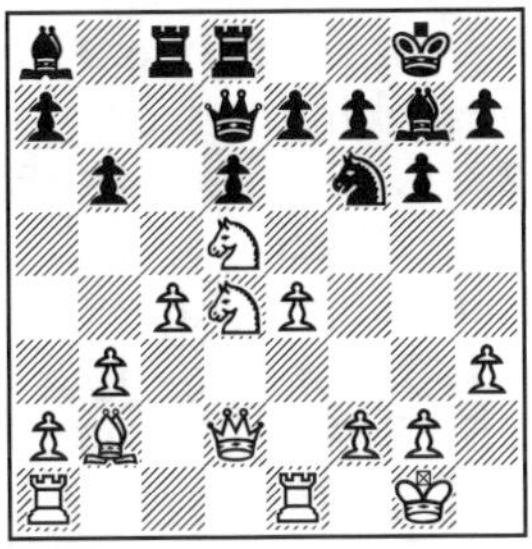

16. ... e6?

White had achieved an ideal position in the placement of his forces, though ideal doesn't mean a winning one. Black could defend persistently, but on the condition of not creating weak points. 16... Nxd5 17. exd5 Re8 coincided with this aim to defend. Black's position was passive yet, at the same time, firm enough. Unfortunately, Black couldn't "stop the jolt," and he fatally weakened the main diagonal.

17. Nf5!

Effective, and instructive. Black would part with his black-squared Bishop, and the result would be the same as when we take the pendulum out of a clock!

17. ... Bxd5

The sacrifice of the piece was quite correct: 17... exd5 18. Nxg7 Kxg7 19. Qd4 Qe6 20. exd5 Qf5 21. g4 Qg5 22. f4 Qh4 23. Kg2 h6 24. g5.

18. Nxg7 e5

19. exd5 Kxg7

20. f4!

Black was helpless against this simple undermining, since he couldn't afford to open the long diagonal. He was forced to surrender the pawn, and at that point the fight came to an end.

20. ... Ne8

21. fxe5 dxe5

22. Rxe5 f6

23. Qe3!

An artist is always an artist! Of course

any retreat of the Rook would be enough to win, but at the moment Nezh was not interested in the score.

23. ... fxe5
24. Qxe5† Kf7

Alas, the King had no escape.

25. Rf1† Qf5
26. Rxf5† gxf5
27. Qxf5†

Black surrendered soon **(1-0)**.

35.

Super Nezh—Y. Estrin

C 78

Semi-finals 19th USSR ch.
Baku 1951

1. e4 e5 2. Nf3 Nc6 3. Bb5 a6 4. Ba4 Nf6 5. 0-0 b5 6. Bb3 d6 7. c3.

In his notes Nezh recommended A. Rabinovich's line: 7. Ng5 d5 8. exd5 Nd4 9. Re1 Bc5 10. c3! (R.N.) Nxb3 11. Rxe5† Kf8 12. axb3 Ng4 13. d4 "with enough compensation for the material." Later V. Hort and J. Pribyl found the refutation: 12... Bxf2†! 13. Kh1 Ng4, and White dies!

7. ... Be7
8. Re1 0-0
9. h3 Be6

By a transposition of moves, the game follows the regular lines of Chigorin's System in the Ruy Lopez and, by playing 9... Na5 10. Bc2 c5 instead, it would've been possible to continue following that strategy, tested in many games. The text, played by Estrin [an outstanding analyst and lover of rare, lesser-known lines, and at the same time a future world corespondence champion] was second-rate, since Black can't hope for equality.

10. d4 Bxb3
11. Qxb3

11. axb3 was considered to be the stronger move, but Nezh aimed to get a position he had prepared in advance.

11. ... Qd7
12. Nbd2 Rfe8
13. Nf1 exd4?!

A voluntary surrendering of the center. In the game *Smyslov—Bolbochan, Helsinki (Ol.) 1952*, Black played the better: 13... h6 14. Ng3 Bf8 15. d5 Na5 16. Qc2 c6 with the chances of success being approximately equal.

14. cxd4 Na5
15. Qc3

Nezhmetdinov was eager to get to this position. It was evidently in White's favor. He had a strong mobile center, under the cover of which it was possible to prepare an attack on the kingside.

15. ... Nc4
16. Ng3 c5
17. b3 Nb6
18. Bb2 b4?!

Black drove the Queen to a place it was eager to be—on the kingside. It would have been better to play either 18... a5, or 18... Bf8, in order to move the Bishop to a defensive post.

19. Qd2 a5
20. dxc5 dxc5
21. Qg5! h6
22. Qf4 c4?!

The d4-square shouldn't have been given to White before the attack. Better would have been 22... Qe6, protecting the Knight and then a5-a4.

23. Bd4 Ra6?

23... Qe6 was necessary, to have 24... Nbd7 against 24. Nf5.

24. Nf5

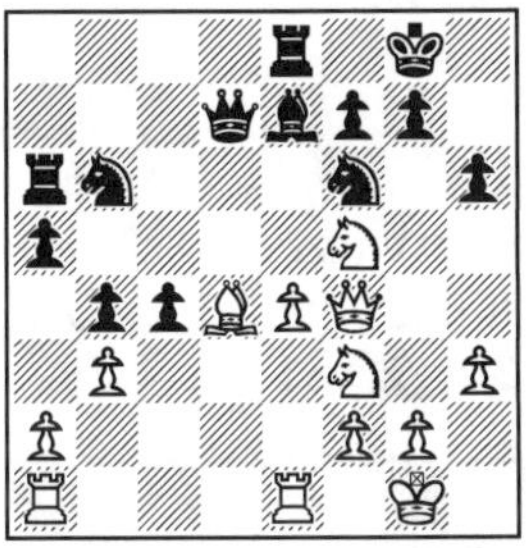

24. ... Qe6

If it had been possible to play 25... Nbd7, Black would have been okay.

25. Bxb6!!

Suddenly, White exchanges his pride and joy, his attacking Bishop. Of course, it was done for a definite reason: Rashid had planned a decisive combination, using the insecure g7-square. To bring it to life the d4-square must be made free for his Knight.

25. ... Rxb6
26. Nxg7! Kxg7
27. Nd4 Qc8

Another, almost identical variation was: 27... Qd7 28. Nf5† Kg8 29. Qg3† Ng4 30. Qxg4† Rg6 31. Nxh6† and 32. Qxd7.

28. Nf5† Kg8
29. Qg3† Ng4
30. Qxg4†

Black surrendered **(1-0)**, as on 30... Rg6, 31. Nxe7† would follow.

36.
Super Nezh—G. Borisenko
C 60
21st USSR ch.
Kiev 1954

1. e4 e5 2. Nf3 Nc6 3. Bb5 a6 4. Ba4 Nf6 5. 0-0 d6 6. d3 b5 7. Bb3 Na5 8. Nc3 Be7 9. h3 0-0 10. Re1 c6 11. Ne2 Kh8 12. Ng3 Ng8 13. d4 exd4 14. Nxd4 g6 15. c3 Bb7 16. Bc2 Bf6 17. Nf3 Re8 18. h4 Nc4 19. Ng5 Nh6.

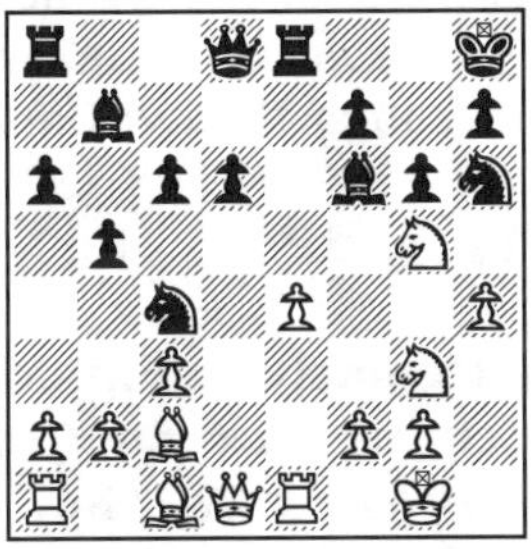

G. Borisenko had the reputation as an outstanding theorist who had published much opening analysis.

He participated in 8 USSR championships, and later was a successful correspondence player [becoming an ICCF grandmaster]. That's why Nezh had deliberately chosen an unpretentious opening variation and obtained a considerable advantage.

> **This tactic often brings success against the theorists, who rely upon their knowledge of openings too much.**
>
> *R.N.*

White got the initiative on the kingside and now he was going for a direct attack.

20. Nh5!

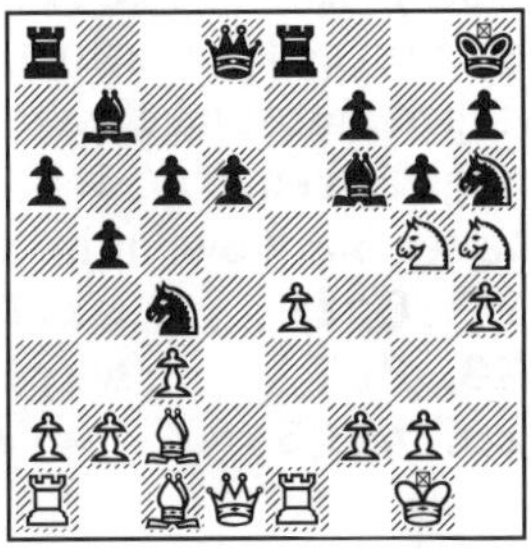

20. ... gxh5

After taking the Knight, things happened quickly and there was no escape. It would have also been bad to exchange the f6-Bishop for the Knight. Probably best was 20… Be7 followed by f7-f6, though this was also difficult.

21. Qxh5 Bg7

Unfortunately, I didn't deliberately sacrifice my Queen in this game: 21… Kg7 22. Qxh6†!! Kxh6 23. Ne6† Kg6 [or 23… Kh5 24. Bd1†, and mate is achieved one move earlier] 24. e5† Kh5 25. Bd1† Kg6 [25… Kxh4 26. g3† Kh3 27. Nf4#] 26. h5† Kf5 27. Nd4#.

R.N.

22. e5!

A white-squared Bishop also joined the attack and the threat 23. Nxf7! appeared. 22… Nxe5 wouldn't stop it: 23. Rxe5!, and on 22… Qd7, the reply 23. e6! was a very strong move. Then 23… fxe6 24. Nxh7.

22. … f5
23. Nxh7! Re6!

On 23… Kxh7, 24. Bxf5† would follow. Then 24… Kg8 25. Bxh6, and the King would have been helpless.

24. Nf6 Rxf6
25. exf6 Qxf6
26. Bg5 Qf7

Having returned the extra material, Black escaped mate and even managed to exchange Queens, but White organized the second wave of his attack.

27. Qxf7 Nxf7
28. Re7 Nxg5
29. hxg5

Everything was calculated up to this point. Yet, White still had to win.

R.N.

29. … Rb8

Not likely was 29… Bc8 30. Re8† Kh7 31. Rxc8! Rxc8 and 32. Bxf5†.

30. Rae1

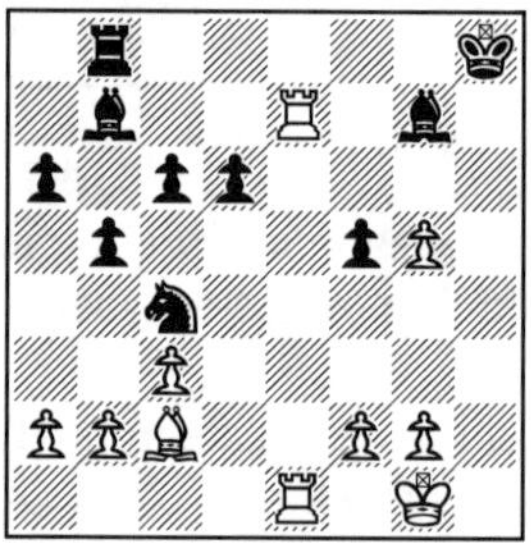

30. … Ne5

Because of the threat 31. Re8 and 32. Bf5#, Black had little choice, but 30… Be5! would have been better. Nezh gave the following line: [30… Be5] 31. f4 Bxf4 32. Re8† Rxe8 33. Rxe8† Kg7 34. Re7† Kg6 35. Rxb7, thinking, that after he took the Bishop everything would have been easy. After 35… Nxb2 36. g4 Kxg5 37. gxf5 Be5 38. Rb6 c5 39. Rxa6 Nc4, the victory might have been in doubt. However, this line could not serve as a refutation of White's attack. Instead of 31. f4, 31. Bxf5 was stronger, with a new threat, namely 32. Re4 and 33. Rh4, uniting the Rooks for the attack.

If 31… c5, good enough would have been 32. f4 Bxf4 33. Re8† Rxe8 34. Rxe8† Kg7 35. Re7† Kf8 36. Rxb7, and this endgame was easily won.

31. f4 Bf8

After 31… Ng6 32. Re8† Rxe8 33. Rxe8† Kh7 34. Bxf5 resigning would have been okay.

32. Rc7

If White had won two pieces for the Rook: 32. Rxb7? Rxb7 33. fxe5 dxe5 34.

Rxe5, it could have turned into a loss—an extra doubled pawn with Bishops of opposite colors not being enough of an advantage for victory.

32. ... Ng6
33. Bxf5 Nxf4
34. Re4 Nxg2
35. Rh7† Kg8
36. g6!

No further comment.

36. ... Bc8
37. Bxc8 Rxc8
38. Kxg2 a5
39. Rd7 d5
40. Re6 Bh6
41. Rdd6 Bc1
42. b3 c5
43. Rxd5 Bb2
44. Rd7 Bxc3
45. g7 Kh7
46. Re3 Bxg7

Black resigned **(1-0)**.

37.

Super Nezh—R. Romanovsky
Semi-finals 24th USSR ch.
Kharkov 1956

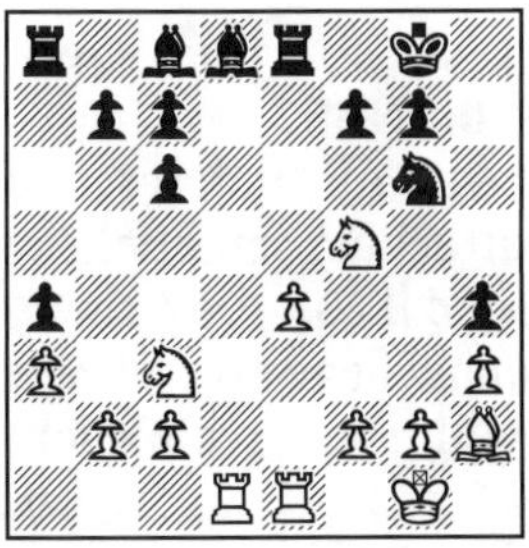

It is easy to recognize the outlines of the Exchange Variation of the Ruy Lopez. Usually White, having extra pawns on the kingside, develops there, and what is left for Black is to move his pawns on the queenside in the hope of creating a passed pawn. Black has some compensation for the bad pawn structure in the form of the Bishop pair.

19. g4!

Nezh felt the inner workings of "Ruy Lopez" positions through his "fingertips." Before starting a massive offense using the e- and f-pawns, he reinforced his pressuring piece, the Knight on f5.

19. ... hxg3
20. Bxg3 Nf8?!

Black was going to transfer the Knight to e6, freeing the Bishop from protecting the c7-pawn. This plan was too slow. White was already beginning the offensive, so Black should have played more actively: 20... Bf6!, and if 21. Bxc7, then 21... Bxc3 22. bxc3 Bxf5 23. exf5 Rxe1† 24. Rxe1 Nh4, taking the f5-pawn and having enough chances in the endgame.

21. Kh2 Ne6
22. f4 b5
23. Rg1 g6

By failing to address the issue that passive defense was not enough, Black was eager to make more serious weakenings. The defense should have been more cool-headed: 23... Kh7, preserved the opportune g7-g6 for a more convenient time.

24. Nh6† Kg7
25. Ng4 f6

26. Ne5 or 26. f5 was threatened, that's why the position had to be weakened again.

26. f5 Ng5
27. Rgf1 c5

The situation had grown even more agitated. The counterthreat b5-b4 had appeared, and it forces White to accelerate his plans.

28. e5! Bxf5

Black was now at the edge of the abyss and inexact play will bring defeat. So, 28... fxe5 29. Bxe5† Kh7 30.

Rxd8! Rxd8 31. fxg6† Kxg6 32. Rf6† Kh7 33. Rh6† Kg8 34. Rh8† would have won by force. The only precise way across this chasm was 28… gxf5! 29. Nxf6 Bxf6 30. exf6† Kxf6! [Damsky] 31. Bh4 Rh8, and it was possible to equalize, for example: 32. Ne4† Kg6 and it would have been quite unlikely to have won the Knight. Or 32. Rf4? Rxh4!. Finally, after 32. Nd5† Kg6 33. Bxg5 Kxg5 34. Rg1† Kh6 35. Nxc7 Ra7 36. Rd6† Kh7! [36… Kh5 37. Nd5 Ra6 38. Nf4† and White would have won.] 37. Nd5 Ra6 38. Nf6† Kh6, and the black King would have been in an extremely precarious position, but White can't achieve more than a draw.

The move in the game was not enough to come to the rescue.

29. exf6† Kf8

29… Bxf6 could not have be played on account of 30. Nxf6 Kxf6 31. Bh4 Rh8 with 32. Nd5† and 33. Bxg5.

30. Ne5! b4

On 31… Bxf6 there would have been: 32. Nd7† Kg7 33. Nxf6 Kxf6 and 34. Bh4.

31. Nd5 Bxc2

A last defensive chance was 31… Nf7!.

32. f7 Re6

32… Rxe5 would not have helped. After 33. Bxe5, 33… Bxd1 wouldn't have done anything because of 34. Bg7†.

33. Nd7†

Black surrendered **(1-0)**.

38.

B. Gurgenidze—Super Nezh

C 60

24th USSR ch.

Moscow 1957

1. e4 e5 2. Nf3 Nc6 3. Bb5 a6 4. Ba4 Nf6 5. Qe2 b5 6. Bb3 Bc5 7. c3 d6 8. 0-0 0-0 9. Rd1 Qe7 10. h3 Bb6 11. d4 Bb7 12. d5 Na5 13. Bc2 c6 14. dxc6 Nxc6 15. Bg5 h6 16. Bxf6 Qxf6 17. Nbd2 Ne7 18. Nf1.

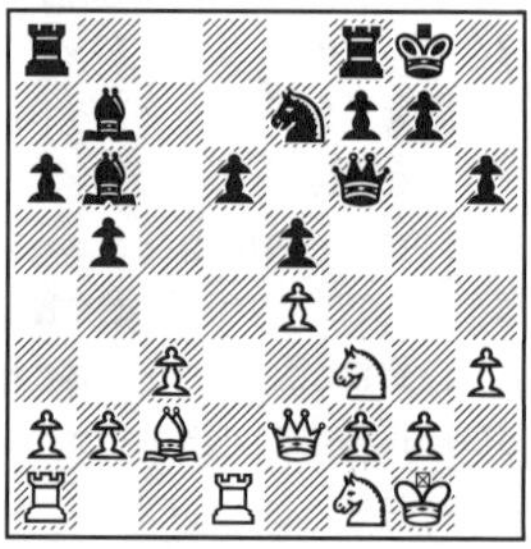

Nezh played the opening better and grabbed the initiative. Now his aim was to open up the diagonals for the Bishops and point them at the white King's position.

18. … Ng6

19. g3

After 19. Ne3, 19… Nf4 20. Qf1 Qg6, would follow stopping 21. Nd5, because of 21… Bxd5 22. exd5 Qxc2.

R.N.

19. … Qe6

20. Ne3?

This was an underestimation of Black's attacking potential. Better was 20. Bb3, and if 20… Qd7, then 21. Bd5!, which would have neutralized the dangerous white-squared Bishop.

20. … Qxh3

21. Rxd6

Poor was 21. Nd5 because of the Queen take on g3, and if 21. Nf5 Nezh planned 21… d5! 22. exd5 Bc8 and 23… f5, rolling out the attack. White was obliged to go along with the plans of his opponent.

21. … Bc5

22. Rxg6

It turned out that it was too late to retreat the Rook: 22. Rd2, then 22… f5!. For example, 23. Nxf5 Rxf5 24. exf5 Qxg3† 25. Kf1 Qh3† 26. Ke1 Bxf3 and the fat lady would have been warming up.

22. ... fxg6
23. Nxe5 Kh7!

Nezh complained about not playing 23… Rxf2 at once, and showed as proof: 24. Qxf2 Rf8 25. Nf7! Kh7 "with the unavoidable threat of …Rxf7 [26. Bb3 Bxe4]." But after 26. Re1! Rxf7 27. Qxf7 Qxg3† 28. Kf1 Bxe3 29. Bb3! he would have missed the win!

24. Rd1?

Unfortunately, none of the commentators [including Nezh] mentioned this error. From the previous note it can be seen that 24. Re1! was correct because it overprotected the Knight. In that event …Rxf2 wouldn't work, and Black would have had to work hard to prove his advantage.

24. ... Rxf2!

Now this combination led to a quick victory.

25. Kxf2

The same result would come after 25. Qxf2 Rf8! 26. Qe1 [26. Nf3 Bxe3 27. Qxe3 Qxg3†] Rf1†! 27. Qxf1 Bxe3†.

25. ... Qh2†
26. Ke1 Qxg3†
27. Kd2 Qxe5
28. Nd5 Qg5†

White surrendered **(0-1).**

39.

Super Nezh—L. Lengyel

C 78

Russia—Hungary

Budapest 1963

1. e4 e5 2. Nf3 Nc6 3. Bb5 a6 4. Ba4 Nf6 5. 0-0 Be7 6. Re1 b5 7. Bb3 d6 8. c3 0-0 9. h3 Be6 10. d4 Bxb3 11. Qxb3 Qd7 12. Nbd2 Re8 13. Nf1 h6.

Up to this move Game No. 35 [N.—Estrin] was repeated.

14. Ng3 Bf8
15. Qd1 Na5
16. b3 c5
17. Bb2 Nc6
18. a4 Qb7?

Until this move, both sides enjoyed equal chances in combat maneuvers, but now Black allowed his opponent to lock up the queenside, and on the kingside, according to the usual themes of the Ruy Lopez, White was in charge of the position. 18… cxd4 was necessary in order to open the c-file for counterplay.

19. d5! Ne7
20. a5 g6
21. Nh2 Bg7
22. Bc1 Nd7

Black was taking measures to prevent f2-f4, but let the white Knight get to g4. More precise would have been 22… Kh7, for to reply to 23. f4 by 23… exf4 would have met with 24. Bxf4 Nd7!.

23. Ng4 Kh7
24. h4 h5?!

White's pressure was tangible, but it was not so great that Black could afford to weaken his position allowing his opponent such good objects of attack: the h5-pawn, the weak point g5, and with it all the black squares near the King. 24… Ng8 should have been considered.

25. Nh2 Rh8
26. Bg5 f6
27. Be3 Raf8

The King could not stay on the weakened wing any longer, that's why it was high time to evacuate—27... Kg8 and then move towards the closed queenside.

28. c4 Rb8
29. Nf3 Ng8?

Black lost his last chance to save his King: 29... Kg8.

30. cxb5! axb5

After 30... Qxb5 31. Nd2 more grief would have been added to Black's problems on his kingside, namely, the c4-square for the Knight on the queenside.

31. a6 Qb6

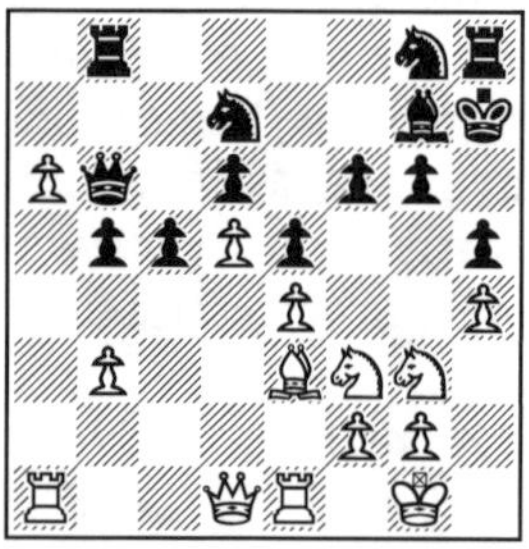

32. Nxh5!

This sacrifice can't be called intuitive, but real. Spielmann, a fine theorist and combinational wizard, referred to the intuitive sacrifice as a sacrifice which doesn't lead at once to the final result.

White only gets a prospective attacking position with the possibilities of various threats, and this was native ground for Nezh.

32. ... gxh5
33. Ng5†! Kg6

It would have been bad to take another Knight: 33... fxg5 34. Qxh5† Nh6 [34... Bh6 35. Qf7† Bg7 36. Qf5† Kh6 37. Bxg5† and 38. g4#] 35. hxg5, and White would have gotten three pawns for the piece without slowing the attack.

34. Qf3 Ne7
35. Ne6 Kf7
36. b4!

A very important resource, which expanded the sphere of attack over the whole board.

36. ... Qa7

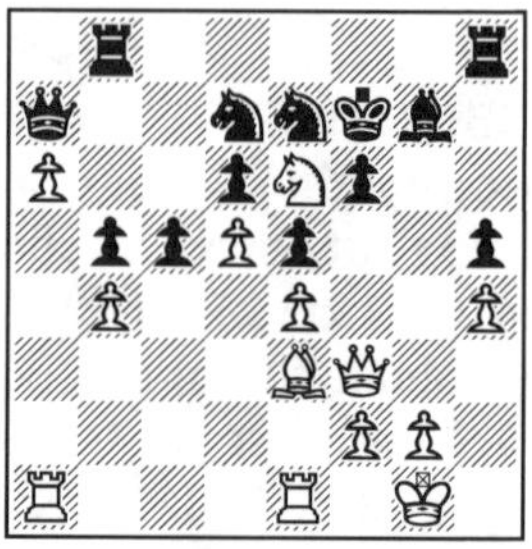

37. Qh3!

After such a sacrificial beginning the further pressing of the attack continues with slow moves which always exerts psychological influences on the opponent, and an aesthetic influence on the audience.

37. ... Bh6
38. bxc5 Bxe3
39. Rxe3 dxc5

Now one more actor appeared on the attacking scene, the passed d-pawn. 39... Nxc5 would have led to a quick defeat after 40. Nxc5 Qxc5 41. Rc3 Qa7 [41... Qd4 42. Qe6† Ke8 43. Rac1] 42. Qe6† Ke8 43. Qxd6. E.g., 43... Rb6 44. Qc7.

40. Rg3 Rhg8
41. Rxg8 Rxg8

Pay attention and know that this is not a good method of attack, owing to the exchanges. These exchanges affected Black badly. The secret was not much of a secret: the pieces needed for the defense should not be exchanged.

42. d6! c4

This was desperation, but on 42... Nc6 or 42... Nc8 there was the unpleasant 43. Nc7.

43. dxe7 Kxe7
44. Qf5 Rh8
45. Rd1 b4
46. Ng7 Nc5
47. Ne8!

Elegance to the end. There were different ways to win, but this move is the stroke of an artiste.

47. ... Qxa6

The Knight could not be taken.

48. Nc7 Qc6
49. Qg6 Rf8
50. Nd5† Ke6
51. Qf5†

Black surrendered **(1-0)**.

40.

Y. Kotkov—Super Nezh
C 76
Gorki 1963

1. e4 e5 2. Nf3 Nc6 3. Bb5 a6 4. Ba4 d6 5. c3 Bd7 6. 0-0 g6 7. d4 Bg7 8. dxe5 dxe5 9. b4.

The play was a bit obtuse, but it defined some things, e.g. that the main fight will be on the wings. More flexible continuations were offered by 9. Be3 or 9. Bg5.

9. ... Nge7
10. Qc2 0-0
11. Rd1 Qe8
12. Bb3

Black threatened 12... Nxb4.

12. ... Kh8
13. Nbd2 f5
14. a4 Nd8

This maneuver can be seen in Game No. 65 [Boleslavsky—N.]. Black not only transfered the Knight to the kingside, but also slowed White's offensive.

15. Nc4

The Knight did not have a good position here, since it blocked the Bishop on b3 and did not let the other Bishop have an active place on b2. 15. Bb2 was preferable.

15. ... Nf7
16. Ne3 Nd6
17. Nd2 f4
18. Nec4 Nf7!

While White shifted his Knights, Black went about activating his kingside, and it was there that a general offensive began, that's why exchanges should be avoided. One thing more: poorly placed enemy pieces should be apprehended.

19. Ba3 g5
20. Nb2 g4
21. Nd3 Ng5
22. Nc5 Bc8
23. b5 f3!

Of course, it would not be good to accept the pawn: 23... axb5 24. axb5 Qxb5? 25. Ba4 Qb6 26. Nd7.

24. g3 Nh3†
25. Kf1 axb5
26. axb5 Ng5

As has been said, taking the b5-pawn was only to White's benefit.

27. Nc4 Qh5
28. Kg1 Ng6
29. Ne3

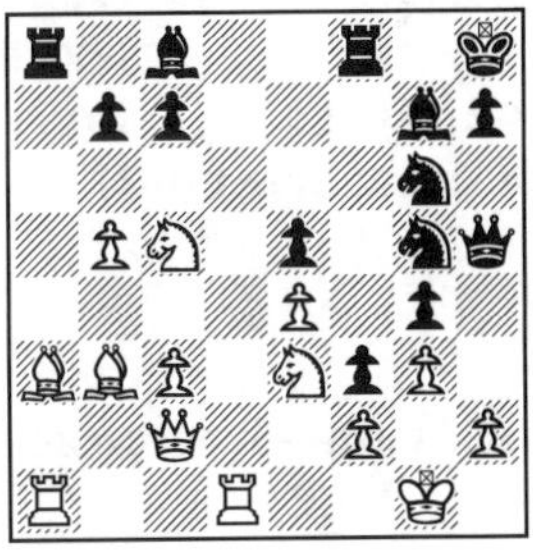

29. ... Nf4!

A thematic sacrifice in this type of position, as 30. gxf4 exf4 was bad for White. Black wanted to play 30... Ne2† 31. Kh1 Nh3 32. Rf1 Bh6, or 30... Ng2.

30. h4

It was possible that 30. Bc4 could have given more defensive chances.

30. ... Ngh3†
31. Kf1 Ng2
32. Ne6 Bxe6
33. Bxe6 Qh6!

With an eye on the e3-square, and because of that, Black wasn't concerned about his own material deficits.

34. Bxf8 Rxf8
35. Bxg4

35. Bf5 Nxe3† 36. fxe3 Qxe3 37. Qh2 Qxc3 38. Rac1 [38. Qd2 Qc5] Qb3 39. Rd5 c6 40. bxc6 bxc6 also fails, and White would have had to let the black Queen give a ruinous check.

35. ... Nxf2!
36. Nf5

On 36. Qxf2 there would have follow 36... Nxe3† and 37... Nxg4 and, the same thing would have happened on 36. Kxf2.

36. ... Nxd1
37. Rxd1 Rxf5
38. Rd8†

If 38. exf5 the rare "quadrangle" fork 38... Ne3† crunches White's pieces.

38. ... Rf8
39. Rxf8† Bxf8
40. Kg1 Ne3
41. Qf2 Nxg4
42. Qxf3 Bc5†

White surrendered **(0-1).**

41.
A. Suetin—Super Nezh
C 78
Yalta 1964

1. e4 e5 2. Nf3 Nc6 3. Bb5 a6 4. Ba4 Nf6 5. 0-0 b5 6. Bb3 Bb7 7. Re1.

Worth some attention was: 7. Ng5 d5 8. exd5 Nd4.

7. ... Bc5
8. c3 d6
9. d4 Bb6
10. a3

A less active move, but 10. a4 also wouldn't have given White an advantage, for example: 10... h6 11. axb5 axb5 12. Rxa8 Qxa8 13. Na3 exd4!, *Kostro—Tseshkovsky, Varna 1969.*

10. ... Qe7
11. Qd3 Na5
12. Bc2 c5
13. Nbd2

Unless Black castled, it would not have been advantageous to play 13. Bg5, because of 13... h6 14. Bh4 g5.

13. ... Nc6
14. d5 c4
15. Qe2 Na5
16. a4

Agreeing that on his 10th move a tempo was lost.

16. ... 0-0

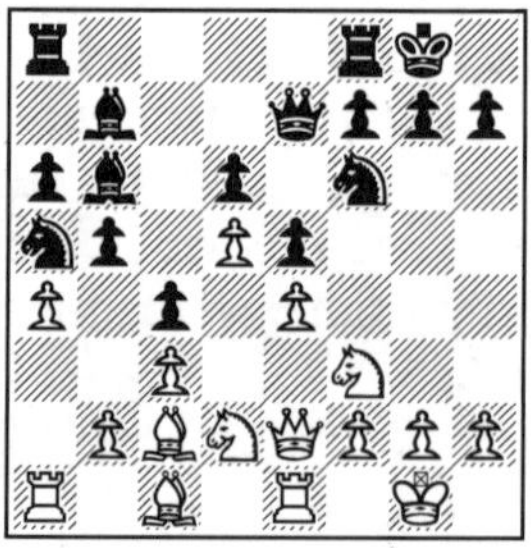

17. Nb1?!

Instead of this slow maneuver it would have been worth paying attention to 17. h3, preparing 18. Nf1. 17. Nf1 at once was worse, because then 17... Ng4 18. Ne3 f5!.

17. ... Nd7!

Black had planned to open the f-file, and was ready to do it, without worrying about the sacrifice of material.

18. Na3 Nc5
19. axb5 axb5

20. Nxb5 f5!
21. exf5 Qd7!

The immediate 21... Bxd5 was weaker because of 22. Nbd4 and 23. Ne6.

22. Na3 e4!
23. Nd4

Of course it would have been dangerous to take on e4.

23. ... Bxd5
24. Be3 Nd3
25. Ne6 Rxf5
26. Bxb6 Qxe6

Wrong was 26... Nxe1 27. Nd4 Nxc2 28. Naxc2, and the Knight and Rook would have been attacked.

27. Bxd3 cxd3
28. Qe3 Nb3
29. Rad1 Qg6
30. Kh1

The Queen was threatened: 30... Rf3!.

30. ... Raf8
31. Rf1 Qh5
32. c4 Ba8
33. Rde1 R8f6

Black owned the elements of space and the initiative, and so he started a direct attack. It's difficult to find a defense.

34. Bd8 Rh6
35. h4 Qg4
36. Kh2

Bad at once was 36. Qh3?, because of 36... Qxh3† 37. gxh3 e3† and 38... e2.

36. ... g5!
37. g3 gxh4
38. gxh4

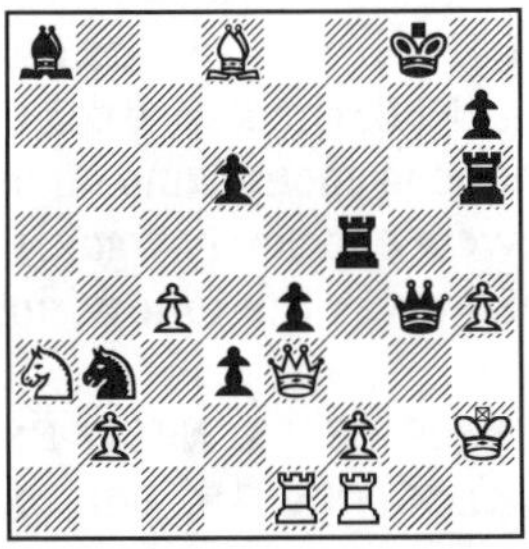

38. ... Rxh4†!

This was an easy material sacrifice, still, it needed calculation.

39. Bxh4 Qxh4†
40. Qh3 Rxf2†
41. Rxf2 Qxf2†
42. Qg2† Qxg2†
43. Kxg2 e3†
44. Kg3 d2
45. Rg1 Kf7!

A careless 45... e2 would have missed a victory—46. Kf2 with check.

46. Nb1 e2
47. Nxd2 Nxd2
48. Re1 Bf3
49. b4 Bh5
50. b5 Nxc4

and Black won **(0-1)**.

42.

Super Nezh—A. Chistyakov

C 12

Semi-finals 24th USSR ch.

Kharkov 1956

1. e4 e6 2. d4 d5 3. Nc3 Nf6 4. Bg5 Bb4 5. e5 h6 6. Bd2 Nfd7.

A connoisseur and adherent of the French Defense, master Chistyakov had prepared a small opening surprise for Nezh—an old move of Tartakower's. Except for the effect of unexpectedness, it had no other value when compared with the traditional 6... Bxc3 7. bxc3 Ne4.

7. Qg4

Another good plan was shown in the game *Alatortsev—Bondarevsky, Moscow 1945:* 7. Nce2 Bxd2† 8. Qxd2 b6 9. Nf4 [Keres' opinion: 9. f4 c5 10. c3 with 11. Nf3 was more natural.] Ba6 10. Bxa6 Nxa6 11. Nf3 c5 12. c3 with a small, but firm advantage for White. Nezh was unaware of this idea. He said that the move 7. Nce2 came to mind only after the game.

7. ... Bf8

In the old game *Réti—Vukovich, Vienna 1922*, after 7... Kf8 8. f4 c5 9. a3 Bxc3 10. bxc3 Nc6 11. Qd1! White had an obvious advantage.

8. Nf3

Nezh considered this continuation stronger than 8. f4, basing this on the game *Vasiukov—Chistyakov* from *Moscow ch. 1956*, in which after 8. f4 c5 9. Bd3?! Nc6 10. Nf3 c4 11. Bg6? Nb6 12. f5 Qd7 13. 0-0 fxg6 Black took the piece and then rejected the attacking attempts of his opponent. Stronger was 9. dxc5! Nxc5 10. Nf3 Nc6 11. 0-0-0 a6 12. Be3 Qa5, with some advantage to White, owing to the possession of the important d4-square, *Kogan—Chistyakov, Moscow 1956*.

8. ... c5?!

A careless move which allowed White to make an unpleasant Knight move. However, White's next move wasn't a surprise for Chistyakov, as 30 years earlier this move had been analyzed by Tartakower and was thought advantageous to Black.

Instead of 8... c5, Nezh recommended playing 8... a6 first, even though that "could be replied to by 9. b4!, with the initiative." This advice was tested in the game *Nikitin—Chistyakov, Moscow 1957:* 8... a6 9. b4! b6 10. Na4 c5 11. bxc5 bxc5 12. Nxc5 Nxc5 13. dxc5 Qc7 14. Be2 Nd7 15. 0-0 g6 16. c4!, and White got the advantage.

9. Nb5 g6?

This was a mistake, as the whole kingside was seriously weakened. As a rule, such a move is always bad in similar positions. It's difficult to explain this choice of move by an experienced master. Maybe he'd just forgotten Tartakower's analysis. He should have played 9... cxd4 anyway. Tartakower offered the following: 10. Nd6† Bxd6 11. Qxg7 Bxe5! 12. Nxe5 Qf6. In reality, this position was advantageous for Black.

The fact was, Nezhmetdinov didn't know this analysis and hadn't planned to play in such a way. After 9... cxd4, he would've sacrificed the pawn: 10. c3! dxc3 11. Bxc3 with enough compensation, as now the e5-pawn was strengthened.

10. Bd3

10. ... Rg8

There was the threat of a sacrifice on g6. If 10... h5, then 11. Qxe6!! fxe6 12. Bxg6† Ke7 13. Bg5† Nf6 14. exf6† Kd7 15. Ne5#!.

R.N.

11. c4!!

A bold shot, ruining the center. Owing to Black's lack of development, there was the threat of a quick catastrophe.

11. ... cxd4

If 11... Nb6, then 12. dxc5 Bxc5 13. Bxh6 was good enough and all the black squares were hopelessly weak. On 11... dxc4 Nezh gives the following:

12. Bxc4 a6 13. Nd6†! Bxd6 14. exd6 Qb6 15. 0-0 Qxd6

16. dxc5 Nxc5 17. Bxh6, and Black is helpless in defense. He can't transfer the King into safety and pull up the reserves.

R.N.

12. cxd5 Nc5

These two lines are bad: 12... exd5 13. e6! Nc5 14. exf7† Kxf7 15. Ne5† [or 13... Nf6 14. exf7† Kxf7 15. Ne5†]; 12... a6 13. dxe6 axb5 14. exf7† Kxf7 15. e6† with total devastation.

13. Qxd4 exd5

Nezh considered this move as the decisive mistake, offering instead: 13... Nc6!.

Now 14. dxc6 Nxd3† 15. Ke2 gives nothing to White because of the handsome *zwischenzug* 15... bxc6!.

R.N.

It's hardly possible to agree with him. Let's continue: 16. Qxd8† Kxd8 17. Ba5† Ke7 18. Kxd3. In the endgame Black couldn't manage to normalize this position, for example: 18... Ba6 19. Nfd4 Kd7 20. Rac1 Bg7 21. Ke4 and White would break through to the 7th rank.

It turned out the fatal mistake was made earlier by Black, probably his 9th move.

14. Nd6†! Bxd6
15. exd6 Qxd6
16. 0-0 Nxd3
17. Qxd3 Nc6
18. Rfe1† Be6
19. Nd4!

Black almost had his development finished and he even obtained an extra pawn, but it was only an illusion of well-being. The attack by White went on without any obstacles. It wasn't profitable for Black to exchange Knights—in this case the black squares will become unprotected—but allowing this Knight to live was also bad.

19. ... g5

Black didn't dare to castle long, as the black diagonals are absolutely unprotected: 19... 0-0-0? 20. Nb5 Qb8 [or 20... Qd7 21. Rac1 Kb8 22. Bf4† Ka8 23. Nc7†] 21. Rac1 Kd7 22. Qf3 Ne5 23. Qg3 [Nezh's analysis]. The idea of Black's move was to take the f4-square away from the Bishop.

20. Rac1 Kd7

20... 0-0-0? was weak because of an easy 21. Nxc6 bxc6 22. Qa6†, and on 20... Rg6 he prepared the thunderbolt 21. Qxg6!.

21. Nf5 Qf8
22. Qb5! Rc8

On 22... Rb8 White planned to play 23. Re5! with an inevitable taking on d5.

23. Qxb7† Rc7
24. Qb5 a6
25. Qd3 Qb8

After 25... Rg6!, it would have been possible to defend much better, and it would be hard for White to go home a winner.

26. Nxh6 Rg6
27. Nxf7! Bxf7
28. Qf5† Kd8
29. Rxc6! Rcxc6
30. Ba5† Qc7
31. Qxf7

Black surrendered **(1-0)**.

43.

Super Nezh—A. Elizarov

C 17

Kazan 1964

1. e4 e6 2. d4 d5 3. Nc3 Bb4 4. e5 c5 5. a3 Ba5 6. Bd2 cxd4 7. Nb5 Bc7 8. Qg4!?.

An interesting gambit continuation, which is not allotted much attention in opening textbooks. They examine only 8. f4 Nh6 9. Qh5 Nf5 10. Nf3 g6 11. Qh3 h5, *Vasiukov—Koc, 29th USSR ch., 1961.*

8. ... Bxe5
9. Nf3 h5
10. Qh3 Bc7
11. Nfxd4 Bd7?!

Preferable is 11... Nc6 or 11... a6.

12. 0-0-0 Na6

[Ed.: Damsky believed that White has the advantage after 12... 13. Nxc7† Qxc7 14. Nb5 Qb8 15. Qf3 Nf6 16. Bf4 e5 17. Bg5 Ne4 18. Bh4 Be6 19. Bc4, but for some reason he "overlooks" 19... Bg4, and Black holds and intimidates.]

13. Re1 Qf6

Hoping to castle queenside.

14. Nxc7† Nxc7
15. Nf3 e5

By preventing the threats of 16. Bg5 and 16. Bc3, Black hoped that having returned a pawn, he would be able to exchange Queens.

16. Qg3 h4

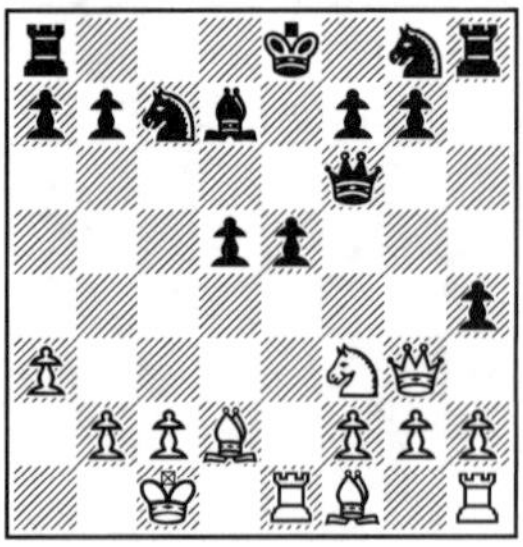

17. Rxe5†!

A surprise. After 17. Qxe5 Qxe5 18. Rxe5† Be6, the endgame was bad for Black, but not hopeless.

17. ... Be6
18. Rxe6†! Nxe6
19. Bb5† Kf8
20. Qd6† Ne7
21. Ne5

The sacrifice had given White a powerful attack. How would Black defend against the threat of 22. Nd7?

21. ... Nc5!

A sharpwitted resource, which allowed the fight to continue.

22. Qxc5 Qxe5
23. Re1 b6
24. Qb4 a5
25. Qg4

Damsky reproached Nezh that the latter missed a chance to win easily: 25. Rxe5 axb4 26. Bxb4 Ra7 27. Rxd5 g6? 28. Rd8† Kg7 29. Bc3† f6 30. Bxf6† and 31. Rxh8. Stronger was 27... Kg8!, and the material can't be won back. Perhaps, Rashid Gibyatovich was right.

25. ... Qf5
26. Qa4 Ng6
27. Bd3 Qf6
28. Kb1 Kg8
29. Bc3 Qxf2?

Beginning with the 21st move, Black defended well, and could have held on after 29... Qg5. Opening the f-file was a suicidal decision.

30. Rf1 Qc5
31. Bxg6!

Black resigned **(1-0)**, as the game would finish: 31... fxg6 32. Qd7 Rh7 33. Rf7.

44.

G. Ilivitsky—Super Nezh

E 68

21st USSR ch.

Kiev 1954

1. Nf3 Nf6 2. c4 d6 3. d4 g6 4. Nc3 Bg7 5. g3 0-0 6. Bg2 Nbd7 7. 0-0 e5 8. e4 exd4 9. Nxd4 Nc5 10. f3 a5 11. Be3 Nfd7 12. Rf2 a4 13. Rb1 c6 14. b4 axb3 15. axb3 Qe7 16. Ra2 Rxa2 17. Nxa2.

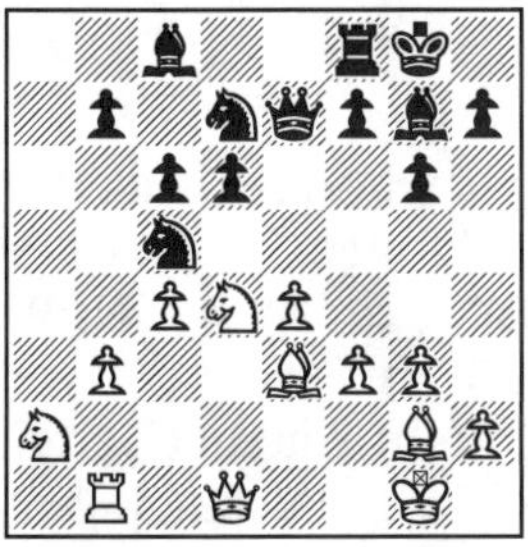

Black had won the opening phase of the King's Indian duel. It was enough to see that the Bishop on e3 was threatened and the Knight on a2 driven back to the flank. Nezh immediately began his attack.

17. ... f5!
18. Nc3 fxe4
19. fxe4 Nf6
20. Qc2 Re8

Through forcing moves, White had been put into a critical situation. The trouble was not in the weakness of his e-pawn, but that his pieces would have no support in the center.

21. Re1 Ng4!

Black had no appetite for the e-pawn. For example: 21... Ncxe4 22. Bg5 or 21... Nfxe4 22. Nxc6! bxc6 23. Bxc5. It was more important to use the lack of coordination of White's pieces without losing time.

22. Nf3 Nxe3
23. Rxe3 Bf5!

Adding a Bishop held in "reserve" finally defined Black's decisive advantage.

24. Qd1 Qf6
25. Qc2

White had no more useful moves.

25. ... Bg4
26. b4 Bh6
27. Re1 Bxf3
28. e5

In case of 28. bxc5 it was possible to play 28... Qd4† 29. Qf2 Qxc3 30. Bxf3 Rf8 31. Kg2 Rxf3! 32. Qxf3 Qxe1. Also weak was 28. Bxf3 Qxf3 with the threat ...Be3†.

28. ... Rxe5
29. Rxe5 Qxe5
30. Bxf3 Qe3†
31. Kg2 Nd3
32. Nd1 Ne1†
33. Kf1 Nxc2

White surrendered **(0-1).**

45.

L. Shamkovich—Super Nezh

E 97

29th USSR ch.

Baku 1961

1. d4 Nf6 2. c4 g6 3. Nc3 Bg7 4. e4 0-0 5. Nf3 d6 6. Be2 e5 7. 0-0 Nc6 8. d5 Ne7 9. Nd2 Ne8.

After the most effective ways of developing an attack on the queenside had been found for White, this continuation was almost abandoned, since it didn't prevent the plan b2-b4, c4-c5, and Nd2-c4. In the plan's foreground will come 9... c5 and 9... Nd7.

10. b4 f5
11. f3 f4
12. c5 g5

13. Nc4 Rf7

The previous moves were clear enough and needed no comment. The Rook's move was a multi-faceted one. It gets ready for the defense of the c7-square, and for participation in the attack via h7 or g7.

14. Bd2?

This feeble move should not have been made in such a dynamic position. There was no time to lose in bringing the plan to life. If the thematic 14. a4! was played, then 14... Ng6 15. Ba3 Bf8 16. b5 would give White chances to be successful with a quicker push than Black.

14. ... Ng6
15. Be1 Bf8
16. Bf2

White used three tempi to establish his Bishop at a place where it could see both flanks—for attack and defense. However, it would have been of no practical importance when defending the King, and the time lost would not be regained.

16. ... h5
17. Rc1 Nf6
18. cxd6 cxd6
19. Nb5 g4
20. Nxa7

If, at the end of its multi-move route, the Bishop had taken on a7, then a possible continuation could have been: 20... Rxa7! 21. Nxa7 Bd7 22. a4 g3, proceeding with a direct attack on the King.

20. ... Bd7
21. a4 g3!
22. Bb6 Qe7
23. Kh1?!

A logical but imprecise move. Better would have been 23. Nb5!, giving Black these choices: either be down a piece, important for his attack, after 23... Bxb5; retreat for defending d6 [23... Ne8]; or sacrifice the pawn, but in that case White would have had a chance to increase his opportunities to invade.

23. ... Rh7
24. Nb5

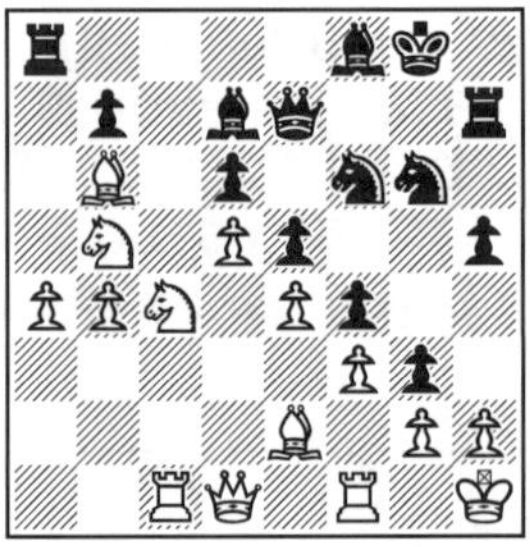

Being late by a move allowed Black to crash through:

24. ... Ng4!
25. h3

The Knight couldn't be taken: 25. fxg4 hxg4 26. Bg1 Rxh2† and 27... Qh4. It became clear that transferring the Bishop was time lost because it had no role in the defense of his King.

25. ... Qh4
26. Qd2 Ne3!

A false trail would exist with 26... Nf2† 27. Kg1 Bxh3 28. gxh3 Qxh3 29. Rxf2 gxf2† 30. Kxf2, and the King would have had time to escape from the chase.

27. Bd3

If 27. Bxe3, then 27... Bxh3! also wins at once.

27. ... Bxh3!
28. gxh3 g2†
29. Kg1 gxf1=Q†
30. Bxf1 Qg3†
31. Bg2 Nh4
32. Qf2 Nexg2
33. Qxg3† fxg3

White surrendered **(0-1).**

46.

V. Zhelyandinov—Super Nezh

E 84

Vologda 1962

1. d4 Nf6 2. c4 g6 3. Nc3 Bg7 4. e4 d6 5. f3 0-0 6. Be3 Nc6.

Nezh always tried to keep himself in the avant garde of the theory of his pet openings. The system with 6... Nc6 was becoming popular at that time.

7. Nge2 a6

8. Qd2 Rb8

9. d5?!

This gives Black an object for his counter-attack—the c4-pawn—and together with that, the initiative. The right way for White was found later—an immediate attack on the kingside—9. h4!.

9. ... Ne5

10. Nd4?!

A logical continuation of the plan used by White, but not a successful one since the Knight was in danger and this circumstance allowed Black to attack for a long time. Better was 10. Ng3, for which there was a good response in 10... h5.

10. ... c5!

11. dxc6

An opening of the file on the queenside can't be averted by White. On 11. Nc2 or 11. Nb3, Black would play 11... b5.

11. ... bxc6

12. Be2

Perhaps clearer was 12. b3 c5 13. Nc2 Qa5 14. Nd1 Qc7 15. Be2 e6 16. 0-0 Bb7, with the initiative belonging to Black, *Ustinov—Stein, 1965.* It was not worth paying much attention to 12. f4, because Black had 12... c5 13. fxe5 cxd4 14. Bxd4 dxe5 15. Bxe5 Qxd2† 16. Kxd2 Rxb2†.

12. ... c5

13. Nb3 Rb4!

This was played because of a profitable change for Black concerning the situation in the center, the result of which will be a combined attack by the dark-squared Bishop and Black's Rook, which intersect at the b2-square. A similar attack is very effective in various King Indian and Indian schemes, and also in the Benko Gambit.

14. Nd5 Nxd5

14... Nxc4 15. Bxc4 Rxc4 16. Na5 Nxd5! 17. Nxc4 Nxe3 18. Nxe3 Be6 was also possible. As compensation Black had the pawn, powerful Bishops, and an opened b-file.

15. cxd5 a5

16. Rb1 f5!

17. f4

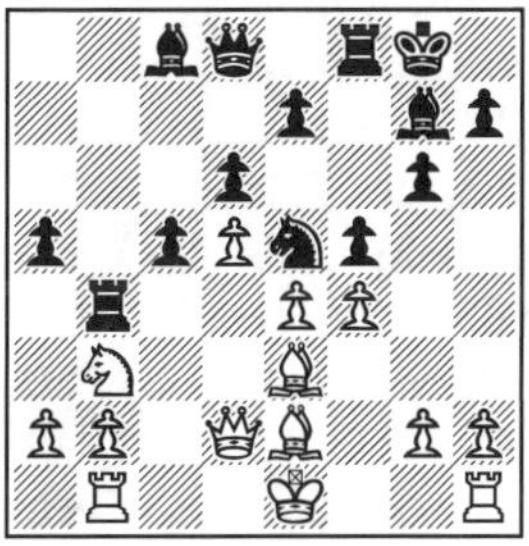

White has not only been defeated in the strategic battle on the queenside, but also in the center. He had run out of normal defensive moves and so he was obliged to complicate matters, hoping to confound the ensuing play.

17. ... a4!

Black's adding oil to the fire. Clearly 17... Nc4 18. Bxc4 Rxc4 19. Nxa5 Rxe4 20. Nc6 and 21. 0-0 would let White hold on.

18. Nxc5 dxc5

19. fxe5 Rxe4

20. 0-0

20. e6 was bad because of 20... Rxe3!.

20. ... Bxe5

21. Kh1

On 21. Bxc5 possible was 21... Bxh2† 22. Kxh2 Qc7† 23. d6 Qxc5 24. dxe7 Qxe7 with a big advantage.

21. ... Qd6
22. Bf3 Rxe3!

A simple sacrifice of material, which ruins the defense of the black squares. It was possible, of course, to play 22... Rb4 or 22... Rh4 23. h3, but Black's decision was more rational.

23. Qxe3 Bxh2
24. Rbe1 Bg3
25. Bd1

On 25. Qxe7 Black would win at once with 25... Qf4 and the threat of 26... Qh6†.

25. ... Rf7
26. Bxa4 Ba6

In this game Bishops had an advantage over the Rooks.

27. Qe6 Bxf1
28. Rxf1

If 28. Qxd6, then 28... Bxg2† and 29... Bxd6.

28. ... Qb8
29. d6 Qb4
30. Rc1 Qxa4
31. d7 Qh4†
32. Kg1 Qd4†

White surrendered **(0-1).**

47.

V. Chernikh—Super Nezh

A 55

Yalta 1964

1. d4 Nf6 2. c4 d6 3. Nc3 e5 4. Nf3 Nbd7 5. e4 g6 6. d5 Bg7 7. Be2 0-0 8. Bg5.

The game transposed to Petrosyan's system. In the 1960s it was played often.

8. ... h6
9. Bh4 g5
10. Bg3 Nh5
11. 0-0 Nf4
12. Ne1?!

This position had been seen before by *Nezh* in his *1961* game with *Yudovich.* In it he obtained the advantage after 12... Nxe2† 13. Qxe2 f5! 14. exf5 Nf6 15. f3 Bxf5 16. Ne4 followed by g5-g4. One of the reasons for Black's success was the bad placement of the white Knight on e1. That's why 12. Nd2 would have been better, to allow the Knight control of e4.

12. ... f5
13. exf5 Nxe2†
14. Qxe2 Nf6
15. Nf3

After 15. f3 the position from the *Yudovich—Nezhmetdinov* game would emerge.

15. ... Bxf5
16. Nd2

After losing two tempi the white Knight reached the desired square.

16. ... Qe8
17. Nde4 Qg6

The first time this plan, the transferring of the Queen to g6, was used was by *Fischer* against *Wexler, Mar del Plata, 1960.*

18. f3 Nh5

Black can play comfortably and he leisurely prepared his attack, as White's counterplay on the queenside doesn't amount to anything.

19. c5 Nf4
20. Qc4 Rf7
21. a4 h5
22. a5 g4
23. fxg4 Bxg4
24. h4

He had to defend against the threat of 24... h4 25. Bxh4 Be2. 24. Rf2 wouldn't have helped because 24... h4 25. Bxh4 Nh3† 26. gxh3 Be2† 27. Rg2 Qxg2† 28.

Kxg2 Bxc4.

24. ... Bf5
25. Rae1 Bh6
26. a6 b6
27. b4 Raf8
28. Kh2 Rg7
29. Rf3?

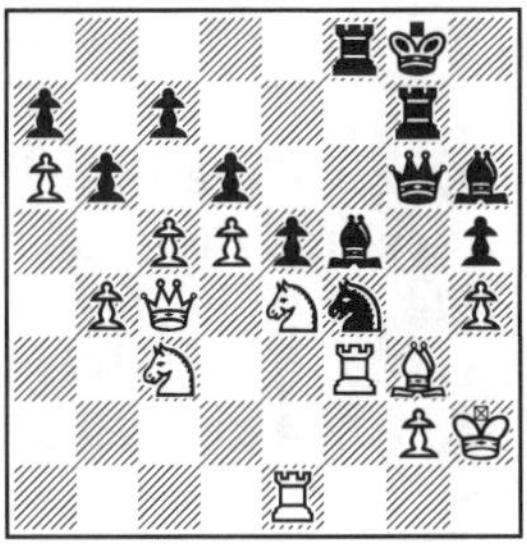

Better was 29. Qa2, but White can't hold on for long.

29. ... Nxg2!

When one has such a big advantage, there must be a combination.

30. Kxg2

30. Rxf5 Qxf5 31. Kxg2 Qf3† 32. Kh2 Bf4 33. Rg1 Rg4 wouldn't have helped either.

30. ... Bh3†
31. Kf2 Rxf3†
32. Kxf3 Qf5†
33. Ke2 Rxg3!
34. Kd1

It was over, as 34. Nxg3 failed because of 34... Bg4†.

34. ... Rg2
35. Rf1 Bg4†
36. Ke1 Bd2†
37. Nxd2 Qc2
38. Nce4 Qd1#!

(0-1).

48.

J. Ruchkin—Super Nezh

E 63

23rd Russian ch.

Kazan 1964

1. Nf3 Nf6 2. c4 g6 3. g3 Bg7 4. Bg2 0-0 5. 0-0 d6 6. d4 Nc6 7. Nc3 Rb8 8. h3 a6 9. Be3 b5 10. Nd2 Bd7 11. cxb5 axb5 12. d5 Ne5 13. b4.

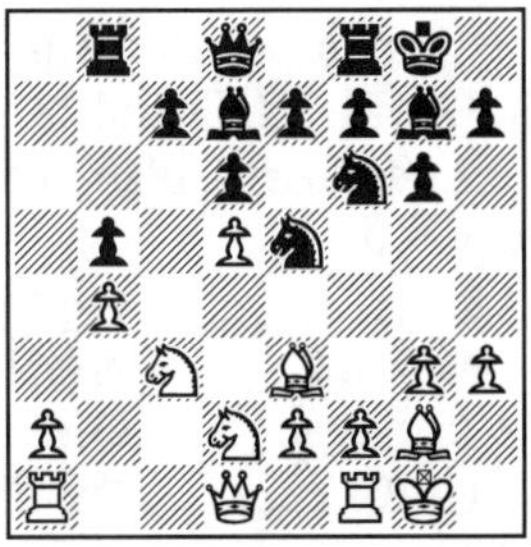

Nezh plays his King's Indian Defense with purpose and so began active play:

13. ... Qc8!
14. g4?!

White was obliged to weaken his King's guard, as they found that the planned 14. Kh2 didn't work because of 14... Neg4†! 15. hxg4 [15. Kg1 Nxe3 16. fxe3 Bxh3] Nxg4† 16. Kg1 Nxe3 and 17... Bxc3. If it was necessary to weaken his position, 14. h4 should have been chosen. On 14... Neg4 [or 14... Nfg4] the response could have been 15. Ba7! Ra8 16. Bd4.

14. ... h5!
15. g5

Worse was 15. gxh5 because of 15... Bxh3. If 15. f4, then it would be strong to take twice by the Knights on g4, but then even 15. f3 hxg4 16. hxg4 Nexg4! would not help White.

15. ... Bxh3!

The sacrifice of the piece came from the previous play.

16. Bxh3

Not 16. gxf6? because of 16... Qg4 with mate next.

16. ... Qxh3
17. gxf6 exf6
18. f3?

Not the best defense, and after this Black quickly progressed. Black's task would have been made more difficult by 18. Nf3!. In that event a pawn attack would have ensued: 18... f5 19. Rc1 g5! and a taking on g5 would have led to the loss of an extra piece: 20. Bxg5 Qg4† 21. Kh1 Nxf3 and 22... Qxg5. At the same time it's also bad not to take the pawn.

18. ... Qg3†
19. Kh1 Ng4!
20. fxg4 Qh3†
21. Kg1 Qxe3†
22. Kg2 hxg4!

Taking the Knight wasn't clear: 22... Qxc3 23. gxh5.

23. Rf2 f5
24. Nf1

Now Black can take the Knight.

24. ... Qxc3

and Black won easily after **25. Rb1 Qc4 26. e3 Qe4† 27. Kg1 Be5 28. Rb3 Kg7 29. Qd3 g3 30. Rc2 Qh4 31. Qe2 Rh8 32. Qf3 Rh5 33. a3 Rbh8 34. Rd2 Qh1† 35. Qxh1 Rxh1† 36. Kg2 R8h2† (0-1).**

49.

V. Ciocaltea—Super Nezh

C 59

Bucharest 1954

1. e4 e5 2. Nf3 Nc6 3. Bc4 Nf6 4. Ng5 d5 5. exd5 Na5 6. Bb5† c6 7. dxc6 bxc6 8. Be2 h6 9. Nf3 e4 10. Ne5 Qc7 11. Ng4?!.

A seldom seen move, though known in the last century. The usual continuations 11. f4, or 11. d4, are better.

11. ... Bxg4
12. Bxg4 Bc5
13. Be2

A tempo would be lost if 13. 0-0?, then 13... h5! 14. Be2 Ng4, and White would be under attack.

13. ... Rd8
14. c3 Nb7
15. 0-0 h5!

It was clear that an attempt to lead his opponent into an unknown line boomerangs—White has had a catastrophic struggle in his play and now he can't stop the attack.

16. d4 exd3
17. Bxd3 Ng4
18. Qe2† Kf8!

Castling was of no importance for Black—the Rook on h8 had become an attacking piece by doing nothing.

19. g3 Qd7
20. Be4 h4
21. Bf4?

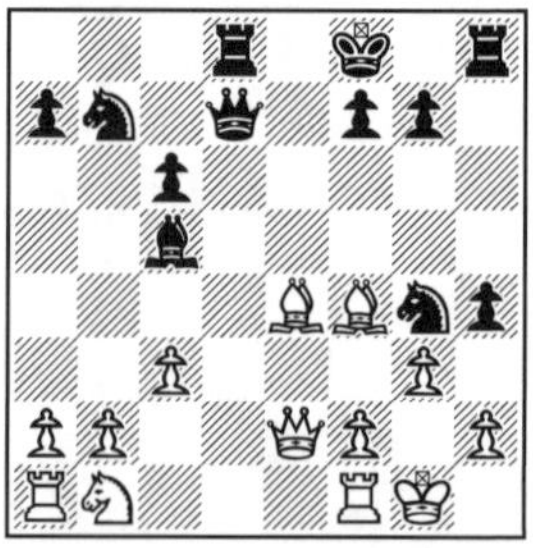

This led to White's immediate defeat. White would also lose in an absurd way after 21. Bxc6? Qxc6 22. Qxg4 h3!.

Obligatory should have been 21. Bg2, though after 21... hxg3 22. hxg3 Qf5 White had no chance to defend against the attack.

21. ... Nxh2!

22. Re1

After 22. Kxh2 hxg3† White would have to give up: 23. Kg1 Qh3 24. Bxg3 Qxg3†.

22. ... Ng4
23. Bf3 Nxf2
24. Be3 hxg3
25. Bxc5† Nxc5
26. Bxc6 Nh3†
27. Kf1 Qf5†

White surrendered **(0-1)** because of the variant 28. Bf3 g2†! 29. Qxg2 Rd3 30. Nd2 Rxd2!.

The 1954 USSR Spartak Team Champions
Tigran Petrosian flanked by Nina Voitsuk and arbiter Yu. Karakhan
In the back, from right to left masters:
S. Furman, V. Simagin, R. Nezhmetdinov, R. Holmov, and I. Lipnitsky

Russian ch. / Moscow/Gorki??? 1950

	Players	1	2	3	4	5	6	7	8	9	10	11	12	13	Points	Place
1	Nezhmetdinov	•	■	▒		▒	▒	■	■		■	■	■	▒	8	1
2	Aronin		•	▒	■	■	■	▒			■	■	▒	■	7.5	2-4
3	Boleslavsky	▒	▒	•	▒	▒	▒	▒	■	▒		■	■	■	7.5	2-4
4	Novotyelnov	■		▒	•	■			▒	■	■	■	▒	■	7.5	2-4
5	Zagorovsky	▒		▒		•	▒	■	■	■	■		▒	■	7	5-6
6	Ilivitsky	▒		▒	■	▒	•	■		■	■		▒	■	7	5-6
7	Kamyshov		▒	▒	■			•		■	■	▒	■	■	6.5	7
8	Dubinin		■		▒		■	■	•	▒			■	■	6	8-9
9	Kan	■	■	▒					▒	•		■	■	■	6	8-9
10	Shaposhnikov			■					■	■	•	■	▒	■	5.5	10
11	Kavtorin					■	■	▒	■			•		■	4.5	11
12	Grechkin		▒		▒	▒	▒				▒	■	•		3.5	12
13	Tetelbaum	▒											■	•	1.5	13
		1	2	3	4	5	6	7	8	9	10	11	12	13		

Semi-finals, 18th USSR ch. / Gorki 1950

	Players	1	2	3	4	5	6	7	8	9	10	11	12	13	14	15	16	Points	Place
1	Aronin	•	■	▒	■	▒	■	■	▒			■	▒	■	■	▒	■	10.5	1
2	Lyubinsky		•	■			▒	▒	▒	▒	■	■	■	■	■	■	■	10	2-3
3	Petrosyan	▒		•		■	▒	▒	■	■		▒	■	■	■	■	■	10	2-3
4	Furman		■	■	•	▒			■	▒	▒	■	■	■	■	▒	▒	9.5	4
5	Nezhmetdinov	▒	■		▒	•	■	▒	▒	■	▒	▒	■	▒	▒		■	9	5-6
6	Ufimtsev		▒	▒	■		•	▒	▒		■	▒	■	▒	■	■	■	9	5-6
7	Konstantinov		▒	▒	■	▒	▒	•	■		▒	■	■	▒	▒	▒	▒	8.5	7
8	Dubinin	▒	▒			▒	▒		•	■	▒		■	▒	▒	■	■	7.5	8
9	Levenfish	■	▒		▒		■	■		•		■		▒		■	▒	7	9-10
10	Soloviev	■		■	▒	▒		▒	▒	■	•	▒	▒	▒	▒			7	9-10
11	Bivshev			▒		▒	▒		■		▒	•	▒	▒	▒	■	■	6.5	11
12	Makarov	▒								■	▒	▒	•	■	■		■	5.5	12-13
13	Ratner					▒	▒	▒	▒	▒	▒	▒		•	▒	▒	■	5.5	12-13
14	Sidorov					▒		▒	▒	■	▒	▒		▒	•	■		5	14-15
15	Estrin	▒			▒	■		▒			■		■	▒		•		5	14-15
16	Guldin				▒			▒		▒	■				■	■	•	4.5	16
		1	2	3	4	5	6	7	8	9	10	11	12	13	14	15	16		

5

Defense and Counterattack

Nezh didn't like to defend, namely, he couldn't stand positions in which one had to carry out a passive, heavy defense. His play was weaker in such contests. Being aware of this, most rivals (not even the leading ones) often succeeded by offering him long, arduous play, aimed at pressuring Nezh's position.

Obliged to defend, Nezh was always on the lookout for counterplay, or a tactical subtlety, a sudden turnover. When he found it, he was truly inspired and played with great energy.

50.

G. Medvedev—Super Nezh

Kazan 1934

The preliminary moves are not known.

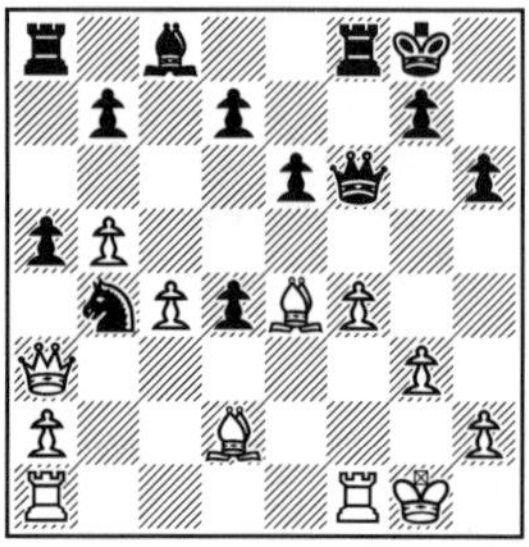

It seems that the opening was profitable for White: the pawns clearly outstripped Black by their advances. The threat of 19. Bb4 was on, and 18... Qe7 19. Rab1 would not have helped. However, Black has a hidden resource:

18. ... d5!

which changed the estimation of the position.

19. Bxb4?

Not having seen the danger, White decided to take the material. Stronger was 19. cxd5. I'm sure that what Nezh had in mind was not the recommendations of the commentators, namely 19... Nxd5 and after 20. f5! White would still hold on to his threats. Instead he would have seen 19... exd5!. Now White was obliged to play 20. Bxb4, and after 20... axb4 [Worse was 20... dxe4 21. Bxf8 Qxf8 22. Qb3† Qf7 (bad was 22... Kh8 because of 23. Qd5 with the taking of one of the pawns) 23. f5! b6 24. Rac1, and Black would not have been able to keep the pair of center pawns.] 21. Bxd5† Be6 and Black would have had active play. 22. Bxe6† Qxe6 23. Qxb4 Qe3†, or 22. Qb3 Bxd5 23. Qxd5† Kh8 24. Qxb7 Rfd8.

19. ... axb4

20. Qxa8 dxe4

21. Qa4

Better was 21. Qa7, keeping control over the a7-g1 diagonal.

21. ... d3

22. Qxb4 Qd4†

23. Kg2 e3

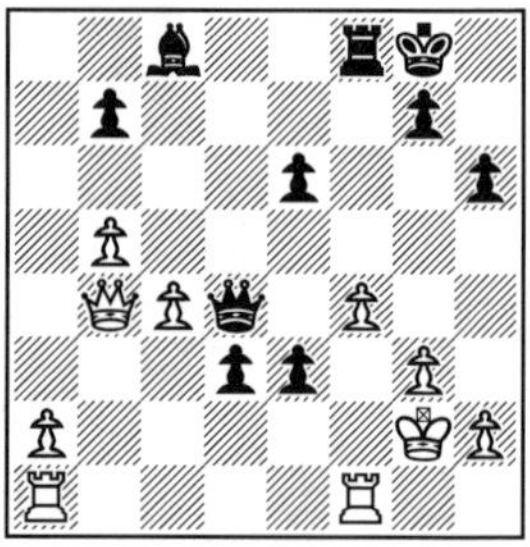

It's difficult for Rooks to fight against an advanced pair of pawns. This position was an ample illustration. Inspite of Black's poor development, he had an easy win due to the dangerous pawns.

24. Qe1 Qe4†

25. Rf3 e2

26. Qd2 Rd8

27. Re1 e5

28. Kf2

The four strongest pieces stand near the pawns, but were helpless to counteract them.

28. ... Bg4

29. Re3 Qd4

30. fxe5 Rf8†

31. Kg2 Rf1!

32. R3xe2

Or 32. Rxf1 Bh3† followed by 33... exf1=Q† or 32. R1xe2 Bxe2 33. Rxe2 Qg1† and then 34. Kh3 dxe2.

32. ... Qg1#!

(0-1).

51.

L. Aronin—Super Nezh

A 53

7th Russian ch.

Kuibyshev 1947

1. d4 Nf6 2. c4 d6 3. Nc3 e5 4. e4 c6.

Concerning 4... exd4, see Game 1.

5. Nge2 Nbd7

6. d5?!

Releasing the tension in the center, White let Nezh finish his development without trouble. Aronin planned a setup similar to Sämisch's system and he went this way.

6. ... cxd5

7. cxd5 g6

8. f3 Bg7

9. Be3 0-0

10. Qd2 Nc5

11. b4?

Having an undeveloped queenside, White started the attack on the a7- and d6-pawns.

> **In the beginning this errant tactic seems to achieve it's goal, but then there's my revenge—active black pieces attack his rash play, and White is doomed.**
>
> *R.N.*

Instead of this hasty attack how should White have moved his King away from the center? For this he should have chosen between 11. 0-0-0 and 11. g3 with the further Bg2 and 0-0.

11. ... Ncd7

12. Nb5 Nb6

13. Nec3 Nh5!

Paying no particular attention to the activity of his opponent, Black calmly continued with his play. This counterplay was typical for such a structure, but at the same time was very effective because of the backwardness and lack of development of White's pieces, especially the insecure position of the King. 13... a6 was a loss of time because of 14. Qf2.

14. Qf2 f5

15. Nxa7 Nd7

16. Nab5

The threat of 16... Rxa7 and 17... b6 maked White move his Knight away. Nezh recommended 16. Qd2, trying to neutralize the pressure on the f-file, but it would have hardly helped.

16. ... fxe4

17. Nxe4 Ndf6

18. Nbxd6

In other continuations Black would have had an increasing initiative: 18. Qh4 Nf4!; 18. Nexd6 e4!.

18. ... Nxe4

19. Nxe4 Bf5

20. Bd3 Ra3!

White wanted to castle, but Black's constant prickliness would not have let him do that.

It was interesting that Black used threats typical of King's Indian positions for the entire game.

21. Bc2 Bxe4

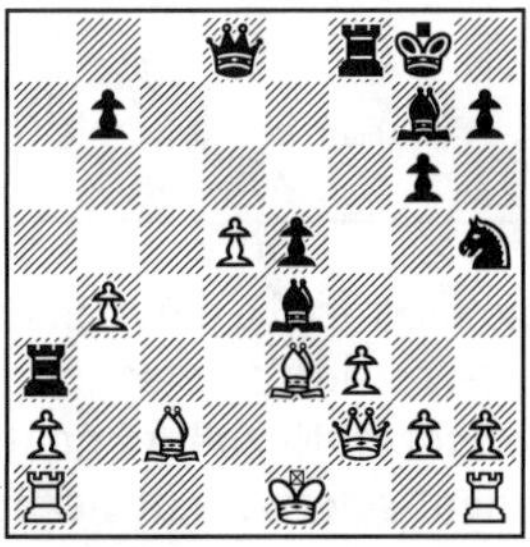

22. Bb6

On 22. Bxe4 Nezh gave the following pretty line: 22... Nf6 23. Qe2 Nxe4 24. fxe4 Qh4† 25. Bf2 Rxf2! 26. Qxf2

Qxe4† 27. Kf1 Ra8! with a decisive attack. It was really true, for example: 28. Re1 Qc4† 29. Qe2 Rf8† 30. Kg1 Qd4† 31. Qe3 e4!, and there was no protection from 32... Qxe3† and 33... Bd4.

22. ... Qc8
23. Rc1 Qc3†
24. Qd2 Qxd2†
25. Kxd2 Bh6†

White resigned **(0-1).**

52.

M. Shishov—Super Nezh

C 91

USSR Team ch.

Leningrad 1953

1. e4 e5 2. Nf3 Nc6 3. Bb5 a6 4. Ba4 Nf6 5. 0-0 Be7 6. Re1 b5 7. Bb3 0-0 8. c3 d6 9. d4 Bg4 10. h3 Bxf3 11. Qxf3 exd4 12. Qd1 dxc3 13. Nxc3 Na5 14. Bc2 c5 15. f4 Nc6 16. Be3 Rc8 17. Kh2 Re8 18. a3 Bf8 19. Bf2 g6 20. g4.

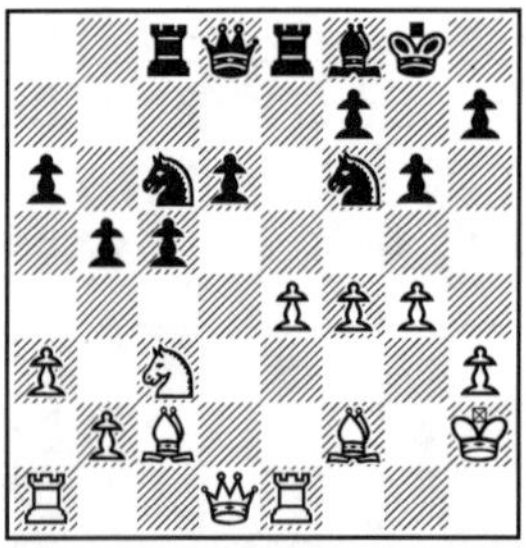

Having sacrificed a pawn in the opening, White couldn't get enough compensation for it. Nezh had neutralized his opponent's activity by accurate defense, and from this point on you will see how he activated his play.

20. ... Nd4!
21. Bxd4

In fact, this was forced. On 21. Bd3 Black would have had both an extra pawn and a very fine position.

21. ... cxd4
22. Qxd4 Nxg4†!
23. Kg2

After 23. hxg4 Qh4† 24. Kg2 Qxg4† 25. Kf1 Qxf4† Black had three pawns for the piece, and a good deal of various opportunities to press on with the attack.

23. ... Qh4
24. Bb3 Bg7
25. e5

The end would be nigh if 25. Qd2 Bxc3 26. bxc3 Rxc3!.

25. ... Nxe5
26. Qe4 Nd3!

Black had no desire to win like an inchworm with 26... Nc4 27. Qxe8† Rxe8 28. Rxe8† Bf8 29. Bxc4 bxc4 30. Nd5. Nezh began complicating matters, matters which had to be carefully calculated.

27. Bxf7†! Kf8!!

This retreat should have been foreseen since after 27... Kxf7 28. Qd5† Kf8 29. Qxd6† Kg8 30. Qd5† Kh8 31. Rxe8† Rxe8 32. Qxd3 Qxf4 Black would only get one extra pawn and there are some problems concerning the use of it.

28. Bxe8 Nxf4†!
29. Kf3

White had few choices. In the endgame after 29. Qxf4† Qxf4 30. Rf1 Qxf1† 31. Rxf1† Kxe8 White would be absolutely hopeless.

He could have thought over 29. Kf1 [on 29. Kg1 there is 29... Bd4†!] Qxh3† 30. Kf2 Nd3† 31. Ke2 Nxe1 32. Rxe1 [on 32. Bc6 good enough is 32... Qd3†!] Rxe8 33. Rf1† Qxf1†.

29. ... Rc4!

The move that made everything clear. White was obliged to give up his Queen.

30. Bd7 Rxe4

31. Rxe4 Be5
32. Nd5 Qd8
33. Nxf4 Qxd7
34. h4 Qf7
35. Rae1 Kg7
36. b4 Qf5
37. Rg1 d5
38. Rxe5 Qxe5
39. Rg5 Qe4†
40. Kg3 d4
41. h5 d3
42. hxg6 hxg6

White surrendered **(0-1).**

53.

Super Nezh—L. Aronin

B 50

13th Russian ch.

Saratov 1953

1. e4 c5 2. Nf3 d6 3. g3 Nc6 4. Bg2 Bg4.

A rare instance in Nezh's practice—he chooses a continuation which is far removed from the regular systems of the Sicilian Defense. Perhaps, this decision was made for psychological reasons.

5. h3 Bh5

Preferable is 5... Bxf3.

6. d3 e6
7. Nc3 Be7
8. 0-0 Bf6?!

It's not clear why Aronin liked this maneuver better than the normal 8... Nf6.

9. Ne2 Bxf3

This is the consequence of Black's previous move. The point here is that the move 9... Nge7 is dangerous. 10. g4 Bg6 11. g5 Be5 12. Nh4 d5 13. f4 Bc7 14. f5. So, Black had lost a tempo, though it was not so important.

10. Bxf3 Nge7
11. Bg2 d5
12. exd5?!

The tension in the center was gone and this was good for Black. Perhaps White didn't want to exchange Queens: 12. f4 dxe4 13. dxe4 Qxd1 14. Rxd1, but here White's chances were better. At this point the position of the Bishop on f6 could have been justified.

12. ... Nxd5
13. Nf4 Nxf4
14. Bxf4 Qd7
15. c3?!

White lessened the activity of the black pieces, but created a weak pawn. Instead, it would have been better to play 15. Rb1, offered later by Nezh, followed by a2-a3 and b2-b4. This plan would underscore the importance of the possession of the two Bishops.

15. ... 0-0
16. Qa4 Rac8
17. Rad1 Rfd8
18. Rfe1 b6
19. Qa6!?

The idea of this maneuver was to discourage the transfer of the Knight via e7 to d5. On 19... Ne7, 20. Bb7 would have followed.

19. ... g5?

Black's position was good, but not good enough to allow such a weakening. It wasn't worth paying much attention to 19... e5? 20. Bxc6 Rxc6 21. Bxe5 Bxe5 22. Rxe5 Qxh3 23. Rde1! Rf8 24. Qb7 with White still having had the advantage. That's why there was no point to sudden movements. 19... h6 or 19... Re8 would have been better.

20. Bc1 Na5

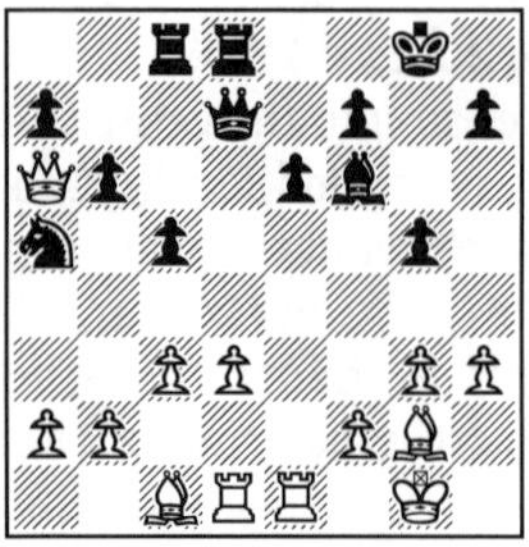

21. d4!

An excellent sacrifice of a pawn. The idea was to have opened the way for the Queen to the kingside which had been weakened voluntarily by Black.

21. ... cxd4
22. Qe2 h6

Nezh gave: 22... Qe7 23. Qh5! dxc3 24. Be4 cxb2 25. Bxg5!.

23. Qh5 Kg7
24. h4 Qe7
25. cxd4 Nc4
26. b3 Nd6
27. d5 e5

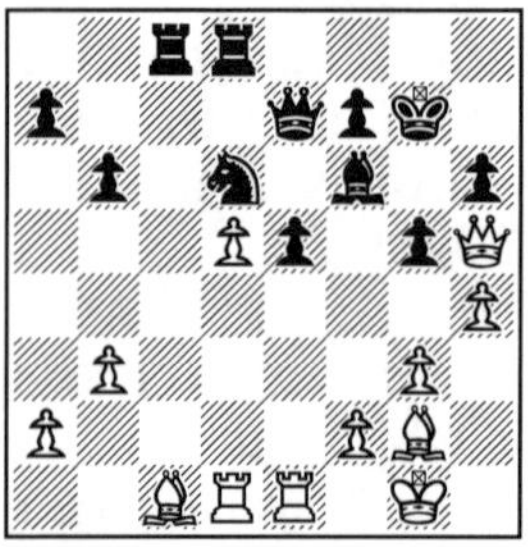

28. f4!!

This explosive move resolved everything. The opening of the King's position was inevitable.

28. ... gxf4
29. Bxf4 Rh8
30. Rxe5! Qd7

30... Bxe5 was bad because of 31. Qxe5†!.

31. Re2 Rh7?

Time trouble, but Black was still down a pawn and under strong pressure.

32. Bxd6

Black resigned **(1-0)**, because 32... Qxd6 would have been stopped by 33. Qg4†.

54.

Super Nezh—E. Geller
A 07
21st USSR ch.
Kiev 1954

1. Nf3.

A rare beginning in Nezh's praxis. In this game his choice can be explained by his tournament position. It was the 4th round and his debut in the first three rounds was modest: a loss in the first round then two draws. Taking into account that the tournament length was considerable (19 rounds), Nezh decided to play with restraint and to conserve his strength in this game. Did he succeed in this task against one of the world's greatest openings theorists?

1. ... Nf6
2. g3 d5
3. Bg2 Bf5
4. 0-0 e6
5. d3 Be7
6. Nc3

White was eager to play e2-e4. Usually White plays for this by 6. Nbd2, then Qe1 and only then e2-e4. Maybe even 6. Qe1!?.

6. ... 0-0
7. Nh4 Bg4
8. h3 Bh5
9. g4 Bg6
10. Nxg6

The plan of forcing the retreat of the Bishop with its ultimate exchange by the Knight was used often by Chigorin, though, only when he had the black pieces. Nezh wasn't afraid of weakening his King's position as a result of the g-pawn move.

10. ... hxg6
11. e4 dxe4
12. Nxe4 c6
13. c3?!

13. Bf4 was preferable.

13. ... Nbd7
14. Qe2 Nxe4
15. Bxe4 Bd6!

An unexpected sacrifice of a pawn for the initiative.

16. Bxg6?

The pawn shouldn't have been taken, as Black would have gotten a good compensation for it. 16. d4 would have been good.

16. ... Qh4
17. Kg2 Ne5
18. Be4 f5!
19. Bf3 Rf6
20. d4 Nxg4!

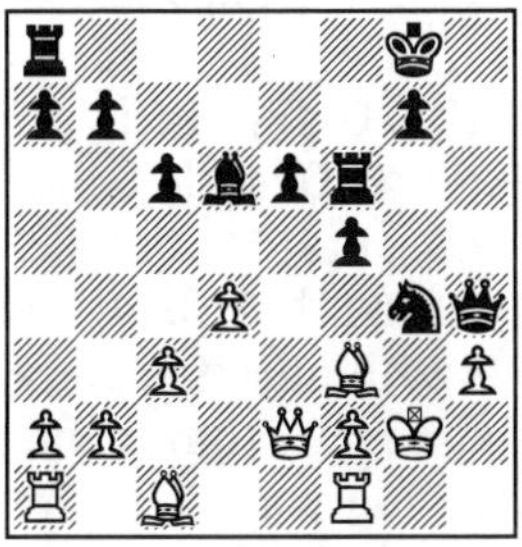

Black was very energetic in this part of the game and now White must play accurately or he will be swatted like a fly.

21. Rh1!

Worse would have been 21. Bxg4 because of 21... Rg6!.

21. ... Nh6
22. Kf1 Nf7
23. Be3 Re8
24. Rd1 f4?

Black had two ways to strengthen his position:

A. 24... g6 [recommended by Nezh], then Kg7 would have created threats on the h-file;

B. To play 24... e5!? at once. 25. dxe5 Nxe5 and Black's threats on the e- and f-files would have quickly become dangerous.

Problems with the game move: the f-file would remain closed, and the black Queen would have lost its influence in the center.

25. Bc1 e5
26. dxe5 Rxe5?!

26... Nxe5 was stronger since it would not have let the white Queen get active.

27. Qc4 Bc5
28. Rh2 b5

It was worth thinking about 28... g6, to have had a shelter on g7 for the King.

29. Rd8† Bf8
30. Qb3 Rfe6
31. Rd1 Rg6
32. Rd7 Be7
33. Bd2

After Black's inaccurate 24th and 26th moves White had managed to counterattack and the tension of the fight had increased considerably. A calm move could not have been made though Nezh had dreamed about it. At that moment both players were into *zeitnot*.

33. ... a5
34. a4 bxa4

Black shouldn't take on a4 since the pawns on the queenside would have become weak.

35. Qxa4 Reg5
36. Qb3 Rg1†
37. Ke2 Qf6
38. Rd4 c5
39. Qb8†

39. Rxf4 would have been better at

once because it would have preserved the pin of the Knight on f7.

39. ... Kh7
40. Rxf4 Qa6†
41. c4 Bd6?

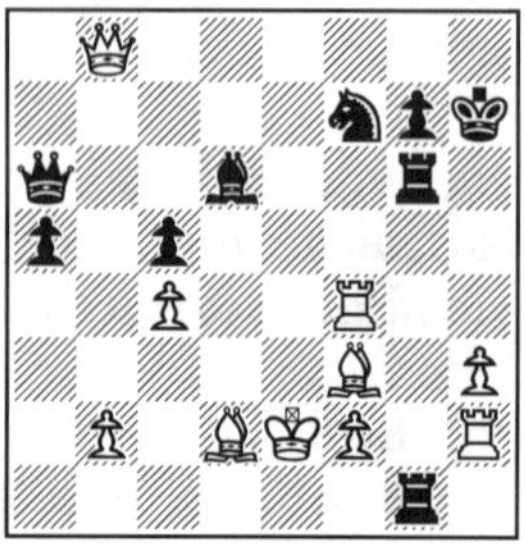

Time trouble was over, but Black automatically made one more move, and as so often happens, a bad one. Moreover it was a move that brought defeat! Black lost the game because he lost control over h4. After the right move, 41... Bg5, the position remained tense and a good deal of interesting fight would have remained after 42. Be4. For example: 42... Qxc4† 43. Bd3 Bxf4! 44. Qxf4 Qxf4 45. Bxf4 Kg8 46. Bxg6 Rxg6 47. Kd3 and the endgame would have been in White's favor, but it would have been scarcely a winning one.

After 41... Bd6 the game was adjourned. The sealed move was clear:

42. Rh4†

It turned out during the analysis after the game that Black had placed himself under an irresistible attack.

42. ... Nh6

The most interesting of all the variations could have been: 42... Rh6 43. Be4† g6 [43... Rgg6 44. Rxh6† Nxh6 45. Bxg6† Kxg6 46. Rg2† Kh7 47. Qb5, and White would have won without any trouble.] 44. Qe8! Qxc4† 45. Bd3 Qb3 [45... Qxh4 46. Qxf7† Kh8 47. Bc3†; 45... Qd5 46. Bxh6] 46. Rh1! [Mikenas & Ragozin offered 46. Bc2! Qd5 47. Bxh6 (47. Rh1 Rxh1 48. Rxh6† Nxh6 49. Qxg6† Kh8), as a possible way to win faster.] Qd1† [46... Rxh1 47. Rxh6† Nxh6 and 48. Qxg6†. If 46... Rxh4, then an easy 47. Rxg1] 47. Ke3.

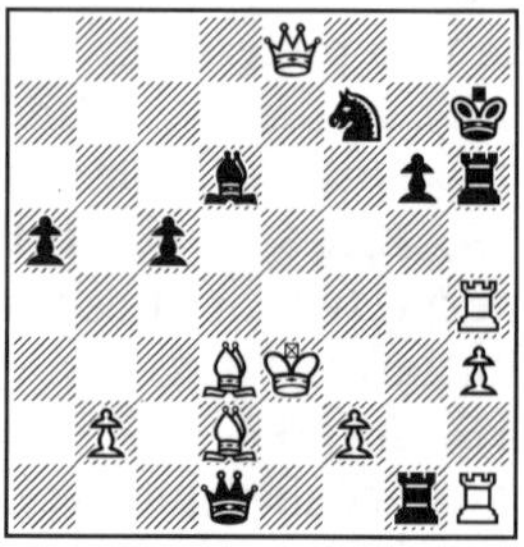

(Analysis after 47. Ke3)

This position looked more like the product of a chess composer than a position in a tournament game between masters. Here were, for example, variations mentioned by Nezh: 47... Ne5 48. Rxh6† Kxh6 49. Qh8† Kg5 50. Rxg1† Qxg1 51. Ke4#!; or 47... Ng5 48. Qxg6†; or 47... Rxh4 48. Qxf7† Kh6 [48... Kh8 49. Qf6†] 49. Rxg1 Qxg1 [49... Rxh3† 50. Ke4†!, or 49... Bf4† 50. Qxf4!] 50. Kf3†! Bf4 51. Bxf4† Rxf4† 52. Qxf4†, and White remained with an extra piece. It was interesting to note that in many lines the white King was an active player in the execution of his opponent.

43. Qe8 Qa7

The Rook was untouchable: 43... Bxh2 44. Bd5!.

44. Be4 Qe7
45. Qxe7 Bxe7
46. Rg4!

Black gave up **(1-0).**

On 46... Nxg4 the victory would have been easy: 47. hxg4† Bh4 [47... Kg8 48. Bd5† with mate looming.] 48. Rxh4† Kg8 49. Bxg6.

55.

A. Lilienthal—Super Nezh

A 56

21st USSR ch.

Kiev 1954

1. d4 Nf6 2. c4 c5 3. d5 d6 4. Nc3 g6 5. e4 Bg7 6. Bd3 0-0 7. Nge2 Nbd7 8. Ng3 e6 9. dxe6!?.

White had shown some of his hand: to attack immediately on the kingside. However, in the normal system 9. 0-0 exd5 10. cxd5, it would have been hard for him to rely upon his advantage as the position of the Knight on g3 and the Bishop on d3 wouldn't have worked well with the existing pawn structure.

9. ...	**fxe6**
10. h4!	

It was the beginning of a flank attack, which could have been enough provided Black hadn't yet created a counterstrike in the center.

10. ...	**Ne5**
11. Be2	**a6**
12. h5	**Qe7**
13. hxg6	**hxg6**
14. Bg5	**b5!?**

Black was in a hurry to create counterplay as his opponent had managed to open the h-file. This counterattack would be effective, if and only if, when the center pawns were moved forward, Black would sacrifice a pawn on the wing. However there was an alternative, 14... Nf7, with the aim to escape, whether the Bishop retreated or White played 15. Qd2.

15. cxb5	**axb5**
16. Nxb5	

16. Bxb5 might be preferred for creating troubles for Black when he counterattacked with d7-d5 in the center, but White had his own plan.

16. ...	**Nf7**
17. Qd2	**d5**
18. exd5	**exd5**
19. 0-0	

It seems like there was a contradiction here—White had opened the h-file and then moved the Rook away from it. Actually, nothing could be done on that file. Simultaneously the center would get opened and on the queenside the King would have had nothing to do.

19. ...	**Bb7**
20. a4!	

This had been done for two reasons: to overprotect the Knight and to open an outlet for the a-Rook and to transfer it to the kingside.

20. ...	**Qd7**
21. Bxf6	

White was eager to start a tactical operation which had as its aim to leave the black King without an escort. Black managed, in an unimaginable way, to counteract the pressure. 21. Ra3 was worth attention.

21. ...	**Bxf6**
22. Qc2	**Kg7**

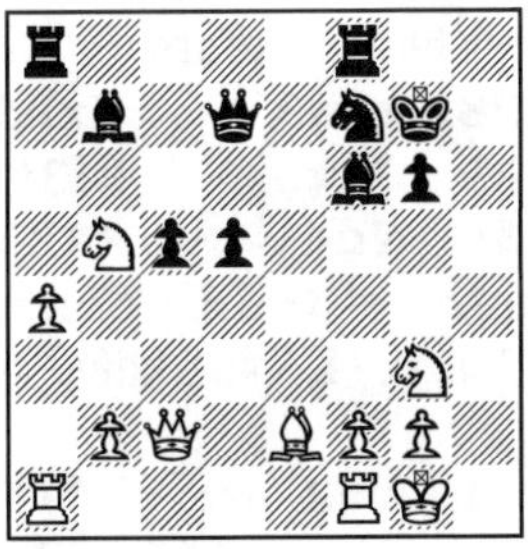

23. Bh5!?

Lilienthal was very resourceful. If he had estimated the consequences of his attack more definitely, he would have chosen the simple 23. Qxc5, and it would not be easy for Black to prove he had compensation for the pawn.

23. ...	**Nh8**

24. Ra3 Be5
25. Bxg6?

White was carrying out his plan, but it would have been better to include one more Rook—25. Re1, and thereby preserve good chances to do better.

25. ... Nxg6
26. Nh5† Kh6
27. Rh3?

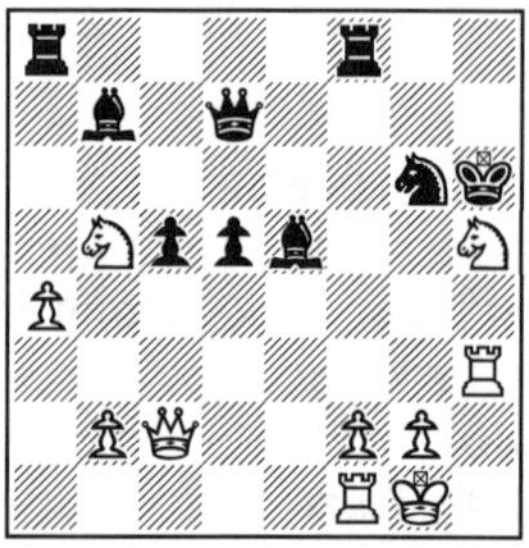

27. ... Qxh3!

This refuted White's attack. Moreover, Black proceeded to create active counterplay. Right would have been 27. Qe2 Qf5, and only now 28. Rh3 d4 29. Ng3† Qxh3 30. gxh3 Rf3.

In this case [compared to the continuation in the game] White would have kept both Knights.

28. gxh3 Kxh5
29. Qxc5 Rf3!
30. Nd4 Rxh3

The threat of 31... Bh2† 32. Kg2 Nf4† 33. Kh1 Bg1†! 34. Kxg1 Rg8# was created.

31. Ne2 Nf4

On 32. Ng3† there was 32... Rxg3† 33. fxg3 Bd4† 34. Qxd4 Ne2† and 35... Nxd4.

32. Nxf4† Bxf4
33. Kg2 Rc8!

The concluding point, after which White resigned **(0-1).**

The idea of the move was, that if instead 33... Rg8† 34. Kxh3 Bc8† 35. Qxc8 Rxc8, then White could still prolong the game after 36. Rd1 Rd8 37. a5.

Now, after the text move, White would have been obliged to take the pressure off the c8-square and lose at once.

56.

Super Nezh—M. Filip

C 64

Bucharest 1954

1. e4 e5 2. Nf3 Nc6 3. Bb5 Bc5 4. 0-0 Nd4 5. Nxd4 Bxd4 6. c3 Bb6 7. d4 c6 8. Bc4 d6 9. a4 Nf6 10. dxe5 dxe5 11. Qxd8† Bxd8 12. Re1 0-0 13. Nd2 Bc7 14. h3 Rd8 15. Nf3 h6 16. g4 g5 17. Kg2 Be6 18. Bxe6 fxe6 19. Nd2 a5 20. f3 Rd3 21. Rh1 Kg7 22. h4 Nh7 23. hxg5 hxg5 24. Kf2 Bb6† 25. Ke2 Re3† 26. Kd1 Rd8 27. Re1 Rxf3 28. Re2 Rf4 29. Kc2 Rxg4.

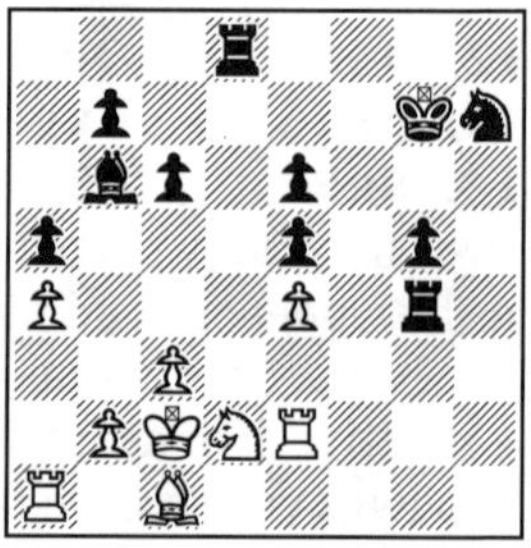

White's position looked absolutely hopeless. His pieces were not developed, two pawns have been lost, and his opponent had a passed pawn. Nezh refused to lose his optimism.

30. Ra3 Bc5?

Black was in a good mood and he didn't believe that his opponent had any counterplay. If he had it together, he would have played 30... Bc7, protecting the e5-pawn and the whole complex of black squares on the queenside.

31. Rb3 b5

32. Nf3

Of course 32. axb5 was unplayable because of 32... a4!.

32. ... Kf6

33. c4! b4

Damsky didn't like this "normal" move and offered the sharper 33... bxc4, and he agreed that the weakening of his pawn structure for the sake of activity was good: 34. Rb7 Rd3, but after 35. Nd2! Rh3 [Black's main trouble was not the bad pawns, but the very poor position of his Knight.] 36. Nxc4 Bd4 37. Nxa5 Black was placed in a very difficult situation.

34. Rh2 Nf8

This Knight was of no use, but it still caused enough problems. 34... Rd7 wouldn't have worked because of 35. Rh6† Kg7 36. Rxe6, which would have won the pawns back and preserved the advantage. Nezh gave an interesting variation: 34... Rxe4 35. Rxh7 Rxc4† 36. Kb1 Rd1 37. Rf7†! Kxf7 38. Nxe5† and 39. Nxc4 would be victory at last. By the way, the motif with the Knight fork on e5 could have been seen in other lines.

35. Nxg5!

A nice shot. White could find resources for a mating attack even in the endgame. Tactical proof: 35... Rxg5 36. Rf3† Kg6 37. Bxg5 Kxg5 38. Rg2† Kh4 39. Rf1 Kh3 40. Rg8 Kh2 41. Rf6 with the inevitable mate.

35. ... Kg6?

On 35... Ng6 Nezh had prepared the following: 36. Rh6! Rg2† 37. Kb1 Rd1 38. Rf3† Kg7 39. Rf7†! with mate in two. If instead of 37... Rd1, stronger would have been 37... Rxg5 38. Rf3† Rf5! 39. exf5 exf5. If 40. Rg3 Rg8 41. Bg5† Kf7 White's attack would have exhausted itself, and the pair of pawns in the center would compensate for the loss of material very nicely. This was exactly how Filip had to play. Having lost this opportunity, he put himself in a lost position.

36. Rbh3 b3†

37. Kxb3 Rd1

Having noticed the danger, Black tried to create counterthreats, but he could not change the game to his advantage.

38. Nf3 Bd4

38... Rxc1 wouldn't have worked because of 39. Nxe5† Kg5 40. Rh5† Kf4 41. Nxg4 and the Bishop on c5 would "hang." 38... Rxe4 was also bad: 39. Rh6† Kf5 40. R2h5† Kg4 41. Nxe5†.

39. Kc2 Rf1

40. Be3!

One more tactical prick which aimed to create an advantageous exchange.

40. ... Kf6

41. Nxd4 exd4

42. Bxd4† e5

43. Bc3

It was time to adjourn the game. Home analysis won't help Black. The game entered the easy technique stage.

43. ... Rff4

44. Rd3 Rxe4

45. Rd6† Ke7

46. c5 Rxa4

47. Rxc6 Rac4

48. b3 Rce4

49. Rh8 Rh4

50. Rc7† Kd8

51. Rxh4 Rxh4

52. Bxa5 Ke8

53. c6 Rh6

54. Rc8† Kf7

55. Bb4! Ne6

56. c7 Rh2†

57. Kb1 Nxc7

58. Rxc7†

Black surrendered **(1-0).**

57.
Super Nezh—J. Kluger
C 85
Bucharest 1954

1. e4 e5 2. Nf3 Nc6 3. Bb5 a6 4. Ba4 Nf6 5. 0-0 Be7 6. Bxc6 dxc6 7. d3 Nd7 8. Nbd2 0-0 9. Nc4 f6 10. a4 Nc5 11. b3 Bg4 12. Ne3 Bc8 13. Bb2 g6 14. Nd2 Ne6 15. Kh1 Bc5 16. Ndc4 Bd4 17. c3 Ba7 18. b4 Rf7 19. Qf3 Qf8 20. Rad1 Bd7 21. a5 Rd8 22. Nc2 c5 23. N2e3 cxb4 24. cxb4 Bc6 25. Nd5 Bxd5 26. exd5 Nd4 27. Qe4 Nf5 28. Bc3 Rfd7 29. g4 Nd6 30. Qg2 Nb5 31. Ba1 Rxd5 32. f4 exf4 33. Rxf4 Bd4 34. Bxd4 Rxd4 35. Rff1 c6 36. Rde1 Rxd3 37. Qe2 Qf7 38. Ne5 Qd5† 39. Nf3 Kh8 40. Kg1 Qc4.

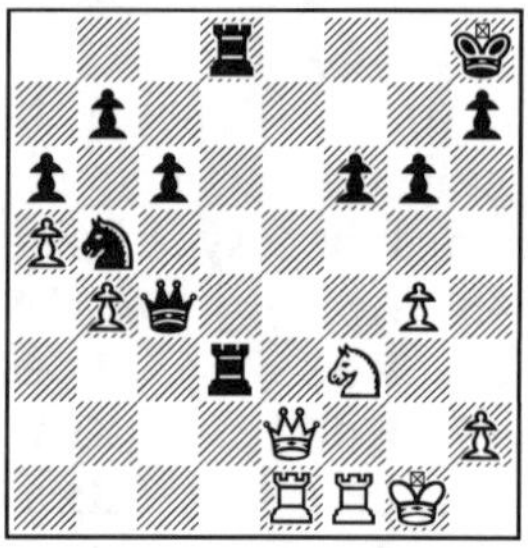

White had two fewer pawns and two others were hanging. Not everything was lost: the ever optimistic Nezh mentioned that the black King was isolated.

41. Qe7! Kg8

Black didn't feel obliged to take on g4: 41... Qxg4† 42. Kh1 Qd7 43. Qxf6† Qg7 44. Qh4! R3d7 45. Ne5, or 42... R3d6 43. Ne5!.

42. Re4! Qd5

On 42... Qc3 there would have followed 43. Ne5!, and then there would have been nothing better than to agree to a perpetual check after 43... fxe5 44. Qf7†. 42... Qf7 failed because of 43. Qxf7† Kxf7 44. Ne5†.

43. g5! f5

Trying to overcome the problems of the position by means of 43... Rxf3 44. Rxf3 Qxg5† 45. Kf2 Rd2† 46. Ke1 Rxh2 47. Qe8† Kg7 48. Qd7† Kh6 49. Rh3† Rxh3 50. Qxh3† Kg7 51. Qd7† or 51. Re7† which would have led to a draw.

44. Rh4 Qd7
45. Rxh7 Qxe7
46. Rxe7 R3d7
47. Rfe1

White managed to achieve a lot: one pawn was won back, but the main thing was that his pieces were active.

47. ... Nc3
48. R1e6 Rd1†
49. Kg2 Nd5
50. Re8†

No good was 50. Rxg6† Kf8 as both Rooks would have hung.

50. ... Rxe8
51. Rxe8† Kg7
52. Rb8 Nf4†
53. Kg3 Nh5†
54. Kf2 Rd7
55. Ne5 Re7
56. Nd3 Kf7
57. Nc5 Nf4
58. Nxb7

Black finally agreed to a **draw** after 29 more moves **(1/2-1/2). 58... Nd3† 59. Kf3 Ke6 60. Ke3 Nxb4 61. Kd4 Rd7† 62. Kc5 Nd3† 63. Kxc6 Re7 64. Kb6 f4 65. Rf8 Nb4 66. Nc5† Ke5 67. h4 Nd5† 68. Kxa6 Kd4 69. Kb5 Ke3 70. Kc6 Nb4† 71. Kd6 Ra7 72. Re8† Kf3 73. Rb8 Na6 74. Rb3† Kg4 75. Nd3 Nc7 76. Rb4 Kxh4 77. Rxf4† Kxg5**

78. Ra4 Kf5 79. Rf4† Kg5 80. Ra4 Kf5 81. Ra1 g5 82. Rf1† Ke4 83. Nc5† Ke3 84. Ra1 g4 85. Kc6 Na8 86. Ra3† Kf4.

58.

E. Vasiukov—Super Nezh

Semi-finals 24th USSR ch.

Kharkov 1956

The preliminary moves are not known.

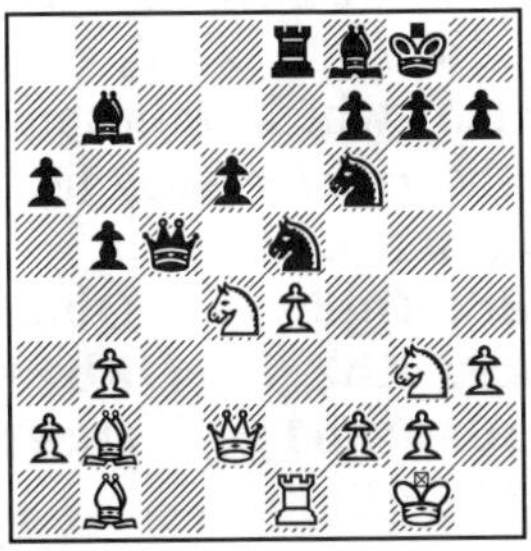

In this game Nezh wasn't able to solve the opening problems in his favorite "Ruy Lopez." White was more active, so on the next move he started attacking the King.

23. ... d5!

The counterpunch in the center was just in time.

24. f4

After 24. exd5 all of Black's troubles would have flown away: 24... Qxd5 25. Ne4 Ned7!.

24. ... Ng6

25. e5 Ne4!

Of course not 25... Nd7?, that would have lost chances for counterplay.

26. Nxe4 dxe4

27. Kh1

On 27. Bxe4 possible was 27... Bxe4 28. Rxe4 f6! 29. e6 Qd5 30. Re1 Bc5, and a pawn most likely would have been won.

27. ... f6

28. exf6 Qh5!

The sacrifice of the pawn was forced: 28... gxf6 29. f5!.

29. fxg7 Bxg7

Black got active play immediately for his pawn, and then White went on the defensive. Psychologically this would be very difficult, even though his position was objectively better.

30. Qe3 Nh4

31. Rc1?

31. Rg1 should have been played right away.

31. ... Qg6

32. Rg1

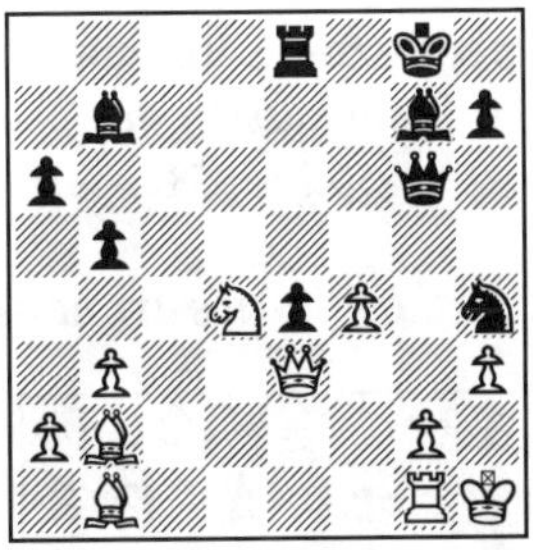

32. ... Bxd4!!

More than a surprise move, this was required by the position: the threat from the f5-square must be eliminated, as that would have allowed the black Knight to remove the Queen blockade of the e-pawn, and then add a white-squared Bishop to the attack.

When everything was explained, the brilliance of Black's play became clear. And how was it explained? Was it easy to give a valuable Bishop away and weaken the long diagonal that led to the black King?

33. Qxd4 Nf5

34. Qd1

The check on h8 was a pernicious mirage: 34. Qh8†? Kf7 35. Qc3 Ng3† and then 36... Ne2 with a loss of material.

34. ... e3

35. Be5?

Losing. It was necessary to play 35. Bxf5! Qxf5 36. Qg4† [but not 36. Qe2 Qh3#!] Qxg4 37. hxg4 Rd8 38. Bc3!, and White wouldn't have lost.

35. ... e2!
36. Qe1 Ng3†
37. Kh2 Nf1†
38. Kh1 Qg3!

It was inevitable, either mate, or the appearance of a new Queen: 39. Qxg3† Nxg3† 40. Kh2 Nf1† and 41... e1=Q.

White quit **(0-1).**

59.

Super Nezh—I. Veltmander

18th Russian ch.

Sochi 1958

The preliminary moves are not known.

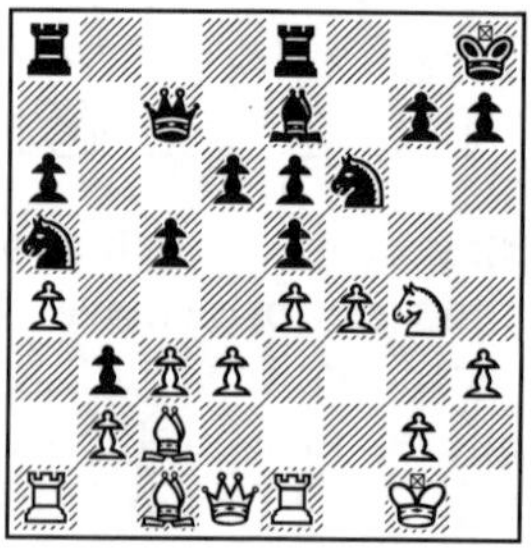

Black has played 21... b3?! thinking that he will get the initiative.

22. Bxb3! Nxg4
23. hxg4 exf4

Black's intention, after 24. Bxf4, was to play 24... Rab8. The pawn on b2 was a weakness since White would hardly play 25. Ra3. As for the e6-pawn, Black had prepared ...Bh4 with a double threat if it would have been taken. Yet...

24. Bxe6! Bh4
25. Bd5 Bxe1
26. Qxe1

The material should have been given back as on 26. Bxa8? Bg3 27. Bd5 Qe7 Black would get a dangerous attack.

26. ... Rab8
27. Bxf4! Rxb2?

Black still continued to force the play, even though the position should be seriously reevaluated. Things became alarming: White had two strong Bishops; besides threatening the d6-pawn, he threatened to advance the g-pawn up the board, after which the black King would be doomed. Careful defense with 27... Nc6! should have been played. On 28. Qg3, then 28... Rbd8, hampering White's play which was connected to e4-e5. In that case the whole fight would have continued.

28. Qg3 Qb6
29. Kh2 Rb1
30. Rxb1 Qxb1
31. g5

Black had no satisfactory defense as the Knight on a5 was out of play and the Queen was far away and could not have helped.

31. ... Qd1

It was too late for 31... Nb7 because of 32. Qh3 with threats 33. g6 or 33. Qd7.

32. Qh3 Qf1
33. Bxd6 Qf2
34. g6 h6
35. Be5!

The threat was 36. Qh6#. If 35... Qd2, then 36. Qd7 would have followed.

Black resigned **(1-0).**

60.

B. Pozarsky—Super Nezh

C 41

Russian Spartakiade

Joshkar-Ola 1963

1. e4 e5 2. Nf3 Nc6 3. Bc4 d6.

It's the Half ("Lesser") Giuoco Piano, introduced to new audiences by Alekhine.

4. d4 Bg4
5. h3 Bh5

5... Bxf3 was preferable.

6. d5

White closes the position and it has the familiar shape of schemes from the Old Indian Defense.

6. ... Nb8
7. Bd3

White disclosed his plan—to strengthen his spatial advantage by building a powerful pawn center, and then to attack on one of the flanks under its cover. It was difficult for Black to create counterplay but, his position was very firm.

7. ... Nf6
8. c4 Nbd7
9. Be3 Nc5
10. g4!

White had been right in avoiding 10. Bxc5 Bxf3! 11. Qxf3 dxc5. Both sides would have had "bad" Bishops and few prospects for interesting and pithy play.

10. ... Nxd3†

A forced exchange. On 10... Bg6 11. Bxc5 dxc5 12. Nxe5 Bxe4 13. Bxe4 Nxe4 White could have chosen charming replies among 14. Qe2 Bd6! 15. Qxe4 Qe7 16. f4 f6 17. Nc3 fxe5 18. f5, or 14. Qa4† Ke7 15. Qc2. In both lines he would have had an obvious advantage.

11. Qxd3 Bg6
12. Nc3 Nd7
13. h4 h5
14. g5 Be7

Some preliminary observations can be made here: White had managed to restrict his opponent, Black's Bishops had nothing to do yet, Black's position looked like a compressed spring, that's why White could not let up the pressure. On the whole, White's chances for a positive result were quite high.

15. 0-0-0 0-0
16. Rhg1 Re8
17. Nd2 c6!

Black had only one hope for counterplay: to prepare, and to promote b7-b5, but that would have been difficult because of his lack of space. White's best target was the h5-pawn. To attack it three tempi would be needed: transferring the Knight to g3 and playing Qe2. Black had to hurry, he had little time to create counterthreats.

18. Nf1 Qa5
19. Ng3 Nc5
20. Bxc5?!

A premature exchange, which made Black's life easier. Correct was 20. Qe2, and only after 20... b5, then 21. Bxc5! dxc5 22. cxb5 cxd5 [22... cxb5 23. Qxb5] 23. Rxd5 a6 24. b6!, and White would have gotten chances to win.

20. ... Qxc5
21. Qe2 b5!

Black had improved his opportunities to create counterplay. 22. Nxh5 b4 would not have helped White.

22. dxc6 a6!

After 22... bxc4 White could have comfortably taken on h5. If 22... Qxc4 23. Qxc4 bxc4 24. Nd5 it would have been a hard endgame for Black. So, taking into consideration that "normal" continuations are not enough, Nezh decided to sacrifice material, hoping to get chances of getting his Bishops free and improving his game.

23. cxb5 axb5
24. Qxb5 Qxf2

Of course the endgame with 24... Qxb5 25. Nxb5 Rxa2 26. Kb1 wouldn't have promised anything good.

25. c7 Rec8
26. Nd5 Bd8!

27. Kb1 Bxc7
28. Ne7† Kh7
29. Nxc8

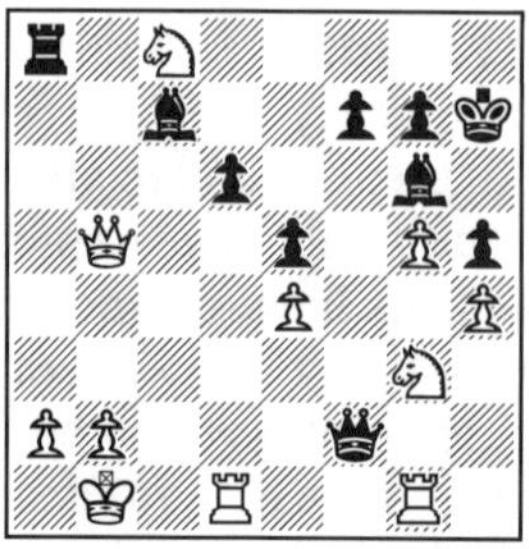

29. ... Rxc8?

A long forced series of moves had brought White extra material and, objectively, a won position. It became won after this mistake by Black. The intermediate move 29... Rb8! should have been played. After 30. Qe2 Qxe2 31. Nxe2 Bxe4† 32. Ka1 Rxc8 33. Rc1 Bf5 34. Ng3 Bg4 Black had a pawn for the Exchange and good chances in a sharp endgame. Now White had the advantage, which was enough to win. Black must rescue his white-squared Bishop, and for this the d6-d5 move must be played.

30. Qf1

Now White played with uncertainty. Perhaps the onset of *zeitnot* had begun. 30. Qc4 would have been okay, and if 30... Rb8, then 31. Qc2.

30. ... Qa7
31. Nf5

31. Qc4 was good.

31. ... Rb8
32. Rg2?!

White could not stand the heat, and so Nezh continued the pressure without letup.

32. ... Qa4!
33. Qd3?!

Black's dream came true. 33. Qe2 would have been right.

33. ... d5!
34. Qc2

Panic seized White and he ceded his position little by little. It was hard to find a good way to defend from the surprise threats. Of course, 34. Qxd5? was poor because of 34...Rd8. Also dangerous was 34. exd5 e4! 35. Qf1 e3 with an increased initiative in Black's hands.

34. ... Rb4!
35. Qxa4

White exchanged Queens to ease his position, but in reality it would not solve his problems. That's why 35. b3 would have been better.

35. ... Rxa4
36. Re2 Rxe4

The same move would have been played on 36. Ng3 or 36. Rxd5.

37. Rf2 Rxh4
38. Rxd5 Rg4
39. Kc1 Bb6
40. Rf1 Rxg5
41. Rxe5 h4

The time scramble had ended, and a non-standard endgame appeared on the board. The material correlation of forces had no importance. It was crucial to outrun his opponent in the pawn-promotion. In such play Bishops would be as strong as Rooks, especially when they are played as a pair. Right off White, who had been worn out by the pinning of his Knight, was eager to exchange Rooks.

42. Rb5 Be3†!
43. Kd1 Ba7
44. Nd6 Rxb5
45. Nxb5 Bb8
46. a4

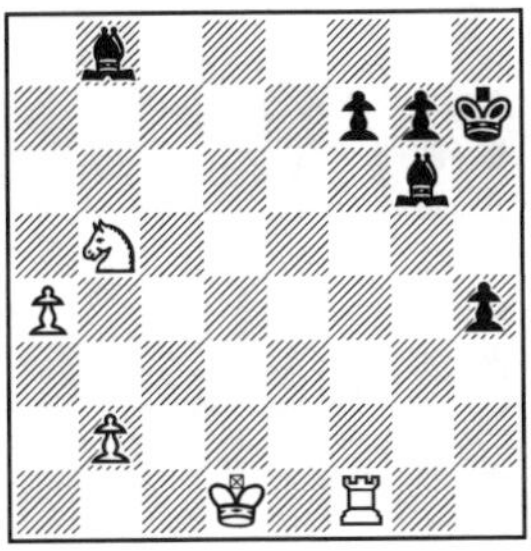

46. ... Be4!

A splendid move which clarified the position. It turned out that the queening squares are controlled by the far ranging white-squared Bishop [a8 and h1]. The Rook could not do it. The h-pawn will have cost White a piece and end the game.

47. Ke2 h3
48. Nd4

White had no time to move his pawns, and even his three pieces could not have averted the fatal promotion of Black's pawns.

48. ... Bg2!

Hindering the closing of the long diagonal by the Knight.

49. Nf3

Alas, material should have been returned, otherwise there would be no chance to stop the pawn.

49. ... Bxf1†
50. Kxf1 Kh6
51. a5 g5
52. a6

It would have been useless to move the b-pawn, the black g-pawn is further along.

52. ... g4
53. Nd4 g3!

An elegant, even study-like decision: Black sacrificed his pawn, but made his King extremely active.

54. Nf5† Kg5
55. Nxg3 Ba7!

An educational example: how strong was the Bishop by pawns at different flanks against the Knight. It neither let the white King go, nor missed the pawns.

56. Ke2 Kg4
57. Nf1 Kf4
58. b4 f6
59. b5 Kg4

Zugzwang.

60. Nh2† Kg3
61. Nf3 f5
62. Nd2 Bb6

The Bishop had one other advantage over the Knight: it could give its turn of the move to the opponent, but the Knight could not.

63. Nf3 Bc5
64. Nd2 Ba7
65. Nf3 f4
66. Nd2 Kg2

Everything was ready for the end: the f-pawn was moving forward, and the Bishop was so far away that the Knight could not reach it.

67. Nf3 Bf2
68. Nh4†

White had nothing else.

68. ... Bxh4
69. a7 f3†
70. Kd3 h2
71. a8=Q h1=Q

White resigned **(0-1)**.

Beginning from the 30th move, Nezh played with great resourcefulness.

Board 1 Team ch. / 1953

	Players	1	2	3	4	5	6	7	8	Points	Place
1	Lipnitsky	•	■	▒	▒	▒	▒	■	■	5	1
2	Furman		•		■	▒	■	▒	■	4	2-3
3	Shishov	▒	■	•	■	■			▒	4	2-3
4	Antoshin	▒			•	■	■	▒	▒	3.5	4-5
5	Suetin	▒	▒			•	■	■	▒	3.5	4-5
6	Nezhmetdinov	▒		■			•	■	▒	3	6
7	Arulaid		▒	■	▒			•	▒	2.5	7-8
8	Koblents			▒	▒	▒	▒	▒	•	2.5	7-8
		1	2	3	4	5	6	7	8		

Semi-finals, 21st USSR ch. / Rostov-on-Don 1953

	Players	1	2	3	4	5	6	7	8	9	10	11	12	13	14	15	16	Points	Place
1	Livshin	•		■	▒		▒	■	■		▒	■	■	■	■	■	■	10.5	1-2
2	Furman	■	•	■	▒	▒	■	▒	■	▒	▒	■	▒	▒	■	▒	▒	10.5	1-2
3	Bannik			•	■	▒	■	▒	■	▒	▒	▒	▒	■	■	▒	■	9.5	3-4
4	Nezhmetdinov	▒	▒		•	▒	■	▒	▒	■	■		▒	▒	■	■	■	9.5	3-4
5	Koblents	■	▒	▒	▒	•		■		▒	■	■		▒	■	■	▒	9	5
6	Antoshin	▒				■	•		▒	■	▒	▒	■	■	▒	▒	■	8	6-8
7	Kotlerman		▒	▒	▒		■	•	▒	■	▒		▒	■	▒	▒	■	8	6-8
8	Shamayev				▒	■	▒	▒	•	▒			■	■	■	■	■	8	6-8
9	Budo	■	▒	▒		▒			▒	•	▒	■	■			■	■	7.5	9-11
10	Fridshtein	▒	▒	▒			▒	▒	■	▒	•	▒	■		■	▒	▒	7.5	9-11
11	Chistyakov			▒	■		▒	■	■		▒	•		■	▒	■	▒	7.5	9-11
12	Reshko		▒	▒	▒	■		▒				■	•	▒		■	▒	6	12
13	Kasparyan		▒		▒	▒				■	■		▒	•	▒		■	5.5	13
14	Konstantinov						▒	▒		■		▒	■	▒	•		■	5	14
15	Zagorovsky		▒	▒			▒	▒			▒			■	■	•		4.5	15
16	Bagin		▒			▒					▒	▒	▒			■	•	3.5	16
		1	2	3	4	5	6	7	8	9	10	11	12	13	14	15	16		

Strategy

Rashid Gibyatovich knew very well, down to the smallest details, the strategic themes of the Ruy Lopez, Sicilian, French and King's Indian Defenses. For many years he was kept busy with his analysis, "polishing" their topicalness, and managing to find among them many interesting and entertaining ideas. Sometimes Nezh won in his favorite openings against such well-known GMs as Spassky, Tal, Boleslavsky, and Geller, and they doubtlessly felt his heavy hand.

Nezh's brilliant mastery in attack was based on a well-prepared strategic drill of these opening plans, plans which contained the core of his opening repertoire.

The strategic treatment of the openings by Nezh reminds us of an approach to the problems of the famous theorist Vsevolod Rauzer: the same aim when preparing attacks; the same connection of an opening line with the choice of strategic plans in the middlegame, and finally, the same conviction in the correctness of his ideas.

This coin has, unfortunately, another side. His conviction in the rightness of his ideas sometimes turned out to be an overestimation of his own chances and an underestimation of the hidden resources of his opponent. This tendency cost Nezh many games, though this deficiency is characteristic of many chessplayers with such an active attacking style—their results depend on how much they can keep their emotions under control and think objectively.

61.

V. Zurakhov—Super Nezh

C 99

14th Russian ch.

Rostov-on-Don 1954

1. e4 e5 2. Nf3 Nc6 3. Bb5 a6 4. Ba4 Nf6 5. 0-0 Be7 6. Re1 b5 7. Bb3 0-0 8. c3 d6 9. h3 Na5 10. Bc2 c5 11. d4 Qc7 12. Nbd2 cxd4 13. cxd4 Bb7 14. Nf1 Rac8.

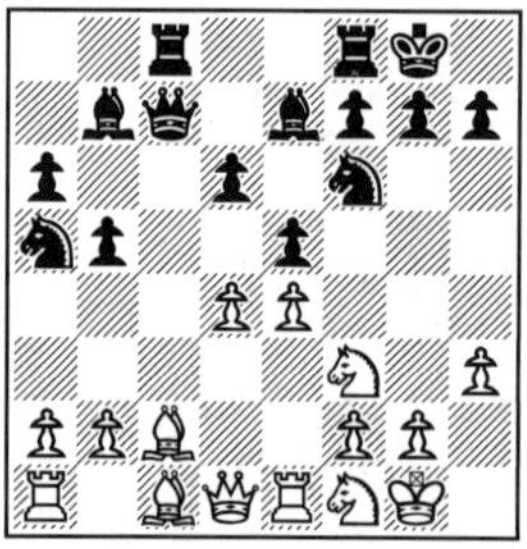

At that time this was one of the main positions in Chigorin's variation of the Ruy Lopez. This setup of black pieces (Bb7, Rc8) with the exchange of pawns in the center, was introduced into tournament practice before the war.

15. Bb1

Simagin's continuation. Here 15. Re2 or 15. Bd3 are often used.

15. ... g6

In the *Moscow championship, 1944,* Panov struck in the center with: 15... d5!? 16. exd5 e4 17. Bxe4 Nxe4 18. Rxe4 Bxd5. For the pawn he got two active Bishops and ideas to create different attacking positions, *Verlinsky—Panov.* Later the correct reaction was found to 16... e4: 17. Ng5! and 18. Nxe4, and White has the better chances. That's why instead of a sharp pawn sacrifice Black usually plays more calmly. Together with the plan of regrouping pieces chosen by Nezh [with the same aim as 15... Rfe8], 15... Nh5, the transfer of the Knight to f4 could also be made.

16. Ng3 Rfe8

17. Bd3 Bf8

18. a4?!

This was a violation of one of the most important strategic principles of chess: never start play on the wing when you don't have the advantage, or a least a calm situation, in the center. That's why a strengthening of the center by means of 18. d5 was necessary.

18. ... b4

19. Bd2

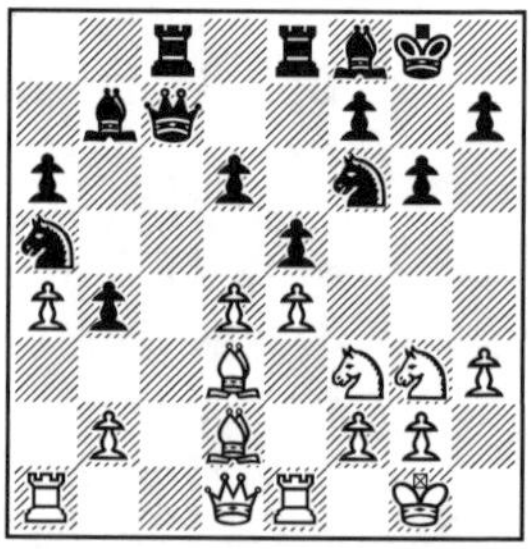

19. ... exd4!

It was inconvenient to defend the pawn at b4: 19... Qb6 20. Be3 with the threat 21. dxe5, and it's not necessary, as there was an opportunity given by his kind opponent to begin active play in the center.

20. Bxb4

This pawn should have been taken, as on 20. Nxd4 there was 20... d5, and Black would grab the initiative.

20. ... Nc6

21. Bd2 Nd7

22. a5

Nezh recommended 22. b4, but most likely there was no big difference between these two continuations.

22. ... Nde5

23. Nxe5 Nxe5

A move which demonstrated Black's aggressive intentions. Others would have chosen 23... dxe5, returning to a regular pawn structure, and they... would also have been right.

24.	**Rc1**	**Qd7**
25.	**Bf1**	**Bg7**
26.	**f4**	**Rxc1**
27.	**Bxc1**	**Nc6**
28.	**Bd2**	

In case of 28. Qa4, Black would have used the back rank for protection by the Rook and would have played 28... d5, after which White would then go on the defensive.

28.	**...**	**Nd8**
29.	**Qb3?**	

The maneuvers of the Queen were unfruitful, as the small threats created by it, were not dangerous. Simpler is 29. Bd3 Ne6 30. b4.

29.	**...**	**Ne6**
30.	**Qb6**	**d3!**

The clumsy moves of the Queen only created tactical troubles for White.

31.	**Be3**	**Nc5**
32.	**e5**	

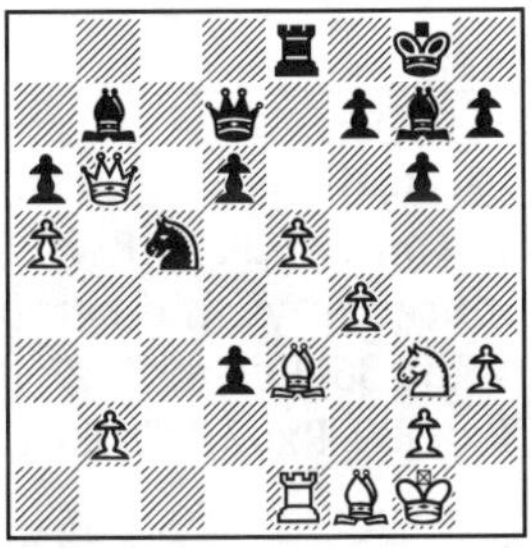

Bad was 32. b4? Na4 33. Qa7 Ra8 catching the Queen. After 32. Bxc5 dxc5 33. Kh2 c4 Black would have had a decisive advantage.

32.	**...**	**dxe5!**

This foreseen sacrifice of a piece led to a quick victory. The motif of the combination was the passed d-pawn.

33.	**Bxc5**	**d2**
34.	**Rd1**	**exf4**
35.	**Nh1**	

White refused to play 35. Ne2 because of the ruinous 35... f3 36. gxf3 Bxf3 37. Qxa6 Qd5 with an unrelenting attack.

35.	**...**	**f3!**
36.	**g3**	**f2†!**

The long diagonal was clear and there were no means to stop the threats.

37.	**Nxf2**	

37. Bxf2 Qd5.

37.	**...**	**Bf3**
38.	**Qb3**	**Bxd1**
39.	**Nxd1**	**h5**
40.	**Bf2**	**Re1**

White surrendered **(0-1).**

62.

Super Nezh—A. Matsukevich

B 01

Riga 1955

1. e4 d5 2. exd5 Qxd5.

In spite of the obvious defect—the loss of tempo as a result of the attack by the Knight on the Queen—the Scandinavian Defense didn't vanish from tournament practice. It's also [if not popular] an exciting and healthy opening.

3.	**Nc3**	**Qa5**
4.	**d4**	**c6**
5.	**Bc4**	**Nf6**
6.	**h3**	

White doesn't want a pinning of the Knight after it's arrival to f3, though 5. Nf3 Bg4 6. h3 is a main system used against the Scandinavian Defense.

6.	**...**	**Bf5**
7.	**Nf3**	**Nbd7**
8.	**0-0**	**e6**
9.	**Bf4**	

9. Re1 was worthy of attention.

9.	**...**	**Nd5**
10.	**Bd2**	**Nxc3**
11.	**Bxc3**	**Bb4**
12.	**Bxb4**	**Qxb4**

13. Bb3 0-0
14. Re1 c5?

An overestimation of the position. The activity in the center was in White's favor. Black's position would be solid if the maneuvering would remain accurate. Good would have been 14... Rad8, 14... h6 or 14... Qd6 [the last one was recommended by Nezh].

15. c3 Qb6
16. d5! Rad8

Black's mistake had brought him trouble—he should have played more accurately. 16... exd5 [16... Nf6? 17. g4] 17. Qxd5 Be6 18. Rxe6! Qxe6 19. Qxe6 fxe6 20. Bxe6† Rf7 21. Ng5 wouldn't have worked for Black either.

17. g4 c4!

Black was resourcefully defending a hard position. The pawn was sacrificed as a temptation: in case of 18. Bxc4 there would have been 18... exd5, getting rid of the object of attack on e6.

18. gxf5! cxb3
19. fxe6 fxe6
20. Rxe6 Qb5
21. axb3 Nc5
22. Nd4 Qd7

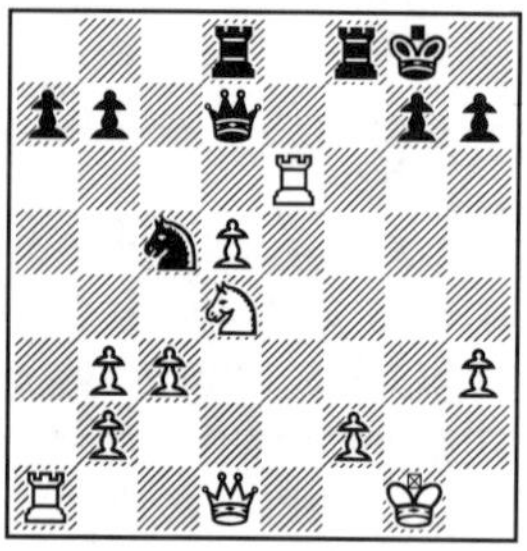

23. Qe2!

The sacrifice of material was forced. At the same time it was strong enough to preserve and strengthen the center. A retreat of the Rook would not have been profitable because of the shots at d5 and h3.

23. ... Nxe6

Black did not want to take the Rook, but he had to: on 23... Qxd5 the Knight would be lost after 24. Re5 and 25. Qc4.

24. Nxe6 Rfe8
25. c4 Ra8
26. Kh1 Re7
27. Qe5 a6
28. Rg1 Rae8
29. Rg3 Rf7
30. Kg2 Qe7
31. f4 g6

This, of course, was a serious weakening, but Black had almost no useful moves.

32. f5 Qf6
33. Qxf6 Rxf6

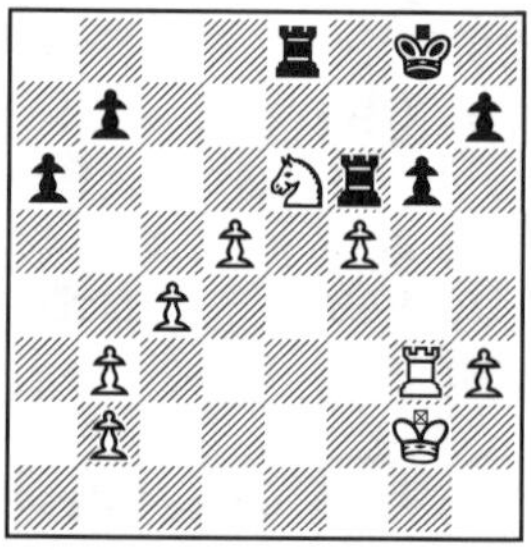

34. d6! Rexe6

The alternative 34... Rf7 wouldn't have promised anything better: 34... Rf7 35. c5 Kh8 36. Rd3 gxf5 37. d7 Rxd7 38. Rxd7 Rxe6 39. Rxb7 Re2† 40. Kf3 Rxb2 41. c6 Rc2 42. c7.

35. fxe6 Rxe6
36. Rd3

Black had no chances here.

36. ... Re8
37. b4 Rd8
38. c5 Kf7
39. Rf3† Ke6
40. Re3† Kd5
41. Re7 b6
42. Rc7 a5
43. cxb6 axb4
44. b7

Black surrendered **(1-0).**

63.

Super Nezh—M. Tal

C 17

24th USSR ch.

Moscow 1957

This game was played in an atmosphere of high anxiety. It was the 6th round of the championship. The 20-year old master Tal, having 4.5 points of 5, was suddenly leading the tournament. He had defeated such GMs as Taimanov and Bronstein. Now, a not young, nor famous master, was on his way. Tal knew Nezh was strong in attack and was good at playing the Sicilian Defense with White. That's why he chose the French Defense as an opening surprise for Nezh. However, Tal was playing this defense only for the second time in his life—a mixture of reckless bravery and giddiness from success. At this point Tal's opening "preparation" was over.

1. e4 e6 2. d4 d5 3. Nc3 Bb4 4. e5 c5 5. Bd2 Ne7 6. a3 Bxc3 7. Bxc3 b6 8. b4.

This was a novelty, from the times Nezh worked together with his pupils.

The aim is to "enliven the black-squared Bishop" (in Nezh's words). After 8. Qg4 Nf5 9. Bd3 h5 10. Qh3 Qg5! Black equalized the play in the game *Krogius—Furman, sf. 24th USSR ch., 1957.*

8. ... Qc7

Only not 8... c4?. In this case Black would have gotten zero counterplay.

9. Nf3 Nd7?!

The novelty by White brought results. A year later [at *13th Olympiad]* in the game *Sanguinetti—Fuchs* Black played more precisely: 9... cxb4! 10. Bxb4 Ba6 11. Bd3 Bxd3 12. Qxd3 Nbc6 13. Bd6 Qd7 14. a4 Na5 and equalized.

10. Be2 Nc6

11. 0-0 0-0

On 11... cxd4 Rashid Gibyatovich had planned to sacrifice a pawn: 12. Nxd4 Ncxe5 [12... Ndxe5 13. Nxc6 Nxc6 14. Bxg7] 13. Nb5 Qb8 14. f4 Ng6 15. f5, starting an attack.

12. bxc5 bxc5

13. dxc5

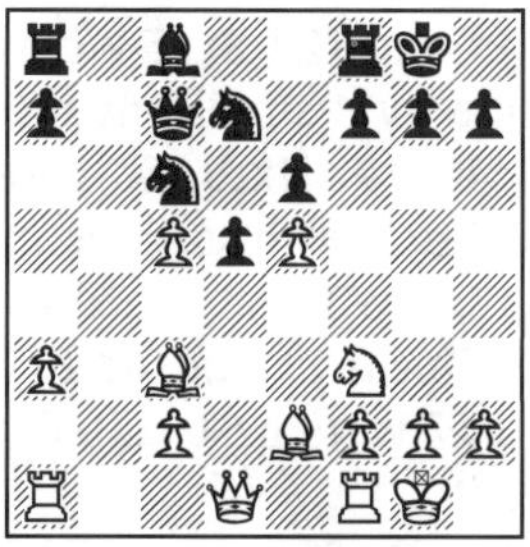

One of Nezh's favorite ways of opening the center in "French" positions. In this situation this opening was justifiable after Black's castling.

13. ... Ncxe5?!

Brave, but very optimistic.

Black agreed to open the diagonals for the white Bishops, relying upon his strong center. But as the further development of events showed, the black pawns in the center couldn't move and were put under fire.

—R.N.

Correct would have been 13... Nxc5 14. Bd3 Ne4! [After 14... Nxd3 15. Qxd3 White's position was better.] 15. Re1 Bb7! [offered by Keres] with enough chances by Black.

14. Nxe5 Nxe5

15. Qd4 f6

16. f4 Nc6?

The pawn on c5 was disagreeable for Black and it should have been attacked: 16… Nd7. Nezh planned to respond 17. f5 or 17. Bg4, because a capture on c5 would be unlikely due to the pin by the Bishop. In case of 17. f5 Re8 18. fxe6 Nxc5, 19. Rxf6? could not have been played because of 19… Ne4 [19… gxf6? 20. Qxf6 Bxe6 21. Rf1 with an unavoidable mate, or 20… Rxe6 21. Qh8† and 22. Qg7† with the win of the Queen]. And after 19. Bf3 Bxe6 20. Bxd5 White would have had only a small advantage. As for 17. Bg4, 17… Nxc5 18. f5 Ne4! also provided Black with satisfactory play.

17. Qe3 Rd8

It was time to defend, and 17… Ne7 or 17… Bd7 were best suited for this purpose.

18. Rad1

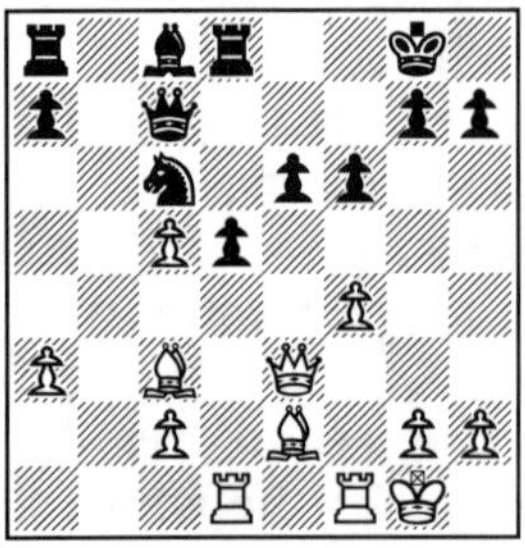

18. … e5?!

This was a continuation of the same optimistic scenario. The opening of the game, and two strong Bishops, would give the advantage to White. Black's handsome pawn center will bring White some problems.

19. fxe5 fxe5
20. Bb5 Bb7

It became an accepted reality that the counterattack had failed.

20… d4 would have been bad, as after 21. Bc4† [Ed.: Tal thought 21. Qe4! was better and he was correct. E.g., 21… Bb7 22. Bc4† Kh8 23. Rf7 Rd7 24. Rdf1 Rxf7 25. Rxf7 Ne7 26. Qg4 Rg8 27. Bb4! and White is winning.] Kh8 22. Qg5 Be6 [Ed.: Tal gave 22… h6! 28. Qg6 Ne7 as unclear.] 23. Bxe6 dxc3 24. Bd5, Black's central pawns would have fallen.

21. Qg3

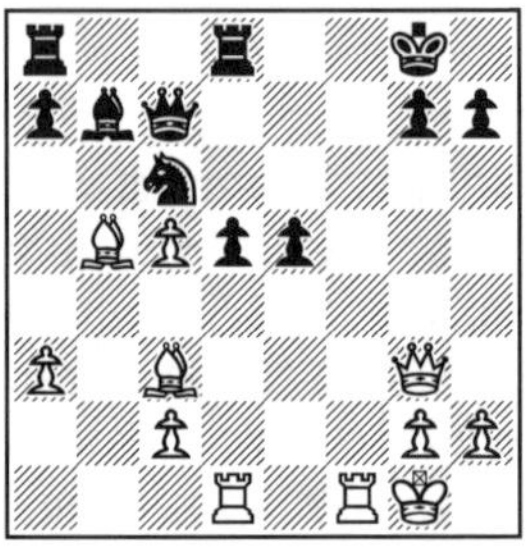

21. … Rd7?!

Neither Nezh, nor Damsky commented on this move. Black had missed his last chance for a counterattack: 21… Rf8! [offered by A. Hasin]. For example: 22. Rxf8† Rxf8 23. Rxd5? Nd4!, and Black would have had the advantage—24. Rxd4 [24. Rd7 Qxd7! 25. Bxd7 Ne2†; 24. c6 Bxc6 25. Rxd4 Bxb5; 24. Bc4 Ne2† 25. Bxe2 Bxd5] Qxc5 25. Bc4† Kh8 26. Qg5 h6 27. Qh5 Rc8, and White would lose material. After the better 23. Bxc6 Qxc6 24. Bxe5 [but not 24. Qxe5? d4] Qxc5† 25. Bd4 Qe7 26. Re1 Qd7 27. Bxa7 White gets an extra pawn, but it's difficult to do anything with it.

22. Rf2!

Taking on c6 at once won't score a point: 22. Bxc6 Qxc6 23. Qxe5 Qxc5 [with check].

22. … Re8
23. h3 Ba8
24. Ba4 Bb7
25. Kh1

In his opponent's approaching *Zeitnot*, White was not in a hurry. This tactic was not pleasant for Black, who was pressed not only by time, but also for space.

25. ... Ba8
26. Rf5 e4

Black couldn't stand the pressure, and preferred to reinforce his play instead of engaging in aimless maneuvering. All the same, it was impossible to hold the position: 26... d4 27. Bb3† Kh8 28. Rdf1 Qd8 29. Rf7 Rxf7 30. Rxf7, or 26... g6 27. Bxc6 Qxc6 28. Rxe5 Rf8 29. Bd4. In both cases Black's position was beyond redemption.

27. Qxc7 Rxc7
28. Rfxd5 e3
29. Rd7 e2
30. Bb3† Re6
31. Bxe6† Kf8
32. Bxg7†

Black surrendered **(1-0).**

64.
Super Nezh—B. Spassky
B 31
24th USSR ch.
Moscow 1957

1. e4 c5 2. Nf3 Nc6 3. Bb5 g6 4. 0-0.

This system, with the devlopment of the Bishop to b5 was used by Nezh many times in different situations. For example, in the semi-final in this *USSR championship he* played 4. c3 in the game with *Boleslavsky,* but the experienced theorist of the openings managed to get a good position, playing [as Black]: 4... d5 5. Qa4 [later Nezh offered 5. e5] dxe4 6. Ne5 Bd7 7. Nxd7 Qxd7 8. Qxe4 Nf6.

4. ... Bg7
5. c3 Nf6

5... e5 could also have been played. Its aim would have been to stop White's play in the center. Still, White would play 6. d4! cxd4 7. cxd4 exd4 8. Bf4, taking the initiative.

6. Qe2

Nowadays 6. Re1 0-0 7. d4 cxd4 8. cxd4 or even 8. e5 Nd5 9. cxd4 d6 10. Nc3! is more often played.

6. ... 0-0
7. e5 Ne8

That, as Nezh confessed later, was why he played 6. Qe2.

He suggested that on 7... Nd5, 8. Qc4 would have been unpleasant due to the loss of the c5-pawn. Later it was discovered that in playing 8... Nc7 9. Bxc6 dxc6 10. Qxc5 Qd3! Black got compensation for the pawn.

8. d4 Nc7
9. Ba4

White could have won the pawn: 9. Bxc6 bxc6 10. dxc5, but after 10... Ba6 11. c4 d5 12. cxd6 exd6 13. Rd1 Re8 14. Be3 d5! Black would have gotten active play.

9. ... cxd4
10. cxd4 d5

Nezh admitted that 10... d6 was weaker because of the line 11. Rd1 Bg4 12. h3 Bxf3 13. Qxf3 dxe5 14. Bxc6 bxc6 15. dxe5 and White would have had the better chances. After 15... Nd5 16. Nc3 e6 there was no advantage.

11. h3 Rb8
12. Bc2 b6
13. Bd2 Ba6
14. Bd3 Bxd3
15. Qxd3 Qd7

The chances for both sides were approximately equal, although Nezh evaluated [in his commentaries] the whole plan for Black, concerning the exchange of white-squared Bishops, as the wrong one. He thought that it would be hard to undermine White's center by means of f7-f6 without a Bishop.

16. Nc3 Nb4?!

After this unnecessary move, which

will give White tempi to invade his space, the play became easier for White. The most logical move would have been 16… f6.

17. Qe2 Rbc8

Still, 17… f6 should have been played.

18. a3 Nc6
19. b4 Ne6
20. Qd3 f6

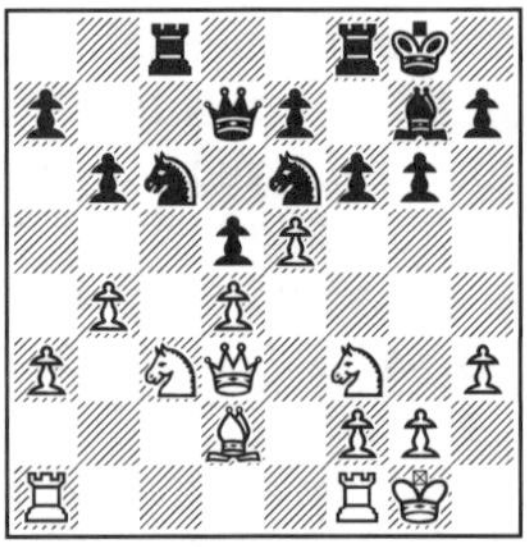

Now the interesting sacrifice of a piece won't work: 20… Nexd4 21. Nxd4 Nxe5 because of 22. Qb5! Qxb5 23. Ndxb5 Nc4 24. Nxd5 Nxd2 25. Nxe7† Kh8 26. Nxc8 Nxf1 27. Rxf1 Rxc8 28. Nxa7 Ra8 29. Nb5 Bb2 30. Rb1 with an extra pawn.

R.N.

21. exf6 Bxf6?

For the sake of easily repelled threats to the pawn on d4, Black gave himself a serious weakening on the e-file. After 21… exf6 he had a comparatively good position.

22. Ne2 Bg7

There was an absence of counterplay due to the d-pawn, and it became more and more difficult for Black because of White's opportunities to attack by h3-h4-h5.

23. Rac1 a5
24. b5 Nb8
25. Rxc8 Rxc8
26. Nf4 Rc4
27. Nxe6 Qxe6
28. Re1 Qd6

28… Qd7 wasn't better because of 29. Bf4. Nezh offered the following variation: 29… Rc8 30. Qe2 Bf6 31. Qe6†! Qxe6 32. Rxe6 Nd7 33. Rc6! Re8 34. Rc7 with a winning endgame.

29. g3 Nd7
30. Bf4 Qf6
31. Bg5 Qf8
32. Rxe7 Nf6
33. Qe2! h6

Alas, 33… Ne4 would have failed, because 34. Rxe4 would have followed, and there would have been no check at c1.

Without waiting for Nezh's response, Black resigned **(1-0)**, as there would have been no defense after 34. Qe6† Kh8 35. Bxf6 Bxf6 36. Rf7. Instead of this line Nezh offered the following poetic variation: 35. Ne5 Qg8 36. Bxf6 Qxe6 37. Nxg6† Kh7 38. Rxg7#!.

65.

I. Boleslavsky—Super Nezh

C 76

USSR Team ch.

Vilnius 1958

1. e4 e5 2. Nf3 Nc6 3. Bb5 a6 4. Ba4 d6 5. c3 Bd7 6. d4 g6 7. 0-0 Bg7 8. Be3.

Both players, as was known, were great researchers in the openings, and they made many discoveries, especially in the Ruy Lopez. As for this very position, the players used it three times during their meetings. It first happened in the *24th USSR ch., Moscow 1957*, where *Nezh* preferred 8… Nge7, but *Boleslavsky* used the novelty 9. dxe5! [Earlier 9. c4 exd4 10. Nxd4 0-0 11. Nc3 Nxd4 had been played with equal chances, *Keres—Capablanca, Buenos-Aires, 1939.]* dxe5 10. Bc5! b6 11. Ba3 b5 12. Bc2 0-0 13. Nbd2 a5 14. Bc5 and owing to the strong position of the Bishop on c5 he got the better game.

Then in the *semi-finals* of the *25th USSR ch., Kiev 1957,* this position was seen again. Remembering the problems caused by the Bishop on c5, Nezh played 8... b6 at once. Not long before that time, master *Ussov* had played against him in the *17th Russian ch., Krasnodar 1957. Boleslavsky* gained an advantage by purely positional means: 9. d5! [He mentioned that the c5-square should be taken under control by Black only after the pawn exchange on e5. This is a splendid example of the way a great strategist thinks: *not to use variations, but schemes, structures, and setups!]* Nce7 10. Bxd7† Qxd7 11. c4 h6 12. Nfd2 f5 13. f3 Nf6 14. Nc3 0-0 15. b4. The game took shape for White as a kind of King's Indian Defense:

> **Black is still preparing his forces on the kingside, and White has already prepared a breakthrough on the queenside. It's also in White's favor that there are no white-squared Bishops on the chessboard.**
>
> *—Boleslavsky*

8. ...	**Nf6**
9. Nbd2	**0-0**
10. dxe5	**dxe5**

10... Nxe5 11. Nxe5 dxe5 12. f3 Bxa4 13. Qxa4 Qd3 brought equality in the game *Jansa—Filip, Marianske Lazne 1960.*

11. Bc5?

Perhaps Boleslavsky was caught off guard by his pleasant memory of this move in the game from the 24th championship. The difference here was that in that game, the Bishop pinned the Knight and owing to this, it handcuffed Black's forces, and here there was no pin. That's why the Bishop's move was aimless. Moreover, White had lost control over the important square f4.

Some other, more useful continuations [11. Qc2, 11. b4, 11. Bxc6] could be made in this position. Perhaps the most preferable would have been 11. Re1, vacating the f1-square for the Knight.

11. ...	**Re8**
12. Re1	**b6**
13. Ba3	

It would have been better to accept his mistake and return the Bishop to e3.

13. ...	**Qc8**
14. Nf1	**b5**
15. Bc2	**a5**

It became clear that the Bishop's wandering maneuvers brought nothing but trouble to White.

16. Bc5 **Nd8!**

The Knight moves with tempo to f4.

17. a4	**Qb7**
18. axb5	**Bxb5**
19. Ba3	

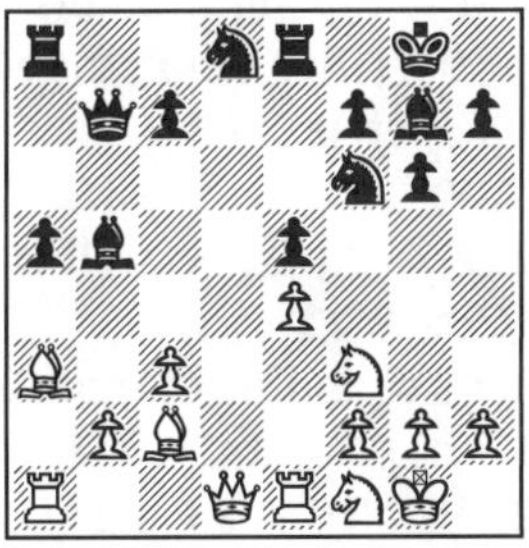

19. ... **Ne6!**

Black sacrificed a pawn, and because of that almost all of his pieces appeared in attacking positions.

20. Nxe5	**Rad8**
21. Qc1?	

21. Qf3 was obligatory, as the basic

events should happen on the kingside. Black planned to play 21... Ng5 22. Qf4 h6 with the threat 23... Nh5 and get the initiative for the pawn. Now the Queen turns out to be a passive bystander.

21. ... Nh5
22. Nf3 Nhf4
23. Ng3 h5
24. h4 Bh6
25. Kh2 Kg7
26. Qb1 Qb6
27. Kg1

Alas, the simple attack on the pawn at f2 can't be repelled: 27. Re3 Nxg2! 28. Kxg2 Bxe3 29. fxe3 Qxe3, or 27. Nh1 Nxg2! 28. Kxg2 Nf4† 29. Kg1 Qe6 and the Queen would have rushed to the h3-square.

After the continuation of the game the same sacrifice would have put an end to the battle.

27. ... Nxg2!
28. Kxg2 Nf4†
29. Kh1

The logical ending of the game was: 29. Kg1 Nh3† 30. Kg2 Qxf2† 31. Kxh3 Bd7† 32. Nf5† Bxf5† 33. exf5 Qxf3† and 34... Rd2 with mate.

29. ... Qxf2

White surrendered **(0-1).**

This is a good example of how clichés and false associations influence even the greatest chessplayers, and perhaps, even more so than less practical players. I believe that if Boleslavsky had played this opening system for the first time, he would never have played the move 11. Bc5.

66.

Super Nezh—A. Shestoperov

B 94

21st Russian ch.

Omsk 1961

1. e4 c5 2. Nf3 d6 3. d4 cxd4 4. Nxd4 Nf6 5. Nc3 a6 6. Bg5 Nbd7 7. Bc4 Qa5 8. Qd2 e6 9. 0-0 Be7 10. Rad1 h6 11. Bh4 Ne5 12. Be2 b5 13. Bxf6 gxf6 14. f4 b4 15. Nb1 Qc5 16. Kh1 Nc4 17. Bxc4 Qxc4 18. b3 Qc5.

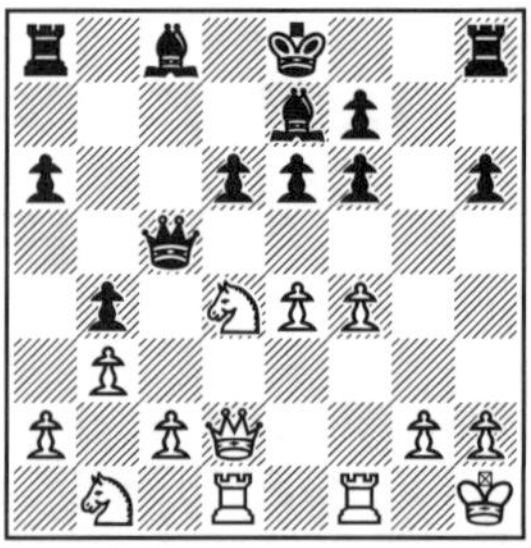

White's position was more active, but he should "hurry up," as Black was eager to quickly finish his development.

19. c3! Bb7!

Black was ready to sacrifice a pawn, as after 19... bxc3 20. Nxc3 Bb7 21. f5! White would have begun an offensive.

20. cxb4 Qb6
21. Nc3!

White also considered that activity was more important than material. The clumsy 21. Rfe1 allowed 21... d5!.

21. ... Qxb4
22. Nc2 Qa5
23. Ne3 Rg8

Black still can't solve the problem of shelter for his King: 23... 0-0 is just bad, and on 23... 0-0-0 the attack 24. b4! would commence.

24. Nc4 Qc5?!

Black shouldn't have allowed the loss of a tempo with an attack on his Queen. 24... Qc7 was better.

25. f5!

Winning the pawn by 25. Nxd6† Bxd6 26. Qxd6 Qxd6 27. Rxd6 Ke7 would have let the black King get rid of his problems.

25. ... 0-0-0
26. Na4 Qb5
27. Qf4 Kb8!

A good defensive move, based on a tactical point: 28. Nxd6? Bxd6 29. Rxd6 Qxf1†! 30. Qxf1 Rxd6, and Black would have gotten two Rooks for the Queen. In the opened position, that would also have been in his favor.

28. Rfe1 h5
29. h3 e5

White's pressure forced Black's uneasy decision. An attempt to open the diagonal [h1-a8] wouldn't have worked: 29... exf5 30. Nc3! and 31. Nd5.

30. Qf2 d5

The pawn sacrifice was needed because of the threat to occupy the d5-square.

31. Nc3 Qc5
32. Qxc5 Bxc5
33. Nxd5 Bxd5
34. exd5

Wrong would have been 34. Rxd5? Rxd5 35. exd5 Rg5 36. Rf1 Rg3, with serious counterplay for Black.

34. ... Bd4
35. d6 Rg5
36. Rf1 Kc8
37. Nd2!

A decisive transfer of the Knight would be made to e4. The Knight would be strong both in attack and defense on this square.

37. ... Rdg8
38. Rc1† Kb7

38... Kd8 39. Ne4 Rxg2 40. Nxf6 R8g3 41. d7 isn't any better and there would be no defense from 42. Rc8.

39. Ne4 Rxg2
40. d7 Rxa2
41. Nd6† Ka7
42. Rc8 R8g2

Black lost with honor—with his last blink he had also created a mate threat.

43. Ra8†

Black surrendered **(1-0).**

21st USSR ch. / Kiev 1954

	Players	1	2	3	4	5	6	7	8	9	10	11	12	13	14	15	16	17	18	19	20	Points	Place
1	Averbakh	•	▒	▒	▒	▒	▒	▒	■	■	■	■	▒	▒	■	■	■	■	▒	■	■	14.5	1
2	Korchnoy	▒	•	▒		▒	▒	■		▒	■	■	■	■		■	■	▒	■	■	■	13	2-3
3	Taimanov	▒	▒	•	▒	▒	▒	▒	■	▒	■	■	▒	▒	■	▒	▒	■	▒	■	■	13	2-3
4	Lisitsin	▒	■	▒	•	▒	■	■	■	▒		▒		▒	▒	▒	■	■	■	▒	■	12.5	4-5
5	Petrosyan	▒	▒	▒	▒	•	▒	■	▒	▒	▒	■	■	▒	■	▒	■	▒	▒	▒	■	12.5	4-5
6	Holmov	▒	▒	▒		▒	•	■	▒		■	■	■	▒	▒	▒	▒		▒	■	▒	10.5	6
7	Nezhmetdinov	▒		▒				•	▒		▒	■	■	■		■	■	▒	■	■	▒	10	7-9
8	Suetin		■			▒	▒	▒	•	■	■	▒	■	▒	▒	■		▒	■		▒	10	7-9
9	Furman		▒	▒	▒	▒	■	■		•			▒	▒	▒	▒		■	■	■	■	10	7-9
10	Bivshev				■	▒		▒		■	•		▒	■	▒		■	■	▒	■	■	9.5	10-11
11	Geller				▒				▒	■	■	•		■	■	■	■	■		■	▒	9.5	10-11
12	Borisenko	▒		▒	■					▒	▒	■	•	▒	▒	▒	▒	▒	■		■	8.5	12-13
13	Flohr	▒		▒	▒	▒	▒		▒	▒			▒	•	■	▒	▒	▒	▒	■	▒	8.5	12-13
14	Bannik		■		▒		▒	■	▒	▒	▒		▒		•	■	▒			▒	■	8	14-16
15	Ilivitsky			▒	▒	▒	▒			▒	■		▒	▒		•	▒	▒	■	▒	■	8	14-16
16	Lilienthal			▒			▒		■	■			▒	▒	▒	▒	•	▒	■	■	▒	8	14-16
17	Ragozin		▒			▒	■	▒	▒				▒	▒	■	▒	▒	•			▒	6.5	17-18
18	Shamkovich	▒		▒		▒	▒				▒	■		▒	■			■	•		▒	6.5	17-18
19	Livshin				▒	▒			■				■		▒	▒		■	■	•		6	19
20	Sokolsky						▒	▒	▒			▒		▒			▒	▒	▒	■	•	5	20
		1	2	3	4	5	6	7	8	9	10	11	12	13	14	15	16	17	18	19	20		

Board 4 USSR Team ch. / 1954

	Players	1	2	3	4	5	6	7	8	9	10	Points	Place
1	Nezhmetdinov	•			■	■	■	■	■	■	■	7	1
2	Mikkov	■	•		■	▒	▒	■		■	■	6	2
3	Cherepkov	■	■	•		▒	▒		■	■	▒	5.5	3
4	Sokolsky			■	•	▒	■	■	■	▒		5	4
5	Zilber		▒	▒	▒	•	■	▒	■		▒	4.5	5
6	Kots		▒	▒			•	▒	▒	■	■	4	6-7
7	Sorokin			■		▒	▒	•		■	■	4	6-7
8	Antoshin		■				▒	■	•		■	3.5	8-9
9	Ostrauskas				▒	■			■	•	■	3.5	8-9
10	Hodzhaev			▒	■	▒					•	2	10
		1	2	3	4	5	6	7	8	9	10		

7

Opening Novelties

Nezhmetdinov's longstanding work on opening theory was responsible for his reputation as a great expert. He managed to find and use many opening discoveries, some of which became the cornerstones of well-known and popular opening systems. In this chapter only Nezh's most famous and successfully used discoveries are presented.

67.

M. Shishov—Super Nezh
C 74
Tbilisi 1947

1. e4 e5 2. Nf3 Nc6 3. Bb5 a6 4. Ba4 d6 5. c3 f5.

This sharp pawn move was introduced into practice by Capablanca. Now the system has lost its popularity, but it was developed and used often after the war.

6. exf5

The continuation 6. d4 was also seen in Nezh's practice. It begins a hand-to-hand fight at once: 6… fxe4 7. Nxe5 dxe5 8. Qh5† Ke7 9. Bxc6 bxc6 10. Bg5† Nf6 11. dxe5 Qd5 12. Bh4 Kd7!? [After 12… Ke6 13. Bxf6 gxf6 14. Qe8† White announced perpetual check in the game *Foltys—Kottnauer, Amsterdam 1950.]* 13. Qg5 Be7! 14. exf6?! [Stronger was 14. Na3, preserving the sharpness of the position.] Bxf6 15. Qxd5† cxd5 16. Bxf6 gxf6, Black has a considerable advantage, *Natarius—Nezhmetdinov, Kazan 1948.*

6. … Bxf5
7. d4

Another, and perhaps the best, possibility was 7. 0-0, without being bothered by 7… Bd3, on which both 8. Re1 and 8. Qb3 would have been possible. In the last variation, 8… Bxf1 would be weak because of 9. Qxb7 Bb5 10. Bxb5 axb5 11. Qxc6†.

7. … e4
8. Ng5

When playing this line as Black, I was always apprehensive, and at the same time [as I tried it on the chessboard] waited for the piece sacrifice—8. 0-0 exf3 9. Qxf3. Unfortunately, not one of my opponents wanted to go there. And in vain! The sacrifice of the Knight could give White the chance for a very dangerous attack.

R.N.

This was written by Nezh in 1958. It's interesting that theorists, headed by Keres, had a very skeptical attitude toward this Knight sacrifice. In 1961, playing with *Shianovsky* [Black], *Rashid Gibyatovich* had a chance to prove his theories. After 9. Re1† Be7 10. Qxf3 Bxb1 11. Bg5? [Correct was 11. Rxb1 Nf6 12. Bxc6† bxc6 13. Qxc6† Kf7 14. Bg5, White had two pawns for a piece and chances for an attack.] Bg6 12. Bb3 [Ed.: 12. Rxe7† can lead to winning the Queen but the price is too high.] Nf6 13. Bxf6 gxf6 14. Re3, and then 14… Kf8. Black can hold onto his position and win.

It should be mentioned that he didn't manage to do this. Later a more definite refutation of the sacrifice was found: 10… Bg6! 11. Bg5 Nf6 12. Bxf6 gxf6 13. Bb3 Kf8 14. Nd2 Kg7.

At any rate, Nezh's ideas should have been examined, as he wasn't afraid of trying even the most speculative ones.

8. … d5
9. f3 h6

9… e3 was usually played. The most famous example was the game *Euwe—Keres* from the match-tournament for the *1948 World Championship:* 9… e3 10. f4 Bd6 11. Qf3? [A weakness. Correct was 11. Qh5† g6 and only then 12. Qf3.] Qf6 12. Qxe3† Nge7 13. Bxc6† bxc6 14. 0-0 0-0. Black got active play for his pawn.

10. fxe4 hxg5
11. exf5

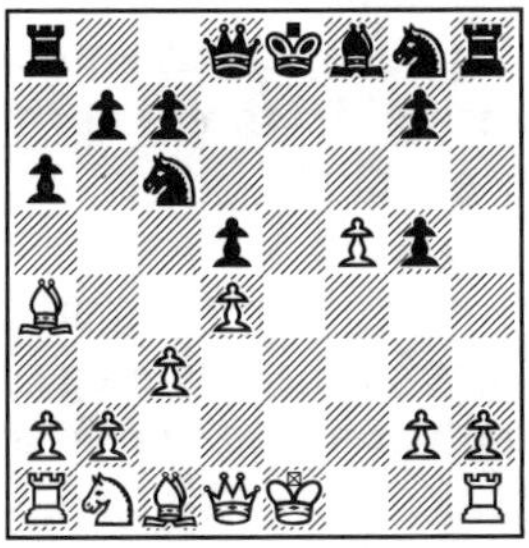

11. ... Bd6!

A considerable strengthening of the whole line, which was considered as incorrect for Black [using the game *Alexander—Aitken, England 1938]*. In that game Black played 11... Qd6 12. Bxg5 Be7 [12... Rxh2? 13. 0-0] 13. Qg4 b5 14. Bf4 and received no compensation for the two pawns. Unfortunately, neither the Yugoslavian *ECO*, nor any other opening books, mention that the authorship of this idea belonged to Nezhmetdinov.

12. Qg4

It isn't our aim to analyze in detail this interesting position, since it can be found in opening monographs on the Ruy Lopez. We'll just point out that besides the continuation in this game, there are other lines met in tournament practice: 12. Qe2† Kf8 13. Kd1 Qf6; 12. Qd3 Kf8 13. Nd2 Nf6; 12. Qf3 g4! 13. Qxg4 Nf6! 14. Qxg7 Rg8 15. Qh6 Rxg2. Everywhere Black gets better chances. Only in 12. Nd2 Qf6 13. Bc2 0-0-0 could White hope for defense.

12. ... Nf6

A good try, but I believe more conclusive was 12... Qe7† 13. Kd1 Nf6 14. Qxg5 0-0-0 15. Re1 Qd7 16. h3 Rde8, and Black whipped up an attack in *Kotkov—Shaposhnikov, Gorki 1963.*

13. Qxg5 Kf8
14. Bxc6

Nezh put a question mark to this exchange, but even after 14. Bf4 Rh5 15. Qg3 Qe7† 16. Kd1 Ne4 17. Qf3 Rxf5 Black had the advantage, *Baturinsky—Estrin, Moscow 1947.*

14. ... bxc6
15. Qg6 Qd7
16. Bg5 Re8†
17. Kd1 Ne4
18. Kc2

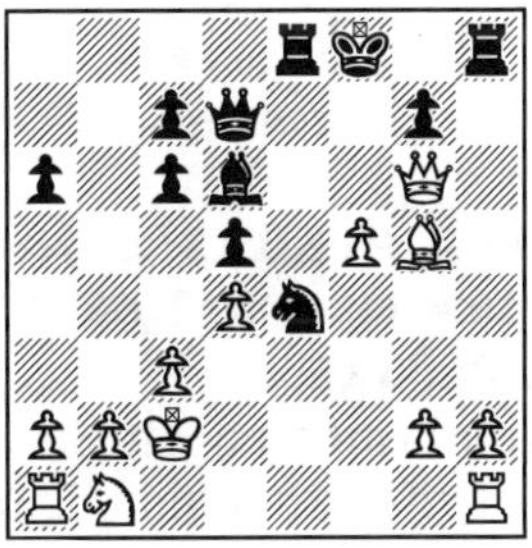

18. ... Qf7!!

Entering the endgame down two pawns! Black rightly considered that without Queens, White could easily be beaten, since his pieces were not developed.

19. Qxf7† Kxf7
20. Bc1 Ng3
21. Rg1 Rxh2
22. Nd2 Ne2
23. Rd1 Rxg2

The material had been won back, but White's problems, connected with the development on his queenside, were not solved, that's why the final result was clear.

24. Kb3 Nxc1†
25. Raxc1 Bf4
26. Nf3

26. Rc2 was useless because of 26... Ree2.

26. ... Bxc1
27. Rxc1 Rb8†
28. Ka3 Rbxb2
29. Ne5† Kf6
30. Rf1 c5
31. Nd7† Ke7

32. Nxc5 Rxa2†
33. Kb4 Rgb2†
34. Nb3 a5†

White surrendered **(0-1).**

68.

Super Nezh—V. Mikenas

B 02

Match, game 11

Kazan 1948

1. e4 Nf6 2. e5 Nd5 3. c4 Nb6 4. c5 Nd5 5. Bc4 e6 6. Nc3 d6 7. Nxd5 exd5 8. Bxd5 c6.

The line beginning with Black's 6th move was the Lithuanian Grandmaster Mikenas' invention. His idea: 8... dxe5 at once was bad because of 9. Qf3.

In the text, after 9. Bc4, 9...d5! would follow, and then 10...Bxc5. On the retreat 9. Bb3, 9... dxe5 is likely.

9. Bxf7†!

The first time Mikenas used his line was in the third game of the match. Rashid, having come across the novelty, understood the position well enough to respond likewise with an unexpected piece sacrifice.

9. ... Kxf7
10. cxd6 Qe8!

In the third game, the source of this variation, Black made the natural move 10... Be6 and on 11. f4 returned the extra piece: 11... Bxd6! 12. exd6 Re8 13. Kf2 Qxd6. It turned out that Black had the advantage, which was used at once. During the analysis after the game Nezh offered the right plan: 11. Nh3!, then d2-d4 with the threat Nh3-g5†. Evaluation of this position as a good one for White, was corroborated in the game *Petriaev—Sholohov, Novosibirsk 1955:* 11. Nf3 Nd7 12. 0-0 g6 13. d3 h6 14. Nd4 Qe8 15. f4 Kg8 16. Bd2, and White soon got the attack.

In this game Mikenas reinforced his play, creating the threat of capturing the piece on d6.

11. Qe2

Details are always important during the fight for the advantage, namely, it's difficult to find them in an unfamiliar position. 11 years later this "detail" was discovered by *E. Vasiukov* in his game with *B. Spassky (26th USSR championship).* He played 11. Qf3† Kg8 12. Qe3!. The subtlety was that Black was not capable of sacrificing back the piece at d6 and destroying the aggressive white pawns. After 12... Be6 13. Ne2 Nd7 White could have created a prospect-filled position by the move 14. f4!.

11. ... c5
12. Nf3 Bxd6!

A timely sacrifice, which can't be accepted by White. After 13. exd6 Qxe2† 14. Kxe2 Re8† 15. Kd1 Bg4 and then ...Nc6, Black has dangerous threats.

R.N.

13. Ng5† Kg6
14. Qd3† Kxg5
15. Qxd6

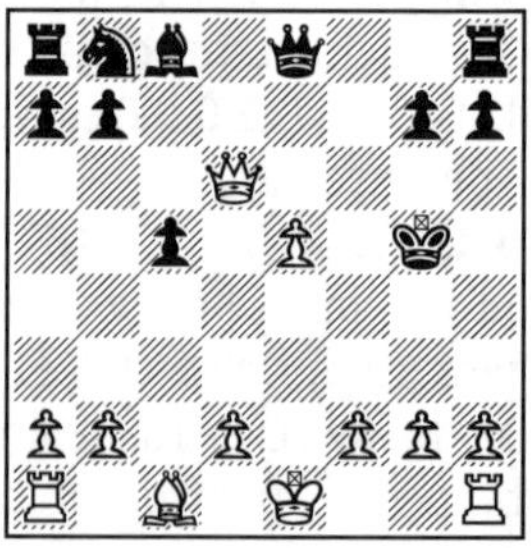

Everyone, who looks at the diagram [being unfamiliar with the moves played], will think: "This was a mistake. The King and Queen should exchange their places." It was not a mistake, and having seen it, it was hard to believe that Black wasn't losing, but actually had a good position after 15... Nc6! 16. d4† Kh5 17. Qxc5 Qe7!.

15. ... Qd8?

"There is one step from hatred to love." Alas, in chess it's enough to take one short step to turn a good position into a hopeless one. Black's King is in a crossfire.

16. d4† Kf5
17. g4†! Ke4

17... Kxg4 18. Rg1† Kh3 19. Qxc5 wasn't better, and nothing can help the King.

18. Qxc5 Rf8

On 18... Qxd4 White could have played 19. f3† Kd3 20. Qa3† Kc4 21. Qb3† Kc5 22. Be3.

19. 0-0 Kf3
20. h3!

This shows how horrible the King's position was.

20. ... b6
21. Qc3† Ke4
22. Qc4!

Mate on the open board is inevitable. Black resigned **(1-0)**.

69.

Super Nezh—V. Shcherbakov
B 97
USSR Team ch.
Riga 1954

1. e4 c5 2. Nf3 d6 3. d4 cxd4 4. Nxd4 Nf6 5. Nc3 a6 6. Bg5 e6 7. f4.

A sharp continuation, which became the basis for the creation of some very popular systems of the Sicilian Defense, played in thousands and thousands of games. It's hard to believe that this game was the first one among them, and that the move 7. f4 got it's baptism by fire here.

Thus, Rashid Gibyatovich was the author of a whole section of the Sicilian Defense.

7. ... Qb6

And master Vitaly Shcherbakov, Nezh's partner, held first claim in the gambit system B97.

8. Qd2 Qxb2
9. Nb3

At once, after this variation had appeared, both the theorists and the practitioners concentrated upon the continuation 9. Rb1. Tal, Fischer, Boleslavsky, Geller, Lilienthal and others participated in its analysis. However, in the Reykjavik match [1972], Spassky brought new life to Nezh's move 9. Nb3. It was a surprise to Fischer.

9. ... Nc6
10. Bd3 d5
11. Bxf6 gxf6
12. Na4 Qa3
13. Nb6

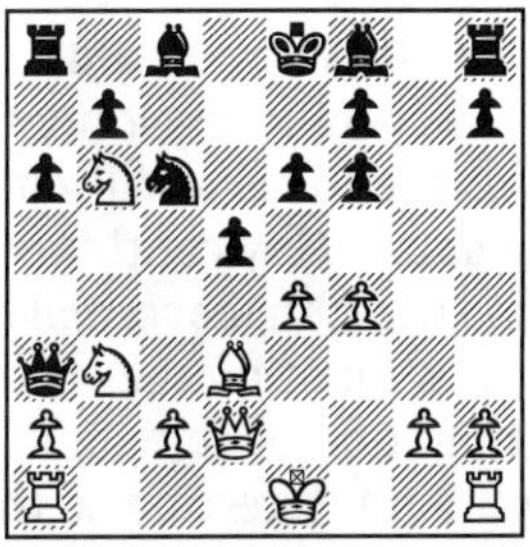

In spite of the lack of any information about this line, and with no home preparation, the players managed to find good continuations. Repeated use of the line, up to White's 13th move in the games of 1970-1980, serve as proof.

13. ... Nd4

Only this move, which was marked with an exclamation mark by Nezh, was refuted many years later, but this refutation was a masterpiece of analytical thought. 14.Rb1!! should have been played and Black would suffer some material losses: 14... Qxa2 15. c3! Qd2 16. Nxd2! won the piece, or 14... Nxb3 15. Rxb3, and the Rook would be lost.

Instead of 13... Nd4, 13...d4 was found for the following sequence: 14. 0-0 Rb8 15. Nc4 Qb4 16. Qe2, and by Boleslavsky's analysis White can count on having the advantage.

14. Kf1

Who would have enough courage to put question marks to the last moves of these chessplayers?

14. ...	**Nxb3**
15. cxb3	**Rb8**
16. exd5	**Qb4**
17. Qxb4	**Bxb4**
18. Rc1	**0-0**
19. Kf2	**Bd2**
20. Rxc8	**Rbxc8**
21. Nxc8	**Rxc8**
22. dxe6	**fxe6**
23. Bc4	**Kf8**
24. Kf3	**Ke7**
25. Rd1	**Ba5**

After the opening revelations the position was equalized and brought to a calm endgame. Play continued a long time, up to the 60th move, and finished as a draw. We'll draw the curtains, as the continuation of the game doesn't add anything interesting to the characteristics of Nezh's creation.

A draw **(1/2-1/2).**

70.

Super Nezh—R. Wade

C 11

Bucharest 1954

1. e4 e6 2. d4 d5 3. Nc3 Nf6 4. e5 Nfd7 5. f4 c5 6. dxc5.

This was the way Steinitz liked to play and we've already seen that in similar "French" schemes Nezh often followed the principles of the first world champion.

6. ...	**Nc6**
7. Nf3	**Bxc5**
8. Bd3	**f6**
9. exf6	**Nxf6**
10. Qe2	**0-0**
11. Bd2	**e5?!**

After this game the push of the pawn to the center was considered premature. In the game *Tringov—Fuchs, Sofia 1958,* considered to be seminal, there was: 11... Bd7 12. 0-0-0 Kh8 13. Rde1 b5!, and Black obtained a position with prospects.

12. fxe5 Bg4

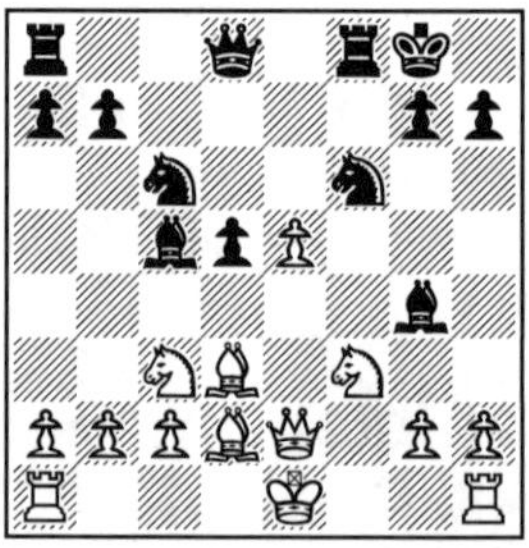

This position was thoroughly analyzed by Nezh. Here's what he wrote:

The last two moves brought immense complications to Black. I had to think a lot, because his moves were quick, and I understood that I could become a victim of home preparation. First, all the lines connected with accepting the sacrifice of the piece should be enumerated. It should be mentioned that in dealing with difficult, tangled, double-edged positions of different kinds, composure and a clear

mind are needed. It's very important not to be carried away by the chase for the "Luck of the mating attack."
R.N.

[Ed.: Nezh noticed this "chase" in the alluring line: 13. exf6 Re8 14. Ne4 (If 14. f7†, then 14... Kxf7 15. Ng5† Kg8 16. Bxh7† Kh8 17. Nf7† Kxh7 18. Nxd8 doesn't work because of 18... Raxd8 19. Kd1 {19. Qxe8 looks like there might be a perpetual check, but after 19... Rxe8† 20. Kf1 Rf8† 21. Ke1 Bf2† 22. Kf1 Nd4 23. Rc1 Bh3! wins} Rxe2 20. Nxe2 Nd4 21. Re1 Re8 22. c3 Bxe2† 23. Kc1 Nc6 and Black has the advantage.) dxe4 15. Bc4† Kf8? 16. Ng5 Bxe2 17. Nxh7#.]

I thought 90 minutes over the next move! Having dealt with variations for the first 15-20 minutes and finding that they were unacceptable, I dove into the position again. The move 13. 0-0-0 strikes the eye at once. But how should the pieces be rearranged successfully after 13... Nd4? It took another 35-40 minutes to find the best defensive moves [it is more difficult to find "tranquil" moves than the forcing ones]. Then I got back to the lines with 13. exf6 again, checked them, and then finally specified the rearranging of the position in the game.
R.N.

This long quotation tells us more about the artistic credo of Nezh than ten of his games. First, we see that the basis of his surprising creations was an astonishing, refined mastery of the details. The last two elements are the very core of "composure and a clear mind."

Secondly, the way Nezh thinks during the game is quite contrary to that of such geniuses of positional flair such as Capablanca and Petrosyan. Undoubtedly, neither Capablanca nor Petrosy0an would spend so much time over the details of the variations connected with 13. exf6. Most likely they would refute this move at once, by intuition.

And thirdly, it's really true that "our deficiencies merit a continued study." Still, one cannot say how Nezh should rationally spend his analytical powers and time during the game [and during the tournament]. A chess-player with a high discipline of thinking [e.g. Karpov] would have never let himself lose energy [like Nezh] on the secondary accounting of a doubtful continuation. That was one of the reasons for Nezh's uneven play: sharp changes between the inspiration and fantasy on the one hand, and the frequent and unexplainable defeats from weaker rivals on the other hand. It was just impossible for a "mere" mortal to perform miracles all the time.

13. 0-0-0 Nd4
14. Qe1 Nh5
15. Be2!

As Nezh said, this was the hardest move to find in the game, or it was perhaps the most labor-intensive. His labor was justified by the fact that White could easily solve the problems around the f3-square. The attempt by 15. Nxd4 Bxd4! 16. Be2 Bf2 would not reach its goal.

15. ... Rxf3!?

This was stronger than 15... Nxf3 16. Bxf3 Bxf3 17. gxf3 Rxf3 18. Qe2 Rf5 19. Rhf1 Rxf1 20. Rxf1 g6 21. Qf3 with a decisive advantage for White.

16. gxf3 Nxf3

Worse would have been 16... Bxf3 17. Bxf3 Nxf3 18. Qe2 Nxd2 19. Qxh5.

17. Bxf3 Bxf3
18. Rf1 Bxd1
19. Qxd1

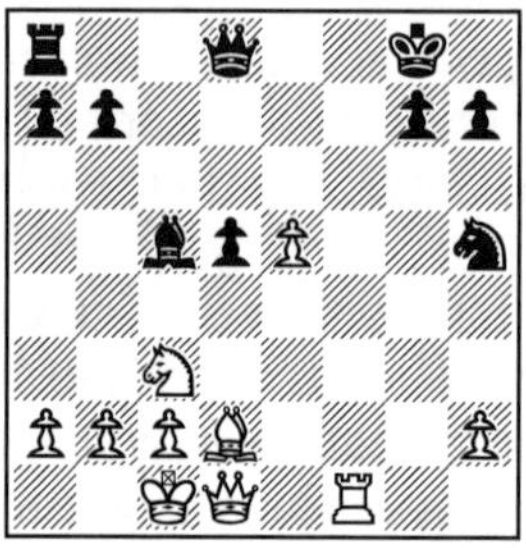

Hard thinking about the various possibilities brought an important result: the d-pawn was very weak, and the black Knight is out of play. These advantages should be enough to win.

19. ... g6

On 19... Qh4, very strong was 20. Qf3.

20. Qf3

The ever self-critical Nezh considered 20. Bh6! to be stronger.

20. ... Qd7
21. Nxd5 Rf8
22. Nf6† Nxf6
23. exf6 Bd4
24. Qd3 Rf7
25. c3 Be5
26. Qe3!

In spite of the preservation of the extra pawn, it was too early to start the endgame since the f6-pawn would be returned.

26. ... Bxf6

Of course, this pawn was more dangerous than the one on h2.

27. Qxa7 h5
28. Rg1 Kh7
29. Qe3 Bg7
30. Qe4 Qf5

Besides the extra pawn, White has strong positional pressure which Black couldn't stand. Black had preferred an endgame. It was a relief for White to achieve victory. 30... Qd6 was better. There was no need to fear 31. Rg5 with the threat 32. Rxh5† because of 31... Bh6!.

31. Qxf5 Rxf5
32. Rg2 Bh6
33. a4 g5
34. b4 g4
35. a5 Rf3
36. Kc2 Bf8
37. b5 Bc5
38. Re2 Rf2
39. Rxf2 Bxf2
40. Kd3 h4
41. Ke2

Black surrendered **(1-0).**

71.

A. Zamikhovsky—Super Nezh

E 81

Semi-finals 24th USSR ch.

Kharkov 1956

1. d4 Nf6 2. c4 g6 3. Nc3 Bg7 4. e4 d6 5. f3 0-0 6. Be3 Nbd7.

Nowadays this continuation isn't the normal line of Sämisch's system. The Knight on d7 is not in a good position as it doesn't participate in the fight for the key square d4. It also closes a diagonal for the Bishop. Black had a definite plan: to play c7-c5, bringing to life the black-squared Bishop, and creating active play on the queenside.

7. Qd2

Nezh's opening idea in this game produced such an impression that, as an alternative, the move 7. Nh3 became popular.

7. ... c5
8. Nge2 a6
9. 0-0-0

For the past ten years or so, White has used many other continuations: 9. Rd1, 9. Ng3, 9. g4, 9. dxc5, and 9. Nc1. The last novelty is 9. Bh6, but let's not get distracted.

9. ... Qa5
10. Kb1 b5
11. dxc5

We'll discuss the continuation 11. Nd5 later.

11. ... dxc5

11... Nxc5 12. Bxc5! dxc5 13. Nd5 Qxd2 14. Nxe7† brings about the loss of a pawn.

12. Nd5

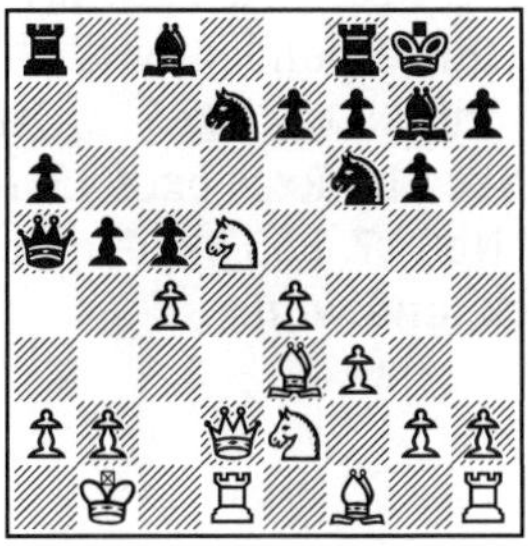

A threatening move because after 12... Qd8 13. Nxf6 Bxf6 14. Nc3 Black just has a bad position.

12. ... Nxd5!

A radical way to solve the problem—with the help of an unforeseen [at that time!] sacrifice of his Queen.

13. Qxa5

It had been supposed for a long time that White should take the Queen if he wanted to fight for the advantage. In the game *Van der Sterren—De Jong, Wijk aan Zee 1990*, White responded with 13. cxd5!?. Not willing to play an endgame, where problems with the pawns on the queenside [after the undermining a2-a4] could arise, Black preferred 13... Qc7. After 14. Bh6! a5 15. h4 Nb6 16. Bxg7 Kxg7 17. h5 White's attack on the kingside turned out to be too impetuous.

13. ... Nxe3
14. Rc1

The most dangerous line for Black was the line 14. Rxd7 Bxd7 15. Qd2 with the offering of two pieces. And then after 15... Nxc4! 16. Qxd7 Rad8 17. Qxe7 Rd1† 18. Nc1 [18. Kc2? doesn't do the job since after 18... Rd2† White is obliged to move the King to b1, and in that case simply 19... Rfd8 with a winning attack.] Bh6 19. Bxc4! Rxh1 20. Bxf7†! Rxf7. White should be satisfed with the perpetual check—21. Qe8† Kg7 22. Qe5†, etc. We will mention that on 15... Nxf1 16. Rxf1 Be6 Black has Rook, Bishop and pawn for the Queen, all placed in active positions.

R.N.

We can add to Nezh's detailed analysis that in the last variation 16. Qxd7 wouldn't work [instead of 16. Rxf1], because of 16... Rad8 17. Qxe7 Rd1† 18. Nc1 Bh6.

14. ... Nxc4
15. Rxc4!

A timely return of material, because after the retreat of the Queen, Black would take on b2 with the Knight and get chances to attack, having almost equal material [two pieces and two pawns for the Queen].

15. ... bxc4
16. Nc3 Rb8
17. Bxc4

This position has been analyzed and practically tested since then.

Geller and Boleslavsky offered 17. Kc2!?, although Boleslavsky thought that White's chances were better, and Geller considered that Black had enough compensation for the Queen.

Geller's thoughts might be more realistic. An indirect proof of this was a comparatively fresh correspondence game *Hempel—Eger, 1989/1991*, in which, after 17. f4 Bd4! 18. Bxc4 Rb4! 19. Nd5 Rxc4 20. Nxe7† Kg7 21. Nxc8 Rb4 22. b3 Rxc8, Black had achieved a decisive advantage.

Zamikhovsky's move was weaker than the one offered by theorists [17. Kc2].

17.	**...**	**Ne5**
18.	**Be2**	**Be6**
19.	**Rd1**	**Bc4?**

A serious inaccuracy, which spoiled Nezh's brilliant opening idea. He could have obtained the advantage by playing 19... Nc6! 20. Qxc5 Nb4. Later Black could choose between the doubling of his Rooks along the b-file, or play along the d-file.

20.	**Rd2**	**Nc6**
21.	**Qa3**	**Be6**

Though he lost two tempi, Black had an idea: he would let White stabilize the position and then [Black] would prove that White's material advantage would not be a decisive factor.

22.	**Qxc5!**	**Nb4**
23.	**a3**	**Rfc8**
24.	**Qxc8†**	**Rxc8**
25.	**axb4**	**Be5**

After 25... Bxc3 26. bxc3 Rxc3 27. Bxa6 Black would have had a bad endgame.

26.	**Bxa6**	**Rb8**
27.	**g3**	**Rxb4**
28.	**Kc1**	**Kg7**
29.	**Bd3**	**Bd4**
30.	**Nd1**	**h5**
31.	**Re2**	**Rb3**
32.	**Kc2**	**Rb6**
33.	**Nc3**	**Bb3†**
34.	**Kc1**	**Rc6**
35.	**Kd2**	**Rc5**
36.	**Re1**	**Ra5**
37.	**Bc2**	**Bc4**
38.	**Bd3**	**Bb3**
39.	**Bc2**	**Bc4**
40.	**Bd3**	**Bb3**
41.	**Bc2**	

Drawn **(1/2-1/2).**

In its time this game didn't gain much attention, but one and a half years later the game *Bobotsov–Tal* caused a furor at the student's team world championship, *Varna 1958.* Here White played 11. Nd5 instead of 11. dxc5, which seemed weaker. Tal responded with the same Queen sacrifice 11... Nxd5 12. Qxa5 Nxe3 13. Rc1 Nxc4 14. Rxc4 bxc4 15. Nc1 Rb8 16. Bxc4 Nb6 17. Bb3 Bxd4, quickly got an attack, and won.

72.

Super Nezh—Y. Sakharov

B 32

Match, Russia—Ukraine

Leningrad 1957

1. e4 c5 2. Nf3 Nc6 3. d4 cxd4 4. Nxd4 e5 5. Nb5 a6.

At that time this line was an innovation. Why was this? Black is giving the d5-square to White, he's also ready to be checked at d6, and is going to play with the backward d-pawn?!

The first time this revolutionary move was played was by the young master *A. Lutikov* [later a grandmaster, alas, now deceased] in his game with *A. Lein* in the *semi-finals* of the *23rd USSR ch., 1955.*

6.	**Nd6†**	**Bxd6**

7. Qxd6 Qf6
8. Qc7

It wasn't easy to decide, which was better here: five (!) continuations [8. Qxf6, 8. Qd3, 8. Qd2, 8. Qd1, or 8. Qa3] were used, not including the move given in this game. It was finally settled: except for the first two lines, these variations would provide White with the advantage. That's why Lutikov's move almost disappeared from modern practice. But at that time nothing was clear and they played relying on intuition.

The move chosen by Nezh is very logical: White is going to block the promotion on the queenside. In the first source game Lein reacted badly to the novelty: 8. Qd2 Qg6 9. f3 d6 10. Bc4 Be6 11. Bxe6 fxe6 12. 0-0 Rd8, and Black had splendid play.

8. ... Nge7
9. Nc3 Nb4
10. Bd3 d5
11. 0-0 d4?!

A strengthening of the center wasn't profitable for Black. Taimanov recommended 11... 0-0 12. exd5 Nexd5 13. Nxd5 Nxd5 14. Qa5 Be6 15. Be4 with a better position for White.

12. Ne2 Nxd3

More exact was 12... 0-0 13. Bd2 and only now 13... Nxd3 14. cxd3 Nc6 with a small advantage to White.

13. cxd3 g5?!

Black was radically blocking the opening of lines by means of f2-f4, but this was too straightforward. Black, of course, was in a weaker position. The more prudent 13... Nc6 14. f4 Qe7 15. Qxe7† Ke7 16. fxe5 Nxe5 17. b3 Rd8 would have let him defend, *Lukin—Gizhdavu, Bucharest 1968.*

14. Bd2 Nc6
15. Rac1 0-0
16. Ng3 h6
17. b4!

Black was defeated in the opening battle, and now the decisive climax began.

17. ... Re8

An attempt to get rid of the Queen by paralyzing the queenside didn't work: 17... Qd8 18. Rxc6! [Damsky recommended 18. Qxd8 Rxd8 19. Rc5 f6 20. Rfc1. That was not very reassuring since Black could defend in a good way.] bxc6 19. Qxe5,

and Black can't repel the coming attack (f4, etc.).

R.N.

18. a4 Nd8

After having protected the e5-pawn, by 17... Re8, 18... Qd8 was playable as it was hard to get a worthwhile position without the Queens. Black still hoped to strengthen his queenside.

19. Rc5! Qg7

The Bishop was still unable to move into the open: 19... Bg4 20. f3 Rc8 21. fxg4.

20. Rd5 Bg4
21. Rc1!

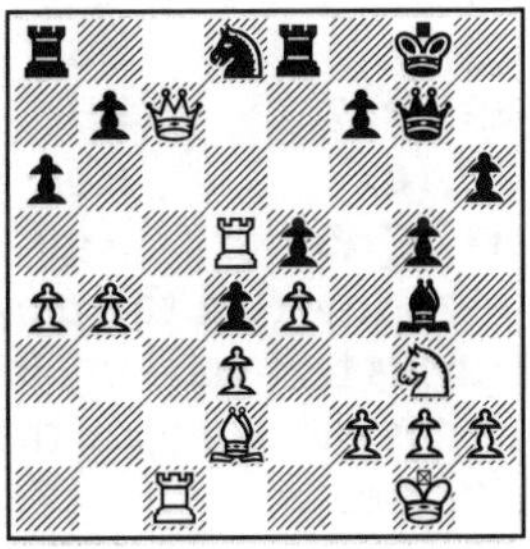

21. ... Kh7?!

Being under pressure the whole game, Sakharov believed White and didn't make his planned move, 21... Rc8. White would obtain a material advantage by force: 22. Qxc8 Bxc8 23. Rxc8 Qf8 24. Nh5 Qe7 [After 24... f6 25. Rd7 Black has no useful moves.] 25. Rd7! Qe6 26. Rcxd8 Rxd8 27. Rxd8† Kh7 28. Kf1! Qb3 29. Ke2 Qxa4. However, Black kept chances to continue the fight in this line. Naturally it was hard to evaluate everything correctly, but Black missed a good practical chance.

22. h3 Be6
23. Nf5!

Again, as in some other games, the text of the game is different in various sources. Nezh himself missed the moves 22. h3 Be6 and pointed at once to 22. Nf5 [R. Nezhmetdinov's *Best Games*]. In this case it leads only to an unimportant rearrangement of the h-pawn. White doesn't distract his attention by taking the pawn: 23. Rxe5? Rc8 24. Qd6 Rxc1 25. Bxc1 Nc6, and Black gets counterplay.

23. ... Bxf5
24. exf5 Qf6
25. g4 Re7
26. Rd7 Rxd7
27. Qxd7 Kg7
28. Rc5

Now Black was obliged to go in for a further weakening of his position because of the threat 29. Qc7, winning a pawn.

28. ... b6
29. Rc7 b5
30. a5 Rb8
31. Qd5 Kg8

Here Nezh inverted the moves Rb8 and Kg8 [in his text version]. It doesn't matter, as it is zugzwang on the board.

32. Bc1 Qg7
33. Qc5 Qf8
34. Qa7

Black surrendered **(1-0).**

73.

Super Nezh—D. Bergin
C 63
Russian Spartakiade
Joshkar-Ola 1963

1. e4 e5 2. Nf3 Nc6 3. Bb5 f5.

Perhaps, Rashid Gibyatovich's reputation as an expert on the Ruy Lopez, against whom it was difficult to play against in the classical lines, influenced the choice of Jaenisch's gambit by the young chess master.

4. Nc3 fxe4
5. Nxe4 d5
6. Ng3

Nezh didn't want to get involved in major complications after 6. Nxe5 dxe4 7. Nxc6 because he was afraid of some trick prepared by his rival at home.

6. ... Bg4
7. h3 Bxf3
8. Qxf3 Nf6
9. 0-0 Bd6
10. Nh5 e4

It was known that 10... Nxh5 11. Qxh5† g6 12. Qf3 a6 13. Ba4 Qh4 14. c4! gives the advantage to White.

11. Qf5 Qd7?

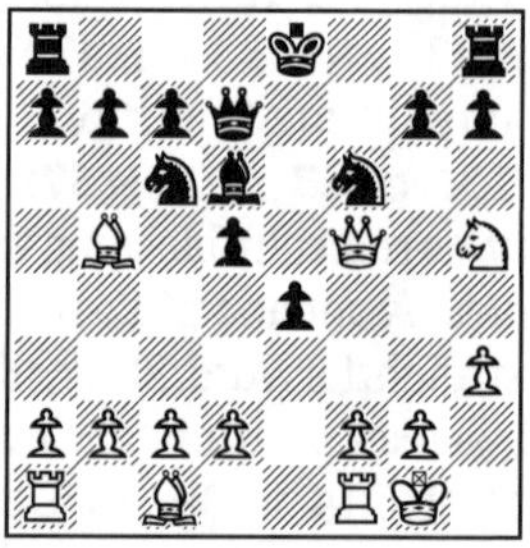

A novelty, in which the main idea is 12. Nxf6† gxf6 13. Qxf6 Rg8, when Black would get the initiative after sacrificing the pawn. Nezh found an opportunity to accept the pawn in another way, which clearly wasn't counted on by Bergin. That's why 11... 0-0 12. Nxf6† Qxf6 13. Qxd5† Kh8 was better since Black would take the initiative into his own hands.

12. Qxf6!

A plain enough refutation and Black was obliged to play the endgame down a pawn [instead of playing his attacking ambitions].

12.	**...**	**gxf6**
13.	**Nxf6†**	**Ke7**
14.	**Nxd7**	**Kxd7**
15.	**d3**	**Rhg8**
16.	**dxe4**	**dxe4**
17.	**Rd1**	**Rg6**
18.	**Bc4!**	

Accuracy was essential in order to extinguish any possible Black initiative.

18.	**...**	**Rf8**
19.	**Bd5**	**Rgf6**
20.	**Be3**	**Re8**
21.	**a3**	

Black couldn't use his advantage in development and the position was becoming volatile. White was able to make use of the extra pawn.

21. ... Kc8?!

This was a desperate attempt to get counterplay at any price. However it quickly turned out that the price of the counterchance was too high. More consistent would have been 21... b6, abstaining from the weakened pawn structure.

22.	**Bxc6**	**bxc6**
23.	**Bxa7**	**c5**
24.	**b4**	**e3**

Continuing in the same search for counterplay at any cost. Perhaps chances would have been better with 24... cxb4 25. axb4 Bxb4, reducing the number of backward pawns.

25.	**fxe3**	**Bg3**
26.	**Bxc5**	**Rf2**

The Rook broke through to the second rank, but the cost was a great deal of material. At the same time White can return some of the extra material to make Black's counterthreats less dangerous.

27.	**Rf1**	**Rxc2**
28.	**Rf8**	**Rxf8**
29.	**Bxf8**	**Bf2†**
30.	**Kh2**	**Bxe3**
31.	**Rf1**	**h5**

31... Ra2 32. b5 Rb2 33. Rf5 also offered nothing. Black's last hope was to make a seige of the white King, but White kept the situation under control.

32.	**Rf5**	**h4**
33.	**Bc5!**	**Bc1**
34.	**a4**	**Rc4**
35.	**a5**	**Bf4†**
36.	**Kg1**	**Bg3**
37.	**a6**	**Rc1†**
38.	**Rf1**	**Bh2†**
39.	**Kf2**	**Rc2†**
40.	**Ke3**	**Ra2**
41.	**b5**	**Ra5**
42.	**Ke4**	**c6**
43.	**Rf8†**	**Kd7**
44.	**a7**	

Black surrendered **(1-0).**

74.

V. Bagirov—Super Nezh

A 21

Baku 1964

1. c4 e5 2. Nc3 f5 3. d4 exd4 4. Qxd4 Nc6 5. Qe3† Kf7!?.

An original novelty of Nezh's, which worked in this game with a ruinous effect. In the game *Matulovich—Kozomara, Sarajevo 1960,* White achieved a clear advantage after 5... Be7 6. Nd5! Nf6 7. Nxf6† gxf6 8. Nf3 d5 9. cxd5 Qxd5 10. Bd2.

Much later, 5... Nce7 was offered

instead of 5... Kf7.

6. Nh3

Later Taimanov offered 6. Nf3 Nf6 7. Nd5!? with the continuation: 7... Nxd5 8. cxd5 Bb4† 9. Bd2 Re8 10. Qf4 Bxd2† 11. Nxd2 Ne7 12. d6! with advantage.

6. ... Nf6

7. Ng5†?

A naïve check which let Black actively develop his forces. The right plan was again offered by Taimanov: 7. Qd2! [stopping d7-d5]. Now on 7... h6 would follow 8. Nf4!, controlling the d5-square for certain and then playing g2-g3, Bg2 and Nf4-d5. In case of 7... Bb4 8. a3 Bxc3 9. Qxc3 d5 10. cxd5 Nxd5 11.Qb3 White's chances would also be better.

7. ... Kg8

8. g3 h6

9. Nh3 d5!

This thrust provides Black with good play.

10. cxd5 Nxd5

11. Qd2

Bad was 11. Nxd5 Qxd5 12. Rg1 Nb4 with dangerous threats.

11. ... Ndb4

12. Qxd8 Nxd8

13. Kd1 Be6

14. Nf4 Bf7

It's strange, but *ECO* rated this position as equal. That is not true, since Black had the initiative in his hands.

15. Be3 Ndc6

16. Bg2 Rd8†

17. Kc1 g5

18. Nd3

White was ready to surrender a pawn. The Knight had no prospects on h3.

18. ... Nxd3†

19. exd3

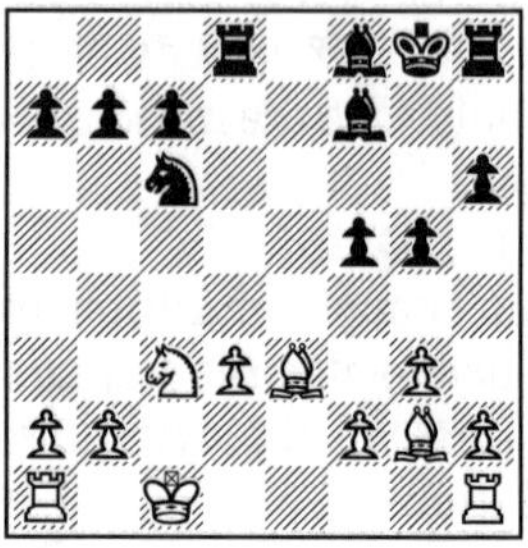

19. ... Nb4!

20. f4

20. Bxb7 was dangerous, 20... c6! 21. a3 Nxd3† 22. Kc2 f4 23. gxf4 Bg6!.

20. ... Nxd3†

21. Kb1 gxf4

22. gxf4

More consistent would have been 22. Bxf4.

22. ... Bg7

There was the threat of 23... Nxb2 24. Kxb2 Rd3.

23. Rd1 Kh7

24. Bxb7

In a good position this move would rarely come to mind, but here White had nothing to lose.

24. ... Bh5

25. Rg1 Rhe8

26. Bxa7 Bxc3

27. bxc3 Re2

28. Rg2 Re1†

White surrendered **(0-1).**

I don't see that White has made a clear mistake in the next game. Perhaps, it's a difficult task to play the King's Gambit against Nezhmetdinov.

V. Simagin

75.

V. Heuer—Super Nezh
C 37
Moscow 1964

1. e4 e5 2. f4 exf4 3. Nf3 h6 4. d4 g5 5. Bc4 Bg7 6. c3.

This modest treatment of a double-edged gambit, such as the King's Gambit, can't create problems for Black. In times of yore preferable was 5. g3 fxg3 6. Nc3, or 5. Nc3 Bg7 6. g3.

6. ... Ne7
7. 0-0 0-0
8. g3 d5!

Black had already obtained better play.

9. exd5 fxg3
10. hxg3 Nf5
11. Kg2 b5!

A struggle for the diagonal (a8-h1) had begun.

12. Bb3 Qd7
13. Qd3 Nd6
14. Rh1 Qf5!

Black was steadfastly imposing his will on his opponent. The Queen exchange was a forced one.

15. Qxf5 Bxf5
16. Re1

There was no wish to let the Bishop go to e4, but to prevent it by any other way [e.g., 16. Nbd2] was bad, as the Knight will stop up the whole queen-side.

16. ... Nd7
17. Be3 a5
18. a4

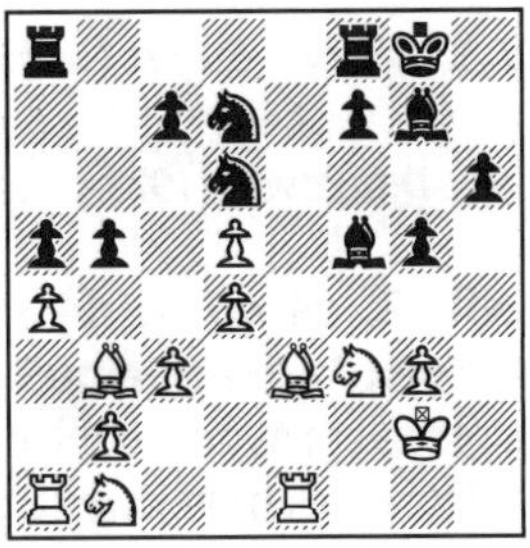

18. ... bxa4!

It's characteristic of Nezh to lead a dynamic fight on both wings.

V. Simagin

19. Bxa4 Rab8
20. b3 Nb6
21. Bc6 Be4
22. Nbd2 Bxd5
23. Bxd5 Nxd5

A sound strategy which brought good fruit, an extra pawn.

24. c4 Nxe3†
25. Rxe3 Nf5
26. Re4 Rfd8
27. Rxa5 Nxd4
28. Nxd4 Bxd4

Here the struggle was finished. Black won easily. For the record, the other moves were: **29. Rf5 Bg7 30. Re2 Rd3 31. Rf3 Rxf3 32. Kxf3 f5 33. Re3 Kf7 34. Rd3 Ke6 35. Nf1 Ra8 36. g4 h5 37. gxf5† Kxf5 38. Ne3† Ke6 39. b4 Rf8† 40. Kg2 Be5 41. b5 g4 42. c5 Rf3 43. b6 cxb6 44. cxb6 h4 45. b7 h3† 46. Kh1 g3 47. Rb3 g2† 48. Kg1 h2† (0-1).**

76.
V. Karasev—Super Nezh
A 32
Daugavpils 1973

1. Nf3 Nf6 2. c4 c5 3. d4 cxd4 4. Nxd4 e6 5. Nc3 Bb4 6. Ndb5.

This is played to avoid doubled pawns, but it also lets Black have an extra tempo for development. Nevertheless, this continuation is considered by theory to be one of the best.

6. ... 0-0
7. Bf4?!

Instead of the logical 7. a3 Bxc3† 8. Nxc3 d5, White chose a way in which tactical complications were not dangerous for Black.

7. ... d5
8. a3

8. Nc7? would not be good because of 8... Nh5 9. Be5 Nc6. Also 8. e3 could be played, but after 8... a6! 9. a3 Ba5 10. Nd6 Nc6 11. Bg3 Bxc3† 12. bxc3 Qa5, Black got excellent chances, *Chernikov—Polugaevsky, Rostov 1971.*

8. ... Bxc3†
9. Nxc3

Preventing the pawn from being doubled, White agrees to lose a tempo again, but it would give the initiative to Black. In the game *Raichevich—Bertok, Yugoslavia 1977,* White preferred 9. bxc3 Nc6 10. Bd6 Re8 11. c5, but after 11... Ne4 12. Nc7 Qf6! 13. Qd3 Qxf2† 14. Kd1 Bd7 15. Nxa8 Rxa8 Black got nice play for the sacrificed material.

9. ... d4
10. Nb5 a6!?

The best move here should be 10... Nc6, which allows Black full control over the center, but Nezh decided to make an interesting sacrifice.

11. Nc7

Practically speaking, White had no choice: 11. Bc7 [11. Nxd4? e5! 12. Bxe5 Qa5†] Qd7 12. Bxb8 axb5 13. Be5 Rd8 14. cxb5 [14. e3? d3] Qxb5 gives him a tough position.

11. ... Ra7
12. Nb5?

The Knight was in danger and, after 12... Nc6, it would have been doomed. That was why White had no time to linger. The lack of protection for the Knight on b8 should be noted. White would have done better by 12. Nd5 exd5 13. Bxb8 Ra8 14. Be5 dxc4 15. Qxd4 Be6, though even there the play of Black would have been much better.

12. ... axb5
13. Bxb8 bxc4!
14. Bxa7 Qa5†
15. Qd2 Qxa7

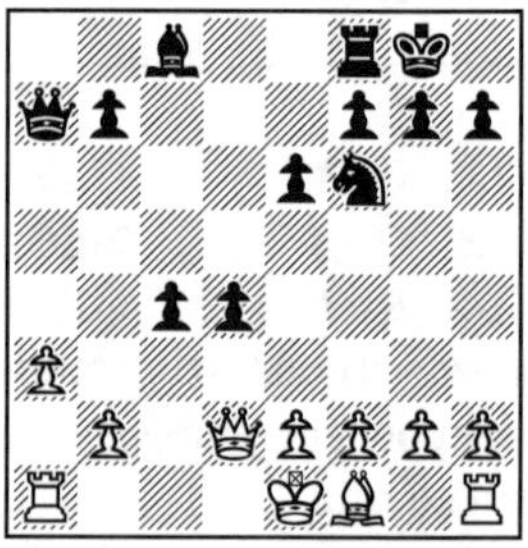

Though it doesn't happen often, even grandmasters can blindly walk into forced opening lines and end up in a disaster.

Why does it happen? Well, in chasing some material or tactical advantages, even an experienced chessplayer can be carried away and forget the basic laws of chess strategy, which are as natural for him as the rules of grammar or arithmetic. Here the strong master Karasev [Leningrad's champion and a participant in three USSR championships] was left with nothing. He either fell victim to some theorist's piece of advice, or had prepared this "strengthening" during his home analysis.

Let's have a look at the position: the white pieces are absolutely undeveloped, and the King has no suitable shelter. At the same time Black has a strong pawn mass in the center and good possibilities for success. All he has to do is just smash the white King who has gotten stuck in the center.

16. e3 d3
17. g3

On 17. f3 Nezh planned 17... Nd5 18. Kf2 f5 19. g3 e5 with a sizeable attack in the center.

17. ... Ne4
18. Qb4 d2†
19. Ke2 Qa6!
20. Kf3

20. f3 doesn't help. 20... c3† 21. Kd1 cxb2 22. Rb1 [22. Qxb2 loses at once to 22... Qa4† 23. Ke2 Rd8, or 23. Qc2 Nf2† 24. Kxd2 Rd8† 25. Kc1 Rd1†.] Qc6 23. Bc4 [23. fxe4 Qc1†] Rd8 24. Rf1 b5! 25. fxe4 bxc4 26. Rxb2 c3 27. Rc2 Qa6! 28. Rf2 [28. Rf3 Qe2!!] e5 and there is no defense from the Bishop's check.

20. ... Qc6
21. Ke2 Qd5
22. Rd1 e5
23. h3 b6
24. Rg1 c3
25. bxc3 Nxc3†!

Mate was inevitable and so White surrendered **(0-1).** One of Nezh's last tournament games and his last prize "for beauty."

Semi-finals 24th USSR ch. / Kharkov 1956

	Players	**1**	**2**	**3**	**4**	**5**	**6**	**7**	**8**	**9**	**10**	**11**	**12**	**13**	**14**	**15**	**16**	**17**	**18**	**19**	**Points**	**Place**
1	Boleslavsky	•	▒	▒	▒	▒	▒	▒	■	▒	▒	▒	▒	▒	■	■	▒	▒	■	■	11.5	1-3
2	Nezhmetdinov	▒	•	▒	▒	▒	▒		■			■	■	■	■	▒	■	▒	■	■	11.5	1-3
3	Tarasov	▒	▒	•	▒	▒	▒	▒	▒	▒	▒	■	▒	▒	▒	▒	■	■	■	■	11.5	1-3
4	Bannik	▒	▒	▒	•	▒	▒	■		■		■	▒	▒	▒		■	■	■	■	11	4-5
5	Holmov	▒	▒	▒	▒	•	■	▒	■		■			■	■	▒	▒	■	■	▒	11	4-5
6	Aronson	▒	▒	▒	▒		•	▒	▒	■	▒	■	■	▒	▒	■		■	■		10.5	6-7
7	Borisenko	▒	■	▒		▒	▒	•	▒	▒	■			■	▒	■	■	▒	■	▒	10.5	6-7
8	Vasiukov			▒	■		▒	▒	•		■		■	▒	■	■	▒	▒	■	■	10	8-10
9	Klarvin	▒	■	▒		■		▒	■	•	▒	■				▒	■	▒	■	■	10	8-10
10	Nei	▒	■	▒	■		▒			▒	•	▒	▒	▒	▒	■	■		■	■	10	8-10
11	Suetin	▒				■		■	■		▒	•	■	■		▒	■	■		■	9.5	11
12	Romanovsky	▒		▒	▒	■		■		■	▒		•		■	■		▒		■	8.5	12
13	Chistyakov	▒		▒	▒		▒		▒	■	▒		■	•	■	▒		■		▒	8	13
14	Vasillchuk			▒	▒		▒	▒		■	▒	■			•	▒	■	▒		■	7.5	14-15
15	Shamkovich		▒	▒	■	▒				▒		▒		▒	▒	•	■	▒	▒	■	7.5	14-15
16	Makarov	▒				▒	■		▒				■	■			•	■	▒	■	7	16
17	Zamikhovsky	▒	▒					▒	▒	▒	■		▒		▒	▒		•	▒		5.5	17-18
18	Livshin											■	■	■	■	▒	▒	▒	•		5.5	17-18
19	Matsukevich					▒	■	▒						▒				■	■	•	4.5	19
20	Simagin	▒	▒	—	—	■	■	—	—	—	—	—	—	—	—	▒	—	▒	▒	—	withdrew	
		1	2	3	4	5	6	7	8	9	10	11	12	13	14	15	16	17	18	19		

The Endgame

Of course, Rashid Nezhmetdinov can't be regarded as a King of the endgame. Still, many interesting endings can be found in his rich tournament practice. Even in them a characteristic of Nezh's handwriting can be felt: a concrete way of thinking, a tendency to solve problems tactically, and his distaste for passive defense.

77.

R. Holmov—Super Nezh

E 61

Yaroslavl 1947

1. d4 Nf6 2. Nf3 d6 3. h3 g6 4. Bf4 Bg7 5. c4 0-0 6. Nc3 Nc6 7. e3 Nd7 8. d5 Nce5 9. Be2 Nxf3† 10. Bxf3† e5 11. dxe6 fxe6 12. 0-0 Ne5 13. Be2 b6 14. Bg3 Ba6 15. f4?!.

White started complications which lead to nothing. Better, to keep equality, were 15. Qb3 or 15. Qa4.

15. ...	**Nxc4**
16. Qa4	**Nxb2**
17. Qxa6	

17. Qb3? doesn't work because of 17... Nd3 18. Qxe6† Kh8 19. Bxd3 Bxd3 20. Rfc1 Qe8!, and the endgame is favorable for Black.

17. ...	**Bxc3**
18. Qa3	**Bg7**
19. Rab1	**Qf6**
20. Rfc1	**d5**

Black had a rather difficult choice at this point. Because of the desperate situation of the Knight on b2, Black had to return some extra material. Nezh chose the way which led to a more active position with material equality. A better possibility was 20... c5. Then 21. Rc2 Qf5 22. Rbxb2 Bxb2 23. Rxb2 d5. Black has a compact pawn mass. White has a Rook and two pawns for the Bishop pair. It is not easy to say which is the way to go. Nezh chose the way which looked "easier."

21. Rxc7	**Rf7**
22. Rc2	**Nc4**
23. Bxc4	**dxc4**
24. Rxc4	**Rd8**
25. Rbc1	**Bf8**
26. Qb3	**Bc5**
27. Kh2	**Rd2**
28. Re4!?	

White had overrated his chances and then Black took the initiative by exchanging Queens. A more accurate idea was 28. R4c2 Rfd7 29. Rxd2 Rxd2 30. Rc2, which would lead to an equal position.

28. ...	**Qb2!**
29. Qxb2	**Rxb2**
30. a4	**Rd7**
31. Rxe6	

It was too late to transfer the Bishop via e1: 31. Be1 Re2 32. Rxe6? Bxe3!.

31. ...	**Rdd2**
32. h4	

Surely, the timid 32. Rg1 would not have helped because of 32... Re2.

32. ...	**Rxg2†**
33. Kh3	**Rge2**
34. Rd1	

White had nothing to do except to attempt to activate his Rooks and to threaten the King, but it was too late for that.

34. ...	**Kf7!**
35. Re4	**h5!**

This locked out the escape square for White's King and created mating threats. This was Nezh's typical way to realize an advantage even in the endgame. There was another choice, for example, 35... Rbd2, aiming to realize the advantage by technical means.

36. Re5	

A more aggressive plan, 36. Rd7† Kf6 37. Rxa7, wouldn't have worked because of the cruncher 37... Rb1.

36. ...	**Kf6**
37. f5!	

The best chance in a difficult position.

37. ...	**Rxe3**
38. Rd6†?	

Most likely it was time trouble which prevented Holmov from finding 38. fxg6!. After 38... Kxg6 39. Rxe3 Bxe3 40. Rd6† Kf5 41. Rd5† Ke4 42. Re5† Kd3 43. a5!

b5 44. Rxh5 and White would keep some chances for a draw. [Ed.: White could also try 39. Rg5† Kf6 40. Rxh5 for drawing chances.]

38. ... Bxd6
39. Rxe3 Bxg3
40. Rxg3 gxf5

Here the game could have ended, but White went on with aimless defense for another 20 moves. The rest of the score was: **41. Rg5 Rb3† 42. Kg2 Rb4 43. Rxh5 Rxa4 44. Kf3 Ke5 45. Rh8 Ra3† 46. Kg2 Kf4 47. h5 Rg3† 48. Kh2 Rg7 49. h6 Rb7 50. Rg8 Rh7 51. Rg6 b5 52. Kh3 b4 53. Kh4 b3 54. Kh5 b2 55. Rg1 Rb7 56. Rb1 a5 57. Kg6 a4 58. h7 Rxh7 59. Rxb2 Ra7 60. Rb4† Ke3 61. Kxf5 a3 (0-1).**

78.
Super Nezh—A. Ivashin
Yaroslavl 1947

The initial game moves are not known.

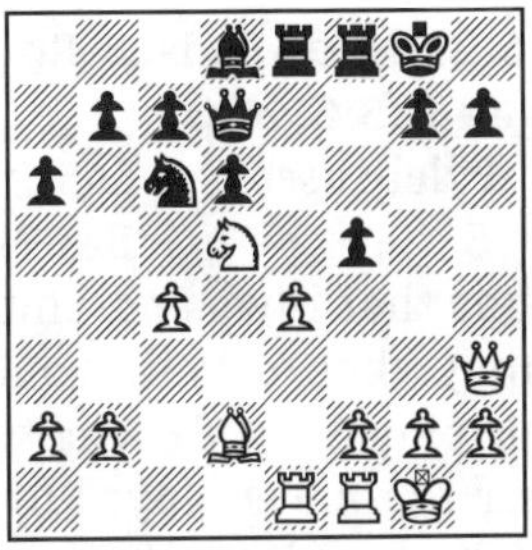

16. Qh3

Black created counterplay with his last move, 15... f5!, and Nezh made the decision to go over to the endgame to shut down this activity.

16. ... Qf7?!

A waste of tempo. Better was 16... Ne5, which would have caused White to return the Queen (17. Qc3).

17. exf5 Rxe1
18. Rxe1 Qxf5
19. Qxf5 Rxf5
20. f4!

From earlier moves Nezh considered that this endgame was good for White.

The ending here is, undoubtedly advantageous to White, whose pieces have a more active position and a pawn advantage on the queenside.

R.N.

20. ... Rf7
21. Re8† Rf8
22. Re3 Kf7
23. Bc3

White is hindering both 23... Re8 and 23... Ne7, because in both instances Black loses the g7-pawn.

R.N.

23. ... Rg8
24. Rh3 h6
25. Kf2 Ne7
26. Ne3 c6
27. a4 Bc7
28. f5 Bb6
29. Rf3 d5
30. f6! gxf6

An attempt to exchange pieces didn't come about: 30... d4 because of 31. fxe7† Ke8 [31... Kxe7? 32. Nf5† and 33. Bxd4] 32. Nd5! cxd5 33. Bb4! and there would have been no defense from 34. Rf8.

31. Rxf6 Ke8
32. Bd2 Rf8†!

Black made the right decision. He didn't rely upon the Rook ending after 32... dxc4 33. Rxh6 Nf5 34. Re6† Kf7 35. Re5 Nxe3 36. Bxe3 Bxe3 37. Rxe3.

In the text the connected passed pawns [g and h] were to bring victory to White. Still, Tartakower said: "All Rook endings are drawn!" Perhaps that's why Nezh approved of this very defense.

33. Rxf8† Kxf8
34. Kf3 Kg7
35. cxd5!

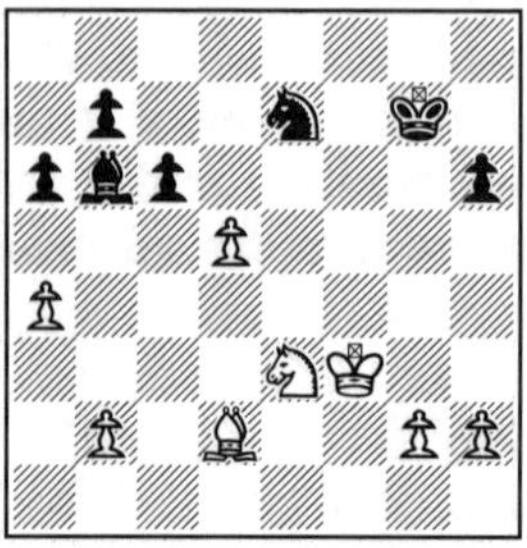

I've put an exclamation mark here because White was again making Black choose: either to play a 4-piece ending after 35… cxd5, or to choose the continuation in the game. There was no third way, 35… Nxd5, because of 36. Nf5† and 37. Nh6.

35. … Bxe3?

Now White should win without any serious problems. His task would have been more complicated after 35… cxd5!. After 36. Bb4 Bxe3 37. Bxe7 Bc1 it would be a same color Bishop ending. After 37. Kxe3 Nc6 Black could have resisted for a long time with his Knight against the Bishop because of the passed pawn.

36. Kxe3!

It was very important to activate the King before Black could respond in kind.

36. … Nxd5†
37. Kd4 h5
38. Ke5

The main square where White had to go in order to have an active King in the center. This was decisive.

38. … Kg6
39. g3 Nb6
40. b3 Nd5
41. Ke6!

The King will win pawns on the queenside and at the same time "push" his opponent away.

41. … Nf6
42. b4 Ne4
43. Be3 a5

White was threatening to play a4-a5 to stop the black pawns, and then to come toward them with his King.

44. bxa5 Nc3
45. Kd6 Kf5
46. Kc7!

This wasn't even the sacrifice of a piece, it was a technical trick: 46… Nd5† 47. Kxb7 Nxe3 48. a6, and the pawn would queen.

Black surrendered **(1-0).**

79.

Super Nezh—V. Mikenas

C 16

Match, game 13

Kazan 1948

1. e4 e6 2. d4 d5 3. Nc3 Bb4 4. e5 b6 5. Qg4 Bf8 6. Nh3.

More widely used is 6. Bg5 or 6. Nf3.

6. … Ba6?!

It seems that it was not important concerning what to do first: move the Bishop or play 6… Qd7. The thing is, that after the move played by Black, he couldn't play a7-a6, that's why the following attack was so strong.

7. Nb5! Qd7

It's worth mentioning the immediate exchange 7… Bxb5 8. Bxb5† c6 since after White's next move it was not convenient to take on b5 because of axb5!.

8. a4 h5?

This weakening of the flank could only be justified in cases of extreme necessity. Development should have continued: 8... Ne7.

9. Qg3 Ne7

10. Qc3!

Now Black was obliged to ruin the coordination in the placement of his pieces.

10. ... Nec6

10... Nbc6 wouldn't have worked because of 11. Nxc7†.

11. Qd2 Na5

12. b3 c6?

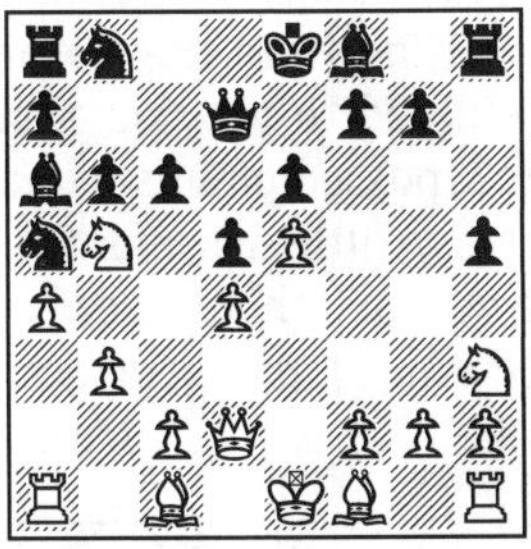

It was not yet time to be in a hurry. It was time to play a preliminarily clumsy move, 12... Nb7. Black has just underestimated the next pawn-sacrifice:

13. Nd6†! Bxd6

The Knight on d6 should be taken, since on 13... Kd8, then 14. Ng5.

14. exd6 Bxf1

15. Kxf1 Nb7

16. Ba3 c5

17. Re1 Nc6

Better was 17... Qxd6, to open the way for the Knight via d7 to f6.

18. dxc5 bxc5

The pawn on c5 should be taken by the pawn, since after 18... Nxc5 19. Bxc5 bxc5 20. Qxd5 the c5-pawn would be lost. It wouldn't be lost if the Queen were on d6.

19. Qg5

After 19. Qxd5 0-0-0 20. Qg5 f6 21. Qe3 Qxd6, and then 22... Nd4, White will have lost the initiative.

19. ... Qxd6

The following set of possibilities would not work: 19... f6 20. Qg6† Qf7 21. Rxe6!, nor 19... g6 20. Nf4 Qxd6 21. Nxd5! [Ed.: Though 21. Qf6 looks strong because of 22. Nxe6, Black has 21... Rh7. Black should consider 19... Kf8.]

20. Nf4 Qe7?!

Damsky recommended 20... Ne7! 21. Qxg7 Kd7 22. Qxf7 e5, and Black would get serious counterplay for the pawn. 22. Qxf7 wasn't mandatory. 22. Nd3 was preferable, since it would preserve some advantage, even though the material was equal. 20... Nd4! should be taken into consideration, since after 21. Qxg7 0-0-0 22. Qxd4 cxd4 23. Bxd6 Nxd6 White has no advantage.

21. Qxg7 0-0-0

22. Nxd5! Qf8

23. Qxf8 Rhxf8

24. Ne3

White won the pawn by tactical means, but his backward development gave Black some counterchances.

24. ... h4!

25. f3 f5

An unnecessary weakening. Better was 25... Kc7 with the idea of ...Nd4 or ...Nb4, to defend the c5-pawn with the King.

26. Nc4 Nd4

27. Kf2 Nxc2

It was also worth White's thinking about 27... Rfe8.

28. Rxe6 Nd4

Black was right in refusing to play 28... Nxa3, because after 29. Nxa3 Na5 30. Rb1 Rd2† 31. Re2 Rxe2† 32. Kxe2 Kd7 33. b4! White would realize his considerable advantage.

29. Re7

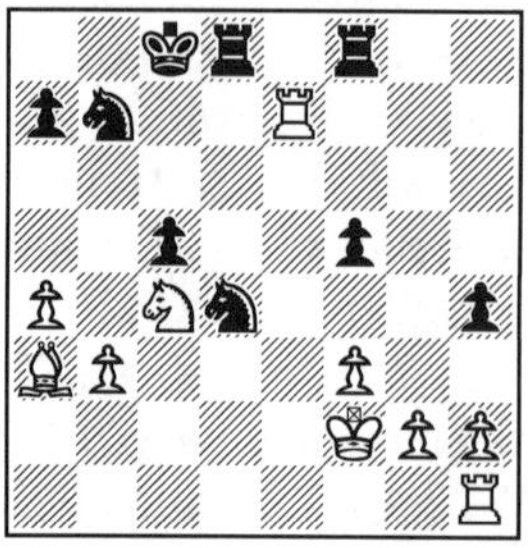

29. ... Rfe8

Dangerous was 29... Nxb3 30. Rb1, and on 30... Rd3, good would have been 31. Rxb7! Kxb7 32. Rxb3† Rxb3 and 33. Na5†. It was also worth looking at 29... Rd7, as the move played allows a combination.

30. Bxc5! Nxc5
31. Rxe8 Rxe8
32. Nd6† Kd7
33. Nxe8 Kxe8
34. b4!

White thoroughly investigated the endgame and prepared the following plan: take the black pawn (a7), even if it costs both pawns on the queenside, and then break up the pawns on the kingside, with the h-pawn being targeted first, having a lack of protection. Lastly, to create two connected passed pawns, against which the black Knights would not have been able to fight.

34. ... Nxa4
35. Ra1 Nb2
36. Rxa7

Perhaps only at this point did Black feel sorry for the mistake on his 25th move [25... f5]. If the pawn had been on f7, it would have been hard for White to keep connected passed pawns.

36. ... f4!

The mobility of the white King and the pawns needed to be reduced as much as possible.

37. Rh7 Nd3†
38. Kf1 Nxb4
39. Rxh4 Nd5
40. Rh7 Ne3†
41. Kf2 Nd1†
42. Kg1 Ne3
43. Ra7 Kf8
44. Ra4

Black had a dilemma: either to respond 44... Nec2! making the Knights temporarily immune, after 45. Rc4, or to play 44... Ne6.

In the first case, White, in order to rescue his King from the "onslaught," will be obliged to play g2-g4, and after ...fxg3, passed pawns [f and g] will result. It was a little easier for the Knights to fight against them than with the pawns [g and h], as in the game.

44. ... Ne6

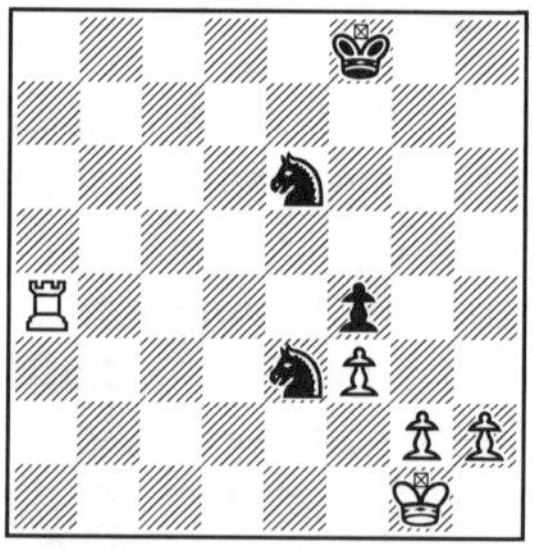

45. g4!

Owing to tactics, White obtained the passed pawns [g and h]. The point was that now 45... fxg3 was bad because of 46. Re4 gxh2† 47. Kh1!. The Knight will be lost and the f-pawn would be left on the board.

45. ... Kg7
46. h4 Kf6
47. h5 Nd5
48. Ra6 Ne7
49. g5† Kf7
50. Ra5 Kf8

On 50... Ng7, White would win even quicker: 51. g6† Kf6 52. h6 Ngf5 53. Ra6†, etc.

51.	**Kg2**	**Kf7**
52.	**Kh3**	**Nc6**
53.	**Rf5†**	**Kg8**
54.	**Kg4**	**Ncd4**
55.	**Rd5**	**Nc6**
56.	**g6**	**Kg7**
57.	**Rd7†**	**Kg8**
58.	**Rd6**	**Ncd8**
59.	**h6**	

Black surrendered **(1-0)**.

The value of the game was in its instructive endgame. It was also interesting that Nezh considered it the best of the match in spite of the abundance of sharp tactical collisions in the other games.

80.
Super Nezh—N. Krogius
C 85
13th Russian ch.
Saratov 1953

1. e4 e5 2. Nf3 Nc6 3. Bb5 a6 4. Ba4 Nf6 5. 0-0 Be7 6. Bxc6 dxc6 7. Qe1.

One more invention of Nezh's. His idea was not only to prevent the Knight from being pinned, but also to put the Queen on the square from which it will be possible to reach the squares g3, h4 or c3.

Original isn't it? This move was shown by its creator to master Bonch–Osmolovsky. Bonch used it for the first time in the Moscow championship of 1948. It would be hard to figure out what the advantage would be in playing with such originality. That's why later Nezh preferred 7. Nc3. Nowadays 7. d3 and 8. Nbd2 are often played.

7. ... c5

Black prevented the move d2-d4 at once. It was not obligatory. *Geller,* for example, just equalized in his game with *Khasin, Kislovodsk 1968,* when he played 7... Nd7 8. d4 exd4 9. Nxd4 Nc5 10. Qe3 0-0 11. Nc3 Re8 12. Rd1 Bd6.

A good plan was shown by *Ragozin:* 7... Be6 8. b3 Nd7 9. Bb2 f6 10. d4 Bd6 11. Nbd2 0-0, equalized in his game with *Fichtl, Prague 1956.*

8. b3

This only gave equality. The fight for the advantage could have continued with 8. Nxe5, a move that was delayed in its use for 15 years and proven worthy by Czech chessplayers headed by Hort. The game could have followed this scenario: 8. Nxe5 Qd4 9. Nd3 [In the game *Kupka—Kozma, Luhacovice 1969,* 9. Nf3 didn't give White any advantage: 9... Qxe4 10. Qxe4 Nxe4 11. Re1 Nf6 12. Nc3 h6.] c4 10. Nf4 g5 11. Ne2 Qxe4 12. d3! cxd3 13. cxd3 Qxd3 14. Bxg5 Rg8 15. Nf4 Qf5 16. Bxf6 Qxf6 17. Nc3! Qxf4 18. Qxe7† with good prospects for White's endgame.

8.	**...**	**Bd6**
9.	**Bb2**	**Qe7**
10.	**Nc3**	**0-0**
11.	**h3**	**Be6**

White didn't justify his Queen's position on e1, that's why Black equalized.

12. Qe3 c4?

For the sake of getting rid of his doubled pawn Black voluntarily gave up his position in the center. A good, solid position could've been obtained after 12... Rad8.

13.	**bxc4**	**Bxc4**
14.	**d3**	**Be6**

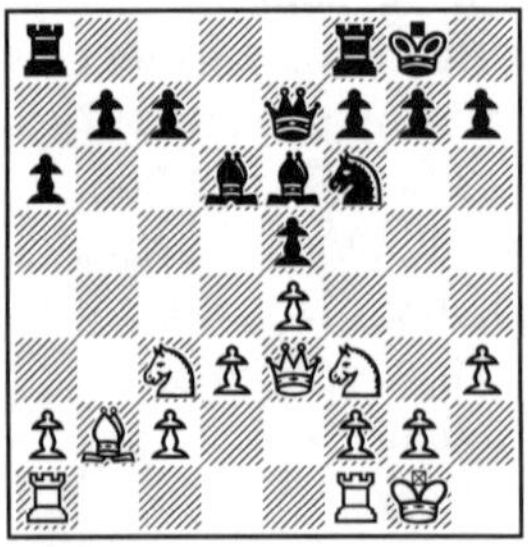

15. d4! exd4
16. Nxd4 Bc5
17. e5 Nd7

17... Nd5? would have been wrong. After 18. Nxd5 Bxd5 19. Nf5! a piece would be lost.

18. Ne4 Ba7

Black had one more trap in: 18... Nxe5? 19. Nxc5 Qxc5 20. Nxe6, and again a piece would be lost.

19. Qg3 Kh8
20. Ba3 c5
21. f4 Bb8

Nezh censured this move, because the c5-pawn became weak. Black's attitude can be explained: something had to be done about the coming pawn advances.

22. Rad1 Bc7
23. Kh1 Rg8?!

23... Rfe8 would have been preferable, though White would have had 24. Nxe6 fxe6 25. Nd6. Black will lose the pawn.

24. Nxe6 fxe6
25. Qg5! Rge8

28... Qxg5?? would have been very bad because of 26. Nxg5.

26. Qxe7 Rxe7
27. Nxc5 Nxc5
28. Bxc5 Rf7
29. f5?

Every chessplayer knows this feeling of impatience, being in a winning position, and the wish to quickly finish the game. Nezh was in a hurry here. There was no reason to hurry since Black had no counterplay. The King could easily be moved to the center, for example, to e4, and only then play g4 and f5.

29. ... Re8!

Of course, as 29... Rxf5 30. Rxf5 exf5 31. e6 was bad for Black. Black must stop the march of the pawn on its way to queening.

30. fxe6 Rxf1†
31. Rxf1 Bxe5
32. Rf7 Kg8
33. Rxb7 Rxe6
34. Rb6 Re8!

After the Rook exchange White would have easily won. That's why Black preferred to sacrifice the second pawn, to get counterchances.

35. Rxa6 Bg3!

Suddenly the white King found himself in an unpleasant position.

36. Bg1 h5!

Why did Black reject 36... Re1 with the threat 37... Bf2 ? Nezh gives the following:

If 36... Re1, then 37. Ra8† Kf7 38. Ra3 Bd6! [38... Be5 39. Re3; 38... Bb8 39. g4] 39. Rf3† Kg8 [39... Kg6 40. Re3 Rd1 41. Rd3] 40. Rc3 Ra1 [40... Bb4 41. Rc8† and 42. g4] 41. g4 Rxa2 42. Rc6 and 43. Kg2.

R.N.

As usual, his analysis was concrete and convincing.

37. Ra3 h4
38. Be3 Rc8!

Neither 38... Rd8, nor 38... Rb8 were good for Black, as White would respond respectively 39. Rd3 or 39. Rb3, and then he would put his Rook on the first rank, which would have removed all threats to his King.

39.	**Kg1**	**Rxc2**
40.	**Ra8†**	**Kf7**
41.	**Kf1**	**Ke6**

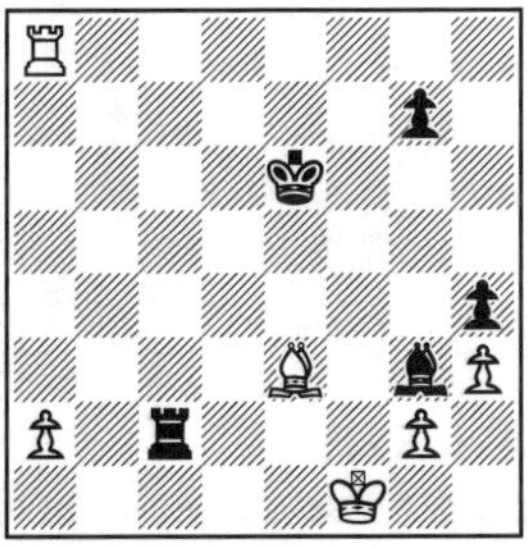

Here the game was adjourned and in the opinion of the majority of the participants, the position would have led only to a draw, as the white King would be hemmed in.

Nezh wrote:

> **During the analysis White was obliged to distract his attention from the enormous number of lines and to talk in general about the peculiarities of this position [a chessplayer should also be a philosopher]. I found out gradually, that instead of the provoking move 42. a4, it would be more convenient to deprive the black King of the 5th rank. The squares d5, e5 and f5 are "critical" for Black, they are needed to approach the white King.**
>
> *R.N.*

42. Ra5!!

Having solved the main "philosophical" problem, White was clearly on the way to the win, though it wasn't easy.

42.	**...**	**g6**
43.	**a4**	**Ra2**
44.	**Bb6!**	**Rb2**
45.	**Rg5!**	**Rb4**
46.	**Rg4**	**Bf4**
47.	**Be3!**	**g5**
48.	**Bxf4**	**gxf4**
49.	**a5**	**Ra4**
50.	**Rxh4**	**Kf5**
51.	**Rh8**	**Ra1†**
52.	**Kf2**	**Ra2†**
53.	**Kg1**	**Kg5**
54.	**Rg8†**	**Kf5**
55.	**Ra8**	**Ra1†**
56.	**Kh2**	**Kg6**
57.	**h4**	**Ra3**
58.	**a6**	**Kg7**
59.	**a7**	**Ra1**
60.	**Kh3**	**Ra2**
61.	**h5**	**Kh7**
62.	**h6!**	

Black surrendered **(1-0).**

81.

Super Nezh—G. Ståhlberg

C 12

Bucharest 1954

1. e4 e6 2. d4 d5 3. Nc3 Nf6 4. Bg5 Bb4 5. e5 h6 6. Bd2 Bxc3 7. bxc3 Ne4 8. Qg4 g6 9. Bd3 Nxd2 10. Kxd2 c5 11. Nf3 Nc6 12. h4 Qc7 13. dxc5!.

A novel opening surprise. The MacCutcheon system had a long history by then and, according to the theory of the day, White tried to hold the pawn center. Here White radically changed the direction of the game, aiming to open the center for an active piece brawl.

13. ... Nxe5?!

Black meets his opponent's wish halfway. It was worth looking at 13... Bd7 and 14... 0-0-0, to finish development, and then proceed to attack White's weak squares.

14. Nxe5 Qxe5
15. Rab1 Qf6
16. Qd4!

This made the Queen exchange obligatory. White now had a convenient endgame with every prospect for developing the initiative on the kingside.

16. ... Qxd4

Black was practically obliged to take on d4 and to correct White's pawn structure. However, after 16... Ke7 17. g4 Rd8 it would not have been clear how to finish his development on the queenside without positional concessions.

17. cxd4 Kd8
18. g4 Kc7
19. h5 g5
20. f4 gxf4
21. Rbf1 e5!

The correct decision by an experienced grandmaster, providing Black with counterplay.

22. dxe5 Bxg4
23. Rxf4 Be6

It was time to take stock of the position. Inspite of the defects of White's pawn structure, the endgame was in his favor owing to the major activity of his pieces and the weak position of the pawns on f7 and h6. Black also had a trump of his own, the g-file.

24. Kc3 Rag8

Nezh recommended 24... d4†!, "to get maneuvering space for his Bishop and to open another line for his Rooks." We'll add that White would lose an ideal place for his King on d4. Thus, Black had to sacrifice the pawn, but on 24... d4† 25. Kxd4 Bxa2?? 26. c4, the f7-pawn would have become terribly weak, and the Bishop would also have been in danger.

25. Kd4 Rg4?

The wrong decision. Black will exchange the active Rook and keep the passive one.

26. Rxg4 Bxg4

27. Rf1!

The main principle in Rook endings is **activity.** Because of that, no sorrow over losing a pawn is necessary.

27. ... Bxh5

Worse was 27... Be6 28. Bf5!. If 28... Bxf5 29. Rxf5 Rh7 30. Kxd5, and Black is out of useful moves. [Ed.: However, 28... Rg8 is not clear.]

28. Rf6 Kd7
29. Bf5† Ke7
30. Rd6 Rb8
31. Rxh6

White had achieved a winning position and now he could've done a little better with: 31. Rd7† Kf8 32. c3! Ke8 33. Rd6.

31. ... Bf3
32. Rd6?

Rashid didn't mention Black's tactical resource which would cost him the advantage. 32. Rh7 also wouldn't have done anything because of 32... Be4! 33. Bxe4 dxe4 34. Kxe4 Rg8 and 35... Rg2 with sufficient counterplay. Instead, 32. e6! would have preserved chances for winning: 32... Rf8 [After 32... Be4 33. Bxe4 dxe4 34. exf7 Kxf7 the Rook endgame would have been good for White.] 33. Rh7 Kf6 34. Rxf7† Rxf7 35. exf7 Kxf7. Further, Nezh continued: 36. c3! [This move was important to block the possible sacrifice of a pawn (d5-d4) after the King would have vacated the d4-square.] Kf6 37. Bh3 [37. Bc8 b6 38. c6 (Ed.: 38. Bb7 looks like it wins a pawn, but the win is probably not there.) Ke7 39. Ke5 Kd8 would do nothing for White because the black King goes to c7 with tempo: 40. Be6 Kc7 41. Bxd5 Be2!, and a draw would be the result.] Bh1 38. a4 Ke7 39. Ke5 and then threatening 40. a5 with the further threats a5-a6 and c5-c6.

32. ... Be4!

33. Bxe4

Black had a trick up his sleeve: 33. Rd7† Ke8 would draw because if 34. Bg4, then 34... Bf3! 35. Bh3 Bg2, etc.

33. ... dxe4
34. Kxe4 Rh8
35. c6 bxc6
36. Rxc6 Rh4†?

The draw would have been easier to achieve after 36... Rh2 or 36... Rh1. By playing about at the rear, the Rook wouldn't have allowed White to activate his King, and the black King wouldn't have been buried on the 8th rank.

37. Kd5 Ra4
38. Rc7† Ke8
39. c4 Rxa2
40. c5 Rd2†
41. Kc6 Re2
42. Rxa7 Rxe5
43. Rb7!

Inspite of it's apparent simplicity, this Rook ending contained serious subtleties which weren't understood by Ståhlberg. Meanwhile, though White had a passed pawn, and the black King was cut off on the back rank, there was no victory against correct defense. For example, after the natural 43. Kb6 Re1 44. c6 Rb1† 45. Kc7 Ke7 46. Kc8† [Ed.: And for basically the same reason, the "obvious" 46. Rb7 doesn't win either!] Kd6 47. c7 f5 48. Kd8 Rc1 49. c8=Q Rxc8† 50. Kxc8 Ke5 and it would be drawn. The move played by Nezh also would not win. He reminded himself, upon seeing no win, that he would make:

> **A waiting [just as it was relayed after the game by S. Furman] move, which produces no threat. This move turned out to be a surprise to Ståhlberg and made him go into a long think.**
>
> *R.N.*

43. ... Re6†

This was played to get the King off of the back rank. Nezh considered this move to be the losing move, yet Black had played correctly.

44. Kc7 f5

In his book Nezh transposed moves and said that Ståhlberg played 44... Ke7. However, that move would lose at once: 45. Kc8† Ke8 46. Rb6, or 45... Kf6 46. Rb6.

45. c6 Ke7
46. Rb5 Kf6?

The losing move! Inspite of its outward simplicity, the ending turned out to be a stumbling block not only to Ståhlberg, but also for many other masters who analyzed it later, including Rashid to some extent. Black's idea was correct: to promote the pawn with the help of the King and to sacrifice a Rook for the white pawn, but the implementation was wrong. Correct was 46… f4!. At this point possible was: 47. Rf5 Re4 48. Kb6 Rb4† 49. Kc5 Rb1 50. Rxf4 Kd8, which would have achieved a theoretical draw, or: 47. Kb7 Kd6! [Nezh offered 47… f3? 48. c7 f2 49. Rf5 Rf6 50. Rxf6 Kxf6 51. c8=Q f1=Q 52. Qf8†.] 48. Rf5 Re7† 49. Kb6 Re1 50. Rf6† Ke5 51. c7 Rb1† 52. Ka7 Rc1 and it would have been drawn.

47. Kb7

47. Kd7 would also have won. 47… Re7† 48. Kd8 Re1 49. c7 Rd1† 50. Ke8 Rc1 51. Kd7 Kg5 52. Kd6! with the threat of 53. Rc5.

47. … Kg5
48. c7 Re8

48… Re7 wouldn't haved saved Black either: 49. Kc6 Rxc7† 50. Kxc7 Kg4 51. Kd6 f4 52. Ke5 f3 53. Ke4 f2 54. Rf5 Kg3 55. Ke3.

49. Kc6 Rc8
50. Rb8 Rxc7†
51. Kxc7 Kf4

Or 51… f4 52. Kd6 Kg4 53. Ke5 f3 54. Rf8 Kg3 55. Ke4 f2 56. Ke3.

52. Kd6

Black resigned **(1-0)**.

The correct evaluation of the ending, beginning with the 43rd move, was first given by V. Smyslov in the third issuance of his monograph (written together with G. Levenfisch), *Rook Endings*, Moscow 1986.

82.

S. Flohr—Super Nezh

E 60

21st USSR ch.

Kiev 1954

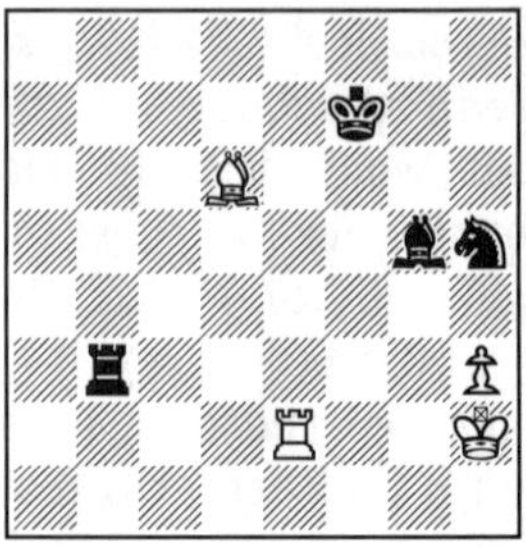

Black has an extra piece, but not a single pawn. A draw? No! Nezh was playing for mate. [Ed.: See page *xi* for the beginning moves.]

67. … Be3!
68. Bc7 Kg6
69. Ra2 Nf6
70. Kg2 Nd5
71. Bd6 Kf5
72. Ra3 Rb6
73. Bg3 Ke4
74. Ra4† Kd3
75. Ra5 Nc3

Black managed to activate his pieces, and most important of all, his King.

76. Kf3 Rf6†
77. Kg4 Rf8
78. Bd6 Rf7
79. Ra3 Bc1
80. Ra1 Bd2
81. Ra8?

After this White couldn't escape losing. Correct was 81. Ra3! and on 81… Ke4, 82. Bb4! Rg7† 83. Kh5. There was no mate, but Black couldn't avoid the exchange.

81. … Ne4
82. Bh2 Nf2†
83. Kh5 Rf6
84. Rh8

An important achievement for Black. The white Rook must take a passive position because of the mate threat, and yet the King had to be moved up.

84. … Ke4
85. Bc7 Kf5

86. Bd8

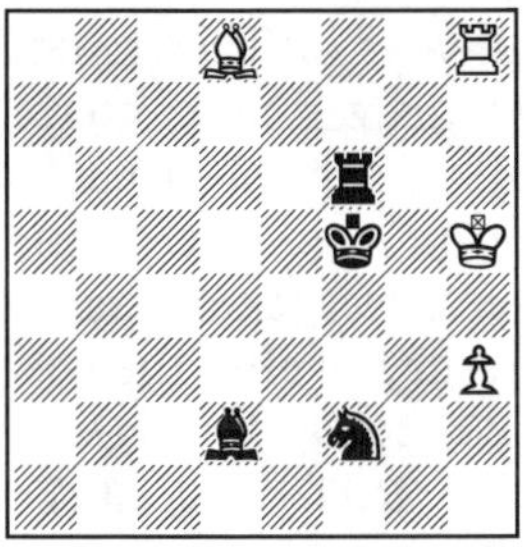

86. ... Ne4!!

A small raisin, based on the fact that White's own pawn was in the way, as it took a square which was needed for the King's escape. The Rook could not have been taken because of mate in two.

87. Bc7 Bg5
88. Rh7 Rf8

There was no defense from 89... Nf6†, so White gave up **(0-1).**

83.

A. Matsukevich—Super Nezh

Semi-finals 24th USSR ch.
Kharkov 1956

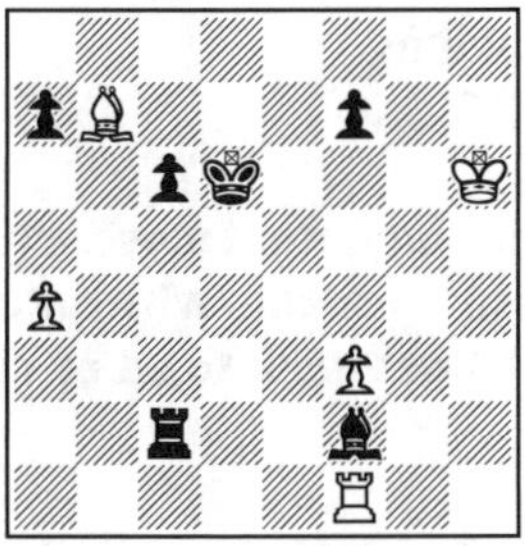

A deep endgame, where a normal plan would be to make something of the c-pawn. But, Bishops of opposite colors were present, and this "detail" made it hard to bring the plan to life. Nezhmetdinov's refined tactical feeling offered another way: the white King was at the edge of the board, and in this case the presence of opposite-colored Bishops was very useful for the organization of an attack, even in a position with few pieces.

41. ... Be3†
42. Kg7

The path to the center was closed: 42. Kh5 Rc5† 43. Kg4 Rc4†, which would another pawn.

42. ... Ke7!
43. f4

43. Re1 would have failed because of 43... Rg2† 44. Kh7 Kf8!, and the mating net would be ready.

43. ... Rh2

43. Rh2 is good play. There was another, more intensive, way, namely 43... Rg2† 44. Kh7 Kf8! 45. Kh6 Rb2! 46. Rf3 Bxf4† 47. Rxf4 Rxb7.

44. Re1

Another defensive attempt, 44. Kg8, had more possibilities. Nezh planned 44... Bd2 with the continuation 45. Bxc6 Bc3 46. Rh1 Rb2 47. Bb5 a6 48. Rh3 Bd4, and Black would be winning a piece, as the Bishop could not leave the b5-square, and the Rook could not leave the h-file. However, stronger was 45. Rf3! and the mating attack would disappear. Perhaps Black would have played 45... c5 and returned to the plan of promoting his c-pawn. This plan had all the earmarks of success because of the uncomfortable position of the white King, but it would mean a long game.

44. ... Rg2†
45. Kh6 Kf6
46. Kh7

On 46. Kh5, simply 46... Bxf4 with the variation 47. Bxc6 Rg5† 48. Kh4 Bg3†, or 47. Rf1 Kf5 48. Bc8† Ke4 49. Bb7 Rh2† and 50... f5#.

46. ... Bd2!

47. Rh1?

This accelerated the defeat, which can be delayed by playing 47. Re4.

47. ... Rg7†
48. Kh8 c5
49. Rh5

The Rook exchange would not have worked: 49. Rh6† Rg6 50. Rxg6† fxg6, as the f4-pawn would have been lost.

49. ... Be3
50. Be4 Bd4
51. Rd5 Rg4

White surrendered **(0-1)**.

84.

A. Kolarov—Super Nezh

E 63

Sofia 1957

1. d4 Nf6 2. Nf3 g6 3. c4 Bg7 4. g3 0-0 5. Bg2 d6 6. 0-0 Nc6 7. Nc3 Rb8 8. b3 a6 9. Bb2 b5 10. cxb5 axb5 11. Ne1 Na5.

Here the Knight has nothing to do. Better was 11... d5.

12. Nd3 b4
13. Nd5 Nxd5
14. Bxd5 Qd7
15. Bg2 Qb5
16. d5 Bb7
17. Bxg7 Kxg7
18. Rc1 c5
19. dxc6 Bxc6
20. Bxc6 Nxc6
21. Qd2 Rb7
22. Rc4 Ne5?

It is always difficult to defend, especially if there is no counterplay. Here Nezh had such a problem, but the ability to defend in a passive position is an obligation of every skilled master. It was not necessary to offer the pawn.

23. Rxb4 Qa5
24. Rd1 Ra7
25. Rh4

Convincing is 25. Nxe5.

25. ... Qxd2
26. Rxd2 Nxd3
27. exd3

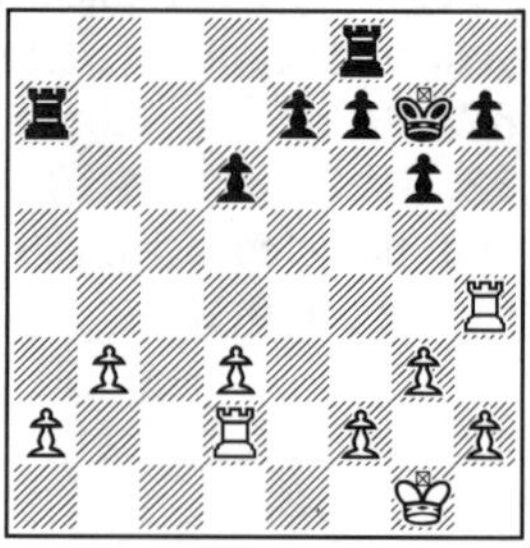

The ending seems to be hard for Black—he was not only minus a pawn, but he had to fight against the pair of passed pawns.

27. ... d5!

A very important move, which doesn't let the white Rook on h4 get back to e4 or c4.

R.N.

28. Rb4! Ra3
29. Rb7

Nezh recommended 29. Rb5, and after 29... e6 30. Rc5, and then Rcc2, White had chances to win, but stronger was 29... Rd8, and if 30. Rc2, then 30... Rd7 and 31. Rcc5 Rxa2 32. Rxd5 Rxd5 33. Rxd5 Rb2 34. Rb5 Rd2! will draw.

29. ... Kf6

30. Rc7 Rfa8
31. Rcc2 e5
32. Kf1

It would have been hard for White to move the a- and b-pawns without help from his King. When the King moves to help, Black would have had time to create counterplay on the other wing.

32. ... Ke6
33. Ke1 Kd6
34. Kd1 f5
35. f3

The pawns shouldn't be moved where Black had been advancing.

35. ... g5
36. Kc1 h5
37. Kb1 R3a7
38. h3?

After this White probably had no chance of winning. Moreover, further play shows that he should have played more accurately to avoid problems. The pawn should be advanced. 38. a4 Rb7 39. Ka2.

38. ... Rh8
39. Kb2 h4
40. Rg2 Rg7!
41. g4

Forced, as 41... hxg3 42. Rxg3 f4 and 43... Rxh3 will threaten.

41. ... Rf8
42. gxf5

The sealed move. The other opportunity was 42. b4 fxg4 43. fxg4 Ra7!. An important detail: the white pawns shouldn't get far. 44. a3 [44. Rgf2 Rf4! 45. a3 Raf7 (Ed.: I believe, however, that White can play 46. Rxf4, and his two passers on the queenside stall Black's queening. See the disk for lengthy details.)] Rf3 45. Rgf2! Rxd3 46. Rf6† Ke7 47. Rh6 Rdxa3 48. Rh7†, and it's a draw, since Black risks getting mated and therefore must keep his King on the d-file.

42. ... Rxf5
43. Rcf2 Rgf7
44. Re2 d4!

44... Rxf3 45. Rxg5 would have brought unfavorable exchanges.

45. Kc2 Ra7
46. Kb2 Rag7
47. Ref2 Rgf7
48. Re2 Rxf3
49. Rxg5 Re3
50. Rxe3 dxe3

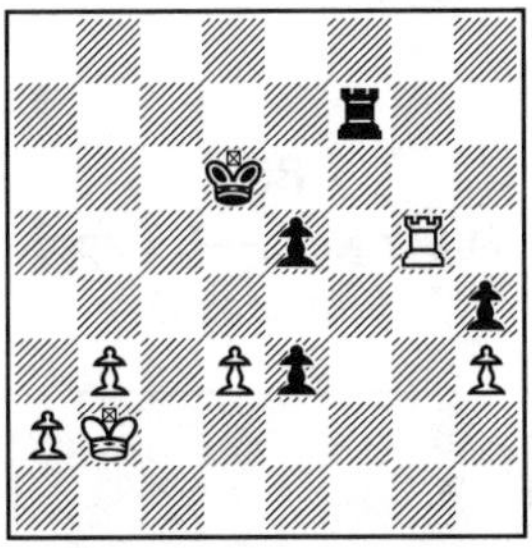

51. Rg4!

A subtle move which preserved the balance.

51. ... Rf4
52. Rg6† Kd5
53. Kc3

If the Rook had been on f7, there would have been a check [on the c-file], which would have brought the King back.

53. ... Rf1
54. Rg2 Rc1†
55. Rc2 Rh1
56. a4 Rxh3
57. Re2!

Mandatory. The a-pawn couldn't be advanced immediately: 57. a5 Rh1 58. Ra2 Rc1† 59. Kb4 Kd4 60. a6 Rc8 61. a7 Ra8.

57. ... Rg3
58. a5 h3
59. a6 Kc6
60. d4!

Guaranteeing the draw.

60. ... exd4†
61. Kxd4 Kb6

62. Ke4 Rg8!

The last attempt to win.

63. Kf3!

The careless 63. Kf4? would have brought defeat: 63... Rh8 64. Re1 [64. Rh2 e2] h2 65. Rh1 e2. Also bad is 63. Rh2 e2! 64. Rxe2 Re8†.

63. ... Rh8

64. Rh2 Re8

65. Ke2

Drawn **(1/2-1/2).**

85.

Super Nezh—I. Slepoi

Frunze 1959

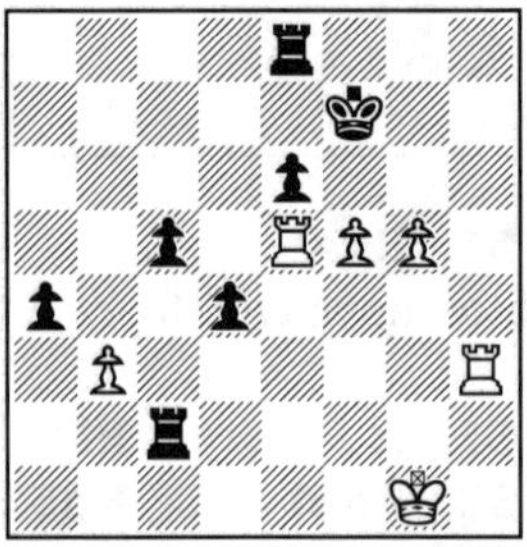

You can see in this position that White was attacking the King, irrespective of action by Black on the queenside, and even not caring that his own King remained vulnerable. Black managed to exchange Queens, and after playing 40... a4, he was eager to go after the King in the event of 41. bxa4?, then 41... Rb8.

Here the game was adjourned and many people thought Black had the better chances. Meanwhile, Nezh was seriously thinking about the sealed move, and after having sealed the envelope he said that ...White would win! After the resumption there was:

41. Rh7† Kg8

42. g6 Rf8

A forced series of moves would bring defeat after 42... axb3 43. f6 b2 44. f7† Kf8 45. fxe8=Q† Kxe8 46. Rxe6† Kd8 47. Rb6 Rc1† 48. Kg2 b1=Q 49. Rxb1 Rxb1 50. g7.

43. fxe6 Rc1†

And again there would be no time for 43... axb3 because of 44. e7 Re8 45. Rf5! b2 [or 45... Rxe7 46. Rxe7 b2 47. Rb7 Rc1† 48. Rf1 wins] 46. Rf8†! Rxf8 47. Rh8† Kg7 48. exf8=Q† with mate coming. However, if we back up and look at what might be Black's best chance, viz., 45... Rc1†, we will see that it too ultimately fails. Now, 46. Kg2 Rxe7 47. Rxe7 b2 48. g7! [48. Rd5? Rg1†=] Rg1† 49. Kh3 Rh1† [49... Rxg7 doesn't help, because 50. Re8† Kh7 51. Rb8 c4 52. Rxb2 c3 53. Rc2 Rd7 54. Rg5 Rd6 and 55. Kg4 stops Black cold due to the mate threat.] 50. Kg4 Rg1† 51. Kh5 [a nice advance] Kh7 [If Black keeps checking with 51... Rh1† 52. Kg6 Rg1† he runs into a looming mate after 53. Kf6.].

In a show of intensity, White will queen the pawn, sac it, and force the win, all while keeping the black pawn mass at bay. Thus, 52. g8=Q†! Kxg8 53. Kh6 Rh1† 54. Kg6 Rg1† 55. Kf6, and a neat piece of "doom" will be delivered with: 55... Kf8 [55... Rh1 loses to 56. Rg5†] 56. Ke6† Kg8 57. Re8† Kh7 58. Rf7† Rg7 59. Rb8 and the pawns are stopped!

44. Kg2

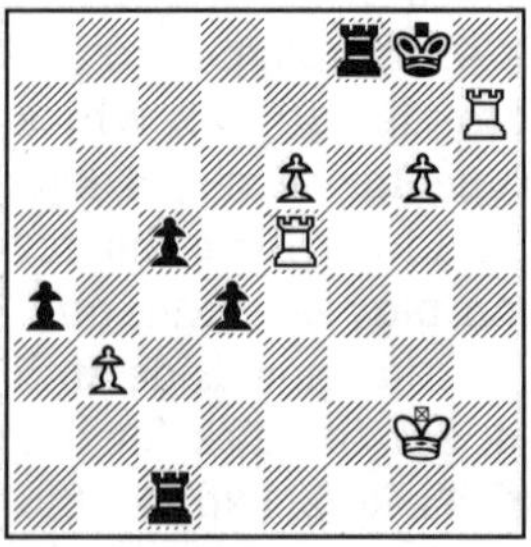

44. ... Rff1

[Ed.: A complicated, but handsome, winning line (for White) after 44... Rc2† would have been 45. Kg3 Rc3† 46. Kg4 Re3 47. e7!! Re8 (47… Rxe5 48. Rh8!! and 49. exf8=Q#) 48. Kf5! Rxe5† (if 48… axb3 49. Rxe3 dxe3 50. Kf6 b2 51. Rg7† Kh8 52. Rf7 Kg8 53. g7 b1=Q 54. Rf8† Rxf8† 55. exf8=Q† Kh7 56. g8=Q#) 49. Kxe5 axb3 50. Kf6 b2 51. Rg7† and the rest like in the note.]

45. e7 Rg1†
46. Kh3

Damsky considered in his book that only this move would win, and that the variation 46. Kf3 Rcf1† 47. Ke4 Re1† 48. Kd5 Rxe5† 49. Kxe5 Re1† 50. Kf6 axb3 meant that White should look for help. White's help comes with a killer: 51. Rh1! Re2 52. e8=Q† Rxe8 53. g7! Re6† 54. Kxe6 Kxg7 55. Kd5.

46. ... Rh1†
47. Kg4 Rhg1†
48. Kf5 Rcf1†
49. Ke6

After 49. Ke4 Re1† 50. Kd5 Rxe5 51. Kxe5, the variation from the notes to the 46th move would appear again.

49. ... Rxg6†
50. Kd5 Kxh7
51. e8=Q axb3
52. Rh5† Rh6
53. Qe7†

Black surrendered **(1-0)**.

86.
Super Nezh—H. Luik
B 30
Kharkov 1958

1. e4 c5 2. Nf3 Nc6 3. Bb5 Nf6 4. Qe2 a6 5. Bxc6 dxc6 6. d3 Bg4 7. h3 Bh5 8. a4 b5 9. g4 Bg6 10. Ne5 Nd7 11. Nxd7 Qxd7 12. f4 f6 13. h4 e5 14. f5 Bf7 15. Nd2 Be7 16. g5 Qd6 17. Nf3 c4 18. axb5 cxb5 19. Be3 cxd3 20. cxd3 Rd8 21. Kf2 Qxd3 22. Qxd3 Rxd3 23. Rxa6 0-0 24. Rc1 Rfd8 25. Rc7 R3d7 26. Rxd7 Rxd7.

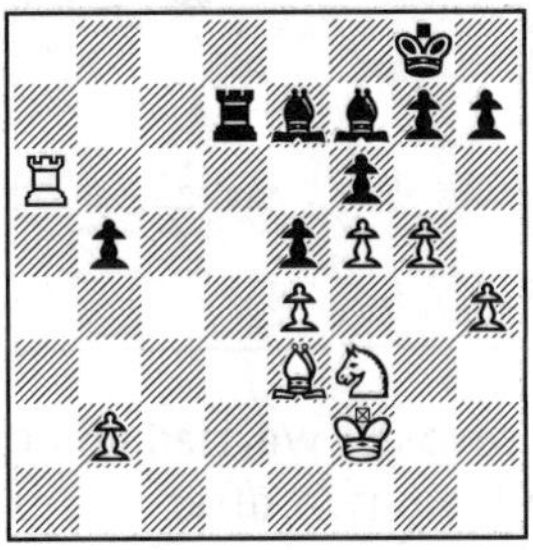

It would have been hard to believe that White's spatial advantage was a decisive one. Nezh proved it in short order.

27. b4!

White conquered the outpost c5, because 27… Bxb4 was weak due to 28. Ra8† Bf8 29. Bc5.

27. ... Be8
28. Bc5 Kf7

28… Bd8 was more consistent, though in this case the lack of air told upon Black's defensive capacity.

29. g6†!

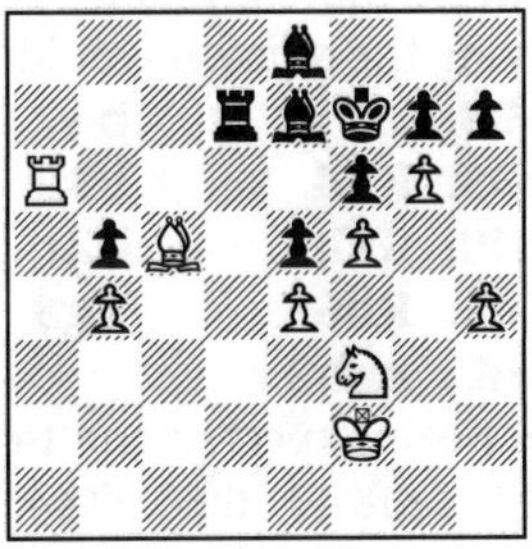

A tactical stroke which fettered Black completely.

29. ... hxg6
30. fxg6† Kf8

30… Kxg6 was bad because of 32. Nxe5†.

31. h5!

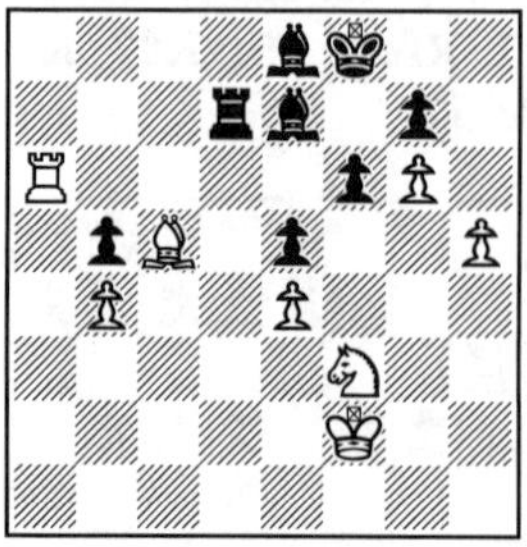

White wasn't worried about the attack on his pawn after the exchange on c5. The possession of the f5-square was more important, as it was to there the Knight would go.

31.	**...**	**Bxc5†**
32.	**bxc5**	**Rc7**
33.	**Ra8**	**Rxc5**
34.	**h6!**	**gxh6**
35.	**Nh4**	

It was too soon to play 35. g7† Kxg7 36. Rxe8 Kf7 37. Rb8 f5! 38. exf5 Kf6 39. Rf8† [39. Nh4 Kg5] Kg7 40. Rb8 Kf6.

35.	**...**	**Rc6**
36.	**Nf5**	**Re6**
37.	**Rb8**	**h5**
38.	**Kg3**	

The King's march finished the fight, and moving the b-pawn wouldn't help.

38.	**...**	**b4**
39.	**Kh4**	**b3**
40.	**Kxh5**	**b2**
41.	**Kh6**	**Kg8**
42.	**Rxb2**	

(1-0). Nezh expected the following finalé: 42… Kf8 43. Rb8 Kg8 44. Rc8 Kf8 45. g7† Kg8 46. Rxe8† Rxe8 47. Kg6 and 48. Nh6#.

87.

V. Sergievsky—Super Nezh

21st Russian ch.

Omsk 1961

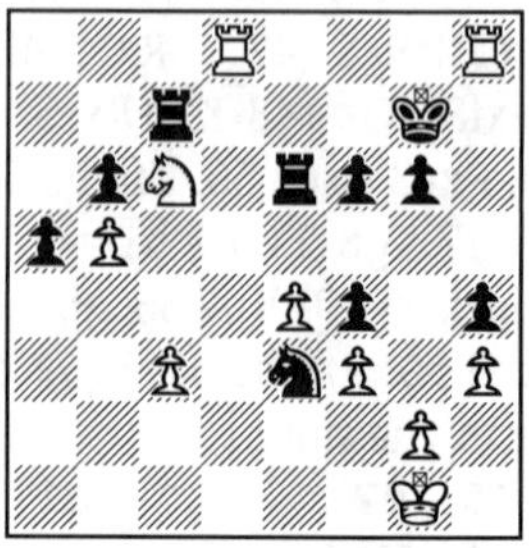

In this position the game was adjourned and Nezh sealed his move. Sergievsky and many masters figured this situation was a winning one for White. Nezh didn't lose hope. After the resumption there was:

42.	**...**	**Rd6!**
43.	**Rxd6**	

It was discovered that Black had strong counterplay in the line 43. Rdg8† Kf7 44. Nd8† Rxd8 45. Rxd8 Rxc3. For example: 46. Rh7† [Ed.: 46. Rc8 is a quagmire. However, it seems that 46… Rb3 47. Rh7† Ke6 48. Rc6† Ke5 49. Rxb6 Rb1† 50. Kf2 Rb2† 51. Ke1 a4! 52. Re7† Kd4 53. Rd7† Kc4 54. Rc7† Kb4 55. Ra6 Kxb5 56. Ra8 Kb6! saves the day because of the vulnerability of White's kingside pawns.] Ke6 47. Rdd7 Rc1† 48. Kf2 Rc2† 49. Ke1 Nxg2† with perpetual check.

43.	**...**	**Kxh8**
44.	**Rxf6**	**Kg7**
45.	**Rd6**	

The f4-pawn was untouchable: 45. Rxf4? g5.

45.	**...**	**Nc4**
46.	**Rd4**	**Na3**
47.	**c4**	**Nc2**
48.	**Rd6**	

It was worth trying 48. Rd3 Ne3 49. Rc3, or even 49. c5, to restrict the Knight's activity.

48.	**...**	**a4!**

Black had more than enough play in this demonstration.

49. Rd2 Ne3

50. c5?

White was still hoping to win. As often happens in these cases, he was too obstinate in his chasing the miracle of happiness. Now he couldn't even hope for a draw, which could have followed after 50. Ra2 Rd7 51. Rxa4 Rd1† 52. Kf2 Rd2†.

50. ... bxc5

51. e5

Another line: 51. Ra2 Rd7 52. Rxa4 Rd1† 53. Kf2 Rd2† 54. Ke1 Rb2, also wouldn't give any chances for survival. [Ed.: Extensive analysis seems to show that 55. Ra7†, 55. e5, 55. Nd8, 55. Ne5, and 55. Ra6, White's best moves, draw! See the disk for many details.].

51. ... c4

52. Ra2 c3

53. Rxa4 c2

54. Ra1 Rd7

White surrendered **(0-1)**.

24th USSR ch. / Moscow 1957

	Players	**1**	**2**	**3**	**4**	**5**	**6**	**7**	**8**	**9**	**10**	**11**	**12**	**13**	**14**	**15**	**16**	**17**	**18**	**19**	**20**	**21**	**22**	**Points**	**Place**
1	Tal	•	■	■	▒	■	▒	▒	■		▒	■	▒	■	■		▒	▒	▒	■	■	▒	▒	14	1
2	Bronstein		•	▒	▒		▒	▒	▒	▒	■	▒	▒	▒	■	■	■	■	■	■		■	■	13.5	2-3
3	Keres		▒	•		■	▒	▒	▒	■	▒	▒	■	■	▒	▒	■	▒	▒	■	■	■	▒	13.5	2-3
4	Spassky	▒	▒	■	•	▒	▒	▒	▒	▒	▒	▒	■	▒			▒	■	■	■	■	■	▒	13	4-5
5	Tolush		■		▒	•		▒		▒	■	■	■	▒	■	▒	■		■	■	▒	■	■	13	4-5
6	Holmov	▒	▒	▒	▒	■	•	▒	■	▒			▒	▒	■	▒	▒	■	▒	■	▒	▒	■	12.5	6
7	Korchnoy	▒	▒	▒	▒	▒	▒	•	▒	■		▒	▒	▒	▒	■		■		▒	■	■	■	12	7-8
8	Petrosyan		▒	▒	▒	■		▒	•	▒	▒	■			■	▒	■	■	▒	■	▒	■	▒	12	7-8
9	Boleslavsky	■	▒		▒	▒	▒		▒	•	▒	▒	▒	▒	▒	■	▒	▒	■	▒	▒	■	▒	11.5	9
10	Aronin	▒		▒	▒		■	■	▒	▒	•	▒	■			▒	▒	▒	■	■	■		▒	11	10-11
11	Taimanov		▒	▒	▒		■	▒		▒	▒	•	▒	▒	■	▒	■	▒	▒	▒	■		■	11	10-11
12	Furman	▒	▒				▒	▒	■	▒		▒	•	■	▒	▒	■	■		▒		▒	■	10	12
13	Bannik		▒		▒	▒	▒	▒	■	▒	■	▒		•	■	▒	▒	▒		▒		▒	▒	9.5	13-15
14	Klaman			▒	■			▒		▒	■		▒		•	■		▒	■	■	■	▒	▒	9.5	13-15
15	Nezhmetdinov	■		▒	■	▒	▒		▒		▒	▒	▒	▒		•	■	■			■	▒		9.5	13-15
16	Antoshin	▒			▒		▒	■		▒	▒			▒	■		•		■	■	■	▒	▒	9	16
17	Stolyar	▒		▒		■				▒	▒	▒		▒	▒		■	•	▒	▒	▒	▒	■	8.5	17
18	Mikenas	▒		▒			▒	■	▒			▒	■	■		■		▒	•		■			8	18
19	Aronson							▒		▒		▒	▒	▒		■		▒	■	•	■	▒	■	7.5	19-22
20	Gurgenidze		■			▒	▒		▒	▒			■	■				▒			•	■	■	7.5	19-22
21	Tarasov	▒					▒				■	■	▒	▒	▒	▒	▒	▒	■	▒		•		7.5	19-22
22	Hasin	▒		▒	▒				▒	▒	▒			▒	▒	■	▒		■			■	•	7.5	19-22
		1	2	3	4	5	6	7	8	9	10	11	12	13	14	15	16	17	18	19	20	21	22		

Small Raisins

In this chapter are games or endings which can hardly be relegated to any other chapter. In some of them the attacks are too impetuous to be included in the chapter "Attack." Among them there are miniatures, but the whole chapter can't be classified as "Miniatures." On the whole, each of the games included here contain some "small raisins," which I would like to bring to the attention of the reader.

88.

A. Korchmar—Super Nezh

D 31

Odessa 1931

1. d4 d5 2. Nf3 Nf6 3. Bg5 e6 4. e3 Be7 5. Bd3 0-0 6. Nbd2 c5 7. c3 b6 8. Ne5 Bb7 9. f4 Nbd7.

The players, not being so up-to-date in opening theory, played the popular, at that time, Colle System. The Belgian master had many successes with it as White. His plan usually included preparation for a piece attack against the King. To achieve that he castled short and transferred the pieces through the f3-square to attack. In this game White decided to "strengthen" Colle's plan: he decided to castle long to make a considerable advance, including pawns, on the kingside.

10. Qf3?! Nxe5
11. fxe5

Allowing the dangerous move of the black Knight. Correct would have been 11. dxe5.

R.N.

11. ... Ne4!
12. Bxe7 Qxe7
13. 0-0-0

Bad was 13. Nxe4 dxe4 14. Bxe4 because of 14... Qh4†, but it wasn't too late to repair the damage done by castling long: 13. Bxe4 dxe4 14. Qe2 [14. Nxe4? Qh4†] cxd4. In this instance White lost the initiative but had a solid position.

13. ... f5!

Nezh suppressed White's hope of attacking the pawn base. Now 14. exf6 Rxf6 would have been bad because the fork on f2 would have been inevitable, 15. Qh5 g6 or 15. Qh3 Rh6 16. Qf3 Rf8.

14. Rdf1?

White continued to "attack" with stubborness, though it was high time to think of defense. Right was 14. Kb1.

14. ... Rac8
15. Rhg1?

Alas, White still remained aggressive and didn't see that Black had prepared everything necessary for a decisive combination. There was a last chance to defend: 15. Bxe4.

15. ... cxd4
16. exd4

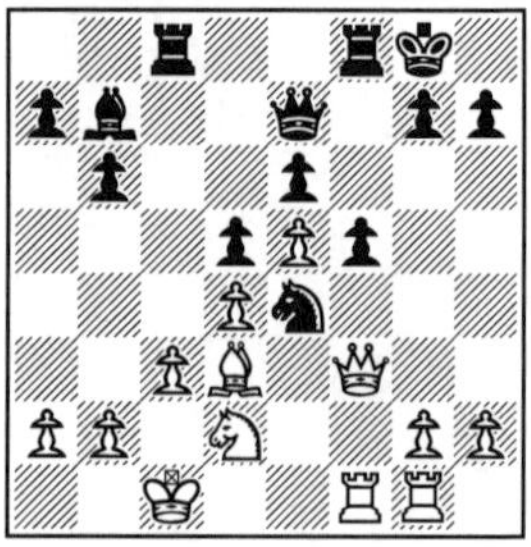

16. ... Nxc3!
17. bxc3 Rxc3†
18. Kb1

Moving towards the center wouldn't have helped: 18. Kd1 Qa3 19. Ke2 Rxd3! 20. Qxd3 Ba6.

18. ... Qa3
19. Nb3 Ba6
20. Rd1 Bc4!

That was all. White was finished.

21. Nc1 Rxc1†!
22. Rxc1 Qxa2#

89.

Super Nezh—S. Pimenov

C 13

Rostov-on-Don 1936

1. e4 e6 2. d4 d5 3. Nc3 Nf6 4. Bg5 Be7 5. e5 Nfd7 6. h4 h6?!.

This is not the best reaction to the Alekhine-Chatard Attack chosen by White. More circumspect responses are 6… c5, 6… f6, or even 6… Qxg5.

7. Qh5

Besides this enterprising move, White could afford retreats of the Bishop to e3 or f4.

7. … a6
8. Bd3 Nf8?

8… c5 was necessary. Black was afraid of the "awful" sacrifice 9. Nxd5 exd5 10. e6. After 10… Ne5! 11. dxe5 Bxe6 there was nothing dangerous for him.

R.N.

9. Bxe7 Qxe7?

This move would lead to hard consequences. If Black had seen the threat, he would have chosen 9… Kxe7! with a defendable position.

10. Qg4!

Besides taking at g7 there was the threat of 11. Nxd5.

10. … f5
11. exf6 gxf6
12. Nh3

Not 12. Nxd5? because of 12… exd5 with check.

12. … h5?!

A worthless move. The pawn would have been weak here. Moreover, the white Queen will get a stronger position. Right was 12… Nc6 or 12… Bd7.

13. Qg3 Qf7
14. Nf4 Rg8
15. Qe3 Kd8
16. 0-0-0 Bd7
17. Be2

The weak pawns at h5 and e6 were good targets for attack.

17. … Rh8
18. Bf3 Nc6
19. Qe2 Be8
20. Rhe1 Kd7

Black protected the weak pawns with great effort. It didn't matter, White had some additional resources.

21. Na4 Rd8

The white Knight will be allowed to go c5 because, if 21… b6, a strong blow to the center would be 22. c4!.

22. Nc5† Kc8
23. Nxa6!

The elementary 23. Ncxe6 would bring victory without any troubles, but as usual, the artist in Nezh was awakened. He preferred to not calculate a long variation, but to carry out a smart combination.

23. … bxa6
24. Qxa6† Kd7

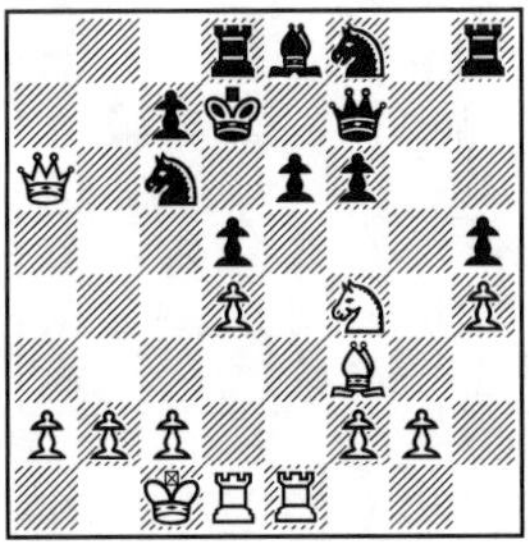

24… Kb8 would have lost at once: 25. Re3 Nb4 26. Rb3 Qe7 27. a3.

25. Nxe6! Qxe6

On 25… Nxe6 there was 26. Bxd5.

26. Rxe6 Kxe6

On 26… Nb8, then 27. Rd6†! should be foreseen (!). 25… cxd6 [27… Ke7 28. Re1 Kf7 29. Rxf6† etc.] 28. Qb7† Ke6

29. Qxd5† Kd7 30. Qb7† Ke6 31. Re1† Kf5 32. Qe4#.

27. Re1† Kf7
28. Rxe8 Nb8
29. Rxd8! Nxa6
30. Ra8 Nb4
31. a3

Black surrendered **(1-0).**

So, instead of a dull victory after 23. Ncxe6, Nezhmetdinov preferred to sacrifice: a Knight, another Knight, the Exchange, and finally, the Queen!!

90.

N. Kosolapov—Super Nezh

C47

Kazan 1936

1. e4 e5 2. Nf3 Nc6 3. Nc3 Nf6 4. d3 d5 5. exd5 Nxd5 6. Be2 Bb4 7. Bd2 0-0 8. Ne4 Be7 9. 0-0 f5 10. Ng3 g5 11. Ne1 Nf4 12. f3 Bc5† 13. Kh1 Rf6 14. c3 Be6 15. Nc2 Rh6 16. Be3.

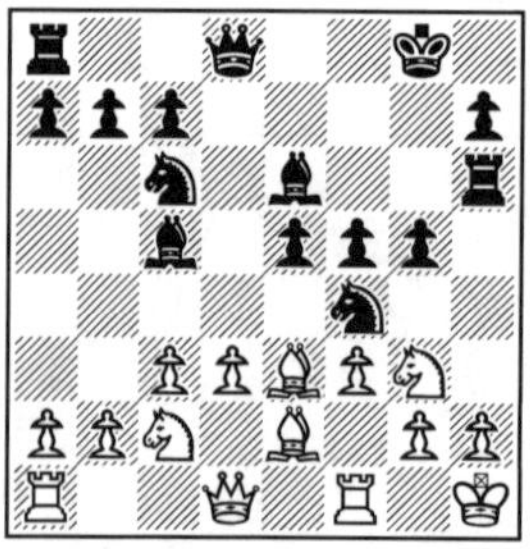

The opening part of the game had practically no value: White had played weakly and imprecisely in the opening. Black had a big advantage. The impending attack should be noted.

16. ... g4!
17. Bxc5 Qh4

17... Rxh2† wouldn't have won for Black. 18. Kxh2 Qh4† 19. Kg1 Qxg3 20. Rf2, and the Rook would've defended [Ed.: for example, 20... Nd4! 21. Bxd4 exd4 22. Qe1 Nh3† 23. Kh1 Nxf2† etc.].

18. Bg1 Qxg3
19. Ne1?

This was the weakest of the three possible defenses. After 19. Rf2 Rxh2† 20. Bxh2 Qxf2 White would have lost a pawn, but would have gone right on playing.

Better was 19. Ne3!. Besides defending against mate, the Knight controlled the squares g4 and d5. Nezh was prepared to continue the attack with the unexpected move 19... Rh4!, preparing ...Nh5. For example: 20. Qe1 Nh5! 21. Qf2 Qxf2 22. Bxf2 g3 23. Bg1 f4, and then 24... gxh2 25. Bf2 Ng3† 26. Bxg3 fxg3, shutting out the King and remaining with an extra pawn. 20. fxg4 fxg4 21. Qe1 Nh5! 22. Qf2 Ne7, transferring the Knight to g6, and then ...Rf8, is stopped by 23. Bxg4 Bxg4 24. Qf7†. Instead, 22... Rd8 gives the edge to Black after 23. d4 Qxf2 24. Bxf2

19. ... Bd5!
20. b4

A useless move, but no other worthy moves remained: 20. c4? Nd4! 21. cxd5 Ndxe2 followed by ...Nxg1 or ...Qxg2†; 20. Qd2 Rf8 21. Bd1 and now Nezh planned 21... Qxh2†!! 22. Bxh2 g3 23. d4 Rxh2† 24. Kg1 Rf6 and 25... Rfh6. On 23. Nc2 [instead of 23. d4] Rxh2† 24. Kg1 Rf6 25. Qf2 gxf2† 26. Kxh2 Rh6† 27. Kg3 Nxd3 28. c4 f4† 29. Kg4 Be6† 30. Kg5 Kg7 with mate looming.

20. ... Nh5

The same idea of the Queen sacrifice was still possible: 20... Qxh2† 21. Bxh2 g3 22. d4 Rxh2† 23. Kg1 Re8, and eventually Re6-h6.

21. Bf2

Mates are threatened everywhere: 21. Be3 f4 22. fxg4 Qxh2† 23. Kxh2 Ng3† 24. Kg1 fxe3! and 25... Rh1#; 21. fxg4

Qxg2†! 22. Nxg2 Ng3#.

21. ... Qf4

22. fxg4

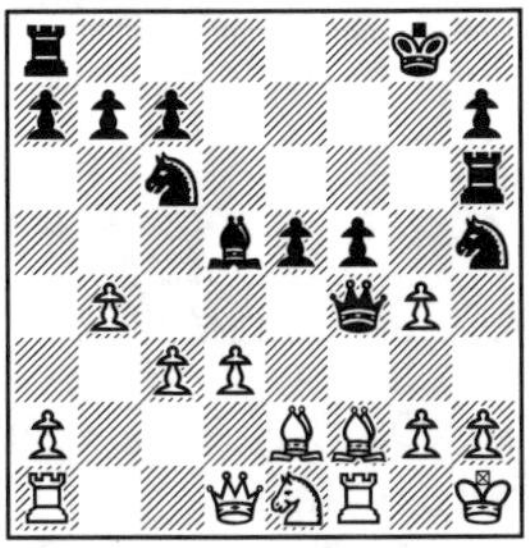

White's torture was at an end. Was it possible to prolong it by 22. Kg1 g3 23. hxg3 Nxg3 24. Bxg3 Qxg3, or 22. Qc1 g3 23. Bg1 Qh4, etc.?

22. ... Qxh2†!

23. Kxh2 Ng3†

24. Kxg3 f4#!

(0-1).

91.

G. Lapin—Super Nezh

Gorki 1938

The preliminary moves are not known.

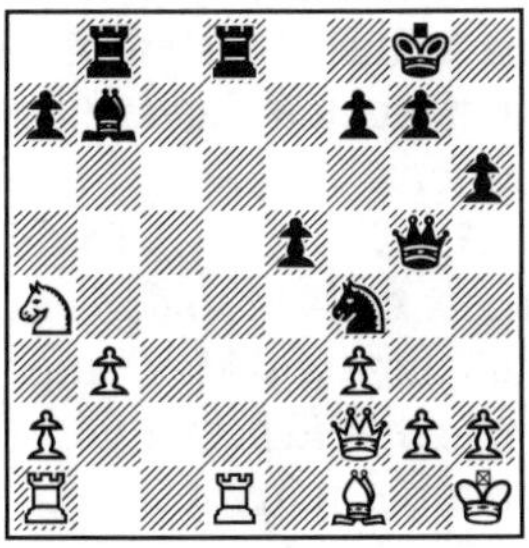

24. ... e4

25. Nc5

If 25. fxe4 Bxe4 26. Nc5 there would have been 26... Nh3!, giving the advantage to Black: 27. Rxd8† Rxd8 29. Qg3 Qxc5 29. Qxh3 Rd2.

25. ... exf3!

26. Nxb7 fxg2†

27. Bxg2 Rxd1†

28. Rxd1 Nxg2

29. Qxa7

The routine 29. Qxg2 Qxg2† 30. Kxg2 Rxb7 would have made it a hard endgame for White, that's why he hoped to get lucky in complications, with lines like 29... Rf8 30. Rg1 or 29... Re8 30. Nd6.

29. ... Nf4!!

The venerable P. Romanovsky wrote after this game:

> **Very nice. Black is not only sacrificing the whole Rook, but he is also letting it be taken with check.**

White was doomed because he would have been unable to reach the diagonal h1-a8 with his Queen.

30. Qxb8† Kh7

31. Rd2 Qg4!

32. h4

How do you defend yourself from the threat 32... Qf3† and 33... Nh3#?

32. ... Qh3†

33. Kg1 Qe3†

White surrendered **(0-1).**

92.

Super Nezh—P. Ermolin

B 71

Kazan 1946

1. e4 c5 2. Nf3 d6 3. d4 cxd4 4. Nxd4 Nf6 5. Nc3 g6 6. f4.

Nezh chooses the old Levenfish Variation, but in his notes, written in the 50s, he considered Rauzer's system the one with the better prospects: 6. Be3 Bg7 7. f3 0-0 8. Qd2 Nc6. He had correctly foreseen the chief direction along which the "Dragon" would later be developed.

6. ... Bg7

Nezh put a question mark to this move, and considered it the losing move. Such a "wholesome" developing move wouldn't lead to defeat, though the better move was 6... Nc6.

7. e5 dxe5
8. fxe5 Nd5?

This seemed to be the most reasonable Knight retreat but it was wrong. Later *Averbakh* found the correct move: 8... Nfd7! 9. e6 Ne5 10. Bb5† Nbc6 11. exf7† Kxf7 12. 0-0† Bf6 13. Nxc6 bxc6 in the game against *Kamyshov, Moscow 1948.* Later Boleslavsky mentioned that after 14. Qxd8 Rxd8 15. Ba4 White's chances would have been preferable. In the 70s, Black, in a correspondence game, played 10... Nec6! [instead of 10... Nbc6] 11. exf7† Kf8! 12. Nxc6 Qxd1† 13. Nxd1 Nxc6, and he solved his opening problems.

9. Bb5† Kf8
10. 0-0 Bxe5

Bad would have been 10... Nxc3, because of 11. Ne6†!, as played in one of Nezh's games. Taking the pawn would also lead to defeat. After 10... e6 there were some fighting chances though the position would remain difficult.

11. Bh6† Kg8

Better would have been 11... Bg7 12. Bxg7† Kxg7 13. Nxd5 Qxd5 14. Nf5† Qxf5 15. Rxf5 Bxf5, but now 16. Qd4† f6 17. Re1 e5 18. Rxe5! would quickly end Black's suffering.

12. Nxd5 Qxd5
13. Nf5 Qc5†

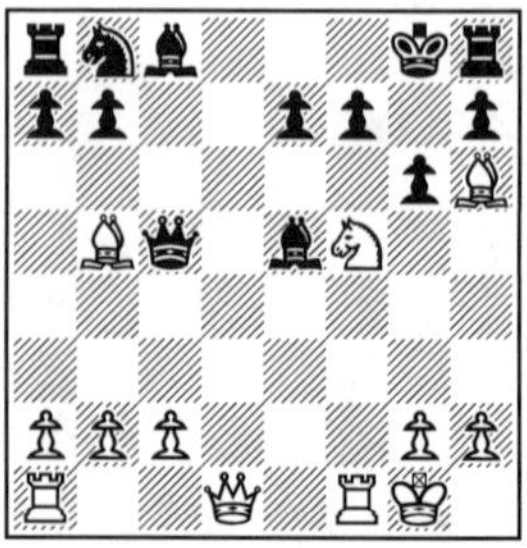

On 13... Qxb5 or 13... Qxd1 there was a mate in one.

14. Be3 Qc7
15. Nh6†

and mate on the next move **(1-0).**

93.
Super Nezh—V. Baskin
C 55
Moldovian ch.
Kishinev 1948

1. e4 e5 2. Nf3 Nc6 3. Bc4 Bc5 4. 0-0 Nf6 5. d4?!.

By transposing moves, White had chosen a somewhat doubtful variation of the Two Knights Defense. The alternative, 5. Nc3 d6 6. d3, would have lead to the "calmest" system of the Italian game, but it wouldn't have suited Nezh's temperament.

5. ... Bxd4

After 5... exd4 6. e5 d5 7. exf6 dxc4 8. fxg7 Rg8 there was Max Lange's sharp attack, which had been analyzed over 100 years ago in great detail.

6. Nxd4 Nxd4
7. f4 d6
8. fxe5 dxe5
9. Bg5 c6?!

An unlucky novelty. The theoretical reference books offered 9... Qe7, and only after 10. Nc3, then 10... c6. [Ed.: 10... Qc5 was played in *Pesitz—*

Sterk, Temesvar 1912. The game continued 11. Bxf7† Kxf7 12. Bxf6 (12. Qh5† doesn't go anywhere either) gxf6 13. Qh5† and White made no headway.] Black would get good chances in this variation, that's why instead of 10. Nc3 Nezh had prepared 10. Kh1. It wasn't known whether this novelty changes anything in its evaluation, but it hadn't been played in anyone's praxis.

10. Qd3 Bg4
11. Nc3 b5

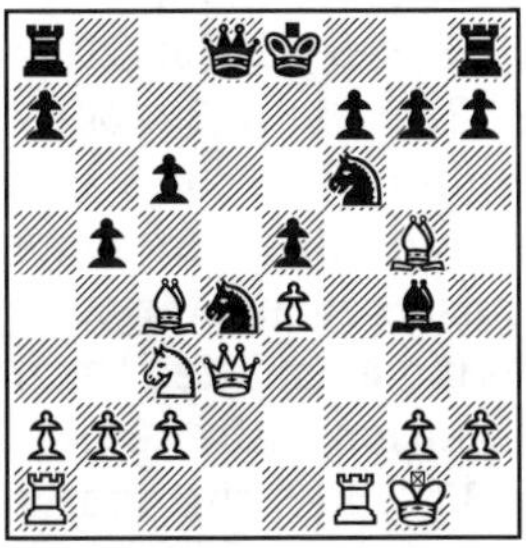

Black was optimistic and planned to win no less than the Exchange: 12. Bb3 b4, and after the Knight's move, 13... Be2. 11... Qe7 would've been much better, to prepare to castle long.

12. Qg3! Qb6

Black continued with tactical complications, an area where it was almost impossible to beat Nezhmetdinov. Since Black decided to weaken the queenside, then that decision should have been justified by 12... bxc4. After 13. Bxf6 gxf6 14. Qxg4 Qb6, Black had good play, owing to a powerful centralized Knight.

13. Be3!

Avoiding the trap 13. Bxf7† Kxf7 14. Qxg4 Nf3†! which would lose the Queen.

13. ... Qc5
14. Bd5!

White wouldn't have gotten anything special from 14. Bxf7† Kxf7 15. Qxg4 Rad8.

14. ... 0-0-0
15. Rxf6! gxf6
16. Qxg4† f5
17. Qxf5†! Nxf5
18. Bxc5 cxd5
19. exf5 a6

This forced variation gave White two pieces for the Rook. Having moved his pawns into the center, Black could still hope for stubborn resistance. There was a fatal problem: there was the threat of a2-a4, after which the queenside would have been ruined.

20. Kf2

Nezh put an exclamation mark after this move and wrote in his notes:

> **How surprising this is, but this "tranquil" King's move strengthens White's threats, which are connected with the move a2-a4.**

In fact, this move effectively brought an end to the game. Actually, the King's move hardly strengthened the threat of a2-a4. It was more like a loss of tempo. This could have given Black another chance: 20... Kb7! 21. a4 Rc8! 22. Bd6 [Ed.: 22. b4 seems stronger.] d4. For example, 23. Bxe5 dxc3 24. Bxh8 cxb2! 25. Bxb2 Rxc2†. That's why 20. a4 should have been played immediately. For example, 20... bxa4 21. Rxa4 Kb7 22. Rb4† Kc6 23. Ba7! Rc8 24. Rb6†.

20. ... Rhg8?
21. a4 bxa4

On 21... Rg5, 22. f6 was playable.

22. Rxa4 Kb7
23. Rb4† Kc6
24. Rb6†! Kxc5

Having a hopeless position, Black made up his mind to lose "to the music."

25. Na4† Kc4

26. b3† Kd4
27. Rb4#
(1-0).

In the final mate all the white pieces took part. The game was awarded the prize "for beauty."

94.
Super Nezh—Y. Sakharov
B11
Semi-finals 25th USSR ch.
Kiev 1957

1. e4 c6 2. Nf3 d5 3. Nc3 Bg4 4. h3 Bxf3 5. Qxf3 Nf6 6. d3 e6 7. g3 Be7 8. Bg2 0-0 9. 0-0 Na6 10. Qe2 Nc7 11. f4 Nfe8 12. Kh2 b5 13. Nd1 f5 14. exd5 exd5 15. c4 bxc4 16. dxc4 Nf6 17. cxd5 cxd5 18. Ne3 Ne4 19. Rd1 Qd7 20. Bd2 Bc5 21. Rac1 Bb6.

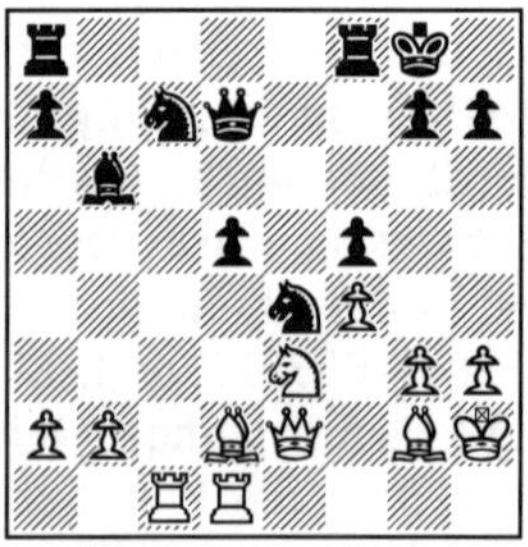

Black seems to have a huge spatial advantage, and his Knight and Bishop were active, but in reality, his position was not an easy one. Nezh proved this very energetically.

22. Bxe4! fxe4
23. Bc3 Rad8

Of course bad was 23... d4 because of the obvious 24. Bxd4 Bxd4 25. Nc2 Ne6 26. Nxd4 Nxd4 27. Qc4†.

24. Be5 Qf7
25. Rc6!

The picture had been forcefully changed. It turned out that White had created real threats: 26. Ng4 with the further Nh6†, or 26. Qg4 and Nf5.

25. ... Ne6

Hoping to complicate matters Black sacrificed his pride and joy, his central pawn.

26. Nxd5 Nd4

The best continuation was 26... Rxd5! 27. Rxd5 Nxf4 28. gxf4 Qxd5. Nezh proved, in his notes, that after 29. Rd6! White had the advantage everywhere, including the line 29... Qc5! [our mark] 30. Qg2 Rf7 31. Re6 Rd7 [or 31... Qc8 32. f5 Qxe6 33. fxe6 Rf2 34. b4! with the better ending] 32. Bc3 e3 33. Qe4 Qd5 34. Re8†, etc. Alas, but sometimes a master misses elementary refutations, after having calculated the most difficult variations. After 30... Qf2! [instead of 30... Rf7] the analysis of all other lines became unnecessary and Black's position wasn't worse. Still his intuition didn't let Nezh down! Instead of 29. Rd6, he should have played 29. Qg2! at once, and after 29... Qf7, take with 30. Qxe4, gaining a healthy extra pawn. The thing was, that on 30... Qxa2, 31. Bxg7! was possible, and after 31... Kxg7 32. Qe5† Kg8 [32... Kf7? 33. Rf6† and 34. Qg5†] 33. Rc2! there would have been no satisfactory defense to 34. Rg2.

27. Rxd4! Bxd4
28. Rc7 Bxe5

After 28... Qxd5 there was a mate: 29. Rxg7† Kh8 30. Rxh7† Kxh7 31. Qh5† Kg8 32. Qg6#.

29. Rxf7 Rxf7
30. Qxe4 Rfd7

Worse was 30... Bxb2, as it would have been very dangerous to allow the Knight to accompany the Queen.

31. fxe5 Rxd5
32. h4 R5d7

33. Qc4† Kf8

The extra pawns provided White with a simple victory, as even the connected Rooks wouldn't have seriously changed the position.

34. Kh3 Re8
35. Kg4 Rf7
36. Qc5† Kg8
37. h5 h6
38. Qd5 Kf8
39. a4 R8e7
40. b4 Re8
41. b5 Rc8

Black surrendered **(1-0).**

95.

Super Nezh—A. Zaitsev

B 27

23rd Russian ch.

Kazan 1964

1. e4 c5 2. Nf3 g6.

Black didn't want a theoretical duel in the main lines of the Sicilian Defense, a defense in which Nezh was an authority. The Vladivostok master, who later became the first grandmaster in the Eastern part of the USSR, usually tried to get through the opening quickly, relying on his tactical abilities in the middlegame.

3. c3 Nf6
4. e5 Nd5
5. d4 cxd4
6. Qxd4

6. cxd4 was no problem for Black.

6. ... Nc7
7. e6!?

A tempting continuation, but it didn't give any advantage. Good would have been 7. Bc4.

7. ... f6
8. exd7† Qxd7

Black was in a peaceful mood and was eager to head for the endgame. 8... Bxd7 was more logical, and after that developing the Knight with an attack on the Queen would win a tempo.

9. Qf4 Nd5
10. Qd2

Everything was done for a continuation of the battle. White would even lose tempi to keep the Queens on the board.

10. ... Bg7
11. Be2 e5

Zaitsev's natural optimism was clear from this move. He had not underestimated his position. Still, 11... 0-0 was preferable, as on 12. Bc4, quite probable was 12... Rd8 13. 0-0 Kh8 14. Rd1 Nb6 with equality.

12. 0-0 Ne7

Bad would have been 12... 0-0 13. Bc4 Rd8 14. Rd1.

13. Bc4 b5?

Black was going to drive the Bishop away from the a2-g8 diagonal by weakening his position. The defect of the text move was that now the black King couldn't have been sheltered on the queenside either. Also, equality couldn't be obtained with a Queen exchange: 13... Qxd2 14. Nbxd2, and then there was the threat of Nd2-e4-d6. Perhaps the best would have been 13... Nbc6 14. Qe2, but even there 15. Rd1 would have provided White with the advantage.

14. Bb3 Na6
15. Qe2 Nc5
16. Rd1 Qc6
17. Bc2 Be6

At this point castling would have been possible, but even then after: 17... 0-0 18. b4 Nb7 19. Be4 Qe8 20. a4 bxa4 21. Qc4† Black would have been under a lot of pressure.

18. Nbd2 Rd8?!

At the very moment that castling

would have been good, Black ignored it! 18… 0-0 19. b4 Nd7 20. Ne4 Bc4 21. Bb3 Rfd8 with a worse, but defendable position.

19. Nb3 Rxd1†
20. Qxd1 Nb7?

This was the last time Black could have castled: 20… 0-0 21. Nxc5 Qxc5 22. Be3 Qc7 23. Bb3 with a hard, but not hopeless position. Zaitsev had missed a disguised White combination, which gave a decisive advantage.

21. a4 a6
22. axb5 axb5

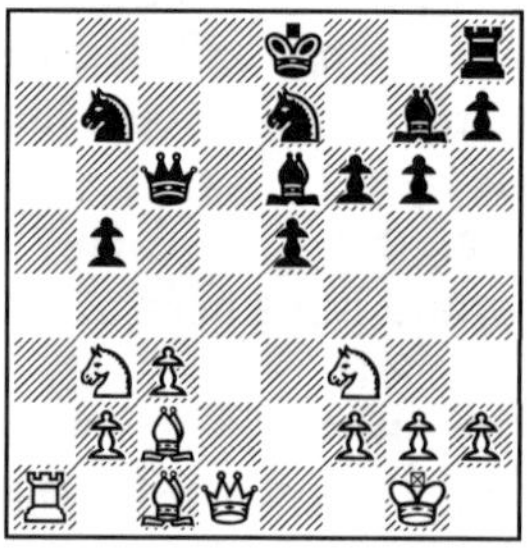

23. Nbd4! exd4
24. Nxd4 Qd7
25. Nxe6 Qxe6
26. Ra8† Nc8

All these moves were forced: 26… Kf7 was terrible because of 27. Rxh8 and 28. Bb3.

27. Bb3! Qd7
28. Qe2† Kd8
29. Be6 Re8

Did Nezh miscalculate, beginning with the combination at the 21st move?

30. Rxc8†!

No, everything was accounted for!

30. … Qxc8
31. Qd1† Ke7
32. Bxc8 Rxc8
33. Qe2†

Black surrendered **(1-0)**.

96.
Super Nezh—V. Tatarintsev
B30
23rd Russian ch.
Kazan 1964

1. e4 c5 2. Nf3 Nc6 3. Bb5 a6 4. Bxc6 bxc6 5. d3 d5 6. Nbd2 e6 7. 0-0 Nf6 8. c3 Be7 9. Qa4 Qc7 10. Re1 0-0 11. Nf1 a5 12. Bg5 h6 13. Bh4 dxe4 14. dxe4 Ba6 15. Ne3 Rfd8 16. Bg3 Qb6 17. Ne5 Bb5 18. Qc2 Nh5 19. a4 Ba6 20. N5c4 Bxc4 21. Nxc4 Qa6 22. b3 Qb7 23. Rab1 Nf6 24. Red1 Rxd1† 25. Rxd1 Nd7 26. Bd6 Bf8 27. g3 Nb6 28. Bxf8 Kxf8.

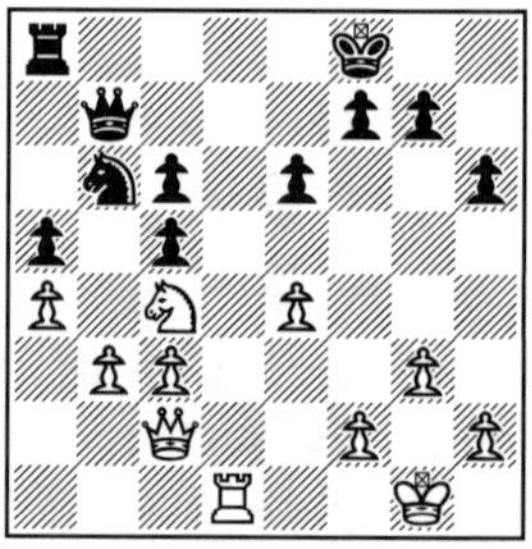

All this maneuvering brought about a decisive positional advantage to White— he was the owner of the open file. Black's pawn structure had been seriously weakened.

Nezh realized this advantage quickly and elegantly.

29. Nd6 Qe7
30. e5 Kg8
31. Qe4 Nd5
32. c4 Nb4
33. Qe3 Qa7

The weak pawns on Black's queenside doomed him, since in trying to defend them, the pieces were obliged to take extremely passive positions.

34. Ne4 Na6

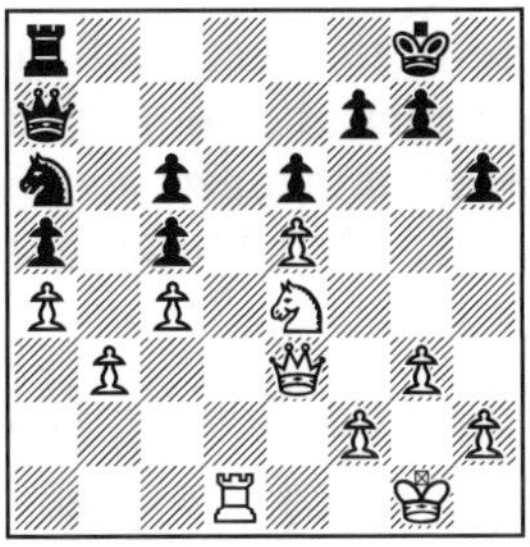

35. Nf6!

Black had left his monarch to die alone, and White realized that Black would be executed immediately. The Knight had to be taken because of the threat of Rd7.

35. ... gxf6
36. exf6 Kh7

By playing 36... Qb8 37. Qxh6 Qf8 38. Qh5, Black looks to prolong. But, 38... Nb4 loses to 39. Re1. On 38... Nc7, White still plays 39. Re1.

37. Qe4† Kh8
38. Qg4

Black surrendered, **(1-0)**, as on 38... Rg8 there was 39. Rd8!.

97.

Super Nezh—B. Rabar
A 04
Baku 1964

1. e4 c5 2. Nf3 e6 3. d3 Nc6 4. g3 g6 5. Bg2 Bg7 6. 0-0 Nge7 7. Re1 0-0 8. e5 d6 9. exd6 Nf5 10. Nc3 Nxd6 11. Bf4 Nd4 12. Be5 Bxe5 13. Nxe5 Bd7 14. Ne4 Nxe4 15. dxe4 Ba4 16. b3 Be8 17. c3 Nc6 18. Nc4 e5 19. Qf3 Kg7 20. Rad1 Qc7 21. Ne3 Ne7.

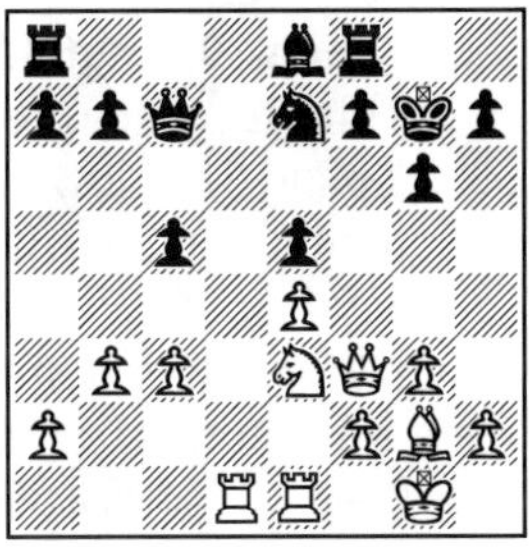

White could have obtained an outpost at d5 and, in combination with the possession of the d-file ["Nimzovich"], this could theoretically provide him with the advantage. Still, no profit could have been gained from it by White, the offensive front was too narrow.

22. h4!

The idea was h4-h5 and h6! with check and a quick mate.

22. ... Bc6
23. Nd5

The straightforward 23. h5 collides with 23... f5, and Black would have gotten considerable counterplay.

23. ... Bxd5
24. exd5 Rad8?

As so often happens, the "natural move" turned out to be the fatal mistake. It was still possible to defend, although the hard-to-find move 24... Nc8, aiming to transfer the Knight to d6, had to be found. 24... Nf5 wouldn't work for this purpose because of 25. Bh3, and then there would be no 25... Nd6 due to 26. Rxe5.

[Ed.: However, Pishkin's idea doesn't work so nicely in all the details. On 24... Nc8 Alex suggests 25. Qe4 as one possible idea, but Black gets the edge there. He also gives 25. h5, which is much better for White. Continuing with 25... f5 26. d6 Nxd6 27. Rxe5 Ne4 28. Red5 he stops at 28... Nf6. But 29. Rd6! is a decent move for White as it puts immediate pressure on Black's b7. Thus, 29... Rf7 and then 30. hxg6 hxg6 31. c4 Ne4 and White has the interesting 32. R6d5. Black plays 32... Re8 to protect his Knight on e4 should White move his Queen away from f3. But, 33. Qe3! anyway, and White has a small but aggravating advantage.]

25. Qe4 f6
26. f4! Nf5
27. fxe5 fxe5

27... Nxg3 wasn't worth playing because of 28. d6! Qb6 [28... Nxe4 29. dxc7 Rxd1 30. Rxd1 and 31. Rd8 or 31. Rd7† followed by 32. Bxe4 if 30... Rc8.] 29. exf6†, and then 29... Rxf6 would have been awful because of 30. Qe7† Rf7 31. Qe5† and 32. Qxg3. A lesser evil would have been 27... Qxe5 28. Qxe5 fxe5 though the ending would have been very bad.

28. d6!

A simple tactical stroke, which will give an irresistible attack.

28. ... Rxd6
29. Qxe5† Kh6

29... Rff6 wouldn't have worked because of 30. g4 and 31. g5.

30. Qf4† Kg7
31. g4 Rf7
32. Qe5† Kg8
33. gxf5 Rxd1
34. Qe8† Kg7
35. Rxd1

Black surrendered **(1-0)**.

98.

K. Langeweg—Super Nezh

E 94

Chigorin Memorial

Sochi 1964

1. Nf3 Nf6 2. c4 g6 3. Nc3 Bg7 4. d4 0-0 5. e4 d6 6. Be2 e5 7. 0-0 c6 8. Rb1?!.

Inspite of the fact that the priority of this move belongs to Larsen, it can't be recommended, as it had no value for White in a fight for the center. The traditional continuations were: 8. Re1 or 8. d5, transposing to the Benoni.

8. ... exd4
9. Nxd4 Re8
10. f3?!

In his *match* against *Donner (1958), Larsen* played without the weakening of the g1-a7 diagonal: 10. Qc2 Na6 11. Be3 Ng4 12. Bxg4 Bxg4 13. Qd2, but he only achieved equality.

10. ... d5!

At once Nezh found an opportunity to create a collision. The Knight on d4 was in an unstable position.

11. exd5 Nxd5!
12. cxd5 Qb6
13. Kh1 Qxd4
14. Qxd4

Not the best decision. The Queen exchange wouldn't solve some of White's problems. He should have had enough courage to sacrifice a pawn, thus 14. Bd3! cxd5 15. Nb5 Qb6 16. Bf4 Na6 17. Qd2 with some activity.

14. ... Bxd4
15. Bc4

15. Bd3 would have been more cautious, as 15... Bxc3 16. bxc3 cxd5 would have preserved chances for White to defend owing to the possession of the two Bishops.

15. ... Bf5
16. dxc6 Nxc6
17. Ne4!

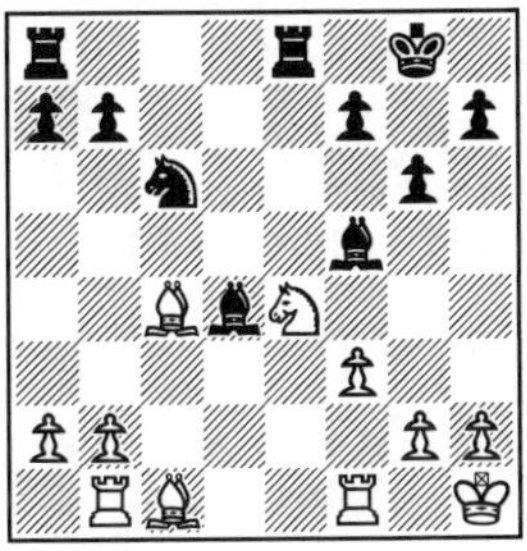

If the Rook went to a1, then 17... Nb4 would have been unpleasant.

17. ... Ne5!

There was a new combinational idea: 18... Nxf3! 19. Rxf3 Rxe4.

18. Bd5?!

This was not enough of a defense. The commentators of this game noted that 18. Bb5 was even worse because of the variation 18... Nxf3 19. Bxe8 Bxe4 20. Bxf7† Kg7 21. gxf3 Bxb1 22. Bh6† Kxf7 23. Rxb1 Re8 with a won ending for Black. Instead of 22. Bh6†?, stronger was 22. Bd5!, and White would have been able to defend. Thus, 18. Bb5! was correct.

18. ... Nd3
19. Bg5 Nf2†
20. Rxf2 Bxf2
21. Rd1 Bxe4
22. fxe4 Rac8
23. Bxb7 Rc2
24. Rd7?

Despite winning the Exchange, Black would have had to work hard to win if White had played 24. Bf6 instead of this. White had forgotten about the weakness of the first rank.

24. ... Bh4!

White surrendered **(0-1).**

After 25. Bh6 Black would have played 25... Rd8 26. Rxd8 Bxd8 and the pawn on b2 would be lost after which it wouldn't have been difficult to realize the advantage.

99.

Super Nezh—A. Cherepkov
A 05
Yalta 1964

1. Nf3 Nf6 2. g3 g6 3. Bg2 Bg7 4. 0-0 0-0 5. d3 d6 6. c3 c5 7. Qa4 Nc6 8. Qh4 Ng4 9. h3 Nge5 10. Nxe5 Nxe5 11. d4 cxd4 12. cxd4 Nc6 13. Rd1 Bf5 14. Nc3 Bc2.

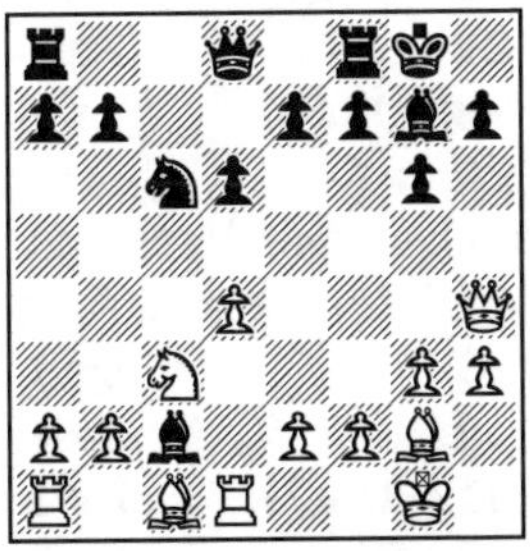

Black expected 15. Rd2 Bf5 16. Rd1 Bc2, forcing the draw. But:

15. d5! Bxc3

Black accepted the challenge and was even ready to part with his black-squared Bishop for the sake of a weak hope to win material.

16. bxc3 Bxd1
17. dxc6 bxc6
18. Bg5!

It was possible to play 18. Bh6 right away, but when there is a chance to weaken the opponents position "free of charge," it shouldn't be missed.

18. ... f6
19. Bh6 Bxe2?

Black will get trapped. Right was 19... Bc2 20. Bxf8 Qxf8 21. Bxc6 Rc8 22. Bd5† Kh8 and it's even.

20. Bxf8 Qxf8
21. Qe4!

An unpleasant surprise. The Bishop was trapped, although it seemed to have plenty squares for retreat!

21. ... Bh5

Worse was 21... Bb5 22. a4 Ba6 23. Qxc6.

22. g4 Bxg4
23. hxg4

Black had three pawns for the piece, but here is exactly that case when the piece is more valuable than the pawns.

23. ... Rc8
24. Qe6† Kg7
25. Qd7 Qd8
26. Qxa7 Ra8
27. Qb7 Ra4
28. Qxc6 Rxg4
29. a4

It was clear that Black had no compensation for the piece. Then:

29. ... Qa5
30. Re1 Rxa4
31. Rxe7† Kh6
32. Qb7 Kg5
33. Qf3 Qf5
34. Qxf5 Kxf5
35. Rxh7 Rc4
36. Rh3

and White soon won **(1-0)**.

100.

Super Nezh—E. Stolyar
Chigorin Memorial
Sochi 1965

The opening moves are not known.

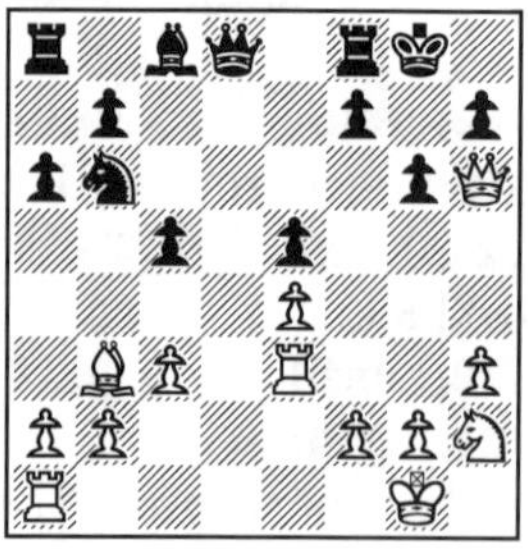

White's advantage was in his prospects of an attack on Black's King position, which was weak along the dark squares. Simultaneously, an open file would have been of great importance.

21. Nf3 Qf6

The only defense to the threat of 22. Ng5.

22. Rd1 c4
23. Rd6! Qe7
24. Rxb6 cxb3
25. axb3 f6
26. Rd3!

Using the open file, White controlled almost the whole chessboard.

26. ... Be6
27. Nh4!

If 27. Rdd6, Black would have had a good defense in 27... Bd7 with the Bishop protecting g6 [after ...Be8].

Now there was the threat of a sacrifice at g6. That's why Black had no time to include the a-Rook in the game.

27. ... Bf7
28. Rg3 Be8
29. Nf5 Qd7

On 29... Qf7, the game would have been decided with 30. Re6.

30. Rd6 Qc7
31. Re6 Rf7
32. h4! Qd8
33. h5 g5
34. Rd6 Bd7
35. Rgd3 Rc8

The slumbering Rook wanted to help, but it was too late.

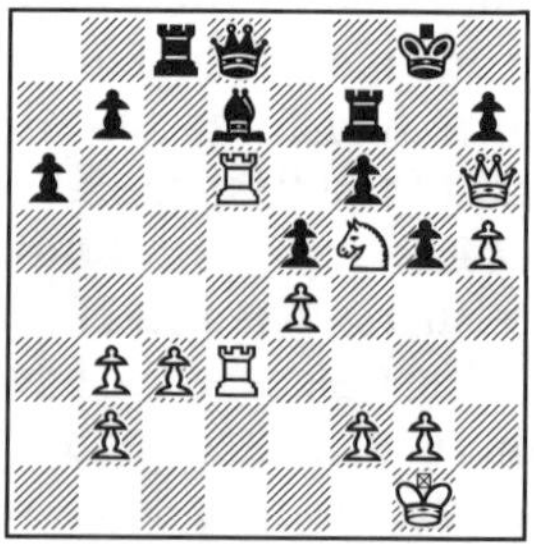

36. Rxd7! Rxd7

37. Rxd7 Qxd7
38. Qxf6 Qd1†
39. Kh2 Qxh5†
40. Kg3

Here the flag had fallen on Black's clock. **(1-0).**

Semi-finals 26th USSR ch. / Rostov-on-Don 1958

	Players	1	2	3	4	5	6	7	8	9	10	11	12	13	14	15	16	Points	Place
1	Nezhmetdinov	•	▒		■		■	▒	■	▒		■	▒	■	■	■	■	10	1-2
2	Spassky	▒	•	▒	■		■	▒	▒	▒	▒	■		■	■	■	■	10	1-2
3	Krogius	■	▒	•	■	▒			▒	▒	■	▒	■	▒		■	■	9	3
4	Makarov				•	■	■	▒	▒	▒	■	■	■	■		▒	▒	8.5	4
5	Borisenko	■	■	▒		•		▒	▒		■	■	▒	▒	■	▒		8	5-9
6	Gurgenidze			■		■	•	■	▒	■		■	▒	■		■		8	5-9
7	Zurakhov	▒	▒	■	▒	▒		•		▒		▒	■	■	▒	▒	+	8	5-9
8	Kots		▒	▒	▒	▒	▒	■	•	■	▒		▒	▒	■	▒	▒	8	5-9
9	Shishkin	▒	▒	▒	▒	■		▒		•	■	■	▒		▒	■	▒	8	5-9
10	Zilber	■	▒				■	■	▒		•		■		■	▒	+	7.5	10
11	Mnatsakanian			▒				▒	■		■	•	▒	■		■	■	6.5	11
12	Aronson	▒	■			▒	▒		▒	▒		▒	•	▒	▒	■		6	12-13
13	Uusi			▒		▒			▒	■	■		▒	•	■		+	6	12-13
14	Zhilin			■	■		■	▒		▒		■	▒		•			5.5	14-16
15	Kopylov				▒	▒		▒	▒		▒			■	■	•	■	5.5	14-16
16	Ufimtsev				▒	■	■	—	▒	▒	—		■	—	■		•	5.5	14-16
		1	2	3	4	5	6	7	8	9	10	11	12	13	14	15	16		

19th Russian ch. / Voronezh 1959

	Players	1	2	3	4	5	6	7	8	9	10	11	12	13	14	15	16	17	18	Points	Place
1	Lutikov	•	■	▒	▒	▒	▒	▒	▒	▒	■	■	▒	▒	▒	■	■	■	■	12	1
2	Shamkovich		•	▒		▒	▒	▒	■	■	▒	■	■	■	■	▒	■	■	▒	11.5	2
3	Polugaevsky	▒	▒	•	▒	▒		▒	▒	▒	▒	▒	■	▒	■	■	■	■	■	11	3
4	Krogius	▒	■	▒	•	▒	▒	▒	■	▒	▒	▒		▒	▒	▒	■	■	■	10.5	4
5	Aronin	▒	▒	▒	▒	•	■	▒	▒	▒	■	▒	▒		▒	■	▒	▒	▒	9.5	5-8
6	Zhilin	▒	▒	■	▒		•	■		▒		▒		■		■	■	■	■	9.5	5-8
7	Nezhmetdinov	▒	▒	▒	▒	▒		•	▒	▒	▒		■	■	▒		■	■	■	9.5	5-8
8	Shahov	▒		▒		▒	■	▒	•		▒	■		■	■	■	▒	■	▒	9.5	5-8
9	Borisenko	▒		▒	▒	▒	▒	▒	■	•	■	▒	■	▒	▒	▒			■	9	9-10
10	Hodos		▒	▒	▒		■	▒	▒		•	▒	▒	▒	▒	■	■	▒	■	9	9-10
11	Ilivitsky			▒	▒	▒	▒	■		▒	▒	•	▒	▒	▒	▒	■	■	▒	8.5	11-13
12	Kotkov	▒			■	▒	■		■		▒	▒	•	▒		▒	▒	■	■	8.5	11-13
13	Stolyar	▒		▒	▒	■				▒	▒	▒	▒	•	▒	■	▒	■	■	8.5	11-13
14	Zagorovsky	▒			▒	▒	■	▒		▒	▒	▒	■	▒	•		■		■	8	14
15	Toprover		▒		▒			■		▒		▒	▒		■	•	▒	▒	▒	6	15
16	Vastrikov					▒			▒	■			▒	▒		▒	•	▒	■	5	16
17	Zhelyandinov					▒				■	▒				■	▒	▒	•	▒	4.5	17
18	Sergievsky		▒			▒			▒			▒				▒		▒	•	3	18
		1	2	3	4	5	6	7	8	9	10	11	12	13	14	15	16	17	18		

Opponents

Aronin, Lev Solomonovich: 51, 53. 1920—1982, master (M) from 1946, IM—1950. 2-4th pl. in 18th USSR ch. (1950), Russian champion—1952, Moscow champion—1965.

Bagirov, Vladimir Konstantinovich: 74. 1936—2000, M—1958, IM—1963, IGM—1978. 13 times champion of Azerbaijan. Now lives in Latvia.

Baskin, V.: 93.

Belov, Lev Andreevich: 9. b.1933, M—1960, 2-6th pl. in Russian ch., 1961.

Bergin, Dmitri: 73. b.1937, M—1964.

Boleslavsky, Isaac Efremovich: 16, 22, 65. 1919—1977, M—1939, GM USSR—1946, IGM—1950. 1-2nd pl. in Candidate's tournament, 1950 (with D. Bronstein), 2nd pl. in USSR ch.—1945, 1947; 3rd pl. in 1944; Russian champion 1946, Ukrainian champion 1938, 1939, 1940; Belorussian champion 1952, 1964.

Borisenko, Georgi Konstantinovich: 20, 36. b.1922, M—1950, IGM ICCF—1966. USSR correspondence champion—1957, 1963.

Cherepkov, Alexander Vasilievich: 99. b.1920, M—1954, IM—1984. Leningrad champion—1967, 1968, 1982.

Chernikh, Valentin: 47. b.1939, M—1965.

Chernikov, Oleg Leonidovich: 12. b.1936, M—1963, IM—1985, 3-4th pl. in Russian ch.—1971.

Chistyakov, Alexander Nikolaevich: 42. 1914—1990, M—1938, Moscow champion—1950.

Ciocaltea, Victor (Romania): 49. 1932—1983, IM—1957, IGM—1979.

Ciric, Dragoljub (Yugoslavia): 11. b.1935, IGM—1965.

Elizarov, A.: 43.

Ermolin, P.: 92.

Estrin, Yakov Borisovich: 35. 1923—1987, M—1949, IM—1975, IGM ICCF—1966. 2-4th pl. Russian ch., 1946; 3rd pl. Moscow ch., 1949; world correspondence champion—1975.

Filip, Miroslav (Czechoslovakia): 56. b.1928, IM—1953, IGM—1955.

Flohr, Salomon Mikhailovich: xi, 82. 1908—1983, GM USSR—1942, IGM—1950. Won 19 international tournaments in the 30s.

Geller, Efim Petrovich: 54. 1925—1998, M—1949, IGM—1952. USSR Champion—1955, 1979; 2-3rd pl. in candidates tournament—1962 (Curaçao); won more than 20 international tournaments.

Gurgenidze, Bukhuti Ivanovich: 38. b.1933, M—1955, IM—1966, IGM—1970. 13 times Georgian Champion.

Heuer, Valter Petrovich (Estonia): 75. b.1928, M—1960.

Holmov, Ratmir Dmitrievich: 77. b.1925, M—1947, IM—1954, IGM—1960. Recurring champion of Lithuania; 1-3rd pl. in USSR ch.—1963; Moscow champion—1987.

Ilivitsky, Georgi Alexandrovich: 44. 1921—1989, M—1947, IM—1955. Russian champion—1948, 1949. Interzonal tourn. 1955: 10—11th pl.

Ivashin, Alexey.: 78. 1915—1958.

Kalinkin, B: 13.

Kamyshov, Mikhail Petrovich: 3. b.1909, M—1945.

Karasev, Vladimir Ivanovich: 76. b.1938,

M—1965, IM—1976. Champion of Leningrad—1974.

Kasparyan, Genrikh Moiseevich: 7. 1910—1995, M—1936, IM—1950, IGM (composition)—1972. 10 times Armenian champion, first Armenian master.

Kluger, Julius (Hungary): 57. b.1914, IM—1954.

Kolarov, Atanas Stefanov (Bulgaria): 84. b.1934, IM—1957.

Korchmar, A.: 88. 1914—1978, M—1964.

Kosolapov, Nikolai Ivanovich: 90. Lived in Kazan.

Kotkov, Yuri Mikhailovich: 8, 40. b.1930, M—1955, IM ICCF—1992.

Krogius, Nikolay Vladimirovich: 80. b.1930, M—1952, IM—1963, IGM—1964. Russian champion—1952, 1964, psychology (PhD).

Langeweg, Kick (Holland): 98. b.1937, IM—1962.

Lapin, G.: 91.

Lein, Anatoly Yakovlevich: 26. b.1931, M—1956, IM—1964, IGM— 1968. Russian champion—1963, 6th pl. in USSR ch.—1966/67. He has lived in the USA since 1975.

Lengyel, Levente (Hungary): 39. b.1933, IGM—1964.

Lilienthal, Andor: 4, 55. b.1911, GM USSR—1940, IGM—1950. USSR champion—1940, now lives in Hungary.

Luik, Helmut (Estonia): 86. b.1928, M—1967.

Lusikal: 5.

Matsukevich, Anatoly Alexandrovich.: 62, 83. b. 1938.

Medvedev, G.: 50.

Mikenas, Vladas Ionovich: 15, 68, 79. 1910—1992, IM—1950, IGM —1987, 4 times Lithuanian champion, Estonian champion—1929, 5-6th pl. in USSR ch. 1944.

Nikitin, Alexander.: 34.

Novotyelnov, Nikolai Alexandrovich: 28. b.1911, M—1945, IM—1951. Russian champion—1947, Leningrad champion—1942.

Padevsky, Nikola Bochev (Bulgaria): 23. b.1933, IGM—1964, recurring Bulgarian champion.

Paoli, Enrico (Italy): 6. b.1908, IM—1951, 3 times Italian champion.

Pimenov, Sergei Ivanovich: 89. 1907—1981.

Polugaevsky, Lev Abramovich: 1, 17. 1934—1995, M—1953, IM—1961, GM USSR—1960, IGM— 1962, USSR champion—1967, 1969; Russian champion 1961, participant in 20 USSR championships.

Pozarsky, B.: 60.

Rabar, Braslav (Yugoslavia): 97. 1919—1973, IM—1950, Yugoslavian champion—1951.

Romanovsky, Rem: 37. b.1929, M—1963.

Ruchkin, J.: 48.

Sakharov, Yuri Nikolaevich: 72, 94. 1922—1981, M—1956, IM ICCF—1971. Ukrainian champion—1966, 1968; 6th pl. in USSR ch.—1967.

Sergievsky, Vladimir Dmitrievich: 33, 87. b.1936, M—1960, IM—1966. Russian champion—1966.

Shamkovich, Leonid Alexandrovich: 18, 19, 27, 29, 45. b.1923, M—1950, IM—1962, IGM—1965. Russian champion—1954, 1956; 5-6th pl. in USSR ch.—1965. He has ived in the USA since 1976.

Shcherbakov, Vitaly Sergeevich: 69. b.1931, M—1954.

Shestoperov, Alexei Nikolaevich: 66. b.1935, M—1960.

Shipov, Boris: 24. b.1941, M—1964.

Shishov, Mikhail Vasilievich: 52, 67. 1910—1981, M—1951, 5 times Georgian champion; coach of N. Gaprindashvili.

Slepoi, Iosef Moiseevich: 85. b.1934.

Spassky, Boris Vasilievich: 64. b.1937, M—1953, IM—1953, IGM—1955, GM USSR—1956. 10th world champion (1969—1972); USSR ch.—1961, 1973. Lives in France since 1976.

Ståhlberg, Gideon (Sweden): 81. 1908—1967, IGM—1950, recurring Swedish champion.

Stolyar, Efim Samoilovich: 100. b.1923, M—1953, 2-4th pl. Russian ch.—1956.

Suetin, Alexei Stepanovich: 2, 41. b.1926, M—1950, IM—1961, GM USSR—1964, IGM—1965. Played in the USSR championship 10 times: 4-6th pl.: 1963, 4-5th pl.: 1965

Tal, Mikhail Nekhemievich: 10, 21, 63. 1936—1992, M—1954, GM USSR—1957, IGM—1957. 8th world champion (1960—1961), 6 times USSR champion.

Tatarintsev, V.: 96.

Timofeev, Vladimir Frolovich: 14. b.1937, M—1967.

Vasiliev, Mikhail Davidovich: 31. b.1945.

Vasiukov, Evgeny Andreevich: 58. b.1933, M—1954, IM—1958, IGM—1961, GM USSR—1962. 3rd pl. in USSR ch.—1967, Moscow champion 6 times.

Veltmander, Ioganess Gugovich: 59. b.1921, M—1953.

Wade, Robert Graham (Great Britain): 70. b.1921, IM—1950.

Zagorovsky, Vladimir Pavlovich: 25. 1925—1994, M—1947, IGM ICCF—1965. World correspondence champion—1965, 2nd pl.—1980. Moscow champion—1952.

Zaitsev, Alexander Nikolaevich: 95. 1935—1971, M—1962, IMC—1964, IM—1965, GMC—1966, IGM—1967, GM USSR—1967. 1-2nd pl. in USSR ch.—1968/69, Russian champion—1968.

Zamikhovsky, Abram Davidovich: 71. 1908—1978, M—1954, Ukrainian champion—1931.

Zhelyandinov, Victor Savelievich: 46. b.1935, M—1962, Soviet Army champion—1966.

Zhilin, Vitaly Valentinovich: 32. b.1934, M—1958, 5-8th pl. in Russian ch.—1959, Soviet Army champion—1962.

Zilber, Iosif Zalmanovich: 30. b.1933, M—1962, Latvian champion— 1958.

Zurakhov, Vladlen Yakovlevich: 61. b.1930, M—1954, Ukrainian champion—1952.

Openings' Index

Bold print indicates Nezhmetdinov had the black pieces.

It should be noted that sometimes the ECO code in the book and the code on the CBH disk do not always match. It depends on "when" the game is saved as it is entered as ChessBase retrieves the position to which that ECO code is assigned. Transpositions can change the ECO code.

26th USSR ch. / Tbilisi 1959

	Players	1	2	3	4	5	6	7	8	9	10	11	12	13	14	15	16	17	18	19	20	Points	Place
1	Petrosyan	•	▒	▒	▒	▒	▒	■	▒	▒	▒	■	▒	■	■	■	■	▒	■	■	▒	13.5	1
2	Spassky	▒	•	▒		▒		▒	▒	■	■	■	▒	■	▒	▒	▒	■	■	■	■	12.5	2-3
3	Tal	▒	▒	•	▒	▒	■	■	▒		■	▒	■			▒	■	■	■	■	■	12.5	2-3
4	Taimanov	▒	■	▒	•			■	▒	▒	■	▒	▒	■	■	▒	▒	■	■	▒	▒	12	4-5
5	Holmov	▒	▒	▒	■	•	▒	▒	■	▒	■	■	▒			■	▒	■	■	▒	▒	12	4-5
6	Polugaevsky	▒	■		■	▒	•	▒		■		▒		▒	■	■	▒	■	▒	▒	■	11	6
7	Averbakh		▒			▒	▒	•	▒	■	▒	▒	■	▒	▒	▒	■	▒	■	■	▒	10.5	7-8
8	Keres	▒	▒	▒	▒		■	▒	•	■		▒	■	▒	▒	▒	■	▒		■	▒	10.5	7-8
9	Korchnoy	▒		■	▒	▒				•	■	■	■	▒	▒		▒	■	▒	■	▒	10	9
10	Geller	▒					■	▒	■		•		▒	▒	■	■	▒	▒	▒	■	■	9.5	10-11
11	Lutikov			▒	▒		▒	▒	▒		■	•	▒	■	▒	■	■		▒	■	▒	9.5	10-11
12	Bronstein	▒	▒		▒	▒	■				▒	▒	•	▒	■	▒	▒	▒	■		■	9	12-13
13	Gufeld			■		■	▒	▒	▒	▒	▒		▒	•	▒	▒	■	▒	▒	▒	▒	9	12-13
14	Yuchtman		▒	■		■		▒	▒	▒		▒		▒	•	▒	■		▒	▒	■	8.5	14
15	Furman		▒	▒	▒			▒	▒	■			▒	▒	▒	•		▒	▒	■	■	8	15
16	Vasiukov		▒		▒	▒	▒			▒	▒		▒			■	•	▒	▒	■	▒	7	16-17
17	Gurgenidze	▒						▒	▒		▒	■	▒	▒	■	▒	▒	•	▒		▒	7	16-17
18	Krogius						▒		*	▒	▒	▒		▒	▒	▒	▒	▒	•	▒	▒	6.5	18
19	Nezhmetdinov				▒	▒	▒						■	▒	▒			■	▒	•	■	6	19
20	Nikitin	▒			▒	▒		▒	▒	▒		▒		▒			▒	▒	▒		•	5.5	20
		1	2	3	4	5	6	7	8	9	10	11	12	13	14	15	16	17	18	19	20		

20th Russian ch. / Perm 1960

	Players	1	2	3	4	5	6	7	8	9	10	11	12	13	14	15	16	17	18	Points	Place
1	Taimanov	•	▒	▒	▒	▒	■	■	▒	■	▒	▒		■	■	■	■	■	▒	12	1-2
2	Tarasov	▒	•	▒	▒	▒	■	▒	■	▒	▒	■	▒	▒	▒	■	■	■	■	12	1-2
3	Lutikov	▒	▒	•	▒	▒	■	▒	▒	■	▒	■	■		▒	■	■	▒	■	11.5	3
4	Borisenko	▒	▒	▒	•		▒	■		■	■	■	▒	■		■	■	■	▒	11	4
5	Krogius	▒	▒	▒	■	•	▒	▒	▒	■		▒	▒	▒	■	■	▒	■	▒	10.5	5
6	Shamkovich				▒	▒	•	■	■	▒	▒		■	■	▒	■	▒	■	■	10	6
7	Vladimirov		▒	▒		▒		•	▒		■	■	■		■		■	■	■	9	7-8
8	Shaposhnikov	▒		▒	■	▒		▒	•		▒	▒	■		■	▒	▒	■	■	9	7-8
9	Aronin		▒				▒	■	■	•	▒	▒		▒	■		■	■	■	8.5	9-11
10	Nezhmetdinov	▒	▒	▒		■	▒		▒	▒	•		▒	▒	■	■	▒	■		8.5	9-11
11	Terentiev	▒				▒	■		▒	▒	■	•	■	■	▒	■			■	8.5	9-11
12	Kotkov	■	▒		▒	▒				■	▒		•	▒		■	▒	■	■	8	12-13
13	Yudovich, Ml		▒	■		▒		■	■	▒	▒		▒	•	▒		■		■	8	12-13
14	Zhilin		▒	▒	■		▒					▒	■	▒	•		▒	■	■	7	14
15	Arseniev							■	▒	■				■	■	•	▒	▒	■	6.5	15
16	Selesniev					▒	▒		▒		▒	■	▒		▒	▒	•	▒	■	6	16
17	Gusakov			▒								■		■		▒	▒	•		3.5	17-18
18	Chernov	▒			▒	▒					■							■	•	3.5	17-18
		1	2	3	4	5	6	7	8	9	10	11	12	13	14	15	16	17	18		

Main
Tournament and Match
Results

Year	Competition	Points	Place
CHESS (incomplete)			
1936	Strongest players first category, Rostov-on-Don	5 (14)	11
1938	Russian tournament first category, Sverdlovsk	12.5 (17)	2
	USSR's tournament first category, Gorki	7 (13)	5 - 8
1939	USSR's tournament first category	9 (10)	1
1940	USSR's tournament for candidates to master	4.5 (11)	9
1941	Baikal-Amur military district championship	15 (16)	1
1946	Soviet military administration championship, Berlin	12 (13)	1
1947	Semi-finals of 8th Russian championship, Gorki	8.5 (11)	1
	7th Russian championship, Yaroslavl	9.5 (13)	2 - 3
	Candidate to Master, Yaroslavl	8.5 (14)	2 - 4
	Championship of "Spartak" club, Riga	13.5 (19)	4
1948	Match with V. Mikenas, Kazan	7 : 7	
	Open championship of Moldavia, Kishinev	10 (12)	1 - 2
	8th Russian championship, Saratov	8.5 (15)	5 - 6
	"Spartak" club championship	4.5 (10)	4
1949	9th Russian championship, Yaroslavl	7 (15)	11 - 12
	Semi-finals of 17th USSR championship, Tbilisi	7 (16)	12
1950	Semi-finals of 11th Russian championship, Arkhangelsk		1
	10th Russian championship, Gorki	8 (12)	1
	Semi-finals of 18th USSR championship, Gorki	9 (15)	5 - 6
1951	Semi-finals of 19th USSR championship, Baku	10 (19)	8 - 10
	11th Russian championship, Yaroslavl	9 (12)	1
1952	1/4 final of 21st USSR championship, Cheliabinsk	9.5 (16)	4
1953	"Spartak" club championship	9.5 (13)	2
	13th Russian championship, Saratov	11 (15)	1
	Semi-finals of 21st USSR championship, Rostov-on-Don	9.5 (15)	3 - 4
1954	21st USSR championship, Kiev	10 (19)	7 - 9
	International tournament, Bucharest	12.5 (17)	2
	14th Russian championship, Rostov-on-Don	11 (17)	2
	Semi-finals of 22nd USSR championship, Gorki	10.5 (20)	10 - 11
	USSR Team championship, Board 4	7 (9)	1
1956	16th Russian championship, Kislovodsk	11 (18)	2 - 4
	Semi-finals of 24th USSR championship, Kharkov	11.5 (18)	1 - 3
1957	24th USSR championship, Moscow	9.5 (21)	13 - 15
	17th Russian championship, Krasnodar	12 (17)	1
	Semi-finals of 25th USSR championship, Kiev	9.5 (19)	11 - 13
	Russia-Ukraine Match		
	Bulgaria-USSR Match		
1958	18th Russian championship, Sochi	13 (19)	1
	Semi-finals of 26th USSR championship, Rostov-on-Don	10 (15)	1 - 2
	USSR Team championships, Vilnius	9.5 (19)	11 - 13

1959	26th USSR championship, Tbilisi	6 (19)	19
	19th Russian championship, Voronezh	9.5 (17)	5 - 8
	Master's tournament, Frunze	12 (14)	1
	USSR Spartakiade, Moscow	2.5 (6)	
1960	20th Russian championship, Perm	8.5 (17)	9 - 11
	Russia-Ukraine Match		
1961	Chigorin Memorial, Rostov-on-Don	7.5 (11)	2 - 3
	21st Russian championship, Omsk	12 (19)	2 - 6
	Complementary match-tournament	4 (6)	1
	29th USSR championship, Baku	7 (20)	19
	22nd Russian championship, Cheliabinsk	10.5 (17)	3 - 5
1963	Open championship of Kazan chess club	6.5 (12)	8
	Semi-finals of Soviet trade-unions, Moscow	9 (13)	2 - 3
	Semi-finals of 34th USSR championship, Moscow	7.5 (17)	12 - 13
1964	"Spartak" club championship, Kazan	12.5 (16)	1
	23rd Russian championship, Kazan	9 (15)	4 - 6
	International tournament, Baku	8.5 (12)	3
	Chigorin Memorial, Sochi	8.5 (15)	6 - 8
1965	Chigorin Memorial, Sochi	7.5 (15)	8 - 10
	International tournament, Ulan-Bator	11.5 (17)	5 - 6
	Semi-finals 34th USSR championship, Irkutsk	7.5 (18)	12 - 13
1966	24th Russian championship, Saratov	10.5 (19)	6 - 9
1967	Russian Spartakiade, Leningrad	7 (11)	8 - 13
	International tournament, Varna	8 (14)	5 - 8
	35th USSR championship (Swiss), Kharkov	7.5 (13)	27 - 40
1969	1/4 finals of 37th USSR championship, Rostov-on-Don	10.5 (15)	1 - 2
	Semi-finals of 37th USSR championship, Rostov-on-Don	9 (17)	7 - 8
	Vasilievsky Memorial, Kaluga	8.5 (13)	3 - 4
1970	International tournament, Kislovodsk	6 (14)	9 - 11
1972	Open championship of Latvia	10 (15)	3 - 4

CHECKERS

1928	Championship of RARO, Kazan	11.5 (14)	2
	Russian championship, Moscow	5.5 (8)	6 - 8
1929	Small USSR championship, Moscow	12 (21)	8 - 9
1934	Russian championship, Moscow semi-finals	7 (9)	1
	finals	2 (5)	4
1938	"Uchiteli" club championship, Saratov	13 (16)	1 - 2
1949	Semi-finals of USSR championship, Kazan	12 (16)	1
1950	Russian championship, Tula	11.5 (17)	2

As the heading on page 211 indicates, these are "main" results. Nezhmetdinov also participated in many team events (Russia—Hungary, Spartak...). There are also personal games that can be found in this book and on the diskette.

Bibliography

Chess: Encyclopedia and Dictionary, A. Karpov (editor-in-chief), Moscow 1990, 176 pp., hardcover, Russian language

My Best Games, Rashid Nezhmetdinov, Kazan 1978, 200 pp., hardcover, Russian language

Oxford Companion to Chess (2nd ed), The, David Hooper & Kenneth Whyld, Oxford/ New York 1992, 483 pp., hardcover

Rashid Nezhmetdinov, J. Damsky, Moscow 1987, 176 pp., Russian language

Shakhmatni Bulletin 1955-1972, Moscow

Shakhmaty v USSR 1947-1972, Moscow

Soviet Chess 1917-1991, Andrew Soltis, North Carolina/London 2000, 450 pp., hardcover

Warriors of the Steppe, A Military History of Central Asia, 500 B.C. to 1700 A.D. by Erik Hildinger, Sarpedon Publishers (Aug. 1997), 272 pp., hardcover

Databases

Chess Assistant 5.1. Helpful on some names and spellings. Does not contain all Soviet tournaments. In fact, the 1961 Russian championship was missing.

ChessBase 7. Sometimes different name spellings, missing records of whole events also.

Ultimate. Occasionally has games the above two do not have. Different name spellings, and too much duplication at times. Does sort by name.

The different name spellings and lack of venue (place) or name of event makes some searches for information difficult. *Chess Asssistant* handles the name spellings the best.

Interestingly, nearly all the Soviet sources consulted had non-duplicative information, most likely they were all controlled by Fizicultura i Sport. The big weakness was often a lack of date and/or name of the place the event was held. The Soviets had a fondness for Roman numeral anniversaries which increases the chance of error.

Colophon

Typeset in Oranda and Thinkers' Press, Inc. chess diagram font, C.R. Horowitz®.

Cover Design: Bass Long
Layout and editing: Bob Long
Translators: Mr. Chuchin, Bob Long, Don Aldrich
Supplemental editing: Don Aldrich
Proofers: Bob Long, Alex Pishkin, Mark Donlan, Nate Long, Dianna Maynard

• • •

Special Thanks to GM Eduard Gufeld and Jakov Damsky for procurring the photographs used in this work. Also a special thanks to Andy Harbert for the loan of Damsky's book. Finally, another special thanks to Bragi Kristjánsson for some detailed works from his library.

DISKETTE

It would be impossible for us to print in this book all the additional analyses contained on the diskette used in producing this book. The diskette contains at least 455 games and fragments (the biggest commercial computer database we know), analyses and evaluations only, in ChessBase and PGN format (CBH). About half the games are annotated: lightly and heavily.

Price: $15 (PGN or CBH format) + $3 for S&H.
Contact Thinkers' Press: 1-800-397-7117.

21st Russian ch. / Omsk 1961

	Players	1	2	3	4	5	6	7	8	9	10	11	12	13	14	15	16	17	18	19	20	Points	Place
1	Polugaevsky	•	▒	▒	■	▒	■	▒	▒	■	■	▒	▒	▒	▒	■	▒	■		▒	■	12.5	1
2	Antoshin	▒	•	▒	▒	▒		▒		▒	▒	▒	▒	▒	■	■	■	■	■	■	■	12	2-6
3	Belov	▒	▒	•				▒		▒	■	▒	■	▒	■	■	■	■	■	■	■	12	2-6
4	Borisenko		▒	■	•	■	▒	▒	■		▒	▒	■		■	▒	■	■	▒	■	▒	12	2-6
5	Lein	▒	▒	■		•	■	▒		▒	■	▒		■	▒	■	■	■	■		■	12	2-6
6	Nezhmetdinov		■	■	▒		•	▒	■		▒	▒	■	■	▒		■	■	■	■	▒	12	2-6
7	Ilivitsky	▒	▒	▒	▒	▒	▒	•	▒	▒	▒	▒	▒	■	■	▒	▒	▒	■	▒	▒	11	7-9
8	Shestoperov	▒	■	■		■		▒	•			▒	■	▒		▒	■	▒	■	■	■	11	7-9
9	Yudovich,Ml		▒	▒	■	▒	■	▒	■	•		▒	▒	▒	▒	■	▒	▒	■	▒	▒	11	7-9
10	Veltmander		▒		▒		▒	▒	■	■	•	▒	▒	■	▒	■	▒		■	▒	■	10.5	10
11	Krogius	▒	▒	▒	▒	▒	▒	▒	▒	▒	▒	•		■	▒	▒	▒	▒	▒	■		9.5	11-12
12	Tarasov	▒	▒			■		▒		▒	▒	▒	•	■	▒	▒	▒	▒	■	■	▒	9.5	11-12
13	Sergievsky	▒	▒	▒	■				▒	▒		■		•	▒	▒	▒	▒	▒	■	■	9	13
14	Arseniev	▒				▒	▒		■	▒	▒		▒	▒	•	▒	■	▒		▒	■	8	14
15	Kotkov				▒		■	▒	▒			▒	▒	▒	▒	•		▒	▒	■	■	7.5	15
16	Zhilin	▒						▒		▒	▒	▒	▒	▒		■	•	■	▒	■		7	16-17
17	Selesniev							▒	▒	▒	■	▒	▒	▒	▒	▒		•	▒	▒	■	7	16-17
18	Ostrovsky	■			▒							▒		▒	■	▒	▒	▒	•	▒	■	6.5	18
19	Gozin	▒				■		▒		▒	▒				▒			▒	▒	•	■	5.5	19
20	Lepeshkin				▒		▒	▒		▒		■	▒				■				•	4.5	20
		1	2	3	4	5	6	7	8	9	10	11	12	13	14	15	16	17	18	19	20		

29th USSR ch. / Baku 1961

	Players	1	2	3	4	5	6	7	8	9	10	11	12	13	14	15	16	17	18	19	20	21	Points	Place
1	Spassky	•	■	▒	▒	■	▒	▒	■	▒	■	▒		▒	■	■	■	▒	■	▒	■	■	14.5	1
2	Polugaevsky		•	▒	■	▒	■	▒	▒	▒		▒	■	■	■	▒	■	▒	■	■	■	■	14	2
3	Bronstein	▒	▒	•		■	▒	■	■	▒	▒	▒	▒	▒	▒	■	▒	▒	■	▒	■	▒	12.5	3
4	Vasiukov	▒		■	•	▒		▒	▒	■	▒		▒	▒	■	■	▒	■	▒	■	▒	■	12	4-5
5	Tal		▒		▒	•	▒	■	▒	▒	▒	▒	■	■	■	▒	■	▒	■		▒	■	12	4-5
6	Averbakh	▒		▒	■	▒	•	▒		▒	▒	▒	▒		■	▒	■	■	■	■	■		11.5	6-7
7	Taimanov	▒	▒		▒		▒	•	▒	▒	■	■	■	■	■		▒	▒		■	▒	■	11.5	6-7
8	Gipslis		▒		▒	▒	■	▒	•	▒	■	▒		▒	▒	▒	▒	■	■	▒	▒	■	11	8-11
9	Keres	▒	▒	▒		▒	▒	▒	▒	•	▒	▒	▒		■	■	■	▒	■	▒	▒	▒	11	8-11
10	Smyslov		■	▒	▒	▒	▒			▒	•	■	■	▒		▒	▒	■	■	■	▒	▒	11	8-11
11	Holmov	▒	▒	▒	■	▒	▒		▒	▒		•		■	■			■	▒	■	■	■	11	8-11
12	Shamkovich	■		▒	▒		▒		■	▒		■	•		■	■	▒	▒	▒		■	■	10.5	12
13	Hasin,Ab	▒		▒	▒		■		▒	■	▒		■	•		■	▒	▒		▒	▒	■	9.5	13
14	Vladimirov			▒					▒		■			■	•	▒	▒	■	■	■		■	8	14-16
15	Kots		▒			▒	▒	■	▒		▒	■			▒	•	■				■	■	8	14-16
16	Shiyanovsky			▒	▒			▒	▒		▒	■	▒	▒	▒		•	▒	▒	■	■		8	14-16
17	Lein	▒	▒	▒		▒		▒		▒			▒	▒		■	▒	•		■	▒	▒	7.5	17-18
18	Savon				▒			■				▒	▒	■		■	▒	■	•	▒	▒	▒	7.5	17-18
19	Nezhmetdinov	▒		▒		■			▒	▒			■	▒		■			▒	•	■		7	19
20	Bagirov				▒	▒		▒	▒	▒	▒			▒	■			▒	▒		•	▒	6	20-21
21	Gurgenidze			▒			■			▒	▒						■	▒	▒	■	▒	•	6	20-21
		1	2	3	4	5	6	7	8	9	10	11	12	13	14	15	16	17	18	19	20	21		

22nd Russian ch. / Cheliabinsk 1963

	Players	1	2	3	4	5	6	7	8	9	10	11	12	13	14	15	16	17	18	Points	Place
1	Lein	•	▒	■			■	▒	■	▒	■	▒	■	■	■		■	■	+	12	1
2	Ilivitsky	▒	•	▒	▒	■	▒	▒	▒	▒	▒	▒	■	▒	■	▒	■	▒	■	11	2
3	Valitinov		▒	•		▒	▒	▒	▒	■	▒	■	▒	■	■	▒	■	▒	+	10.5	3-5
4	Nezhmetdinov	■	▒	■	•	▒	▒	▒	▒	■	▒			■	▒	■	▒	▒	+	10.5	3-5
5	Terentiev	■		▒	▒	•	▒	▒	■		▒	▒	▒	■	■	■	▒	▒	■	10.5	3-5
6	Rusakov		▒	▒	▒	▒	•	▒	▒	▒	▒	▒	■	■	▒	▒	▒	▒	■	9.5	6-7
7	Tarasov	▒	▒	▒	▒	▒	▒	•	▒	▒	■	▒			▒	■	▒	■	■	9.5	6-7
8	Anoshin		▒	▒	▒		▒	▒	•	■	▒	▒		■	▒	▒	■	▒	+	9	8-11
9	Kopylov	▒	▒			■	▒		▒	•	▒	▒	■	■	■		▒	▒	+	9	8-11
10	Selesniev		▒	▒	▒	▒		▒	▒	▒	•	▒	▒	▒	■	▒	■	▒	■	9	8-11
11	Sergievsky	▒	▒		■	▒	▒	▒	▒	▒	▒	•	▒			■	▒	■	■	9	8-11
12	Doroshkevich			▒	■	▒		■	■		▒	▒	•		▒		■	▒	▒	7.5	12
13	Bastrikov		▒				■				▒	■	■	•		■		■	+	7	13-15
14	Belov				▒		▒	▒	▒			■	▒	■	•	■	▒	■		7	13-15
15	Shipov	■	▒	▒				▒	▒	■	▒		■			•		▒	+	7	13-15
16	Kotkov				▒	▒	▒	▒		▒		▒		■	▒	■	•		▒	6	16-17
17	Ostrovsky		▒	▒	▒	▒		▒	▒	▒	▒		▒			▒	■	•		6	16-17
18	Tatarintsev	—		—	—				—	—			▒	—	■	—	▒	■	•	3	18
		1	2	3	4	5	6	7	8	9	10	11	12	13	14	15	16	17	18		

Semi-finals 34th USSR Ch. / Moscow 1963

	Players	1	2	3	4	5	6	7	8	9	10	11	12	13	14	15	16	17	18	Points	Place
1	Nikolaevsky	•	▒	▒	■	▒	▒	■	■	■	■	■	■	■	▒	▒		■	■	13	1
2	Krogius	▒	•		■	▒	▒	■	▒	▒	■	▒	▒	▒	■	▒	■	■	▒	11	2-3
3	Liberzon	▒	■	•		▒	▒	▒	▒	■		■	▒	■	■	■	▒	▒	■	11	2-3
4	Sakharov			■	•	■	▒	▒	▒	▒	▒	■		■	■	▒	■	■	▒	10.5	4
5	Gurgenidze	▒	▒	▒		•		■	■			▒	■	▒	▒	▒	■	■	■	9.5	5-6
6	Shmit	▒	▒	▒	▒	■	•	▒		▒		▒	▒	▒	■	▒	■	▒	■	9.5	5-6
7	Zhidkov			▒	▒		▒	•	▒	■	■	▒	▒	■	▒		▒	■	■	9	7-8
8	Uusi		▒	▒	▒		■	▒	•	▒		▒	■	▒		■	▒	■	■	9	7-8
9	Bakulin		▒		▒	■	▒		▒	•	■	■	■			▒	▒	▒	■	8.5	9-10
10	Danov			■	▒	■	■		■		•			▒	▒	■	■	▒	▒	8.5	9-10
11	Mukhin		▒			▒	▒	▒	▒		■	•	▒	■	▒	■	▒		■	8	11
12	Muratov		▒	▒	■		▒	▒			■	▒	•	▒			■	▒	■	7.5	12-13
13	Nezhmetdinov		▒			▒	▒		▒	■	▒		▒	•	▒	■	■	■		7.5	12-13
14	Kimelfeld	▒				▒		▒	■	■	▒	▒	■	▒	•			▒	▒	7	14-15
15	Kopylov	▒	▒		▒	▒	▒	■		▒			■		■	•	▒		▒	7	14-15
16	Liavdansky	■		▒				▒	▒	▒		▒			■	▒	•	▒	■	6.5	16
17	Kydriashov			▒			▒			▒	▒	■	▒		▒	■	▒	•	▒	6	17
18	Pavlenko		▒		▒						▒			■	▒	▒		▒	•	4	18
		1	2	3	4	5	6	7	8	9	10	11	12	13	14	15	16	17	18		

Russia vs Hungary / 1963

	Players	1	2	3	4	Points
1	Lengyel	■				1
2	Nezhmetdinov		■	■	■	3

International Tournament / Baku 1964

	Players	1	2	3	4	5	6	7	8	9	10	11	12	13	Points	Place
1	Antoshin	•	▒	▒	▒	▒	■	■	■	■	■	▒	▒	■	9	1-2
2	Bagirov	▒	•		■	■		▒	■	■	■	■	■	■	9	1-2
3	Nezhmetdinov	▒	■	•	▒	▒	▒	■	■		■	▒	■	■	8.5	3
4	Gufeld	▒		▒	•	▒	■	▒	▒	▒	▒	▒	■	■	7	4-5
5	Yudovich	▒		▒	▒	•	▒	▒		■	▒	■	■	■	7	4-5
6	Lilienthal		■	▒		▒	•	▒	▒	▒	▒	■	▒	■	6.5	6
7	Rabar		▒		▒	▒	▒	•	■	▒	▒	▒	▒	■	6	7
8	Capello				▒	■	▒		•	▒	■		■	■	5.5	8-9
9	Cvetkov			■	▒		▒	▒	▒	•	▒	■		■	5.5	8-9
10	Khalilbeili				▒	▒	▒	▒		▒	•	■	▒	■	5	10
11	Adamski	▒		▒	▒			▒	■			•	▒	■	4.5	11-12
12	Listengarten	▒					▒	▒		■	▒	▒	•	■	4.5	11-12
13	Hosking													•	0	13
		1	2	3	4	5	6	7	8	9	10	11	12	13		

23rd Russian Ch. / Kazan 1964

	Players	1	2	3	4	5	6	7	8	9	10	11	12	13	14	15	16	Points	Place
1	Krogius	•	▒	▒	▒	▒	▒	■	▒	▒	▒	▒	■	▒	■	■	■	10	1
2	Borisenko	▒	•	■		▒	▒	■	■	■		■	■			■	■	9.5	2-3
3	Lein	▒		•	■	▒	▒	■	▒		■	▒	▒	■	▒	■	■	9.5	2-3
4	Zaitsev	▒	■		•	■		■	■		■	▒		▒	■	■	▒	9	4-6
5	Kotkov	▒	▒	▒		•	■	▒	▒	■	▒	■	▒	▒		■	■	9	4-6
6	Nezhmetdinov	▒	▒	▒	■		•		▒	■	▒		■	■	■	■	▒	9	4-6
7	Belov					▒	■	•			■	■	■	■	■	■	■	8.5	7
8	Gilinsky	▒		▒		▒	▒	■	•	■	▒	■	■	▒	▒		▒	8	8
9	Baranov	▒		■	■			■		•	▒	▒		▒	▒	■	■	7.5	9-10
10	Terentiev	▒	■			▒	▒		▒	▒	•	▒	■	▒	■		■	7.5	9-10
11	Doroshkevich	▒		▒	▒		■			▒	▒	•		■	■	▒	■	7	11-12
12	Ruchkin			▒	■	▒				■		■	•		■	■	■	7	11-12
13	Sokolov	▒	■		▒	▒			▒	▒	▒		■	•	▒	■		6.5	13
14	Kuzimichev		■	▒		■			▒	▒				▒	•	▒	▒	5	14
15	Tatarintsev								■		■	▒			▒	•	■	4	15
16	Ulianov				▒		▒		▒					■	▒		•	3	16
		1	2	3	4	5	6	7	8	9	10	11	12	13	14	15	16		

M.I. Chigorin Memorial / Sochi 1964

	Players	1	2	3	4	5	6	7	8	9	10	11	12	13	14	15	16	Points	Place
1	Krogius	•	■	▒	▒	▒	▒	▒	■	▒	■	■	■	■	▒	▒	■	11	1
2	Damjanovich		•	▒	▒		▒	▒	■	■		■	■	■	■	■	■	10	2-3
3	Holmov	▒	▒	•	▒	▒	▒	■	▒	■	■		▒	■	▒	■	■	10	2-3
4	Spassky	▒	▒	▒	•	▒	▒	■		▒	▒	■	■	▒	▒	■	■	9.5	4
5	Matulovich	▒	■	▒	▒	•		■	▒		▒	▒	▒	▒	■	■	■	9	5
6	Antoshin	▒	▒	▒	▒	■	•	▒	■		■	■		▒	▒	■		8.5	6-8
7	Lein	▒	▒				▒	•		■	▒	■	▒	■	■	■	■	8.5	6-8
8	Nezhmetdinov			▒	■	▒		■	•	▒	▒		■	▒	■	■	■	8.5	6-8
9	Bondarevsky	▒			▒	■	■		▒	•	▒	■			■	■	■	8	9
10	Barcza		■		▒	▒		▒	▒	▒	•		■	▒	■	■	▒	7.5	10-11
11	Uitelky			■		▒			■		■	•	▒	▒	■	■	■	7.5	10-11
12	Doroshkevich			▒		▒	■	▒		■		▒	•	▒	▒	■	■	7	12
13	Gheorghiu				▒	▒	▒		▒	■	▒	▒	▒	•	▒	■		6	13
14	Forintos	▒		▒			▒						▒	▒	•		■	3.5	14
15	Uitumen	▒			▒										■	•	■	3	15
16	Garcia						■				▒			■			•	2.5	16
		1	2	3	4	5	6	7	8	9	10	11	12	13	14	15	16		

M.I. Chigorin Memorial / Sochi 1965

	Players	1	2	3	4	5	6	7	8	9	10	11	12	13	14	15	16	Points	Place
1	Spassky	•	▒	▒	▒	▒	▒	■	▒	■	▒	■	▒	■	▒	■	■	10.5	1-2
2	Unzicker	▒	•	▒	▒	■	▒	▒	■	■	▒	■	■	▒	▒	▒	■	10.5	1-2
3	Ciric	▒	▒	•	▒	▒	■	▒	▒	■	■	▒	▒	▒	■	▒	■	10	3
4	Krogius	▒	▒	▒	•	▒	▒	▒	▒		■	▒	▒	▒	▒	■	■	8.5	4
5	Zaitsev	▒		▒	▒	•	■	▒	■	▒	■	▒		▒	■		▒	8	5-7
6	Ilivitsky	▒	▒		▒		•	▒	▒	■	▒	▒	■	▒	▒	■	▒	8	5-7
7	Flohr		▒	▒	▒	▒	▒	•	▒	▒	▒	▒	■	▒	▒	▒	■	8	5-7
8	Damjanovich	▒		▒	▒		▒	▒	•	■	▒	■	■		▒	■		7.5	8-10
9	Nezhmetdinov				■	▒		▒		•	■		■	■	■	▒	■	7.5	8-10
10	Jansa	▒	▒				▒	▒	▒		•	■	■	▒	▒	■	■	7.5	8-10
11	Antoshin			▒	▒	▒	▒	▒		■		•	▒	▒	■	▒	■	7	11
12	Lein	▒		▒	▒	■						▒	•	▒	■	■	■	6.5	12
13	Kotkov		▒	▒	▒	▒	▒	▒	■		▒	▒	▒	•		▒		6	13-14
14	Malich	▒	▒		▒		▒	▒	▒		▒			■	•	▒	■	6	13-14
15	Uitumen		▒	▒		■		▒		▒		▒		▒	▒	•		4.5	15
16	Garcia					▒	▒		■					■		■	•	4	16
		1	2	3	4	5	6	7	8	9	10	11	12	13	14	15	16		

Ulan Bator 1965

	Players	1	2	3	4	5	6	7	8	9	10	11	12	13	14	15	16	17	18	Points	Place
1	Antoshin	•	▒	■	▒	▒	▒	▒	■	■	■	■	▒	■	■	■	■	■	■	14	1
2	Miagmasuren	▒	•	▒	▒	▒	■	▒	▒	▒	■	■	■	■	▒	■	■	■	■	13	2
3	Uitumen		▒	•	■	▒	■		■	■	■	■	▒	■		■	■	▒	■	12	3-4
4	Shamkovich	▒	▒		•	▒	▒	▒	■	■	■	▒	■	▒	▒	■	■	■	■	12	3-4
5	Vladimirov	▒	▒	▒	▒	•	▒	▒	■	▒	▒	▒	■	▒	■	▒	■	■	■	11.5	5-6
6	Nezhmetdinov	▒			▒	▒	•	▒	▒	■	■		■	■	■	■	■	■	■	11.5	5-6
7	Yudovich	▒	▒	■	▒	▒	▒	•	▒	■	▒	▒	▒	▒	■	▒	▒	▒	■	10.5	7
8	Zita		▒				▒	▒	•	■	▒	▒	▒	▒	■	■	▒	■	▒	8.5	8
9	Tsaagan		▒			▒				•	▒	■	▒	■	■	▒	■	▒	■	8	9-10
10	Cvetkov					▒		▒	▒	▒	•	▒	▒	■	■	▒	■	■	▒	8	9-10
11	Tsend				▒	▒	■	▒	▒		▒	•	▒	▒	▒	▒	■	▒	▒	7.5	11
12	Shatar	▒		▒				▒	▒	▒	▒	▒	•	▒	▒	▒	▒	■	▒	7	12
13	Chalhasuren				▒	▒		▒	▒			▒	▒	•	▒	■		■	▒	6	13
14	Badamgarav		▒	■	▒							▒	▒	▒	•		■	▒	▒	5.5	14
15	Zorigt					▒		▒		▒	▒	▒	▒		■	•		▒		4.5	15-18
16	Pliater							▒	▒				▒	■		■	•	▒	▒	4.5	15-18
17	Purevzhav			▒				▒		▒		▒			▒	▒	▒	•	■	4.5	15-18
18	Tumurbator								▒		▒	▒	▒	▒	▒	■	▒		•	4.5	15-18
		1	2	3	4	5	6	7	8	9	10	11	12	13	14	15	16	17	18		

24th Russian ch. / Saratov 1966

	Players	1	2	3	4	5	6	7	8	9	10	11	12	13	14	15	16	17	18	19	20	Points	Place
1	Sakharov,I	•		■	▒	▒	■	■	■		▒	▒		■	■	▒	▒	▒	■	▒	■	12	1-3
2	Lein	■	•	▒		▒	▒	▒	▒	▒		■	■	▒	▒	■	■	▒	▒	■	■	12	1-3
3	Sergievsky		▒	•	▒	▒			■	▒	▒	■	■	▒	▒	■	▒	■	■	■	■	12	1-3
4	Doroshkevich	▒	■	▒	•		■	▒		▒	▒	▒		▒	■	■	■		■	■	■	11.5	4
5	Rusakov	▒	▒	▒	■	•	▒	▒	▒	▒	▒	▒	▒	▒	▒	▒	▒	▒	■	▒	■	11	5
6	Kopylov,I		▒	■		▒	•	▒	▒	▒	■	■	▒	▒	■	▒	▒	▒	▒	▒	▒	10.5	6-9
7	Nezhmetdinov		▒	■	▒	▒	▒	•	▒	▒	■			▒	▒		■	▒	■	■	■	10.5	6-9
8	Rashkovsky		▒		■	▒	▒	▒	•	■	■		▒	▒		■		▒	■	■	■	10.5	6-9
9	Terentiev	■	▒	▒	▒	▒	▒	▒		•	▒	▒	▒	▒	▒	▒	■	▒	■	▒	▒	10.5	6-9
10	Kotkov	▒	■	▒	▒	▒				▒	•	▒		■	■		▒	▒	■	■	■	10	10
11	Belov	▒			▒	▒		■	■	▒	▒	•	■	▒	■		■	■		▒		9.5	11-13
12	Kopylov,N	■			■	▒	▒	■	▒	▒	■		•		▒	▒	▒	▒	▒		■	9.5	11-13
13	Ostrovsky		▒	▒	▒	▒	▒	▒	▒	▒		▒	■	•	▒	▒	▒	▒	▒	■	▒	9.5	11-13
14	Chernikov		▒	▒		▒		▒	■	▒			▒	▒	•	■	■	■	▒		■	9	14-15
15	Shestoperov	▒				▒	▒	■		▒	■	■	▒	▒		•	▒	■	▒	■		9	14-15
16	Zaitsev,A	▒		▒		▒	▒		■		▒		▒	▒		▒	•	▒		■	■	7.5	16-17
17	Ilivitsky	▒	▒		■	▒	▒	▒	▒	▒	▒		▒	▒			▒	•	▒	▒		7.5	16-17
18	Vasiliev		▒				▒					■	▒	▒	▒	▒	■	▒	•		■	6.5	18-19
19	Titenko	▒				▒	▒			▒		▒	■		■			▒	■	•	▒	6.5	18-19
20	Terpugov						▒			▒		■		▒		■		■		▒	•	5	20
		1	2	3	4	5	6	7	8	9	10	11	12	13	14	15	16	17	18	19	20		

Semi-finals 37th USSR ch / Rostov-on-Don 1969

	Players	1	2	3	4	5	6	7	8	9	10	11	12	13	14	15	16	17	18	Points	Place
1	Zhukhovitsky	•	▒	■	▒	▒	■	■	▒	■		■	▒	■	■	▒	▒	■	▒	12	1
2	Taimanov	▒	•	▒	▒	▒	▒	■	■	▒	▒	■	▒		▒	■	■	■	■	11.5	2
3	Furman		▒	•	▒	▒	▒	■	■	▒	■	■	▒		■	▒	■	■	▒	11	3
4	Bagirov	▒	▒	▒	•	▒		▒	▒	■	▒	▒	▒	▒	■	▒	■	■	■	10.5	4-6
5	Vasiukov	▒	▒	▒	▒	•	▒	▒	▒	▒		■	■	▒	■	▒	▒	■	■	10.5	4-6
6	Kuzmin		▒	▒	■	▒	•				▒	■	■	■	▒	■	■	■	■	10.5	4-6
7	Kanpengut				▒	▒	■	•	▒		■		▒	■	▒	■	■	■	▒	9	7-8
8	Nezhmetdinov	▒			▒	▒	■	▒	•		▒		▒	■	■	■	■	■		9	7-8
9	Kudryashov		▒	▒		▒	■	■	■	•	▒	■	▒	■			▒		▒	8.5	9
10	Dzindzhihashvili	■	▒		▒	■	▒		▒	▒	•	▒	▒		■			▒	■	8	10
11	Ageichenko				▒			■	■		▒	•	■	▒		■	▒	▒	■	7.5	11-13
12	Grigorian, L	▒	▒	▒	▒			▒	▒	▒	▒		•		▒	▒	▒	■	■	7.5	11-13
13	Zaharov		■	■	▒	▒					■	▒	■	•	▒	■		▒		7.5	11-13
14	Pavlenko		▒				▒	▒		■		■	▒	▒	•	■		■	▒	7	14
15	Bukhman	▒		▒	▒	▒				■	■		▒			•	■		■	6.5	15-16
16	Kapelyush	▒				▒				▒	■	▒	▒	■	■		•		■	6.5	15-16
17	Veselovsky									■	▒	▒		▒		■	■	•	■	5.5	17
18	Gusev	▒		▒				▒	■	▒				■	▒				•	4.5	18
		1	2	3	4	5	6	7	8	9	10	11	12	13	14	15	16	17	18		